Managing Data
with Excel

Managing Data with Excel

Written by Conrad Carlberg

with
Kelly Conatser and Shane Devenshire

Managing Data with Excel

Library of Congress Catalog No.: 95-71755

ISBN: 0-7897-0385-8

98 97 96   6 5 4 3 2 1

Interpretation of the printing code: the rightmost double-digit number is the year of the book's printing; the rightmost single-digit number, the number of the book's printing. For example, a printing code of 96-1 shows that the first printing of the book occurred in 1996.

Screen reproductions in this book were created using Collage Plus from Inner Media, Inc., Hollis, NH.

Composed in *Stone Serif* and *MCPdigital* by Que Corporation

Credits

To Toni Messer. For all the right reasons.

About the Authors

Conrad Carlberg is president of Network Control Systems, Inc., a software development and consulting firm that specializes in the statistical forecasting of data network usage. He holds a Ph.D. in statistics from the University of Colorado, and is a three-time recipient of Microsoft Excel's Most Valuable Professional award.

Kelly Conatser creates spreadsheet and database applications for businesses ranging from small restaurants to large oil companies. He writes a regular column for the Lotus edition of *PC World* and has published three books: *Excel Solutions, Spreadsheets for the Small Business*, and the *Lotus Guide to 1-2-3 for the Macintosh.*

Shane Devenshire is a consultant specializing in project management, databases, graphics computer packages, and the scientific and business application of spreadsheets. He is a founding partner of the MAR&SHA Corporation, a computer consulting company providing application development, programming, and training in both the mainframe and personal computer areas. He has written over 230 computer-related articles for twenty journals here and abroad. He has been a guest editor for *PC World* magazine and has been on the product review board of *INFO World*. He has three years experience in the bio-tech arena, five years in business management, and 13 years in computer-related industries. He has coauthored *Excel Professional Techniques, Using 1-2-3 Release 4 for DOS* and *Making Microsoft Office Work.*

We'd Like to Hear from You!

As part of our continuing effort to produce books of the highest possible quality, Que would like to hear your comments. To stay competitive, we *really* want you, as a computer book reader and user, to let us know what you like or dislike most about this book or other Que products.

You can mail comments, ideas, or suggestions for improving future editions to the address below, or send us a fax at (317) 581-4663. For the online inclined, Macmillan Computer Publishing has a forum on CompuServe (type **GO QUEBOOKS** at any prompt) through which our staff and authors are available for questions and comments. The address of our Internet site is **http://www.mcp.com** (World Wide Web).

In addition to exploring our forum, please feel free to contact me personally to discuss your opinions of this book: I'm **76507,2715** on CompuServe, and I'm **karnoff@que.mcp.com** on the Internet.

Thanks in advance—your comments will help us to continue publishing the best books available on computer topics in today's market.

Kathie-Jo Arnoff
Title Manager
Que Corporation
201 W. 103rd Street
Indianapolis, Indiana 46290
USA

Contents at a Glance

Data Management Techniques

Pivot Tables

Scenario Management

Consolidations, Views, and Reports

Managing External Data Sources and Destinations

Contents

II Pivot Tables   127

7 Understanding Pivot Tables   129

IV Consolidations, Views, and Reports   319

17 Consolidating Business Information   321

18 Managing Different Views   343

19 Choosing Between Scenarios and Consolidations 351

20 Putting It Down on Paper   359

V Managing External Data Sources and Destinations 381

21 Importing Data from External Sources 383

22 Sending Data to External Applications 423

Introduction

Welcome to *Managing Data with Excel*!

As an activity, managing data doesn't sound very glamorous. And it's not. You didn't learn how to use Excel to manage data—you learned Excel to analyze data, to create informative reports and attractive charts, to share data with colleagues, to develop applications...well, you had your reasons. Managing data wasn't high on the list.

Nevertheless, you've learned how to enter data into a worksheet. You've learned how to copy it, paste it, cut it, drag it, autofill it, array-enter it, edit it, find it, name it, format it, and clear it. You can do everything with it except make it play Johnny B. Goode on the ocarina, and you're working on that. What more could there be?

Plenty.

Have you ever tried to sort a range of data that contains relative references? They have an annoying way of recalculating when the sort's finished, so they wind up unsorted. *Managing Data with Excel* shows you how to do it.

It's sometimes desirable to hide a formula in a balance sheet. Did you know there's a custom format you can use to make values and formulas invisible in worksheet cells? It's not in the list of built-in formats, but it's in Chapter 6 of this book.

Do you understand data caches? Those are the structures that make pivot tables work. Caches are necessary because if you change the source data, then you have to refresh the pivot table. Did you also know that you can delete the source data to save file space, and then bring it back by accessing the pivot table's data cache? You can find out how in Chapter 8.

What about scenarios? Have you used the Scenario box to create a scenario as fast and easily as you name a range with the Name box? Or have you let Excel do the hard work for you when it comes to combining the data on 15 different worksheets in one location?

How about external databases? New Excel tools make it a piece of cake to enter data into an Excel worksheet and have the data automatically show up in an Access database, *and* automatically show up as a workbook in a colleague's inbox. You can turn VBA loose to manage external databases—either directly or behind the scenes—without ever leaving the Excel environment.

So maybe there's something more to learn about. Here's where to find it:

Part I of Managing Data with Excel covers **Data Management Techniques**. Chapter 1, "Managing Business Data with Lists," describes the basic structure of Excel lists and how to sort them; how to filter, for example, sales data to identify the top sales performers in different regions; and how to use custom lists of your customers to avoid having to enter the same data repeatedly—or, worse, misspelling a customer's name.

Chapter 2, "Using Data Tables To Project Financial Outcomes," introduces Excel data tables. Use them as one way to automate what-if analysis so you can easily see the impact of changing inputs such as loan rates on outcomes like monthly payments.

Chapter 3, "Representing Business Forms on the Worksheet," shows you how to set up data forms that speed data entry and make the entry process more accurate at the same time. Once the data is in the worksheet, you can learn to use Excel data structures to base your analyses on changing subsets of records (see Chapter 4, "Using Excel Databases To Organize Business Information").

Not all of Excel's data management techniques depend on menu commands. Worksheet functions such as TRANSPOSE and OFFSET work in concert with array-formulas to smooth the reorientation of worksheet data. You'll find these topics covered in Chapter 5, "Managing Data with Worksheet Functions."

Much business information is confidential and needs to remain that way. At the same time, it's often necessary to display the results of calculations that depend on formulas and constants that should be protected either from modification or from prying eyes. Chapter 6, "Protecting Business Data from Tampering," shows you how to hide information, prevent people from changing it, and even hide worksheets so thoroughly that they can't be displayed using Unhide commands. (It also shows you how to unhide them, even if you don't know that they're there.)

Part II, **Pivot Tables**, covers the many different ways to bring scattered, diffuse data into focus by properly managing the structure and display of pivot tables. It begins with Chapter 7, "Understanding Pivot Tables," which is an overview of the various options available when you create or modify these tables.

Chapter 8, "Placing Business Data into Pivot Tables," gives you detailed instructions for creating pivot tables from worksheet lists, from external data sources such as relational databases and text files, from multiple worksheets, and from other pivot tables.

The different display options, such as subtotals and running totals, available within pivot tables are described in Chapter 9, "Applying Special Pivot Table Options." Here you'll find techniques such as automatically disaggregating a pivot table into separate worksheets—for example, to distribute customer account information among different members of your sales force.

Particularly when you have designed a pivot table whose source data is updated regularly, such as for a monthly report, you will find Visual Basic for Applications (VBA) a great time-saver. When possible, you should use VBA to automate these routine tasks, and Chapter 10, "Using VBA To Create Pivot Tables," shows you how.

While Excel provides a large number of worksheet functions and analysis add-ins to analyze data sets, these capabilities focus on the analysis of relationships between continuous variables such as revenues, costs, and product units. Because pivot tables are uniquely suited to describing the interactions of non-continuous variables, such as product segments and sales territories, this book covers the analysis of contingency tables and log-linear analysis. See Chapter 11, "Analyzing Pivot Tables."

Part III, **Scenario Management**, contains five chapters that describe the creation, management, and analysis of business scenarios. Chapter 12, "Understanding Business Scenarios," provides an overview of the use of Excel's Scenario Manager. This Manager is a way of creating, storing, and retrieving different assumptions that define a business model, so you can see the impact of different combinations of inputs on an outcome such as break-even points or undiscounted net cash flow.

Chapter 13, "Creating Business Scenarios," describes how to construct a business model on an Excel worksheet, and details the different ways you can bring different sets of input assumptions—the scenarios—into the model.

Excel's Solver, an optimization add-in, can be used in combination with the Scenario Manager, so an optimal balance of input values and constraints can be found and, subsequently, saved as a scenario. Chapter 14, "Solving Business Scenarios," explains how to use the Solver in this context.

There are different ways to report the results of different scenarios in order to view a set of outcomes under different sets of assumptions. For example, you might want to present a worksheet model with different combinations of discount factors, capital budgets, and headcounts to obtain different outcome measures. You can then use all the outcomes simultaneously in a sensitivity analysis. Chapter 15, "Reporting Scenarios," takes you through examples of how to do this using the Scenario Manager. And, when recurring events make it desirable to turn the work over to VBA, you can use the information in Chapter 16, "Using VBA To Create and Manage Scenarios."

Part IV, **Consolidations, Views, and Reports**, begins with an explanation of how to combine information you might have scattered across several worksheets into one, consolidated report. Chapter 17, "Consolidating Business Information," provides the details and examples.

The View Manager is, in a sense, complementary to the Scenario Manager. However, instead of retrieving different sets of data into a model, you use the View Manager to retrieve different views of a worksheet, including hidden rows and columns and print settings. This capability is particularly useful when you want to switch back and forth between a view that's appropriate for detailed financial analysis and one that's appropriate for a report to creditors or stockholders. You can learn how to use this capability in Chapter 18, "Managing Different Views."

There are some subtle (and some not-so-subtle) reasons to consolidate data instead of placing the data in scenarios, and vice-versa. You'll find a discussion of the tradeoffs in Chapter 19, "Choosing between Scenarios and Consolidations." And Chapter 20, "Putting It Down on Paper," explains how to ease the process of moving different views and scenarios from the worksheet to the printer, including an all-Excel solution and alternative reporting methods using Access.

Part V, **Managing External Data Sources and Destinations**, takes you into the world of Structured Query Language and database management from the Excel platform. In Chapter 21, "Importing Data from External Sources," you will learn how to use Data Access Objects to move information from relational databases into Excel. And Chapter 22, "Sending Data to External Sources," explains how to move data from Excel to such databases, whether on your own computer or on a remote server.

Throughout this book, you will find the concepts and techniques illustrated with case studies of typical business situations and problems. (Look for the Case Study icon in the margin next to these special sections.) Using the Solver on marketing models and the Scenario Manager for sales analysis are examples of how you can use the case studies to understand a particular Excel data management capability.

Every chapter has a corresponding Excel workbook on the companion disk. All case studies and figures that employ worksheet data are replicated in these workbooks (a special disk icon points these out). We recommend that you copy these files to your computer when you begin the book, to make it easier for you to follow along with instruction sets and to understand the case studies more fully.

Although *Managing Data with Excel* is intended primarily for Excel 7, and consequently Windows 95, most of its content is compatible with the capabilities of Excel version 5 and Windows 3.*x*. We have, in most cases, used short file names to make it easier for the reader who uses Windows 3.*x*. In a few cases, you might find that you need to mentally convert a long file name to a short file name. Simply keep in mind that the short name is the first six, non-blank characters of the long file name, plus a tilde (~), the numeral 1 and the extension. Thus, the long file name "Data Manager.xls" would become "DATAMA~1.xls".

Conventions Used in This Book

Managing Data with Excel uses a few typeface, terminology, and formatting conventions to denote special information:

- A sequence like this

    Ctrl+Enter

    means you should hold down the Ctrl key as you press Enter.

- When you should select a sequence of options from an Excel menu, you will see this

    Choose Tools, Solver.

    This means you should first select the Tools menu on Excel's main menu bar and then select Solver from the drop-down menu under Tools. The "hot" or "accelerator" keys associated with a menu item are underlined, indicating that you may use Alt+ the underlined letter to choose the command or option. If you want to use two hot keys consecutively (as in Tools, Solver), keep pressing the Alt key as you press T, then V. Do not use Alt+T, then Alt+V.

- Data or formulas that you enter in an Excel worksheet cell are shown like this

  `=SUM(CumulativeNetIncome)/ProductLife`

- New terms, or information that needs special emphasis, are shown in *italic.*

- Data that has to be typed appears in **boldface.**

- Information about performing a task more efficiently or alternative ways to go about a task appears in tips. Tips are set apart from text like this:

  Tip

  To select a range of cells, even if it contains some blank cells, press Ctrl+*.

- Information that is related to the current topic, but that might not apply to it directly, is shown like this:

  Note

  You can find VBA code that automates this process on the disk that accompanies this book.

- Information that warns the reader of potentially hazardous procedures (for example, activities that delete files.)

  Caution

  Excel does not warn you if your data will overwrite existing data.

Now, copy the files from the companion disk to your computer, and turn to Chapter 1, "Managing Data with Lists." Put the ocarina down first.

Part I

Data Management Techniques

1

Managing Business Data with Lists

In Excel, a *list* is a fundamental structure on a worksheet, one that forms the basis for many different data management capabilities. Whether you want to sort, extract, summarize, or analyze data, the Excel tool that you choose usually requires that your data be organized as a list.

This chapter shows you how to sort lists, both by means of the defaults and by means of special options such as custom sorting orders. You'll see how to filter lists—that is, to display only those records that meet your selection criteria. Worksheet outlines, which allow you to quickly display or hide certain rows and columns, are covered at the end of the chapter.

First, you need to know how to structure lists, so they will have the characteristics needed to sort, filter, or outline them. List structures are covered in the following section.

Structuring Lists

A list's structure is simple and intuitive. It has these characteristics:

- It occupies one or more columns and up to 16,384 rows (the maximum number of rows on an Excel worksheet).

- Its first row is termed a *header row*, consisting of one or more *column labels*. Whatever is in a column's header row is the column's name. (A header row is optional. Exercise the option.)

- All rows in the list below the header row contain *records*. The records are values that are in some way similar to one another.

That's it. If your worksheet contains a range of values that correspond to those characteristics, it contains a list. An example is shown in figure 1.1.

Fig. 1.1

Lists are most useful when their columns contain records that share similar characteristics.

You don't need to define a list as you do, for example, a named range. So long as it is structured according to those three characteristics, the Excel tools that you bring to bear on the list will recognize it as a list.

If you're familiar with databases and database management, you might find it convenient to think of a list as a populated field. The header row is analogous to a database field name, and the rows in the list are the same as database records.

In a formal sense, the similarity of the records to one another is as you perceive it. For example, if a column label in your list is "Salary," then it certainly makes sense that all its entries would be numbers. If a column label is "Employee Name," you would expect that all its entries would be text values, each representing the name of an employee. The data management tools at your disposal work best, and return sensible results, if the entries in a list's column all represent the same construct.

But there's no formal or syntactic requirement that says you can't mix names with numbers. In fact, some Excel tools allow for just this sort of situation.

Using Lists for Different Purposes

If you structure your data on a worksheet as a list, a variety of techniques become much easier.

You can *arrange* the list's data in an order that you choose by sorting the records. Usually, the order in which the records are sorted is ascending (1, 2, 3, etc.) or descending ("Smith," "Robertson," "Quigley"). But there are also some custom sorting orders that you can apply. For example, if a list contains the names of the months of the year, you can sort it so that "September" records precede "October" records, even though alphabetic order calls for the reverse.

If you have structured your data as a list, Excel can automatically recognize its header row, and omit it from the records to be sorted. This capability prevents a column label, "Employee Name," from being sorted between "Edwards" and "Etheridge."

Excel can *extract* records from a list, and display them in-place or in a different location. This action is called *filtering*, and there are various ways to filter a list:

- Visually, so that certain records are hidden and others are visible
- Structurally, so that selected records are copied to a new location
- According to a criterion such as the highest ten values, or the highest ten percent, or some other criterion that you specify

You can also *summarize* the values in one column according to values in another column. For example, you might want to view your total sales revenues according to which sales region made each sale. Excel's Subtotal functions are handy for this, and you can create some very sophisticated summaries by using lists as inputs to pivot tables. Because pivot tables have so many options, several chapters in this book are devoted to their use.

The *analysis* of data in lists is simplified by using the Scenario Manager, the View Manager, the Analysis ToolPak and other tools and worksheet functions. These capabilities are also complex enough that they are treated in their own separate chapters.

The remainder of this chapter covers some of the more basic operations that help you arrange records in a list, extract records from it, and summarize its values.

Sorting Lists

Suppose you have data on products manufactured by your company in a worksheet list, as shown in figure 1.2.

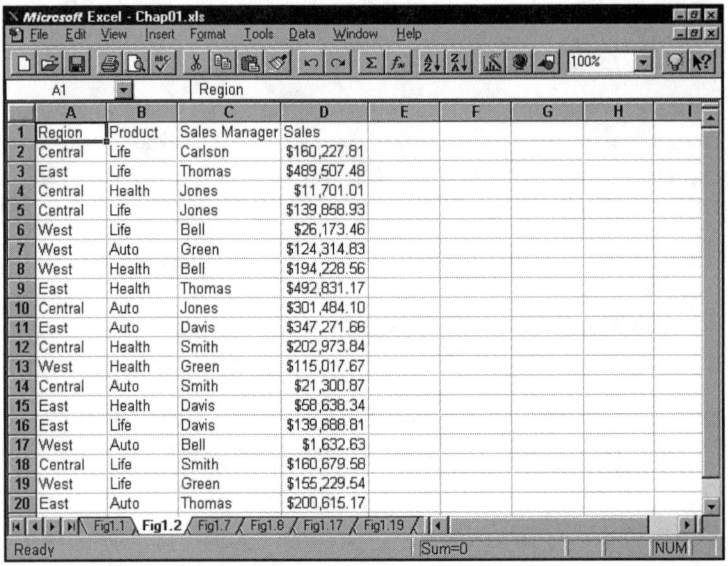

	A	B	C	D
1	Region	Product	Sales Manager	Sales
2	Central	Life	Carlson	$160,227.81
3	East	Life	Thomas	$489,507.48
4	Central	Health	Jones	$11,701.01
5	Central	Life	Jones	$139,858.93
6	West	Life	Bell	$26,173.46
7	West	Auto	Green	$124,314.83
8	West	Health	Bell	$194,228.56
9	East	Health	Thomas	$492,831.17
10	Central	Auto	Jones	$301,484.10
11	East	Auto	Davis	$347,271.66
12	Central	Health	Smith	$202,973.84
13	West	Health	Green	$115,017.67
14	Central	Auto	Smith	$21,300.87
15	East	Health	Davis	$58,638.34
16	East	Life	Davis	$139,688.81
17	West	Auto	Bell	$1,632.63
18	Central	Life	Smith	$160,679.58
19	West	Life	Green	$155,229.54
20	East	Auto	Thomas	$200,615.17

Fig. 1.2
As a first step in a sales analysis, you might want to sort the product line according to the revenue generated by each product.

You want to view the data in figure 1.2 according to the amount of sales revenue generated by each product, without regard to Region or Sales Manager. To do so, follow these steps:

1. Select one or more cells in the range A1:D20.
2. Choose Data, Sort. The Sort dialog box appears (see fig. 1.3, although the drop-down will not appear in the dialog box until you click its down-arrow).
3. Because you want to sort by sales revenue, you want the column label "Sales" to appear in the Sort By drop-down box. If it isn't there, click the down-arrow next to the Sort By edit box, and click "Sales" in the drop-down list.
4. Because you want the record with the highest amount of sales to appear first, choose the Descending option button, as shown in figure 1.3.
5. Choose OK.

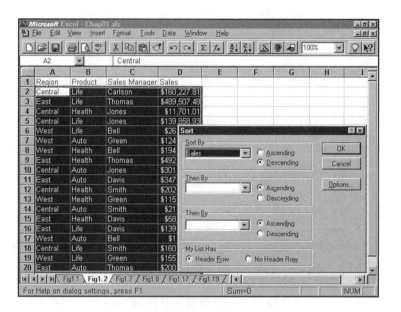

Fig. 1.3
Use the Sort dialog box to identify the range to sort, the sort keys and the direction of the sort.

After you choose OK, the range A1:D20 appears as shown in figure 1.4.

Fig. 1.4
After the list has been sorted according to the sort key (Sales), all records in all columns follow the order specified for Sales.

Several events occur behind the scenes as you complete the previous steps 1 through 5:

- Although you selected only one cell before choosing <u>D</u>ata, <u>S</u>ort, the entire range A2:D20 was highlighted as the Sort dialog box appeared on-screen. Because the list has four contiguous columns, and each column has 19 contiguous records, Excel was able to propose an entire range to sort.

- The header row was omitted from the highlighted sort area. The Sales column contains numbers as entries, and contains text as its column label in the header row. The difference in the types of information, numbers vs. text, in cells D1:D20 enabled Excel to identify the first row as a header. Excel uses that information to eliminate A1:D1 from the sort area, making the assumption that those cells constitute headers.

- Excel placed the names of each column—their headers—in the <u>S</u>ort By and in both the <u>T</u>hen By and the Then <u>B</u>y drop-downs. This makes it more convenient for you to specify sort keys than if a cell or range address had been presented to you as a sort key choice. That is, it's easier to keep track of what's going on if you see "Sales" in the <u>S</u>ort By box than if you see "Column D" in the <u>S</u>ort By box.

The <u>T</u>hen By and the Then <u>B</u>y drop-downs allow you to specify a second and third sort key for the list. Suppose you have a list with three fields: Sales Manager, Month, and Sales Dollars. Further suppose you use Sales Manager in the <u>S</u>ort By box, Month in the <u>T</u>hen By box, and Sales Dollars in the second Then <u>B</u>y box.

All records for the Sales Manager named Smith would be sorted together. Within the block of Smith's records, all of Smith's records for January would be sorted together. And within Smith's records for January, Sales Dollars would be sorted in whatever order, ascending or descending, that you specify.

What if the lists in A1:D20 had no header rows, but Excel had assumed that the first row constituted headers? Then you could have chosen the No Header Ro<u>w</u> option button on the Sort dialog box. And if the list had a header row, but Excel had not been able to identify one, you could have chosen the Header <u>R</u>ow option button to omit the first row from the sort area.

Tip

Excel can't identify a header row automatically if both the header and the records are text; or, if both the header and the records are numbers. In these cases, Excel will propose the No Header Ro<u>w</u> option.

Once you have chosen <u>D</u>ata, <u>S</u>ort with a single cell active, you do not have control over the area that Excel highlights—which indicates the area that will be sorted. Suppose you wanted to sort only the Sales and Sales Manager columns, and leave the Region and Product columns in their existing order. In that case, you would have two options:

■ Insert a column between columns C and D. Click the C at the top of column C, and choose <u>I</u>nsert, <u>C</u>olumns. This makes the columns noncontiguous, and Excel proposes D2:E20 as the sort area if you select one cell in D1:E20 prior to choosing <u>D</u>ata, <u>S</u>ort.

■ Select the range C1:D20, and then choose <u>D</u>ata, <u>S</u>ort. If you do so, Excel assumes that you have already selected the area to sort, and does not attempt to expand it. Excel does, however, attempt to identify a header row for the list in columns C and D.

Using Sort Options

While the Sort dialog box is visible on the screen, but before you choose OK or Cancel, there are additional options available to you. You can access these options by choosing the <u>O</u>ptions button on the Sort dialog box (see fig. 1.5).

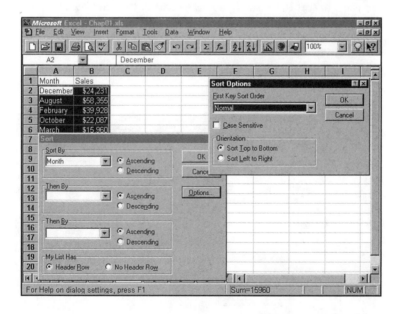

Fig. 1.5
The sort options enable you to choose a custom sort order, change the orientation of the sort, and cause Excel to attend to the case of text values.

Suppose one of the Sales Managers in your list is named E. E. Cummings, and that another is named e. e. cummings. Excel does not normally distinguish between uppercase and lowercase when comparing text values, and if you don't check the <u>C</u>ase Sensitive checkbox, Excel would intermingle the two Sales Managers' records. By checking the checkbox, records for e. e. cummings would precede records for E. E. Cummings in an ascending sort.

Although lists are deemed to be oriented with records in rows, it is not necessary to arrange your data range in that fashion in order to sort it. If, for example, you wanted to put a sorted range in a report, you might want to sort the data left to right instead of top to bottom. You can arrange to do so by choosing the Sort <u>L</u>eft to Right option button in the Sort Options dialog box.

Note

The labels Sort <u>T</u>op to Bottom and Sort <u>L</u>eft to Right are mildly misleading. Choosing one or the other has nothing to do with the order in which the sort takes place: you can sort ascending or descending left to right. Top to bottom simply means that rows switch places; left to right means that columns switch places.

The final option in the Sort Options dialog box pertains to custom sort orders. Suppose you have the names of the months in random order in a list, and you want to sort that list. If you do so without specifying a sort option, the months will be sorted in alphabetical order: April, August, December, and so on.

You can specify a custom sort order in the Sort Options dialog box (see fig. 1.6).

Fig. 1.6
Excel comes with several custom sort orders already established.

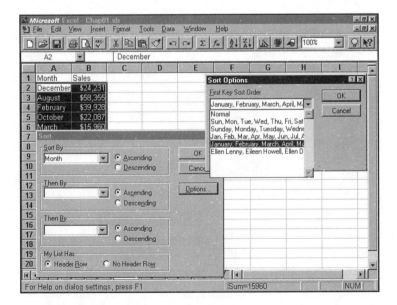

To view the custom sort orders already available to you, click the down-arrow in the First Key Sort Order drop-down box. By selecting one of these options, you can associate that sort order with the *first* sort key. If you attempt to associate a custom sort order with either the second (Then By) or the third (Then By) sort keys, it will not be implemented during the sort.

You can define your own custom sort orders. The process is described later in this chapter in "Managing Custom Lists."

Sorting References

Occasionally, you may want to sort a list that contains not values but references, or pointers to other worksheet cells. See, for example, figure 1.7.

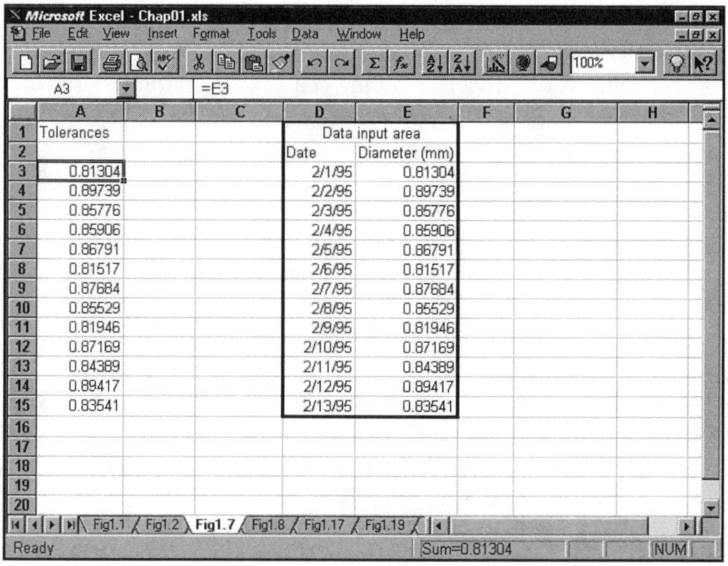

Fig. 1.7
Cells A3:A15 refer to cells E3:E15. For example, cell A3 contains the formula =E3.

If you were to sort the list in A3:A15, Excel would sort it by its values. However, once the sort is complete, the cells would recalculate. Because the formula =E3 is still in cell A3, the value displayed in cell A3 would recalculate to the value in E3, and the list's values would still appear in their original order.

There are several ways to get around this difficulty. One is to convert the relative references in A3:A15 to mixed references. If you understand relative, mixed, and absolute references, you can skip the next section without missing anything. Otherwise, or if you're not sure, it would be a good idea to read it: understanding the different types of references is crucial to using Excel effectively.

Understanding Different Forms of References

Suppose that, on some worksheet, cell C3 contains this formula

=F3

Cell C3 displays whatever value is in cell F3. If you now copy cell C3 into cell C4, then C4 will contain this formula

=F4

The reference is *relative* to the cell where it exists. If you copy it down a row or up a row, or right one column, or left one column, the copied formula adjusts its reference relative to the direction you copy it.

In contrast, suppose that cell C3 contains this formula

=$F$3

Notice the dollar signs in the reference. These signs anchor the reference to the row and column that together define cell F3. No matter where you copy the formula, it will contain the same reference to cell F3. This form of reference, with a dollar sign before both the column letter and the row number, is termed an *absolute* reference.

There are two types of *mixed* reference. One type anchors the reference to a particular column, and one anchors it to a particular row. If cell C3 contains this formula

=$F3

then you can copy it into another column in row 3 (such as A3 or IV3) and the reference will remain the same no matter which column you copy it to. The dollar sign anchors the reference to column F. But if you copy the formula into cell C4, it changes to

=$F4

because it's not anchored to any particular row. And if cell C3 contains this formula

=F$3

then the reference is anchored to row 3. Copy it up or down, and the reference remains the same. Copy it right or left, and the column adjusts relative to the distance and direction that you copy it.

> **Tip**
>
> Typing dollar signs is tedious. As a shortcut, select the cell that contains the reference, highlight the reference in the formula bar and press the F4 key. Pressing F4 repeatedly cycles a reference through, for example, A1, $A$1, A$1 and $A1, and then back to A1.

Converting a Range of References

To convert a range of relative references to mixed references, follow these steps (this example converts relative references to any row in column E into mixed references anchored to specific rows in column E):

1. Select the range A3:A15.

2. Choose Edit, Replace.

3. In the Find What box, enter **E**.

4. In the Replace With box, enter **E$**.

5. Choose Find Next to find the next instance of E, Replace to replace the current instance and prompt you with the next one, or Replace All to replace all instances of E with E$, with no further prompting.

The references in A3:A15 are now anchored to rows. When you sort A3:A15, the row references follow *and stay with* the sort of the values in the range. Try it on a worksheet and verify for yourself that the row portion of the references do move to the appropriate cells.

Sorting Relative References with an Array Formula

Another way to sort A3:A15 (refer to fig. 1.7) is useful if you want to keep the references purely relative. However, to use this method you must create the sort in a different location. Follow these steps:

1. Highlight a blank range consisting of one column and 13 rows.

2. Type this formula so that it appears in the formula bar, but do not yet press Enter:

   `=SMALL(E3:E15,ROW(E3:E15)-INDEX(ROW(E3:E15),1)+1)`

3. Hold down Ctrl+Shift simultaneously, and press Enter.

This formula returns, in the range that contains it, the smallest, then the next smallest, through the largest value in the range E3:E15. If you wanted to sort the range in descending order, instead of ascending order, you could replace the SMALL function with the LARGE function.

> **Note**
>
> The formula will not sort text values, because the values in the first argument to SMALL or LARGE must be numeric. If it's necessary to sort formulas that contain references to cells that contain text values, it's best to convert the relative references to mixed references.

If you have entered the formula properly, you will see that it's surrounded by a pair of curly (sometimes termed *French*) braces in the formula bar. These braces are added by Excel—do not type them yourself or Excel will interpret the entry as text. They indicate that the formula is an *array formula*. Array formulas are a powerful analysis tool in Excel, and you can save yourself considerable time and effort by using them—in fact, several worksheet functions *must* be entered as array formulas.

Array formulas have limited utility for data management, and are not discussed in any great detail in this book, but you can find valuable information about them in Excel's online Help.

Filtering Lists

To *filter* a list is to extract records from it, based on criteria that you set. You can extract records visually, by causing Excel to temporarily hide records that don't meet your criteria, or you can extract them structurally, by causing Excel to move records that do meet the criteria to another part of the worksheet.

There are two menu commands to filter a list, both found in the Filter menu that cascades from the Data menu: AutoFilter and Advanced Filter.

Using AutoFilter

The quickest way to filter a list is by means of AutoFilter. This menu command provides you with some preset criteria and enables only visual filtering. The ease of using AutoFilter means that it offers you fewer options than the Advanced Filter. Figure 1.8 shows an example of using AutoFilter.

To enable AutoFilter, select any cell in a list. Then, choose Data, Filter, AutoFilter.

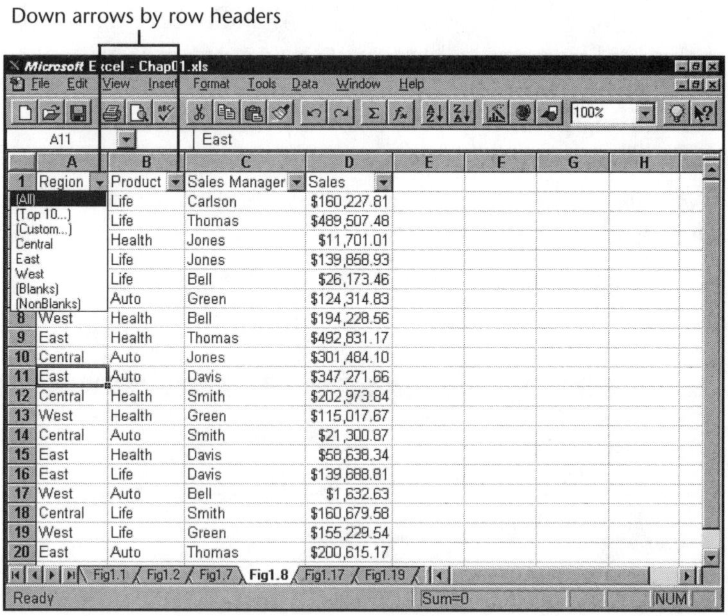

Down arrows by row headers

Fig. 1.8
AutoFilter puts down arrows by the column labels in the header row to display filtering criteria.

Notice in figure 1.8 the drop-down box that appears when you click the arrow beside a column's header (the arrow is called an *AutoFilter control*). When you click the control, a drop-down box appears that contains several options:

■ *(All)*. Displays all the items in the list.

■ *(Top Ten)*. Despite its name, this option allows for the display of 1, 2, 3,... items in a numeric list. You can also choose to display the largest (Top) or smallest (Bottom) items, and the number that you select can be either a number of items or a percentage of the items in the list.

> **Tip**
>
> Top Ten has no effect if a column contains only text values. If the column contains both text and numeric values, it hides the text values and filters the numeric values.

■ *(Custom)*. Provides a way for you to specify one or two criteria to apply to the list. The criteria can be connected by an AND or by an OR.

■ *Specific values*. The drop-down also displays the values found in the list. If a value appears more than once in the list, it appears only once in the drop-down box.

- ■ *(Blanks)*. Most useful if your list contains multiple contiguous columns. Using the Blanks option, you can display records that have missing information in one of the columns. Finding a record with a blank in a column might warn you that information has been omitted, or that an action remains to be taken.

- ■ *(NonBlanks)*. The opposite of the (Blanks) option, the NonBlanks option suppresses the display of records with missing data.

For example, figure 1.9 shows the list in figure 1.8 filtered to show only the records from the Central region.

Fig. 1.9

AutoFilter filters records by hiding rows that do not meet the criterion.

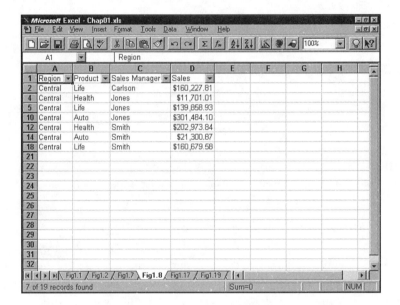

Figure 1.10 shows the list filtered to show only the records from the Central region that belong to the sales manager named Jones. This shows that when you choose a criterion for each of two or more columns, the criteria are treated as connected by an AND. The entries that are displayed must meet all criteria that have been set.

Figure 1.11 shows the five records with the highest values in the Sales field. It also shows the dialog box that appears when you choose the Top Ten option.

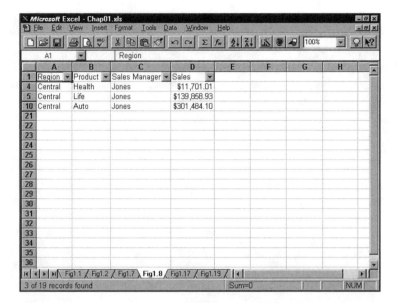

Fig. 1.10
If criteria are set
for two or more
fields, the criteria
are treated as being
connected by an
AND.

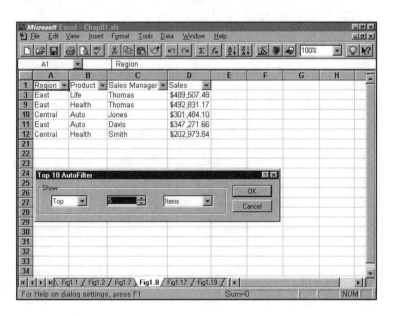

Fig. 1.11
The Top Ten
option is not
limited either to
Top or to Ten.

Data Management

Tip

When you filter a list, Excel changes the color of the AutoFilter control from gray to blue. This is a convenient way to tell which column in a multi-column list the filter applies to. This also occurs with the Advanced Filter (see the next section) when the list is filtered in-place.

Figure 1.12 shows the results of choosing the Custom option. The dialog box provides for one or two custom criteria. The criteria can be treated as connected by an AND—a record is displayed only if it meets both criteria—or by an OR—a record is displayed if it meets either criterion.

Fig. 1.12
You can use the Custom option in AutoFilter if you have no more than two criteria to apply.

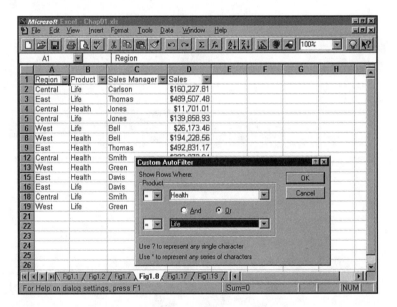

Note

You can specify only one AutoFilter on a worksheet. Selecting AutoFilter a second time on the same worksheet merely removes the first AutoFilter. The same is true of the Advanced Filter (see the next section).

Tip

To remove the AutoFilter controls from the list's header row, toggle the command by choosing Data, Filter, AutoFilter again. To keep the AutoFilter controls but show all the records in a list, choose Data, Filter, Show All.

Using the Advanced Filter

The Advanced Filter command gives you more options than the AutoFilter command. Using the Advanced Filter, you can:

- Choose between filtering the list visually (hiding rows, as with AutoFilter) or structurally (by copying records to another location on the worksheet).

- Apply more complex criteria—including computed criteria—to the list.

- Display unique records only.

When you choose Data, Filter, Advanced Filter, the dialog box shown in figure 1.13 appears.

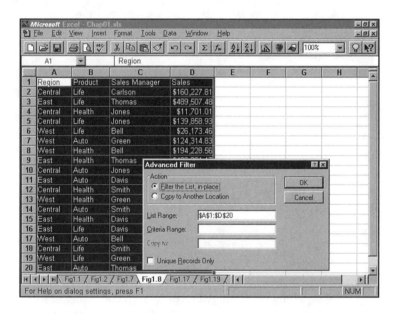

Fig. 1.13
The Advanced Filter is more complex than AutoFilter, but it offers you more options.

If you choose the Filter the List In-place option, the Advanced Filter hides rows containing records that don't meet your criteria, just as the AutoFilter does. If you choose the Copy to Another Location option, the Copy To edit box is enabled, and you can click in a worksheet cell to establish the first cell to contain the copied data.

Note

You can't copy filtered data to another worksheet using the Advanced Filter.

In contrast to the AutoFilter command, the Advanced Filter allows you to modify, in its dialog box, the range that is filtered. If only one cell in a list is active when you start the Advanced Filter, Excel expands the selection to all contiguous rows and columns, just as AutoFilter does. However, you can use the List Range edit box to narrow the selection. The List Range edit box defines the list that is subjected to the filtering process.

For example, if you check the Unique Records Only checkbox, the Advanced Filter ignores duplicate records in the list identified by the List Range edit box. See figures 1.14 and 1.15 for two examples.

Fig. 1.14
This list was filtered for unique records in Region only.

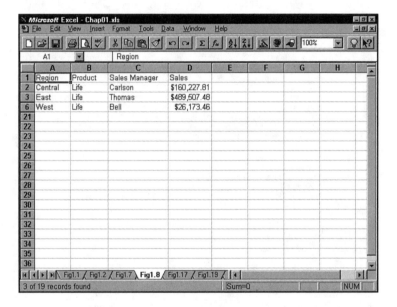

Figure 1.14 displays only three filtered records, each consisting of the first instance of each of the three possible values for Region. It was created by entering A1:A20 in the List Range edit box, and checking the Unique Records Only checkbox.

Figure 1.15 displays nine filtered records, each consisting of the first instance of the *combination* of a unique record for Region and a unique record for Product. It was created by entering A1:B20 (notice that two columns were chosen) in the List Range edit box, and checking the Unique Records Only checkbox.

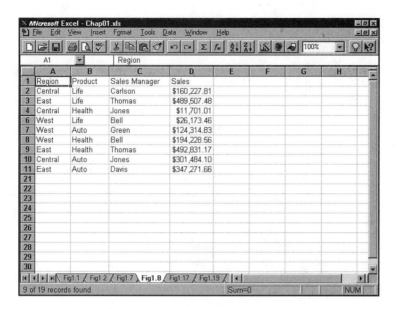

Data Management

Fig. 1.15
This list was filtered for unique records in both Region and Product.

Although two columns were chosen for filtering in the List Range edit box in figure 1.15, all four columns were filtered. This occurs because filtering the list in place causes entire rows to be hidden. If the Copy to Another Location option button had been chosen, the filtered list would appear as shown in figure 1.16.

> **Caution**
>
> Excel clears all cells below the Copy To Location, regardless of how many rows the new list occupies. So if the fields are copied to the range E1:G5, Excel clears cells E6:G16384. Excel does not warn you if you have data in those columns, so be sure that copying to another location will not overwrite anything you can't stand to lose.

Notice, in figure 1.16, that filtered records from only two columns appear in the new location. If you want to filter for unique records in a subset of the list's columns, and yet show their values in all the columns, you must filter the list in place.

The Advanced Filter, as noted at the beginning of this section, allows you to create more complicated criteria than does the AutoFilter. In particular, you can use the Advanced Filter to specify:

- More than the two criteria allowed by the AutoFilter.
- One criterion for one column, and another criterion for another column.

Fig. 1.16
Copying the
filtered list to
another location
prevents rows
from being
hidden.

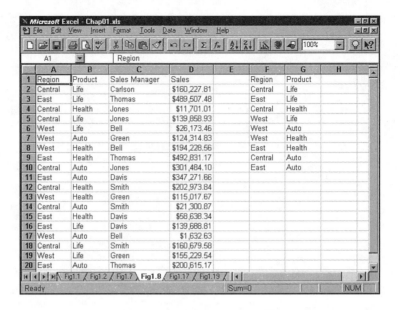

- Computed criteria: for example, "Display only those records whose Sales value is greater than the average Sales value." This is termed a *computed* criterion because Excel must compute, in this case, the average Sales value in order to determine whether a record meets the criterion.

You must enter the criteria for record selection in a range on the worksheet, and refer to that range in the Advanced Filter dialog box's Criteria Range edit box.

Additionally, in all but one situation, you need to repeat the columns' headers as the first line in the criteria range. This is so that Excel knows which column to compare with which criterion.

Figure 1.17 displays some of your options for Advanced Filter criteria.

If you used the range A22:D25 (or just C22:C25) in the Criteria Range edit box, the Advanced Filter would display only those records whose value on Sales Manager is Carlson, Thomas, or Green.

In contrast, if you used the range A27:B28 as the criteria range, the Advanced Filter would display only those records whose value for Sales is over $120,000 and which belong to the Central region.

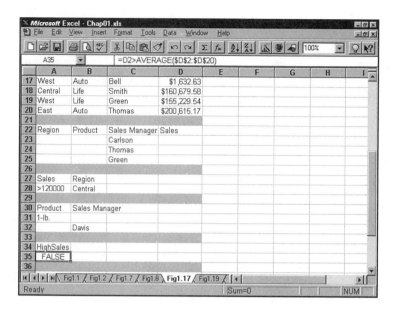

Fig. 1.17
Each of these
criteria ranges
results in the
display of a
different subset
of records.

Data Management

Notice these aspects of the criteria in A22:D25 and A27:B28:

- C22:C25 contain three criteria. Because AutoFilter supports the use of two criteria at most, this selection requires the Advanced Filter.

- A27:B28 make reference to two different columns: Sales and Region. The AutoFilter allows you to specify two criteria, but both criteria must refer to the same column.

- To connect multiple criteria by ORs, enter them in different rows, as shown in C22:C25. Again, the Advanced Filter returns records that match Carlson *or* Thomas *or* Green.

- To connect multiple criteria by AND, enter them in different columns, as shown in A27:B28. Again, the Advanced Filter returns records that match the Central region *and* that have sales values over $120,000.

- To connect multiple criteria by both AND and OR, use both different columns and different rows. For example, in figure 1.17, if you entered **Life** in B23, B24, and B25, and then used B22:C25 as the criteria range, the Advanced Filter would return records that matched (Carlson and Life) or (Thomas and Life) or (Green and Life).

- It's convenient, but not necessary, to put the criteria in the same column as their associated list. It's usually inconvenient to put the criteria in the same rows as the lists occupy, because hiding the rows for unselected records could hide the criteria range.

The criteria range A30:B32 shows how to join criteria that refer to two different columns with an OR. Different rows imply an OR, just as is the case with the range C22:C25. However, in A30:B32, two different columns are involved—Product and Sales Manager. These criteria would return records with the value of 1-lb. for Product, *or* records with a value of Davis for Sales Manager.

Finally, the range A34:A35 contains a *computed criterion*. The formula that returns FALSE in cell A35 is

```
=D2>AVERAGE($D$2:$D$20)
```

The criterion specifies that only those records whose values on Sales exceed the average sales value are to be displayed. Notice about this criterion that:

- The use of D2 is a relative reference. As the Advanced Filter scans the records in the range D2:D20, it adjusts the relative reference to D3, D4, ..., D20. As it finds a record that meets the computed criterion, it displays the row; as it finds a record that does not meet the criterion, it hides the row.
- Cell A34's label is *not* "Sales" but "HighSales." In contrast to other, non-computed criteria, it's important to use a label that isn't identical to any column label in the list's row header. (You can also leave the criterion label blank.) Using the same label for the criterion and the list can cause unpredictable results. Because the criterion specifies a relative reference by its use of D2, the Advanced Filter finds the proper list values to compare to the average of the values in $D$2:$D$20.

Caution

Notice that the computation of the average of the values in D2:D20 uses an absolute reference as its argument. Excel 7.0 terminates with an unrecoverable error if you use a relative reference as an argument in a computed criterion.

In the example above, the criterion is computed by reference to the records in the list that is to be filtered ($D$2:$D$20). This is often the most useful way to employ a computed criterion. However, it isn't necessary to base the criterion on the list itself. This computed criterion would also be legal

```
=D2>AVERAGE($Z$100:$Z$500)
```

as a means of filtering the lists in A1:D20.

Managing Custom Lists

As discussed in the section in this chapter on sorting lists, Excel comes with several custom sort orders already defined. These sort orders are actually *custom lists*, and you can define more custom lists for various purposes. To do so, choose Tools, Options and select the Custom Lists tab from the Options dialog box (see fig. 1.18).

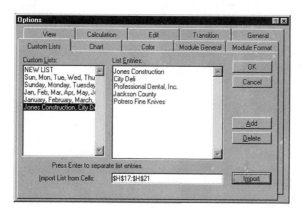

Fig. 1.18
You can create new custom lists for data that you enter frequently, or to establish a new custom sort order.

The custom lists that are supplied with Excel include the names of the days of the week and of the months of the year—both abbreviated and spelled out. This chapter has already discussed how custom lists can be used as custom sort orders; they have other uses.

For example, you might create a custom list of your company's best customers. Doing so makes it very easy to begin a report that analyzes some variable such as sales per customer. To create the list, follow these steps:

1. Type the names of the customers into a range of contiguous cells, such as A1:A20.

2. Choose Tools, Options and, if necessary, click the Custom Lists tab.

3. Click in the Import List from Cells edit box, and highlight cells A1:A20.

4. Click Import, and then choose OK.

Your custom list now appears in the Custom Lists list box. To make use of it, enter the first item in the list in any worksheet cell. Make that cell active, and then use the fill handle (the heavy black square in the bottom-right corner of an active cell) to drag right or down. The list extends to its final item, and then begins again at its first value.

Data Management

Values other than names are useful custom list entries. If there is a report or form that you create on a regular basis, one way to avoid having to type its headings repeatedly is to store them in a custom list. Another way would be to store them in an Excel template—different circumstances would dictate which method you would use.

In the Custom Lists text box, you can also type new values for a list in the List Entries box. After you have typed a new entry, choose Add to establish the new entry if you want to continue with another entry.

Using Outlines

In Excel, an outline is a means of displaying and hiding rows or columns that contain the details that comprise summaries. Figure 1.19 gives an example of an Excel outline.

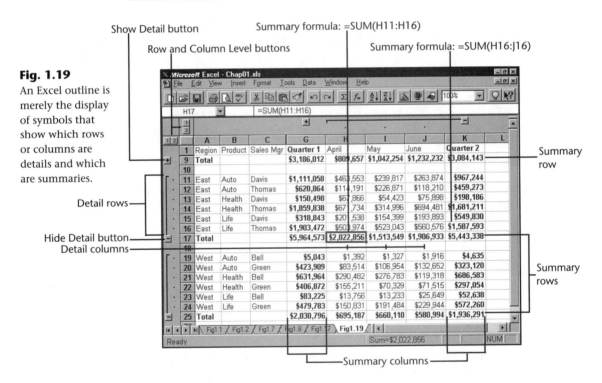

Fig. 1.19
An Excel outline is merely the display of symbols that show which rows or columns are details and which are summaries.

If your worksheet has rows that summarize other rows, or columns that summarize other columns, you can use outlines to quickly display and hide the detail information.

Creating an Outline

You can create an outline automatically by selecting any cell within the range and selecting Data, Group and Outline, Auto Outline. Excel analyzes the formulas in the summary rows and columns, and treats the rows and columns that they refer to as details.

You can also create an outline manually. This is the right procedure if your worksheet does not have summary formulas, as can occur if you import data from a text file or from an external database. You can also modify an outline manually, if your sheet is set up in such a way that Auto Outline does not give you the effect that you want.

To create an outline manually, select a set of detail rows or columns and choose Data, Group and Outline, and then select Group from the cascading menu. (The detail-level rows or columns that compose a summary row or column are termed a *group*.) This action simply defines which records or columns define a group, and displays the appropriate outline symbols in the margin of the worksheet.

Hiding and Displaying Detail

Once you have created the groups, you can use the buttons on the outline symbols to hide and unhide details. For example, in figure 1.19, you could click the Hide Detail button to the left of row 9 to hide rows 2 through 8. Or, you could click the Show Detail button above column G to display columns D through F.

Tip

If you want to hide the outline symbols after you have created the outline, choose Tools, Options and click the View tab. Then, clear the Outline Symbols checkbox and choose OK.

To show or hide all details in all groups, click a Row Level button or a Column Level button. This is quicker than clicking each Hide or Show Detail button individually.

Chapter Summary

In this chapter, you have learned how to manage lists of data on worksheets. In particular, you have learned both the basics and the details of sorting lists, of filtering records within lists to view or to suppress the records according to criteria, and of outlining data in worksheets.

Sorting is a valuable way of managing the data in an Excel worksheet. It helps you bring similar records together, for visual inspection or other purposes such as preparing reports and charting the data.

Filtering the data in a worksheet is a useful way to view a subset of the records that compose a list. Pivot tables, which are covered in detail in chapters 7 through 11, also enable you to view subsets of data, but pivot tables are weak when it comes to applying criteria. Particularly if you want to view or analyze lists according to computed criteria, consider using the AutoFilter or Advanced Filter in preference to using a pivot table.

Outlining a worksheet is useful in only a restricted set of circumstances. A pivot table does a much better job of summarizing the details of lists in a worksheet than does an outline. An outline does make it somewhat easier to toggle back and forth between hiding and showing details than does a pivot table. Furthermore, an outline doesn't require the use of another range in a worksheet to display summaries, as does a pivot table. But apart from these considerations, you will usually find that pivot tables meet your needs and offer much more functionality than does a worksheet outline.

Yet another method of managing data in a worksheet is by means of Data Tables, which are the topic of Chapter 2.

2

Using Data Tables To Project Financial Outcomes

One of Excel's most useful features is the flexibility it provides for making forecasts. After an analysis is set up, you can anticipate different possible outcomes simply by changing the assumptions you used. What will the payments on a fixed-rate mortgage be, for example, if interest rates jump by half a percent before you nail down the financing? What if rates fall by half a percent? How will a 10% rise in unit costs affect the profitability of a product line? How about a 5% decline?

Obviously, you can generate an entire range of possible outcomes for such analyses. The process can become quite tedious, depending on how many possibilities you want to examine. Fortunately, you can construct an entire table of such values in almost no time by using Excel's Data Table command.

The Data Table command speeds up the what-if process by doing the heavy lifting for you. After you set up your initial analysis, you enter a series of alternative values for a key variable in a nearby section of the worksheet. When you issue the command, Excel fills out the table, entering the results that correspond to each different variable value.

The completed table remains in the worksheet so you can quickly look up the outcome associated with a particular variable value. You can also apply many of the list-analysis tools described in Chapter 1, such as the AutoFilter, to the data in the table. And because Excel uses array formulas to generate data tables, the table provides a dynamic reference. If you change some aspect of the original analysis, the change is automatically reflected in the data table.

This chapter explains the simple steps you use to create a data table. We begin with the most basic type of data table, in which only one variable changes, and graduate to more sophisticated data tables, in which you use two variables to create a matrix. We conclude by pointing out some of the tricks that Excel pros use to maximize the value of their data tables.

Using One-Variable Data Tables

The example most commonly used to illustrate the power and versatility of data tables is mortgage-payment calculations, because it's relatively simple and familiar to so many people. Rather than buck tradition, we'll use just such an example (see fig. 2.1).

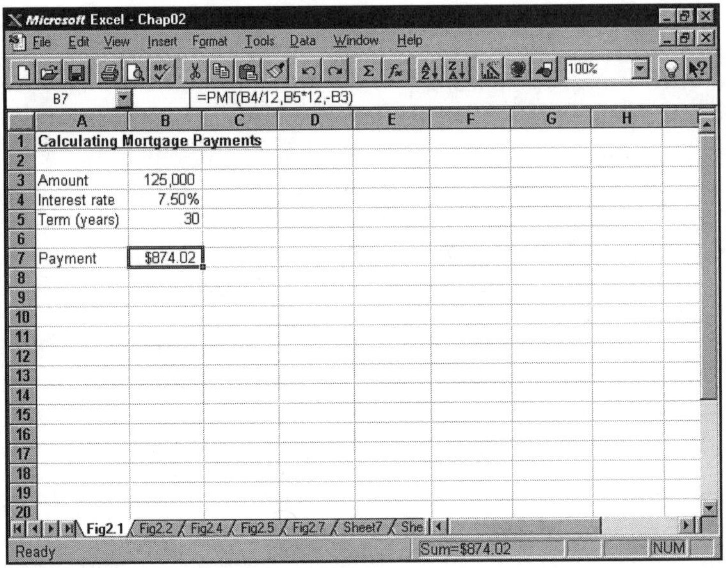

Fig. 2.1
This simple mortgage payment analysis can act as the foundation for a more detailed data table of possible payment amounts.

The worksheet in figure 2.1 shows the mortgage payment for a single scenario, one with a mortgage amount of $125,000, an interest rate of 7.5%, and a term of 30 years. The formula in cell B7

```
=PMT(B4/12,B5*12,-B3)
```

shows that the monthly payment associated with this set of variables is $874.02.

If you're planning to take out a $125,000 mortgage sometime during the next year, you might wonder how changes in the interest rate would affect the payment. Or, if you already had a mortgage at this interest rate, you might wonder about the savings that would be possible by refinancing at a lower rate (see fig. 2.2).

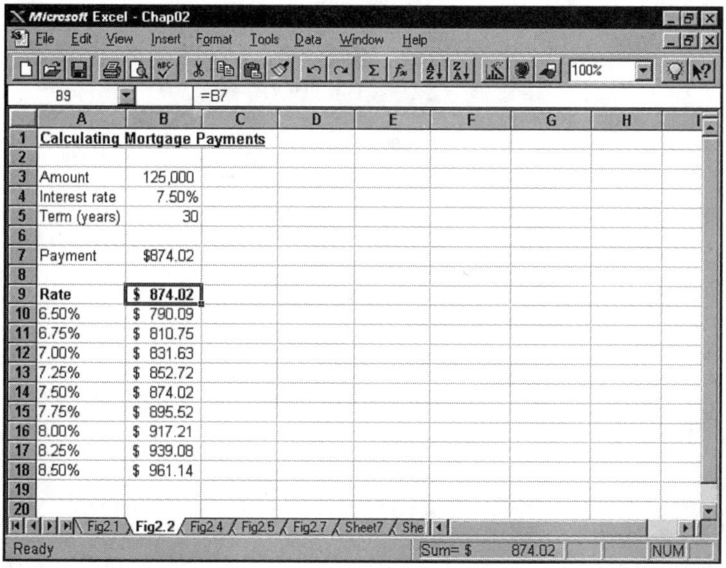

Fig. 2.2

The one-variable data table in range A9:B18 lists mortgage payments associated with different interest rates.

The one-variable data table shown in figure 2.2 answers all such questions at a glance. To set up such a data table, follow these steps:

1. Set up the original analysis, as shown in figure 2.1.

2. Enter the variable values you wish to test in a column. In figure 2.2, a range of possible interest rates is entered in range A10:A18. (The column heading in cell A9 is optional for the purpose of creating the data table, but is necessary if you later want to filter the table.)

3. In the cell one row above and one column to the right of the column of variable values, enter a simple reference to the cell that contains the result of the initial analysis. In figure 2.2, cell B9 contains the formula =B7.

4. Select the range that contains the column of test variable values and the reference formula. In figure 2.2, you would select range A9:B18.

5. Choose Data, Table. The Table dialog box opens.

6. In the Table dialog box (shown in figure 2.3), use the Column Input Cell edit box to indicate the cell in the original analysis that corresponds to the variable values you are testing. In the example, we are testing the impact of different interest rates on the mortgage payment. Since the interest rate variable in the initial analysis is located in cell B4, we entered B4 in the Column Input Cell edit box.

7. Choose OK.

Fig. 2.3

Use the Table dialog box to indicate which cell in the original analysis contains the variable or variables that correspond to the variable values you are testing in the data table.

Excel fills the second column in the data table (range B10:B18) with the mortgage payments that correspond to the interest rates listed in the first column, as shown earlier in figure 2.2. You can now easily determine the payment associated with any given interest rate, for the Amount and Term listed in the original analysis.

Using Two-Variable Data Tables

Once you've mastered the simple technique required to create a one-variable data table, you may find yourself hungry for more. A data table with multiple columns would be even more useful, representing the payment associated with different interest rates—and different mortgage amounts.

The Data, Table command gives you this flexibility by including both a Row Input Cell and a Column Input Cell in the Table dialog box (refer to fig. 2.3). Rather than using one or the other, you can use both to create a matrix of possible outcomes associated with two changing variables rather than just one.

In the mortgage payment example, for instance, you might wonder how the monthly payment varies not only with the interest rate, but with the size of the mortgage as well. If rates go low enough, you may be able to afford a bigger mortgage.

Tip

In a two-variable data table, it doesn't matter which variable goes on the top row of the table and which goes in the first column. It's important, though, to make sure that the inputs in the Table dialog box correspond to the correct cells in the initial analysis.

To model the effect of both changing rates and a changing principal amount, set up a two-variable data table as shown in figure 2.4. Test variables for the interest rate are listed in a column (range A10:A18), just as they were in the one-variable data table. Test variables for the mortgage amount are listed in a row at the top of the table (range B9:G9).

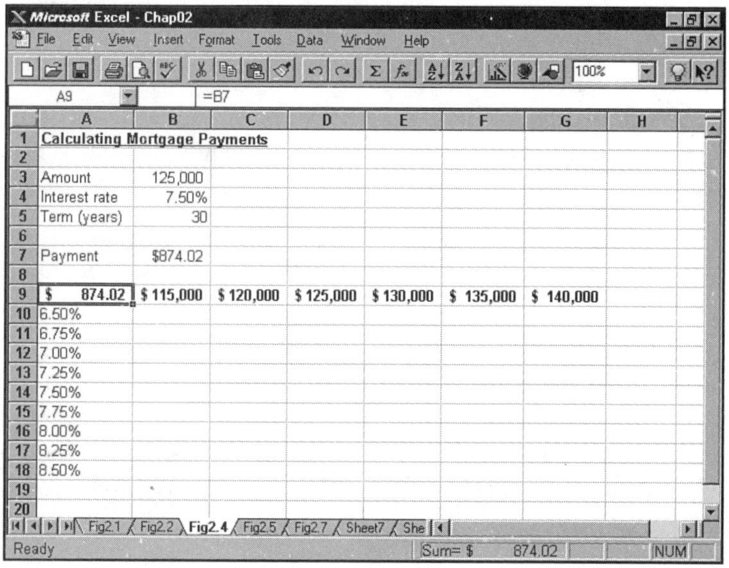

Fig. 2.4
To create a two-variable data table, list one set of test values in the first column of the table and the other in the top row.

The two-variable data table is almost identical in structure to the one-variable data table, with two important differences:

- The reference formula moves from the second column of the table to the first column. It remains in the top row.
- The data table range expands to include all the columns indicated by the test variables in the top row.

Thus, the steps for creating a two-variable data table are very similar to the steps listed above for a one-variable data table. However, it's important to note the different location of the table's reference formula, and to enter both a column input cell and a row input cell in the Table dialog box. The steps required to create a two-variable data table are listed below:

1. Set up the original analysis.

2. Enter the values for the first variable that you wish to test in a column. In figure 2.4, a range of possible interest rates is entered in range A10:A18.

3. In the cell above this column of test values, enter a simple reference to the cell that contains the result of the initial analysis. In figure 2.4, cell A9 contains the formula =B7.

4. Enter the values for the second variable that you wish to test in the row at the top of the data table. In figure 2.4, a range of possible mortgage amounts is entered in range B9:G9.

5. Select the range that contains all test variable values and the reference formula. In figure 2.4, you would select range A9:G18.

6. Choose Data, Table.

7. In the Table dialog box (shown in figure 2.3), use the Row Input Cell edit box to indicate the cell in the original analysis that corresponds to the values along the top row of the table. In the example, these values represent mortgage amounts, so the Row Input Cell is cell B3.

8. While still in the Table dialog box, use the Column Input Cell edit box to indicate the cell in the original analysis that corresponds to the variable values in the left column of the table. In the example, these values represent interest rates, so the Column Input Cell is cell B4.

9. Choose OK.

Figure 2.5 shows a completed two-variable data table. By reading across the top of the table and down the first column, you can find the monthly payment that corresponds to any combination of the mortgage-amount and interest-rate variables you tested. For example, a $120,000 mortgage at 8.25% would run $901.52 per month. A $140,000 mortgage at 6.75% would be just a little more—$908.04 per month.

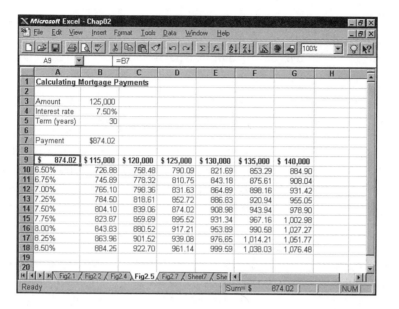

Fig. 2.5
A completed two-variable data table displays a matrix of values.

What a difference a good rate makes.

The test variables you use in the left column or top row of a data table don't have to fall at regular intervals (6%, 7%, 8%...), but it usually makes the table easier to interpret if they do.

Case Study—Fitting Data Tables to Your Business Needs

Typically, data tables are used to gauge the effect of changes on commonplace business variables, such as interest rates, capital expenditure amounts, market share forecasts, and so forth. However, data tables can be as exotic as your business, as one agricultural concern in western Pennsylvania proved in the early 1990s. The company's line of business, breeding unusual animals such as ostriches, monkeys, and snakes, required some unusual forecasting methods.

Data tables came into the picture when the firm bid a contract to breed chinchillas for delivery in approximately two years' time. The question: What quantity of specialized construction material would the firm need to house its product until the delivery date? How many chinchillas might there be by then?

The answer, of course, depended primarily on two variables: The chinchillas' reproductive and mortality rates. A two-variable data table provided a range of possible outcomes. The firm immediately purchased enough construction materials to house the minimum possible number of chinchillas and at the same time procured options for further purchases, up to the maximum possible number of chinchillas.

It was a good thing, too, for the chinchillas turned out to be a hardy (and busy) bunch, pushing the final population near the maximum number forecast by the two-way data table. The breeding firm was protected from increases in the price of construction materials which jumped substantially during the period. The outcome was a happy one for the chinchillas, as well: The breeding firm's contract was with a major pet-store franchise rather than a furrier, and each of the cuddlesome creatures presumably found a happy home.

Working with Data Tables

How does Excel construct data tables? Some other spreadsheets approach this task by repeatedly substituting the variable test values you specify into the Column Input Cell and/or the Row Input Cell, recalculating the worksheet, and placing static results in the data table.

Excel does things a little differently, creating an array that refers to the column input cell, the row input cell, or both. The array is dynamic, which means that any change that affects the contents of the data table is immediately reflected in the table itself.

For example, if you changed cell B5 in figure 2.5 to 15 years, rather than 30 years, the entire array in range B10:G18 would recalculate automatically, displaying mortgage payments that correspond to a mortgage with a 15-year term. This is because the formula used to calculate the data table values, in cell A9, refers to the payment formula in cell B7. When the payment formula recalculates, so does the reference formula in cell A9, and hence, so does the entire table.

Using arrays rather than static values has obvious advantages. Unless you change Excel's recalculation settings, your tables always reflect the latest information in the worksheet; you don't have to reissue the Data, Table command every time you change some aspect of your model. This can save you a great deal of time if your data table depends on a more-complex model than the simple mortgage-payment worksheet we have been using as an example.

There's an additional benefit: You can change the test values in the left column or the top row of the data table and the table updates automatically. Once again, it's unnecessary to reissue the Data, Table command.

For example, if your deadline for making a mortgage commitment is imminent and it appears that your rate will be 7.125%, you could substitute this value in one of the cells in the first column of the data table in figure 2.5. If you substituted this value in cell A12, for example, range B12:G12 would update automatically, showing you the monthly payments associated with the 7.125% rate.

However, in addition to these benefits, using arrays instead of static values in a data table can create some circumstances that you might not anticipate. Recalculation and editing are the two functions that most commonly pose problems for people unaware of data tables' use of arrays.

Recalculating Data Tables

With the power and flexibility that data tables offer, you may be tempted to create them often, and on a grand scale. And why not? They provide an almost effortless way to examine the effect of a wide range of variable values on the outcome of an analysis.

The problem is that too many data tables—and too many arrays—can require substantial resources to recalculate, thus slowing down workbook performance.

Excel's designers recognized this, and included a way for you to turn off automatic recalculation of data tables—while maintaining automatic recalculation for the rest of the workbook (and other open workbooks). It's the Automatic Except Tables calculation option, shown in figure 2.6. To select this option, use the following steps:

1. Choose Tools, Options. The Options dialog box appears.
2. Select the Calculation tab.
3. Select the Automatic Except Tables option button.
4. Choose OK.

Fig. 2.6

The Automatic Except Tables option allows you to turn off recalculation for data tables while maintaining it for the rest of the workbook.

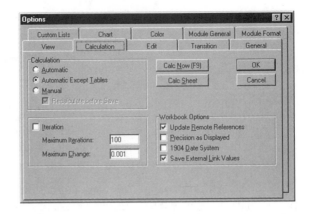

After you select this option, your data tables no longer automatically reflect the current values of cells elsewhere in the worksheet. To update the data tables in a workbook, you must press the F9 key or select the Calc Now button on the Calculation tab of the Options dialog box (shown in figure 2.6).

You can reinstate automatic recalcuation for data tables by selecting the Automatic option button on the Calculation tab of the Options dialog box.

Editing and Deleting Data Tables

Another often unanticipated consequence of using arrays to create a data table is that the cells in the table function as a unit, rather than individually. If you try to move or delete a single cell or a portion of a data table, Excel displays the error message Cannot change part of a table.

As this error message indicates, manipulating an array is an all-or-nothing procedure. For example, to move or delete a data table, you must first select all the cells in the table, including the test values in the left column and/or the top row of the table.

If you really want to rearrange parts of a data table, there are a couple of ways around this problem. The first option is to create a "shadow" data table by entering reference formulas in another part of the workbook, then manipulate the reference formulas. For example, to create a shadow of the two-variable data table shown earlier in figure 2.5, you would enter the formula

        =A9

in a blank cell, then copy it down nine rows and across six columns. You can then rearrange or delete the reference formulas in the shadow table however you like; they will still refer to the proper cells in the data table and will update whenever the data table (and the rest of the workbook) recalculates.

A second, simpler option is similar: Use the Edit, Copy command to copy the data table, then use the Edit, Paste command to paste the copy in a different location. This procedure creates a static version of the data table that has no links to the data table and does not update along with the data table.

Tip

The option to create a static copy of a data table allows you to "freeze" the table's results for a particular set of worksheet conditions. This static copy is often useful as a point of comparison when you later update the original data table.

Using List Features with a Data Table

After you have created a data table, you can use some of the list-manipulation features described in Chapter 1 to further refine the table's usefulness as a reference tool. For example, if you know you can't afford mortgage payments above $900 per month, you can filter the one-variable data table shown in figure 2.2 to exclude all payments that are out of your price range, as shown in figure 2.7. To achieve this display, we used these steps:

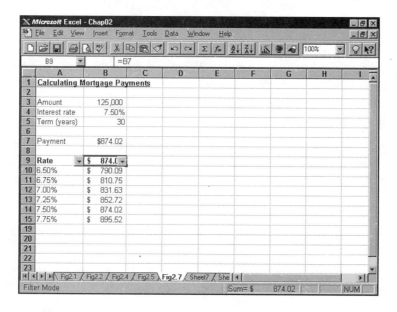

Fig. 2.7
In some one-variable data tables, it may be appropriate to implement the AutoFilter feature to further refine the display.

1. Create the one-variable data table, as described in the earlier section, "Using One-Variable Data Tables."

2. Apply unique formatting to the first row of the table. (In figure 2.7, we used boldface.)

3. Select a cell in the data table.

4. Choose Data, Filter, AutoFilter.

5. Click the drop-down arrow next to the formula in cell B9.

6. Choose Custom from the drop-down list. The Custom AutoFilter dialog box appears.

7. In the Custom AutoFilter dialog box, enter **<900** as the first criterion, as shown in figure 2.8.

8. Choose OK.

Fig. 2.8
This criterion will filter out all rows of the data table whose payment amounts are greater than or equal to $900.

To use the AutoFilter feature with a data table, you must remember to offset the cells in the table's first row with different formatting than the other rows, so Excel will recognize the table as a list. In figure 2.7, for example, we added boldface to range A9:B9.

For practical purposes, the AutoFilter is generally limited to data tables of the one-variable variety, as shown in the example above. Since the different columns of a data table are usually not related, applying a filter to one column often applies a criterion that is meaningless to the other columns of the table. Even when you use an AutoFilter with a one-variable data table, you must be careful not to expect too much—the filter isn't dynamic, so it won't update if the table changes.

Caution

When you use a filter with a data table, be aware that the filter does not update with the table results. If you cause the table to recalculate by changing one of the variable test values or some aspect of your initial analysis, the filtered table might not display the information you were expecting.

Other Uses of Data Tables

Data tables are obviously a valuable and easily generated source of reference material for someone who simply wants to peruse a worksheet for a quick answer. However, when it comes to advanced data analysis, data tables can be used in far more powerful ways. Functions that retrieve values from tables, such as VLOOKUP, HLOOKUP, INDEX, and MATCH, are natural companions to lookup tables.

Since the tables themselves use arrays and functions dynamically, you can be certain that formulas that use these functions will also return the correct values (as long as the data table has been properly recalculated). As you create advanced data analysis tools, be on the lookout for problems that can be solved with dynamic data tables, rather than static tables that you must change yourself or with macro code.

In addition, don't be afraid to use data tables in conjunction with an advanced or complicated analysis. Even if a model contains hundreds of variables and formulas, you can shed new light on the analysis by constructing a data table for one or two key variables in the model.

Chapter Summary

Excel's Data, Table command allows you to generate large quantities of data in tabular format almost instantly. Tables of such data can be used simply for reference within a workbook, but are more commonly used to assess a range of possible outcomes associated with different variable values.

Excel's data tables can test different values for one or two variables. One-variable data tables consist of two columns, with variable test values in the first column and the table formula at the top of the second column. Two-variable data tables can be expanded to up to 256 columns, and the table formula is located in the top-left cell of the table.

Data tables can be filtered, although this is not a common usage. It's far more common, and often invaluable, to use data tables as building blocks in sophisticated data analysis models.

3

Representing Business Forms on the Worksheet

One of the trickiest parts of data management with Excel is seemingly the most trivial: getting the data into a workbook. But entering data into the spreadsheet's native row-and-column grid is extremely tedious and prone to error. If you botch this part of the process, the rest is academic; you'll never get any meaningful information out of the list.

The past several releases of Excel have provided a built-in data form that helps you tame the data-entry process. Excel 7 goes one step further. Its built-in integration with Microsoft Access 95 gives you an entry to the Access form designer right from the Excel menu, providing you with the tools you need to create truly sophisticated and visually appealing forms.

Even the lucky few who have inherited already-constructed Excel lists can benefit from a quick review of Excel's form-designing capability, because a form provides a powerful and easy-to-understand way to filter data. This chapter explains how to use Excel's native data forms for both entering and filtering data, and introduces the powerful form-designing capabilities available to those who also have Access 95 on their systems.

Using Excel's Data Forms

The data forms available within Excel provide a solid, if unspectacular, way for you to enter, view, and filter data. Figure 3.1 shows one such form, which was created for the sales list on the sheet behind the form. Using this form, we can edit or delete the existing records in the list or add new records.

Fig. 3.1

Excel's built-in data forms provide an almost foolproof way to view, enter, and edit list data.

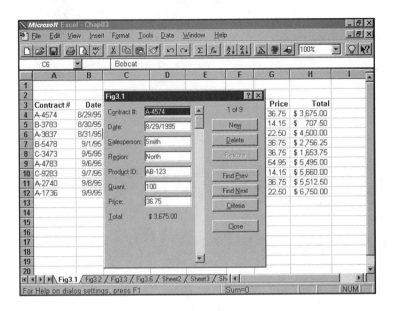

You can generate a form at any point in a list's existence. If the list is brand-new, of course, it's best to generate the form for it immediately, so you can use it to enter the data in the list. However, you can also generate a form for an existing list.

From a forms management point of view, it doesn't really matter when you decide to generate a form, because you can't edit or save the forms you create with the Data, Form command. Excel generates the same form every time; it's a simple columnar arrangement of the fields in the list, as shown in figure 3.1. The layout of the form is dependent on the structure of the list (with one field for each column in the list) and remains the same whether your list contains ten thousand records or none.

With this simple system, there are no form-design and form-management issues to worry about. When you close the form, it disappears. Excel recreates it on the fly whenever you choose the Data, Form command. So you can use the Data, Form command to create a form (as described in the next section), enter a few records into the list, close the form, perform some other tasks in the workbook, and then issue the Data, Form command again to reopen the form and enter more records.

This flexibility removes a lot of the headaches that come with more sophisticated form management. You can even hop from list to list within the same workbook, using the Data, Form command on each list. Whenever you choose the Data, Form command, Excel immediately displays a form appropriate to the list (or list headers) in which the cell pointer currently resides.

Note

You can use the Data, Form command on lists with up to 32 fields (columns). If your list contains more than 32 fields, you can still use the Data, Form command by hiding some of the columns in the list. (To hide a column, right-click the column letter at the top of the worksheet and choose Hide from the pop-up menu.) Since you can't edit a form directly, this is the only way to specify which fields Excel will display in the form.

Creating a Data Form

As the previous section indicates, creating a data form is remarkably easy. Here are the steps:

1. Place the cell pointer anywhere in the list.

2. Choose Data, Form.

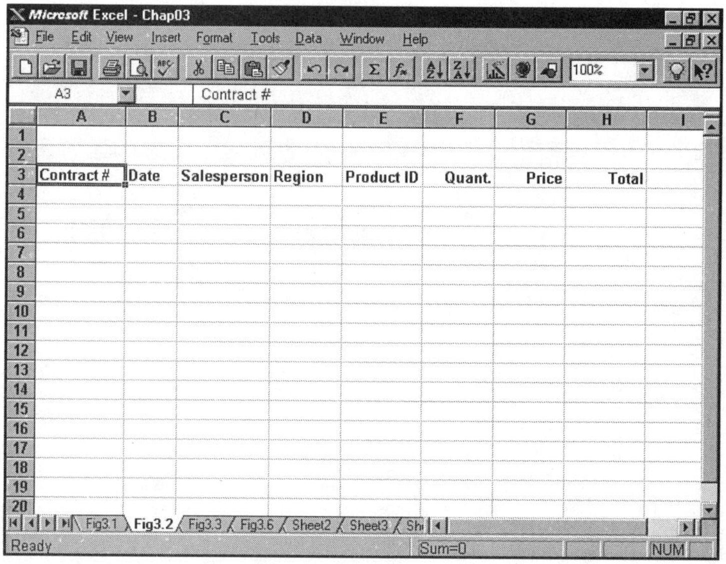

Fig. 3.2
You can create a data-entry form from nothing more than a set of list headings, as shown here.

If the list does not exist yet, you create the data form by entering the list headers, as shown in figure 3.2. Then place the cell pointer on one of the headers and choose Data, Form. Excel responds with a dialog box that reads `No headers detected. Assume top row of selection is header row?` Choose OK in this dialog box to generate the form.

Note

If you use only list headings to generate a form, remember that the list headings must have different formatting from the rest of the entries in the list if you want to take advantage of other list-related features, such as AutoFilter. In figure 3.2, for example, we have formatted the list headings in range A3:H3 in boldface. When we use a data form to enter records for the list, they will appear with normal formatting (no boldface).

Including Calculated Fields in a Data Form

There's one disadvantage to creating a data form from list headings alone. If the list contains calculated fields, the calculations won't appear in the form and won't be included in any records that you add with the form. In figure 3.3, for example, column H contains the total sale amount, which is calculated by multiplying the entry in the *Quant.* field by the entry in the *Price* field. In the figure, we have entered

        =F4*G4

in cell H4 to perform the calculation.

Fig. 3.3

To include calculated fields in a form, enter the formulas for the calculation in the first row of the list, as shown in cell H4.

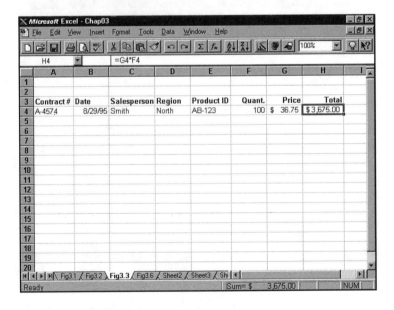

The way to have the form include such calculations (and add them to new records that you enter) is to issue the Data, Form command after one record that contains the calculation has been entered in the list, as previously shown in figure 3.3. When we select a cell in the list shown in that figure, then choose Data, Form, the form appears as shown earlier in figure 3.1. The calculated Total field appears at the bottom of the form (in the same position as it appears in the list), but there is no way to edit it. When you use the form to enter a new record in the list, Excel automatically copies any formulas used in the first record to the new record, saving you the trouble of doing it yourself in the workbook.

Calculated fields in data forms don't update as soon as you enter new data that would affect the calculation. Instead, you must move off the record currently displayed in the form. When you return to the record, the calculated fields are updated. The following section explains how to perform such list navigation within a form.

Using a Form to Navigate Through a List

The built-in controls on an Excel data form make navigating a list easy. After you display a record, you can edit or delete it. The list below summarizes the methods you use to navigate between existing records:

- To move to the previous record in the list, click the up-facing scroll arrow in the form, press the up-arrow key on the keyboard, or use the Shift+Enter key combination.

- To move to the next record in the list, click the down-facing scroll arrow in the form, or press the down-arrow key or the Enter key on the keyboard. (If you scroll past the last record in the list, Excel displays a blank form, giving you the opportunity to enter a new record in the list.)

- To move up ten records within the list, click in the scroll bar between the scroll tab and the up-facing scroll arrow, or press the PageUp key on the keyboard.

- To move down ten records within the list, click in the scroll bar between the scroll tab and the down-facing scroll arrow, or press the PageDown key on the keyboard. (If you scroll past the last record in the list, Excel displays a blank form, giving you the opportunity to enter a new record in the list.)

- To move the cursor between the fields in the current record, use the Tab key (to move forward) or the Shift+Tab key combination (to move backward). You can also move to a particular field by pressing the Alt key plus the key of the underlined letter in the field name. (Excel creates these accelerators automatically when you generate the form.) For example, to move to the Region field in the form in figure 3.1, you would press Alt+E.

When you use one of these navigational techniques to move off a record, any changes you have made are transferred to the list in the Excel sheet.

> **Tip**
>
> The notation in the top-right corner of the form (such as *1 of 9* in the form shown in figure 3.1) tells you the total number of records currently in a list and which record you are currently viewing.

Creating, deleting, and restoring records is a similarly easy task:

- To display a blank, new record in the form, choose the form's New command button. Enter the data for the record. The data will be transferred to the list when you select New again to enter another record, move to another record, close the form.

- To delete the record currently displayed in the form, choose the form's Delete command button. Choose OK when Excel displays the confirmation message. Once you choose OK, the record is permanently deleted from the list and cannot be retrieved using the Edit, Undo command.

- To undo all changes you have made to the record currently displayed in the form, choose the form's Restore command button. This option is available because Excel does not commit the changes you make until you move off the record. Once you move off a record, you cannot use the Restore command to change the record back to its original state.

Using a Form to Filter a List

In addition to entering, editing, and deleting records, you can also use an Excel data form as a filtering tool. After you enter criteria in the form, Excel displays only the records that meet the criteria. Since you can only view one filtered record at a time, this alternative to filtering data generally isn't as efficient as the AutoFilter (described in Chapter 1) or the Advanced Filter (described in Chapters 1 and 4). However, it still can be a useful tool, especially when you're in the middle of a data-entry task and want to ask some quick questions of your list (for example, "Did I already enter that record?").

To use a data form to filter a list, follow these steps:

1. If the data form is not already visible, place the cell pointer in the list that you want to filter and choose Data, Form.

2. Choose the Criteria command button in the form. Excel displays a blank record.

3. Enter your criteria in the appropriate fields. You can enter criteria for as many fields as you like. The criteria in figure 3.4, for example, will find all records in the North region with Totals greater than 5,000.

4. Choose the Form command button. Excel displays the next record in the list that meets the criteria. (The next record is determined by the current record. If the form displays the fourth record after you enter the criteria, Excel will search from that point forward when matching records.)

5. Use the Find Prev and Find Next buttons to display other records that match the criteria.

Fig. 3.4
You can use criteria within a form so that the form displays only selected records. This set of criteria will select records from the North region with sales totals greater than $5,000.

You can alter the filtered records that you display with the Criteria command button. If they no longer meet the criteria, Excel will no longer display them when you use the Find Prev and Find Next command buttons.

To alter the criteria and display a different set of filtered records, click the form's Criteria command button, enter the new criteria, and follow steps 4 and 5 above.

To eliminate the criteria so that all records are again visible from the form, use these steps:

1. Choose the Criteria command button.

2. Choose the Clear command button.

3. Choose the Form command button.

Closing a form also erases any criteria that currently exist within the form.

Using the Access Form Designer

If you're using Excel 95 and also have Access 95 on your system, you have a separate option for generating forms: the Access form designer. The form you design will be available from Excel, to use with Excel lists, simply by clicking a button that the Access form designer places on your worksheet.

The Access form designer gives you complete control over the layout and operation of your forms, but at a price. If you want any functionality beyond simply entering and viewing data, you're on your own to create it. The calculated fields and filtering capabilities inherent in Excel's native data forms aren't automatically included on an Access form.

When you use Access to design a form, you have access to all the tools that a person designing a form within Access itself does. You can reposition fields, change the field labels, specify a new name for the dialog box, and even change the background of the form. The somewhat whimsical form shown in figure 3.5 was created in Access; in fact, the background of billowing clouds is one of the default choices you get when you create a form.

Fig. 3.5
When you design a form in Access, you have control over field place-ment, the dialog box title, and the form's background, among other things.

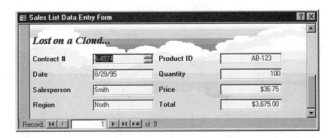

You can also create checkboxes, radio buttons, macro buttons, drop-downs, and more right on the form. However, once you've put these elements on a form, it's up to you how they'll perform—if they perform at all.

In fact, designing a form in Access is such a specialized task that it would take well over 100 pages to describe the many features available. In this book, we'll be content to introduce the Access FormWizard available through Excel and point out a few of the ways that you can quickly create an attractive custom form that performs basic data-entry functions.

Caution

Designing complex forms in Access can be a time-consuming process, especially if you are not familiar with database environments. When using the Access form designer, keep your goals modest, or you may wind up spending a great deal of time creating a form that still doesn't work exactly as you had hoped.

Using the Access FormWizard

To illustrate the use of the Access FormWizard, we'll rely on the sample list shown in figure 3.6. You can create an Access form from an existing list, like the one in the figure, or from a set of new column headers (like the one in figure 3.2).

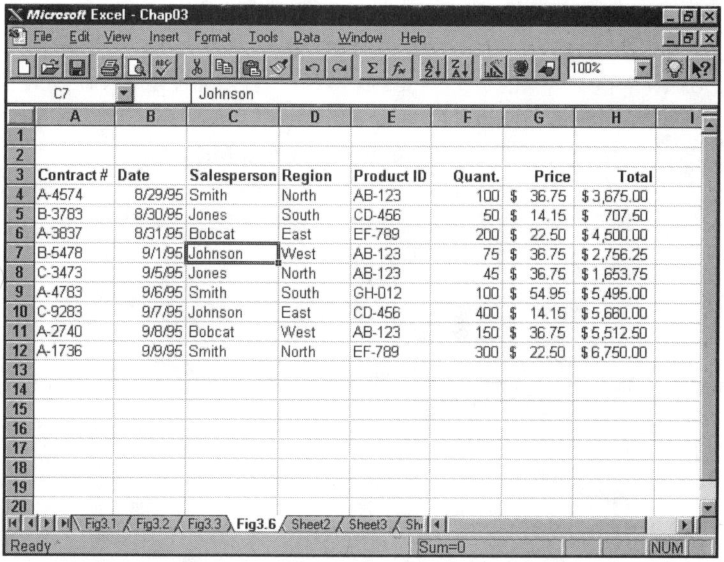

Fig. 3.6
The data in this list can be displayed in an Access form by using the Access form designer.

Note

To use the Access form designer, Access 95 must be installed on your system.

To create an Access form, use the following steps:

1. Place the cell pointer in the list or list headers on which you wish to base the form.

2. Choose Data, Access Form.

3. To confirm that it has detected the correct settings from your list, the Access FormWizard may display the dialog box shown in figure 3.7. The settings shown in the figure are the ones you should select if your list's header row has different formatting than the rows containing the data. Choose OK.

Fig. 3.7
This dialog box insures that your form uses the correct list parameters.

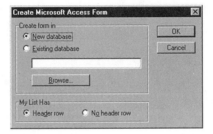

4. The next dialog box lets you choose the fields that will appear on the form, as shown in figure 3.8. (It may take a few moments for this dialog box to appear, while Access loads.) To move fields from one scroll list to the other, click the single-arrow command buttons. To move all the fields at once, click one of the double-arrow buttons.

Fig. 3.8
You can place selected fields from an Excel list in a form or use all the fields.

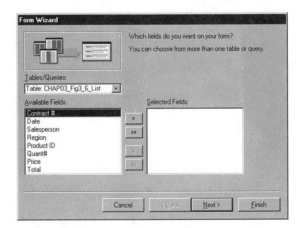

5. Choose a format for the form from the option buttons shown in figure 3.9. In almost all cases you should select the Columnar format. The Tabular and DataSheet formats display fields in a row-and-column grid that's quite similar to the Excel environment you've temporarily left behind.

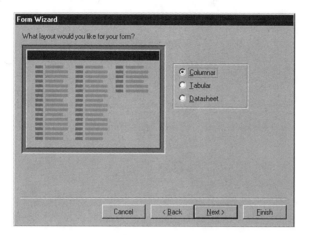

Fig. 3.9
Select the Columnar format to produce a form that has a different look and feel than an Excel worksheet.

6. Choose a style for the form. Figure 3.10 displays the options available. The form shown in figure 3.5 was created with the first style option, Clouds. However, whimsical styles such as this aren't generally appropriate for business applications. The most conservative option is Standard, which produces forms with a look and feel similar to Excel's native dialog boxes.

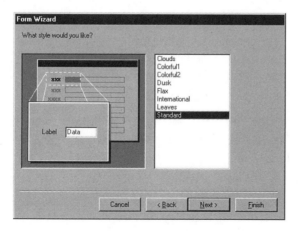

Fig. 3.10
Built-in form styles range from cloudlike to conservative.

7. Finally, enter the title that you want to appear in the form's title bar, as shown in figure 3.11. If you want to begin entering data immediately, select the first option button in figure 3.11. To modify the form's design, select the second option button, as shown in the figure. Choose Finish.

Fig. 3.11
This dialog box lets you specify a title for the form's title bar and gives you the chance to edit it.

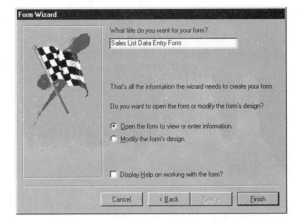

Modifying a Form's Design

If you choose to edit a form in the Access form designer, the options available to you are nearly endless. That much quickly becomes clear when you peruse the form's Properties dialog box, shown along with the form in figure 3.12. The form has dozens of property settings, arranged into five separate tabs in the dialog box. (To display both the form and its Properties dialog box as shown in the figure, maximize both the Access program window and the form window.)

What's more, each component on the form, including the fields from your Excel list, has dozens of available property settings. When you select a component on a form, the Properties dialog box updates automatically to display the properties relevant to that component.

With so many properties to choose from, you can usually achieve the results you want with a little research. Here's a rundown of the properties you'll use most often for the form:

■ The *caption* is the text that displays in the form's title bar when you activate it.

■ The *picture* is a bit map displayed in the background of the form. If you use the Standard form style shown in figure 3.12, there is no picture.

- The *allow edits, allow additions,* and *allow deletions properties* let you specify what activity will take place in the form.

Fig. 3.12
The Properties dialog box allows you to set parameters for the form and the components on it. The slender Toolbox toolbar below the Properties dialog box lets you place additional components on the form.

Tip

To view all properties relevant to a form or a component, display the All tab of the Properties dialog box.

When you select a component, properties relevant to that component appear in the Properties dialog box. For forms that you create to work with Excel lists, the component you'll be dealing with most often is the field (and the separate, but attached, field label that goes with it).

Here are some common tasks you perform on fields:

- To select a field and its field label, click in the field anywhere except on the field label.

- To change the text of the label, double-click it to begin edit mode, then type the changes.

- To resize a field, select it, then drag one of the selection handles on the corner of the field to indicate the new size.

- To move a field, simply drag it to its new position.
- To select several fields, drag the mouse around the fields or Shift+click the fields.

After your fields are in place, you may want to experiment with some of the sophisticated form-management tools that Access provides. Here are some of the properties that are commonly used with edit fields:

- The *decimal places* property indicates the number of decimal places used in numeric fields.
- The *default value* property indicates the default property for a field.
- The *enabled* property indicates whether the field will be available to the user.
- The *font name, font size, font italic, font underline,* and *font weight* properties control the appearance of the text in the field.
- The *input mask* property allows you to specify a miniature template within the field to help guide data entry. For example, a template for a telephone number might include parentheses enclosing three spaces (for the area code) and a hyphen to separate the remaining seven digits. Access features an Input Mask Wizard, shown in figure 3.13, that lets you select from a number of common input masks or design your own.

Fig. 3.13
The Input Mask Wizard helps you design a miniature template within a field to assist data entry.

Experimenting with these properties and others in the Properties dialog box will quickly give you an appreciation of how powerful the Access form designer can be. But as mentioned earlier, immediate gratification isn't the likely outcome of such ad hoc form design. To generate a quick-and-easy conduit for data entry, use Excel's native data form, discussed at the beginning of this chapter.

When you have finished designing your form, save it, then choose File, Exit to close Access. The form remains available to you through means of a graphical button that Excel places in your workbook next to the original list, as shown in figure 3.14. When you click the button, the form you created in the Access form designer reappears.

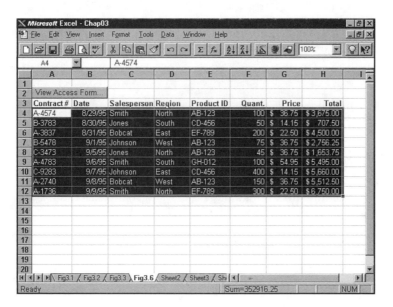

Fig. 3.14
The View Access Form button gives you immediate access to a form you created in the Access form designer.

Note

You can move the View Access Form button or change the text that appears on it. To move the button, right-click it and choose Cut from the pop-up menu. Then select the new location for the button and choose Edit, Paste from the normal Excel menu.

To change the text on the View Access Form button, right-click the button, drag the mouse across the default text to select it, and type the new text.

Chapter Summary

Entering data through a form, rather than directly into the row-and-column grid of a workbook, helps cut down on data entry errors, thus increasing the value of the data in your lists. A form displays one record at a time; you can quickly scroll through records using controls that are built into the form.

Excel's native data forms require no knowledge of form design or form-management techniques. Generating one of these forms is as simple as placing the cell pointer in a list (or in the row of list headers for a new list) and choosing Data, Form. Excel creates an ad-hoc form that corresponds to the fields in the list. (You can prevent fields from displaying in the list by hiding the columns that contain the fields in the workbook.)

The form-design possibilities are far greater for people who have both Excel 95 and Access 95 on their systems. Access's form designer allows you to create forms with a variety of eye-catching backgrounds. You can edit these forms to change field positions and labels, the title of the form dialog box, and even the bit map that appears on the form background. You can also include fields from multiple Excel lists on a single form by selecting both lists before you issue the Data, Access Form command.

Both form types allow you to filter data and create calculated totals. However, when you use the Access form designer, you must add these features yourself, a time-consuming process that may make Excel's native data forms the more attractive option.

4

Using Excel Databases To Organize Business Information

Having all of your important business data carefully recorded in Excel lists is an important aspect of data management, but it's really only half the battle. Getting specific data out of the lists—and doing it quickly and efficiently—is where the data management wars are won and lost. In fact, the innovative AutoFilter feature described in Chapter 1 was a direct result of Microsoft's customer research, which revealed that many Excel users spent a great deal of time unnecessarily sorting and scrolling through on-sheet lists because they didn't know how to use the more advanced features of the product.

The AutoFilter and related features, which are discussed in-depth in Chapter 1, fulfilled their purpose more thoroughly than even Microsoft could have hoped. The point-and-click method of identifying criteria and the concept of filtering a list in place, rather than extracting results to a different part of the workbook, make it simple for almost anyone to focus his or her view of a list on selected records.

However, Excel also includes more complex—and more powerful—ways to get the information you want out of a list. There *are* occasions when it's better to extract data, rather than filter a list in place. Furthermore, Excel offers several functions that return data from a list, such as statistics or individual cell entries, without altering the list. This chapter tells you how and when to use these advanced list features.

Extracting Data to a Different Location in the Workbook

Chapter 1 briefly discussed Excel's ability to extract data from a list to a different part of the sheet, rather than filtering the data in-place. This method of filtering data, which was the standard before the AutoFilter was introduced, now seems so arcane that most people strenuously avoid it. However, there is one compelling reason to use it; extracted records are copies that are physically separate from the original list. You can add formatting, move records around, and perform what-if analysis by changing the values within cells without ever worrying about compromising the integrity of the original data.

To extract records from a list, rather than filtering the list in place, choose Data, Filter, Advanced Filter. Then select the Copy to Another Location option button in the Advanced Filter dialog box, as shown in figure 4.1. When you do this, Excel activates the Copy To edit box, as shown in the figure. You can point to the range or enter a cell reference in the edit box.

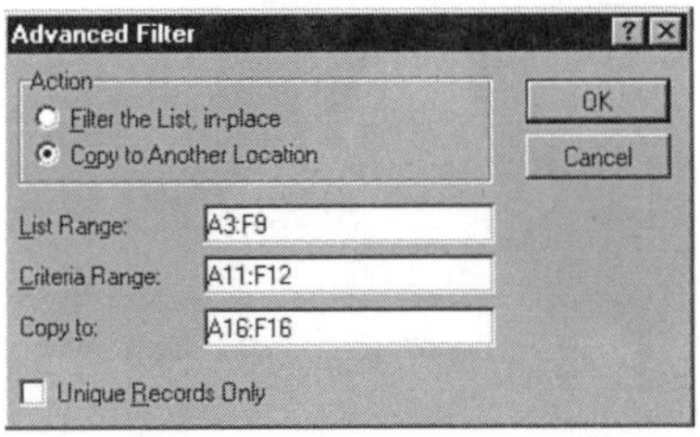

Fig. 4.1
Use the Advanced Filter dialog box to extract data from a list to another part of the sheet.

Tip

The range to which you extract records must be on the same sheet as the list that contains the original data.

The rest of the dialog box settings work the same way they do when you filter a list in place:

- The List Range edit box specifies the range that holds the original list, including the row of column headings at the top of the list. If you have selected a cell within the list before you choose the Data, Filter, Advanced Filter command, Excel enters the list range for you. (If you have selected a range before you issue the command, Excel enters the range, whether it represents a list or not.)

- The <u>C</u>riteria Range edit box specifies the criteria that Excel will use to select which records are extracted. Using a criteria range gives you almost unlimited flexibility in refining your query, as described in Chapter 1. You can specify criteria for several columns in a list, include AND/OR functionality, and even use criteria that compute different values in the extracted records than are contained in the original list.

- The Unique <u>R</u>ecords Only checkbox allows you to specify that if several records meet the criteria in the criteria range, only the first will be copied to the extract range. See Chapter 1 for a more detailed discussion of unique records.

When you choose OK, Excel copies the records that meet the criteria in the criteria range to the range specified in the Copy <u>T</u>o edit box. As figure 4.2 shows, Excel copies the column headings from the original list, which gives you the opportunity to perform list-related operations on the extracted records.

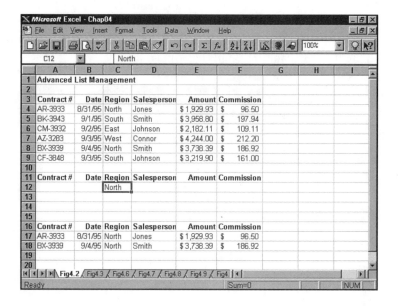

Fig. 4.2

The Advanced Filter dialog box settings shown in figure 4.1 produced the extracted records shown in range A17:F18.

Caution

When you indicate a single, blank cell as the Copy To range, Excel automatically uses as many rows and columns as necessary to create copies of the extracted records, overwriting existing data if necessary. You can use a more precise Copy To setting in the Advanced Filter dialog box to limit the number of rows and columns that the extracted records can occupy.

In the example shown in figure 4.2, the column headings at the top of the extracted records are an exact copy of the column headings at the top of the original list. In addition, the criteria range (range A11:F12) uses the same column headings as the original list in range A3:F9. However, you can use a truncated version of both the Copy To range and the Criteria Range to save room in the workbook and focus your attention on the criteria and list fields that are most crucial to your query.

Figure 4.3 shows such an example. Here, a criterion in the Date field was used to extract records. Only the information in the Salesperson and Amount fields appears in the extract range. In addition, the latter two fields appear in a different order than they do in the original list.

Fig. 4.3
It's not necessary for criteria ranges and extracted records to include all the fields in the original list.

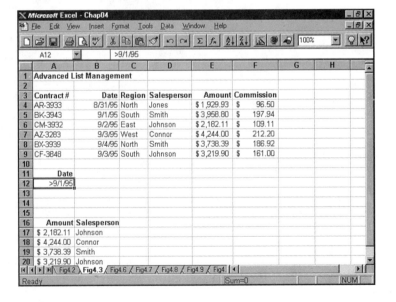

> **Tip**
>
> You can rearrange the order of the columns in a list when you extract data.

Figure 4.4 shows the dialog box settings used to create this extraction. The Criteria Range is limited to a single column (range A11:A12), and the Copy To range comprises range A16:B16, rather than a single, blank cell.

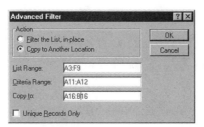

Fig. 4.4
By specifying a range instead of a single, blank cell as the Copy To edit box, you can limit extracted records to specific columns of the original list.

How did Excel know which columns to use in the extracted records and in which order to place them? We entered that information in the worksheet before issuing the Data, Filter, Advanced Filter command. Cell A16 contained the label *Salesperson* and cell B16 contained the label *Amount*. Not coincidentally, range A16:B16 was the range we specified in the Copy To edit box when we performed the filter.

By making further adjustments in the Copy To edit box, you can limit the number of rows in the extracted range, as well as the number of columns. For example, suppose you have important data in range A18:D18, and you expect the Advanced Filter dialog box to extract only one record from the original list. You can enforce a one-record limit by indicating range A16:B17 as the Copy To range—one row of column headings and one row for the extracted record.

What if you specify a limited number of rows in the Copy To range and the criteria you specify selects more records than can fit? Excel lets you decide, with the dialog box shown in figure 4.5.

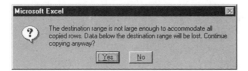

Fig. 4.5
You must decide whether to overwrite existing data—or omit some of the extracted data.

When you see this dialog box, here's what to do:

■ If you want to view all extracted records (overwriting existing data below the range you specified in the Copy To edit box of the Advanced Filter dialog box), choose Yes.

■ If you don't want to overwrite data, choose No to cancel the operation. This is the conservative choice—one which allows you to reexamine your criteria if the extraction produces more records than you had expected.

Functions for Retrieving List Information

In addition to extracting selected records from a list, you can create formulas that return specific information from the list. For example, Excel includes a specialized subset of statistical functions that work specifically with lists, allowing you to calculate statistics only for selected records. Another class of functions, called lookups, is particularly helpful for retrieving information from a list of structured reference information in which each record is unique, such as an inventory database. Two other functions, INDEX and MATCH, also provide specific information from a single cell in a list.

Getting Statistics from List Data

Excel's statistical list functions, sometimes referred to as the 'D' functions (from the good old days when lists were called databases), provide an instantaneous way to measure a number of important list statistics, such as sums, averages, and standard deviations. Because these functions use criteria ranges, you can specify that the calculation include only certain records from the list by entering the appropriate criteria. This structure allows you to make the same formula quickly yield statistics for a number of different sets of records simply by changing the criteria in the criteria range.

Cell I3 of figure 4.6 shows an example of the most commonly used statistical list function, DSUM. In the figure, the criterion in range A11:F12 has been used to extract the two records in range A17:F18. Although the extract range clearly shows which two sales occurred in the North region, you won't know the total unless you create another formula.

The DSUM formula in cell I3 performs this function. It's better than writing a formula specifically for the extracted records, because those records must be updated if the contents of the criteria range change. The DSUM formula, on the other hand, updates automatically to reflect changes in the criteria range. For example, if you entered the criterion "West" in cell C12, the DSUM formula would immediately reflect the total sales for the single West record in the list.

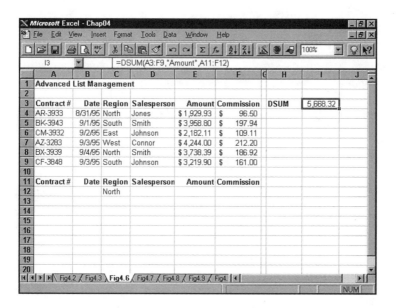

Fig. 4.6
The DSUM formula in cell I3 uses the criteria in range A11:F12 to calculate the total sales amount in the North region.

The generic syntax of the DSUM function is

```
=DSUM(list,field,criteria)
```

Here's what the three arguments represent:

- *List* is the list that you want to perform the statistical analysis. You must specify a range that includes the column headings of the list. In the example, the column headings in range A3:F3 are included in the *list* argument.

- *Field* is the field from which you want to return data. To specify the field, you can use the appropriate column heading from the top of the list, or you can use the position of the field within the list (1, 2, 3, and so forth). In the example, the *field* argument is "Amount," which tells the function to return data from the Amount field in the list. Alternatively, we could have used 5 as the *field* argument, since Amount is located in the fifth column of the list.

■ *Criteria* specifies the criteria range that the function will use to select records on which to perform the calculation. In the example, the *criteria* argument is A11:F12. Since that range contains a criterion that specifies records in the North region, only amounts from those records are summed.

Figure 4.7 expands the statistical repertoire of the sample worksheet to include all of Excel's statistical list functions. Each of these formulas has the same syntax as the DSUM formula in cell I3; each uses the same *list*, *field*, and *criteria* arguments. Only the functions themselves have changed. Table 4.1 provides a brief explanation of each of the statistical list functions.

Fig. 4.7

Range I3:I13 contains Excel's 11 statistical list functions.

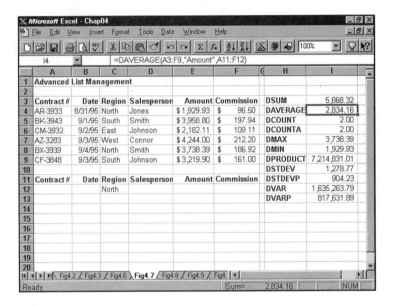

Table 4.1   Statistical List Functions

Function	Returns
DAVERAGE	Average
DCOUNT	Count of cells containing numbers
DCOUNTA	Count of nonblank cells
DMAX	Maximum
DMIN	Minimum
DPRODUCT	Product
DSTDEV	Standard deviation

Function	Returns
DSTVDEVP	Population standard deviation
DSUM	Sum
DVAR	Variance
DVARP	Population variance

The symmetry of the list statistical functions makes them even more powerful, because once you understand one, you understand them all. But the best thing about these functions is their flexibility; whenever the data in a list changes, any statistical list formulas that refer to that list update automatically. The same is true of the criteria range. By changing the criterion in cell C12 of figure 4.7 from "North" to "South", for example, you can immediately display an entirely different set of statistics.

As you can imagine, the ability to calculate such a wide range of statistics can provide important insights into the data in a list. Below are a few ways that you can use list statistical functions to interpret list data and spot potential problems.

- *Check maximum and minimum values.* Unexpected maximum and minimum values often represent data-entry mistakes.

- *Compare maximum and minimum values to the average.* If one of these extremes is significantly further from the average than the other, it can indicate that your data is statistically skewed (assuming there are no data-entry errors).

- *Compare the population standard deviation and population variance for different criteria.* The higher these statistics are, the more variation there is between records. If you expect records to be fairly consistent for a given set of criteria, a high population variance or population standard deviation may be an indication of a problem.

Looking Up Data

Excel's lookup functions, VLOOKUP, HLOOKUP, and LOOKUP, provide you with different (and sometimes overlapping) ways of finding a specific piece of information within a structured list of unique records. The parts list in figure 4.8, for example, is an excellent candidate for the VLOOKUP function. If you want to find the description, the supplier, the price, or the inventory on hand for any particular part number, a VLOOKUP formula will return it immediately, without requiring you to filter the list or scroll through an unfiltered list.

Data Management

Fig. 4.8

The VLOOKUP function can return information from this parts list, which comprises five unique records.

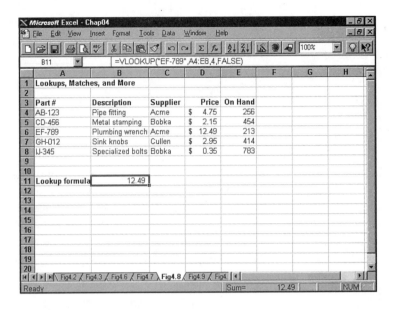

The syntax of the VLOOKUP function is

```
VLOOKUP(lookup_value,list,column,approximate_match)
```

Here's what the VLOOKUP function's four arguments represent:

- *Lookup_value* is the value or text string that you want to find in the first column of a VLOOKUP list. If you're looking up a text string, enclose it in quotation marks, as shown in the example in figure 4.8.

- *List* is the list on which you want to perform the lookup. Unlike the list statistical functions, you do not include the first row, which contains the column headings at the top of the list. (If you're looking up a text value, these can sometimes cause the function to return incorrect results.)

- *Column* specifies the column in the list from which you want to return data.

- *Approximate_match* tells whether you want the lookup function to look for a value in the *list* that exactly matches the *lookup_value* or whether you'll settle for the value that comes closest. A value of TRUE indicates that you'll accept an approximate match; a value of FALSE indicates that you won't.

In figure 4.8, the formula in B11 reads =VLOOKUP("EF-789",A4:E8,4,FALSE). This formula returns 12.49, the price of part EF-789, which is located in the fourth column of the list in range A4:E8. The lookup formula calculates this result by looking for the text value "EF-789" in the first column of the list (range A4:A8). When it finds the row that contains this value, it returns the data in the column in the list indicated by the *column* argument—in this example, the fourth column of the list.

Tip

A lookup formula can return either a number or text; you don't have to specify what you're looking for when you write the formula.

Like all formulas, lookup formulas perform best when you take maximum advantage of their flexibility. The lookup formula in figure 4.8, for example, looks for a particular value in the parts inventory list. To look up the price for another part or the supplier for part EF-789, you'd have to edit the existing formula or write a new one. A better alternative is to write the lookup formula so that at least its *lookup_value* and *column* arguments refer to cells elsewhere in the worksheet. In figure 4.9, for example, the lookup formula reads

```
=VLOOKUP(B13,A4:E8,B14,FALSE)
```

By entering different values in cells B13 and B14, you can return a wide range of different information from the list. In figure 4.9, the formula returns the inventory in stock (column 5) for part CD-456.

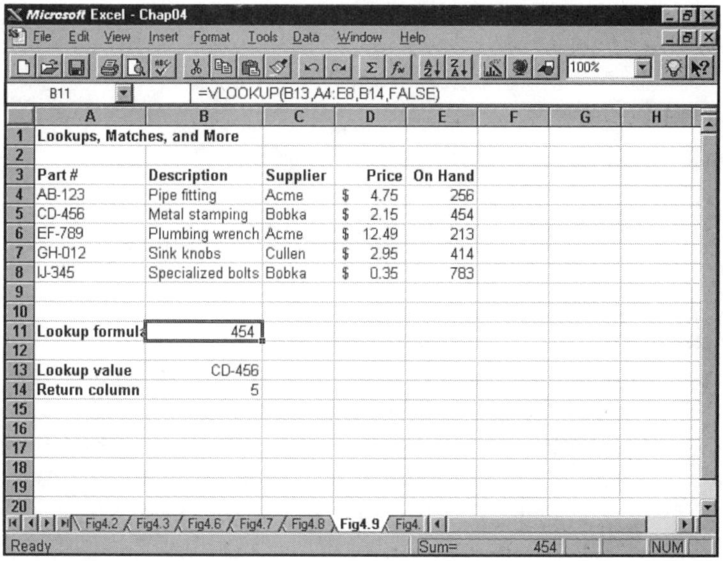

Fig. 4.9
Lookup formulas achieve maximum efficiency when two or more of the arguments refer to outside cells which can be easily updated. The formula in cell B11 uses cell B13 as its lookup_value argument and cell B14 as its column argument.

The analog of the VLOOKUP function is the HLOOKUP function, whose syntax is

```
HLOOKUP(lookup_value,list,row,approximate_match)
```

As you can see, all the arguments are the same as those in the VLOOKUP function, except that the *column* argument has changed to *row*. This provides a clue about the difference between the two functions. The HLOOKUP function checks the first *row* of the list, rather than the first column, for the lookup value. It then returns the entry in the corresponding *row* of the list.

Figure 4.10 shows a common business usage of the HLOOKUP formula. The formula in cell B11

```
=HLOOKUP(B13,B3:F8,B14,FALSE)
```

looks across range B3:F3 until it finds the year indicated in cell B13. It then returns the value for the product line indicated by the row input in cell B14.

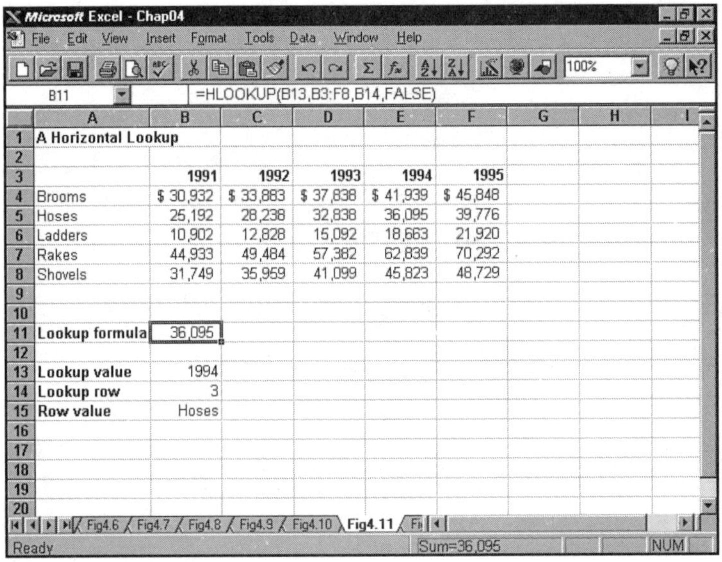

	A	B	C	D	E	F
1	A Horizontal Lookup					
2						
3		1991	1992	1993	1994	1995
4	Brooms	$ 30,932	$ 33,883	$ 37,838	$ 41,939	$ 45,848
5	Hoses	25,192	28,238	32,838	36,095	39,776
6	Ladders	10,902	12,828	15,092	18,663	21,920
7	Rakes	44,933	49,484	57,382	62,839	70,292
8	Shovels	31,749	35,959	41,099	45,823	48,729
9						
10						
11	Lookup formula	36,095				
12						
13	Lookup value	1994				
14	Lookup row	3				
15	Row value	Hoses				

Fig. 4.10 The HLOOKUP function searches the first row of a list rather than the first column.

Using the MATCH Function to Aid Lookups

Writing a lookup formula so that the *lookup_value* and *column* or *row* arguments refer to other cells, as shown in figures 4.9 and 4.10, increases the value of a lookup formula, because you don't have to change the formula to update it. Instead, you can simply enter new information in the cells that the formula refers to. In figure 4.10, for example, you could enter *1994* in cell B13 and *3* in cell B14 to return the 1994 sales of hoses.

However, using "3" to represent "hoses" isn't exactly intuitive. When a lookup list grows, it becomes quite easy to use a mistaken *row* or *column* offset, thus returning incorrect information from the list.

To avoid this problem, use Excel's MATCH function to calculate the *row* or *column* offset. The syntax of the MATCH function is

```
MATCH(lookup_value,lookup_array,match_type)
```

The function returns the *lookup_value*'s position within the *lookup_array*. If the *lookup_value* is the fourth item in the *lookup_array*, for example, the MATCH function returns 4.

The implication for the VLOOKUP and HLOOKUP functions is straightforward. Using the MATCH function, you can specify both the *lookup_value* and the *row* or *column* argument as they naturally occur in the list, rather than figuring out for yourself what integer you should be using for the *row* or *column* argument.

Figure 4.11 shows how this works. Cell B14, which has held an integer in the previous two figures, now holds the formula

```
=MATCH(B15,A3:A8)
```

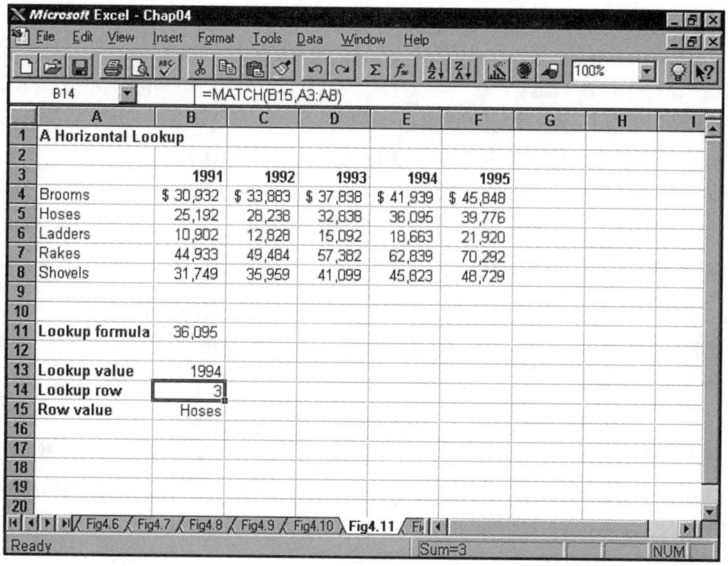

Fig. 4.11
The MATCH function in cell B14 searches range A3:A8 to see where "hoses" falls in the array.

This formula returns 3, which represents the position of the word "hoses" in range A3:A8. The formula in cell B11

```
=HLOOKUP(B13,B3:F8,B14,FALSE)
```

is unchanged from the previous example. It now relies on the MATCH function to determine the *row* argument. We can thus find the 1994 sales for any product line simply by typing the product name in cell B15—a much more intuitive method than entering an integer.

Optional Arguments in Lookups and Matches

The VLOOKUP, HLOOKUP, and MATCH functions all have an optional argument that lets you control how Excel will perform the lookup or match. While this might seem a bit esoteric in a book about Excel's general business capabilities, understanding these optional arguments isn't difficult and can help you correct a lookup or match function that isn't working the way you expected it to.

In the case of the two lookup functions, the fourth argument, *approximate-_match,* is optional. We touched on this option in our earlier discussion. A value of TRUE indicates that you'll accept an approximate match; a value of FALSE indicates that you won't.

It might seem optimal to use TRUE as the *approximate_match* argument, in order to cast as wide a net as possible when looking up data, and indeed this is the Excel default. If you omit the *approximate_match* argument, Excel assumes that it is TRUE. But consider the following scenario: Your parts list contains a record for part number EF-788, but no entry for part number EF-789. You enter a VLOOKUP formula that searches for the price of part EF-789. If you allow an approximate match, Excel will return the price for part number EF-788 (or possibly another part in the list), and you'll be none the wiser.

Here's a second, related scenario: Your parts list does indeed contain a record for part EF-789, but the list is not sorted by part number. Once again, the chances are excellent that your lookup function will return the wrong information. When you use an approximate match, Excel assumes that the list has been sorted by the first column (the first row in an HLOOKUP function). If it comes to an entry that's higher in the alphabet than EF-789, it assumes it has found the closest approximate match—even though part number EF-789 may actually exist somewhere else in the list.

> **Note**
>
> If you're using approximate matches with the VLOOKUP function, the list must be sorted by its first column in ascending order. For the HLOOKUP function, the list must be sorted by its first row in ascending order. See Chapter 1 for further information on sorting.

In most cases, then, it's preferable to use an *approximate_match* argument of FALSE, in order to make your lookups as precise as possible. The exception is when a list of reference information spans a range of values, as shown in the example in figure 4.12. In this case, the formula in cell B18 calculates an agent's commission based on the sale amount in cell B13. But what's the commission rate? It varies by the amount of the sale. Sales under $1,000 garner a 5% commission; those between $1,001 and $1,999 receive 6%; those between $2,000 and $4,999 get 7%, and those above $5,000 get 7.5%.

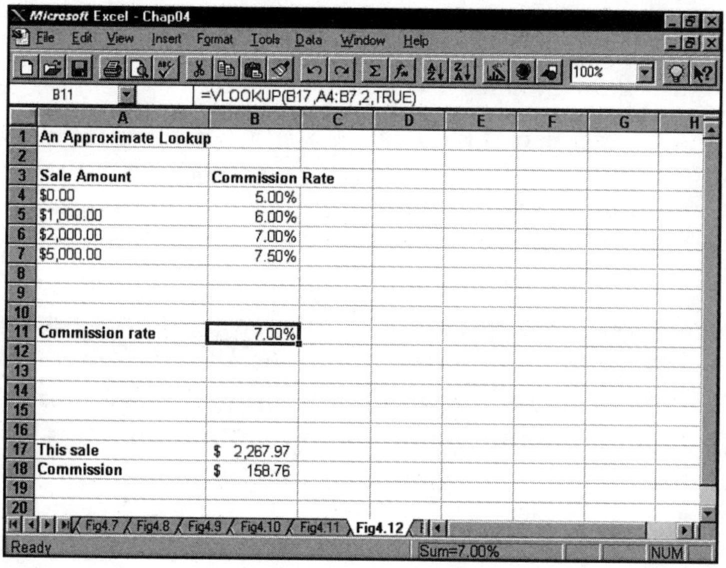

Fig. 4.12
Approximate matches are appropriate in lookups that span ranges of information, rather than exact values.

Obviously, the $2,267.97 sale in cell B17 doesn't exactly match any of the entries in the first column of the list in range A4:B7, so the VLOOKUP formula in cell B11 uses an *approximate_match* argument of TRUE to determine the commission rate. With this setting, the VLOOKUP function looks down the first column of the list until it finds a value that is greater than the *lookup_value*, in this case $2,267.97. It then returns the appropriate value from the *preceding* row.

Thus, an approximate match finds the value in the list that is closest to, but not greater than, the *lookup_value*. It works the same way for a text *lookup_value* as it does for a numeric *lookup_value* and the same for an HLOOKUP formula as for a VLOOKUP formula. This is why a list must be sorted in ascending order, either by column for an HLOOKUP formula or by row for a VLOOKUP formula, for an approximate match to work correctly.

The MATCH function's optional argument, *match_type*, works similarly, except that it can take one of three arguments: 1, 0, and -1. Here's how each of these arguments affects the result of the MATCH function:

A *match_type* argument of 1 is equivalent to an *approximate_match* argument of TRUE in a VLOOKUP or an HLOOKUP function. The MATCH function finds the value in the *lookup_array* that exceeds the *lookup_value*, then returns the position of the previous value in the array. Therefore, the *lookup_array* must be sorted in ascending order for the approximate match to return correct results.

A *match_type* argument of 0 is equivalent to an *approximate_match* argument of FALSE in a VLOOKUP or an HLOOKUP formula; the MATCH argument will return a value only in the case of an exact match.

A *match_type* argument of -1 is the inverse of an argument of 1. In this case, the MATCH function finds the value in the *lookup_array* that is less than the *lookup_value*, then returns the position of the previous value in the array. Therefore, the *lookup_array* must be sorted in descending order for the approximate match to return correct results.

> **Tip**
>
> If you omit the MATCH function's *match_type* argument, Excel uses the default value of 1 and returns an approximate match for a *lookup_array* in ascending order.

Using Lookup Formulas in Business Applications

Obviously, writing a lookup formula for the small sample lists we've used as examples in this section is a bit superfluous. It's a lot easier to look up the value yourself than to write the formula. When a list extends to more than a couple hundred rows, however, lookup formulas become a crucial way to quickly retrieve specific information from a list.

This is typical of many business applications in Excel. Reference information, such as the parts inventory or the commission schedule shown in the earlier examples, is a key component of the application. Often, the data in such reference lists is the starting point for mission-critical computations. For things to work smoothly, you must be able to get information out of the list quickly and reliably.

To make sure you achieve this goal, keep these guidelines in mind when creating lists and designing lookup formulas:

- Put the key fields—the values on which you'll search—in the left column or top row of a list. Where possible, put one key value (such as a product line) in the left column and another (such as the year) in the top row. This allows you to use the MATCH function to pinpoint the lookup data more reliably.

- If you intend to use approximate matches, keep the list sorted in ascending order, both by row and by column. If you're using the VLOOKUP function and one of the values in the left column of the list changes, you'll have to re-sort the list. The same is true if you're using the HLOOKUP function and one of the values in the top row changes.

- If you don't want to re-sort a list every time a key value in a list's left column or top row changes, use 0 as the *approximate_match* argument of the VLOOKUP or HLOOKUP function. (You can also use this setting to force an exact match even when the list is correctly sorted.) Otherwise, the lookup function may return inaccurate results.

Using Additional List Functions: INDEX and LOOKUP

The functions discussed in the previous sections—the list statistical functions, the VLOOKUP and HLOOKUP functions, and the MATCH function—answer the bulk of the questions you'll want to ask of most lists. But two additional functions, LOOKUP and INDEX, can help solve less conventional lookup tasks, such as those involving multiple lists. This section provides a brief explanation of these two functions.

The LOOKUP function comes in handy in the somewhat unlikely event that you want to use a *lookup_value* in one list, yet return a value from another list. The syntax of the LOOKUP function is

```
LOOKUP(lookup_value,lookup_range,result_range)
```

Here, the *lookup_value* and *lookup_range* arguments function similarly to the *lookup_value* and *list* arguments in the VLOOKUP and HLOOKUP functions. But instead of comprising an entire list, the *lookup_range* includes only one column or row of a list.

The *result_range* has the same size and dimension as the *lookup_range,* but it's usually located in a different list. Figure 4.13, for example, contains two lists. (In real life, of course, these lists would likely be located on separate sheets of the workbook or even in separate workbooks.)

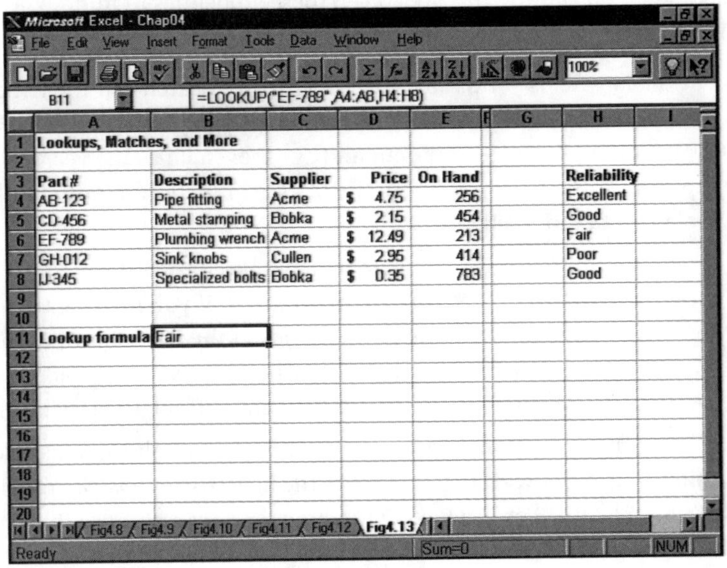

Fig. 4.13
The LOOKUP function can find a lookup value in one list and return a result from a different list.

In the figure, the first list is the parts inventory from figures 4.8 and 4.9. The second rates each part in terms of reliability. Since these two lists haven't been integrated (perhaps for reasons of confidentiality), you can use a LOOKUP formula rather than a VLOOKUP formula to get data from the reliability list. The following formula does the trick

```
=LOOKUP("EF-789",A4:A8,H4:H8)
```

This formula, located in cell B11 of figure 4.13, finds part EF-789's position in the lookup range (range A4:A8), then returns the value from the correspond- ing position in the result range (range H4:H8). Since the LOOKUP formula returns its result based on the relative values in the lookup range and the result range, the two ranges obviously must be of the same dimension and sorted in the same order.

Of course, you can maximize the flexibility of the LOOKUP function by using cell references rather than specific values as arguments for the functions, as explained in the section that covered the VLOOKUP and HLOOKUP functions.

> **Tip**
>
> The LOOKUP function makes it easy to look up information that's stored in a different workbook. Just include a reference to the workbook in the *result_range* argument.

The INDEX function returns a value from a list based on the value's position in the list, rather than on a lookup value. The syntax of the INDEX function is

    =INDEX(range,row,column,which_range)

For example, the formula in cell B11 of figure 4.14

    =INDEX(A4:E8,3,4)

returns the value in the third row and fourth column of range A4:E8 or 12.49 (the price of a plumbing wrench).

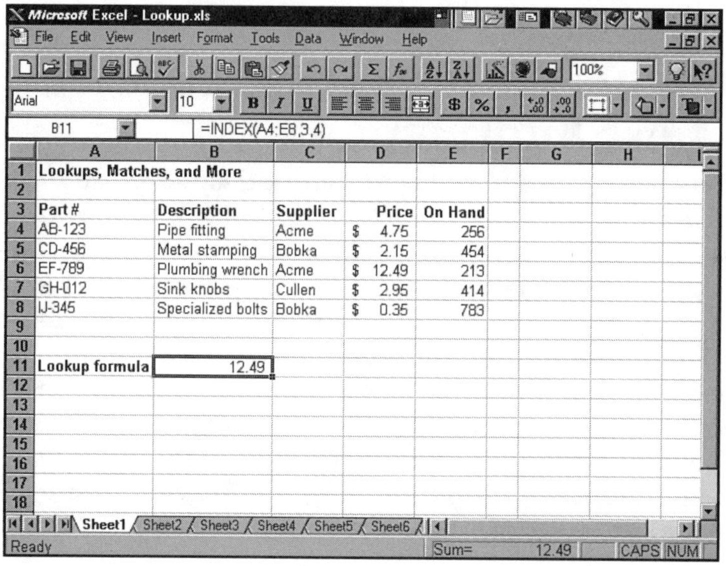

Fig. 4.14
The INDEX function returns a value based on its position within a list.

When would you want to use these somewhat confusing positional arguments, rather than the self-evident *lookup_value, column,* and *row* arguments available with the VLOOKUP, HLOOKUP, and MATCH functions? One instance is in iterative macros, which process a loop a given number of times. Depending on how a list is constructed, it may be possible to create a macro loop that returns the values you want as it iterates.

A less technical scenario (and one more likely for the average business user) is one in which you would use values returned from custom drop-down lists or list boxes that you place on the sheet. The next section explains these features, which are fairly simple to implement and make it far easier for users to interact with list data.

Tip

The optional *which_range* argument gives you the opportunity to specify more than one range in the *range* argument. (You group multiple ranges inside parentheses.) For example, the formula

```
=INDEX((A4:B8,H4:I4),3,1,1)
```

returns the value from the third row and first column of range A4:B8. If you change the last argument to 2, it will return the value from the third row and first column of range H4:I8.

Using On-Sheet Controls To Retrieve Information

Both extracted records and list functions can be easily tailored to respond to Excel's unique on-sheet controls, such as the drop-down list shown in figure 4.15. By using such controls, you can hide the nitty-gritty details of the criteria range from others who use your workbooks. More important, you can place the controls, as well as the formulas that rely upon them, on a different sheet from your original list, thus helping to prevent accidental changes to your data. If you like, you can go further by using Excel's Tools, Protection, Protect Sheet command to place the sheet that contains the original data off-limits to anyone who does not have the password that you specify. (If you use controls to extract data from a list, the extracted records must appear on the same page as the original list.)

The drop-down list shown in figure 4.15 works in conjunction with the sales list introduced earlier in this chapter. When you select a region from the drop-down list, Excel updates the criteria in range A11:F12 (specifically, cell C12). The statistical formulas in column I all update automatically to reflect the new criterion. You can also attach macro code to the drop-down list to make Excel extract the records that match the criterion you have selected, placing them in the rows below range A16:F16.

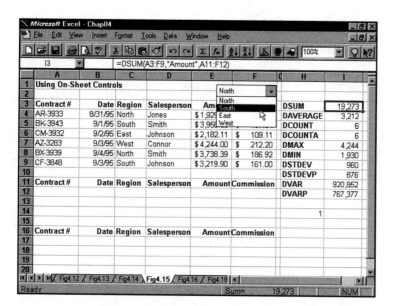

Fig. 4.15
Excel's unique on-sheet controls help to foolproof the process of selecting criteria for extracted records and list-related formulas.

Data Management

Integrating an on-sheet control with a list requires several steps, which aren't difficult, and are usually worth the effort. Basically, the process works as follows:

- Create the on-sheet control.
- Identify the values that will appear in the on-sheet control.
- Tell Excel where to store the user's selection in the control.
- Tell Excel how to interpret the selection and apply it to the list.

The following section explains these steps in greater detail.

Creating an On-Sheet Control

To draw an on-sheet control, use these steps:

1. Choose View, Toolbars.
2. Select the Forms checkbox in the Toolbars scroll list.
3. Choose OK to close the Toolbars dialog box and display the Forms toolbar.
4. In the Forms toolbar, click either the List Box tool or the Drop-Down tool.
5. Drag on the sheet where you want the control to appear.

The control you have created acts like any drawn object; as long as you are in drawing selection mode, you can use the mouse to move or resize it.

Note

If you cannot select a control to edit it, right-click the control, then press the Esc key to clear the shortcut menu that appears. The control remains selected, allowing you to move, resize, or delete it.

The next step is to identify the items you want to appear in the control when the user accesses it. You enter these items in a single-column list, as shown in range H16:H19 of figure 4.16. In this example, the items we have listed correspond to the regions in the sales list, which comprise a natural set of criteria for filtering the list.

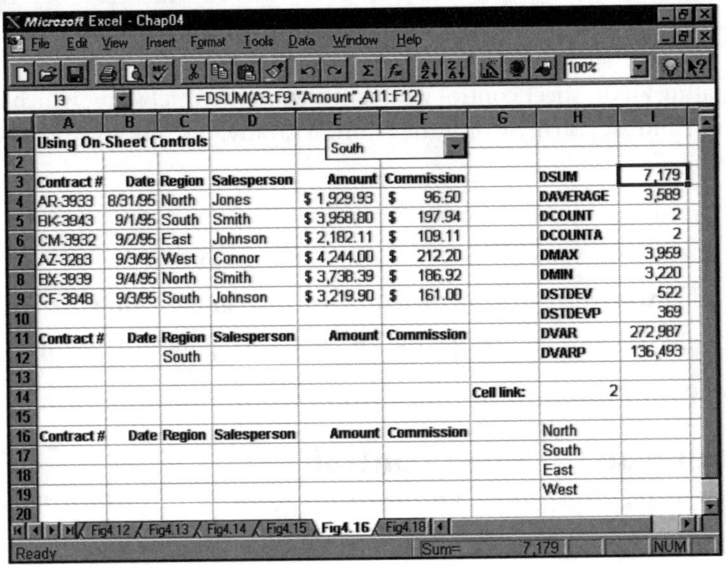

Fig. 4.16

Range H16:H19 contains the four items that will appear in the drop-down list. The user's selection appears in cell H14.

You must also identify a cell where Excel will place the user's selection. In figure 4.16, the selection will appear in cell H14.

Following are the steps you use to specify these settings:

1. Right-click the control.

2. From the pop-up menu that appears, choose Format Object.

3. On the Control tab of the Format Object dialog box (shown in figure 4.17), enter the input range. The input range identifies the entries that will appear in the control when the user activates it. In the example, the input range is range H16:H19, which means that the entries North, South, East, and West will appear in the drop-down when the user clicks it.

4. While still on the Control tab, enter the cell link. This is where the user's selection from the control will be stored. In the example, the cell link is cell H14.

5. Choose OK.

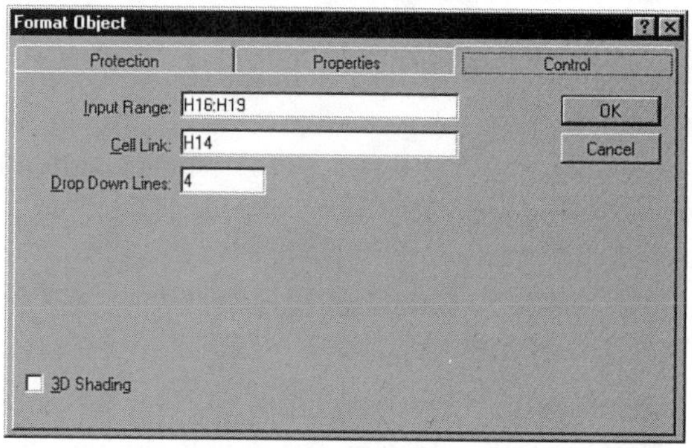

Fig. 4.17
The Control tab of the Format Object dialog box is where you specify what will appear in an on-sheet control and where the user's selection will be stored.

You're now well on your way to using the on-sheet control to place a criterion in the criteria range. There's just one small problem. When you select an item from a drop-down or a list box, Excel returns the position of the selection in the cell that you identified as the cell link, rather than the text of the actual selection.

Fortunately, this small obstacle is easily overcome by the INDEX function described in the preceding section. You enter a formula containing the INDEX function right in the criteria range, where you would normally type a criterion. In figure 4.16, cell C12 contains the formula

```
=INDEX(H16:H19,H14)
```

This formula says, in effect, "Within range H16:H19, find the entry indicated by cell H14." (The *column* and *which_range* arguments are unnecessary in this formula, and therefore are omitted.)

Thus, if the user selects *South*, the second selection in the drop-down, cell H14 will contain the value 2. The INDEX function in cell C12 will then return the second value in range H16:H19—*South*. It's a bit circuitous, but it works.

And best of all, that's all there is to it. By selecting different criteria from the drop-down, you can immediately update all of the list statistical formulas in column I.

Managing Lists and Running Macros with On-Sheet Controls

Now that you know the steps necessary to create an on-sheet control and integrate it with a list, the possibilities for list management are almost endless. In our simple example, you could place additional drop-downs on the sheet. A second drop-down, for example, could be linked to the salesperson field in the list. By creating a separate input range of salespeople, identifying a second cell link, and creating a second INDEX formula in cell D12 of the criteria range, you could integrate this drop-down into the worksheet in figure 4.16. By using both drop-downs, you could filter the list both by region and by salesperson.

Since you can also assign macro code to on-sheet controls, extracting records based on the criteria a user selects from a control is also possible. Figure 4.18 shows the macro code you would use to filter the list in range A3:F9, based on the criteria in range A11:F12, that places the copied records in the rows below range A16:F16. When you assign this macro code to the drop-down shown in figure 4.16, it extracts the records for whatever region the user selects from the drop-down.

Here are the steps you use to create this custom macro code and attach it to an on-sheet control such as a custom drop-down:

1. Choose Insert, Macro, Module.

2. On the blank macro module that appears, enter the code shown in figure 4.18. For your own workbook, alter the three range arguments so that they conform to the list, criteria range, and extraction range in your workbook.

3. Return to the worksheet that contains the custom control and right-click the control.

4. In the pop-up menu that appears, choose Assign Macro.

5. From the Macro Name/Reference scroll list, choose Extractor.

6. Choose OK.

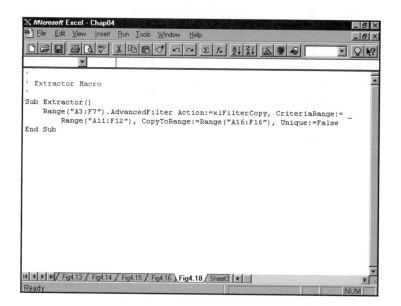

Data Management

Fig. 4.18
This macro code
extracts records
from the original
list when the user
selects an entry
from the custom
drop-down.

Figure 4.16 showed all of the elements necessary to implement an on-sheet
control with a list, including the input list, the cell link, the original list, and
the criteria range for the list—as well as the control itself. This is done for the
purpose of illustration only. Since custom controls are designed to reduce
confusion and the possibility for error, try to place them in an uncluttered
section of a sheet. Where possible, formulas and extract ranges that are updated by the controls should be located in the same view as the controls
themselves, so that users can see how choosing one or more criteria from a
control or controls affects the results of these outputs.

Chapter Summary

Getting data out of a list in a clear and efficient manner is an important part
of the data-management process. Excel has several tools that help you accomplish this task. The Advanced Filter dialog box includes an option to copy
records that match the criteria you specify to another part of the sheet, where
you can manipulate them without affecting the original list.

Several Excel functions return data from a list. The statistical list functions
calculate statistics for only the records in the list that meet criteria that you
specify. The lookup functions help you manage large lists of reference data by
returning information for specific records from specific fields. The MATCH
and INDEX functions give you further control over the data by allowing you
to identify a given entry's position in a list or an array.

On-sheet custom controls can cut down on the confusion and chance for error inherent in criteria ranges, while at the same time adding pizzazz to your application. You can also assign macros to on-sheet custom controls, allowing you or others who use your workbooks to perform specialized list operations, such as extractions, simply by pointing and clicking.

In all of the above features, the criteria range is a central element. Identifying the correct criteria range and establishing the correct criteria is a critical step in extracting list data and performing list calculations. See Chapter 1 for a complete discussion of criteria and criteria ranges.

5

Managing Data with Worksheet Functions

Much of this book is concerned with the management of data by means of special capabilities in Excel, such as pivot tables, the Scenario Manager, and accessing external databases. But there are several techniques available to you that ease the management of data that already exists on a worksheet.

These techniques involve the use of worksheet functions such as OFFSET and TRANSPOSE, as well as menu commands such as Edit, Paste Special and Edit, Go To. This chapter covers these techniques in detail.

These techniques involve the use of the worksheet functions OFFSET and TRANSPOSE. Using OFFSET, you can reach into a worksheet range and return any number of values from that range. This function is particularly useful when you want to deal with a subset of data in a range by means of an array formula.

The TRANSPOSE function helps when you want to interchange the rows and columns of a worksheet range or an array. It's surprising how frequently users of Excel want to enter data in one orientation, but print or display a report that is turned 90 degrees. TRANSPOSE is a valuable way to accomplish this without reentering an entire range of data.

Other techniques involve menu commands such as Edit, Paste Special and Edit, Go To. Using Paste Special, you can easily convert text values to numeric values, and change formulas to values. Go To is a useful way to select a worksheet's Last Cell (the cell defined by the worksheet's lowermost used row and rightmost used column), and to activate only those cells not hidden by an outline or filter. This chapter covers these data management techniques in detail.

Using Worksheet Functions to Manage Data

Assuming that you have at least a little experience using Excel—and if you're still reading this book, you have more than a little—you are familiar with the concepts of linking to other cells, other worksheets, and other workbooks. Earlier chapters have described the use of worksheet functions, such as INDEX, VLOOKUP, and MATCH, to locate data.

There are other worksheet functions available, though, that extend the data management capabilities beyond those you might have already encountered. Two such functions are OFFSET and TRANSPOSE.

Distinguishing between the OFFSET and INDEX Functions

OFFSET and INDEX are ways to obtain values in worksheet ranges or arrays. For example, this formula

```
=INDEX(INVENTORY,5,4)
```

returns the value in the fifth row and fourth column of the range named INVENTORY. If INVENTORY occupies the range A1:E10, the value returned by this INDEX function is the value in cell D5.

OFFSET is similar to INDEX, but it identifies rows and columns slightly differently, and it can return more than one cell in an array. Suppose again that INVENTORY occupies the range A1:E10. Then this formula

```
=OFFSET(INVENTORY,0,0)
```

returns the value in cell A1. Its second and third arguments specify not *which* row and column, but a distance that Excel is to offset the target from the range's uppermost row and leftmost column. The formula above directs Excel to offset zero rows and zero columns from A1, and therefore to return the value that is in A1.

Similarly, this formula

```
=OFFSET(INVENTORY,1,1)
```

returns the value in cell B2, given that INVENTORY's upper-left cell is A1.

By adding a fourth and fifth argument to the OFFSET function, you can define how many cells it is to return. For example

```
=OFFSET(INVENTORY,2,1,2,3)
```

returns the values occupied by a range that is two rows high and three columns wide. The range begins two rows into INVENTORY and one column into INVENTORY. So, if INVENTORY begins in cell A1, the formula returns the values in cells B3:D4. Figure 5.1 depicts these examples of OFFSET and INDEX.

Tip

If you omit the fourth and fifth arguments to OFFSET, the height and width of the array it returns is assumed to be the same as the height and width of its first, reference argument.

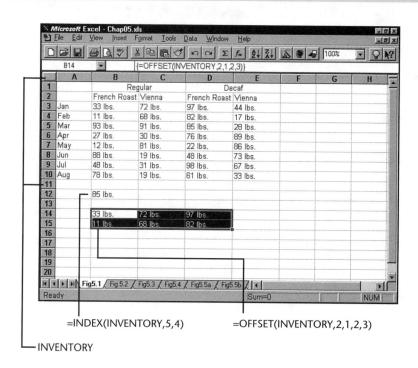

Fig. 5.1
OFFSET, in contrast to INDEX, can return an array of values.

=INDEX(INVENTORY,5,4)   =OFFSET(INVENTORY,2,1,2,3)

INVENTORY

How do you enter a formula that returns multiple values? By means of a special type of entry that is termed an *array formula*. To return the offset range in figure 5.1, you would begin by highlighting the range that will contain the formula.

Then, type the formula as given, but as you press Enter you should simultaneously hold down Ctrl+Shift. This instructs Excel to interpret what you have typed as an array formula, and to return the results to all the cells that you highlighted before entering the formula.

OFFSET is particularly useful when you use it as an argument to another function (see fig. 5.2).

Fig. 5.2
Use OFFSET to access data values in another range, when the value depends on the location of the formula.

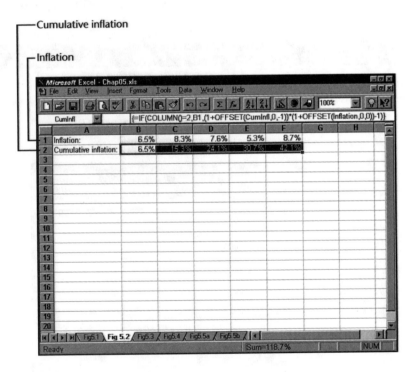

Cells B1:F1 are (hypothetical) values for inflation during each of five years; the range is named *Inflation*. Cells B2:F2 are the resulting values of cumulative inflation during the same five year period (the range is named *CumInfl*). Each value of cumulative inflation is the current year's inflation times the prior year's cumulative inflation.

An array formula is used to calculate the cumulative inflation. In cells B2:F2, the formula is

```
=IF(COLUMN()=2,B1,(1+OFFSET(CumInfl,0,-1))*(1+OFFSET(Inflation,0,0))-1)
```

To understand the use of OFFSET in this formula, consider first this fragment

```
OFFSET(CumInfl,0,-1)
```

This fragment returns an array of values beginning in the same row (row offset = 0) and in the prior column (column offset = –1) as CumInfl. So, since CumInfl occupies B2:F2, this fragment returns the array of values in A2:E2. (Remember: if the fourth and fifth arguments are omitted, the array is assumed to have the same dimensions as CumInfl: one row and five columns.)

Tip

To see the actual values in the OFFSET array, click in cell B2. In the formula bar, drag across OFFSET(CumInfl,0,–1). Then, press F9 to see the values. When you're through, press Esc to avoid entering the values in the formula.

This fragment

```
OFFSET(Inflation,0,0)
```

returns an array of values beginning in the same row (row offset = 0) and the same column (column offset = 0) as Inflation. The array again has one row and five columns.

Because the entries in Inflation are fractional values, 1 is added to the array of values returned by each OFFSET. So doing means that when they are multiplied together, the values increase instead of decrease. At the end of the formula, 1 is subtracted from the products to put the displayed value back into the proper metric.

Multiplying the two arrays together has the desired effect: the current year's inflation times the prior year's cumulative inflation. Array-entering the formula in a one-row, five-column range puts the products of the individual array entries into the proper columns.

The formula begins with this fragment

```
=IF(COLUMN()=2,B1
```

This is to return the first year's cumulative inflation as the first year's inflation: there is no prior year's cumulative inflation to act as a factor in the product.

OFFSET can also help you around a limitation in the INDEX function. Suppose that instead of obtaining each year's cumulative inflation, you simply wanted the cumulative inflation at the end of the fifth year. You might logically expect that this array formula

```
=PRODUCT(1+INDEX(Inflation,1,{1,2,3,4,5}))-1
```

would return that product—the result of multiplying together 1 plus each value in the Inflation range, minus 1. It does not, however, because INDEX does not accept a full array as one of its arguments. You can use this array formula

```
=PRODUCT(1+OFFSET(Inflation,0,0))-1
```

because the full array, Inflation, is implied by the absence of the fourth and fifth arguments to OFFSET. That is, the formula is equivalent to

```
=PRODUCT(1+OFFSET(Inflation,0,0,1,5))-1
```

which explicitly calls for an array of one row and five columns.

Using TRANSPOSE and Edit, Paste Special, Transpose

A question that frequently arises is along these lines: "I have set up a report format that links beautifully to other workbooks and worksheets. After doing all that work, I've decided that the report would look better if I changed its rows to columns and its columns to rows. Is there some way I can do that?"

There are two methods. The first makes use of the TRANSPOSE function. Suppose that you want to reorient the data shown in A1:E4 in figure 5.3 so that it appears as in C7:F11.

Fig. 5.3
By using the TRANS-POSE function, you can put data from rows into columns, and from columns into rows.

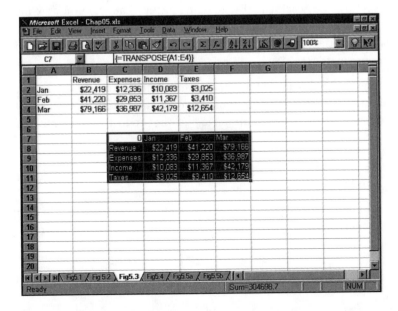

This is accomplished by selecting C7:F11, and array-entering this formula

```
=TRANSPOSE(A1:E4)
```

If you have array-entered the formula correctly, you will see the curly braces surrounding it in the formula bar. Do not enter these braces yourself. If you do so, Excel will interpret your entry as text.

You can use exactly this technique to transpose the data in A1:E4 to another worksheet or to another workbook. To transpose the range into another workbook, follow these steps (the basic approach would be the same for another worksheet):

1. Open the sheet named Fig5.3 in the Chap5.xls workbook on the companion disk.

On the Disk

2. Open the workbook that you want to transpose the data into.

3. Enter the following:

   =TRANSPOSE(

4. Use the <u>W</u>indow menu to switch back to Chap5.xls, and select cells A1:E4. The entry in the formula bar should now look like this

   ```
   =TRANSPOSE([CHAP5]Fig5.3!A1:E4
   ```

5. Enter a closing parenthesis at the end of the formula.

6. Hold down Ctrl+Shift, and press Enter.

You now have the original data range in a new book, with its row-column orientation reversed. You can close the original workbook (in this example, Chap5.xls) as well as the new one. Any changes that you make to Chap5.xls will be reflected in the new workbook. Its links to Chap5.xls are, by default, updated whenever you open it.

An alternative to using the TRANSPOSE function is the Transpos<u>e</u> option in the <u>E</u>dit, Paste <u>S</u>pecial menu. To use this option, follow these steps:

1. Open the workbook that you want to transpose the data into. This example assumes that its name is Book3.

2. Open the sheet named Fig5.3 in the Chap5.xls workbook on the companion disk.

On the Disk

3. Select A1:E4 in sheet Fig5.3.

4. Select <u>E</u>dit, <u>C</u>opy.

5. Use the <u>W</u>indow menu to switch back to Book3, and select cell A1.

6. Select <u>E</u>dit, Paste <u>S</u>pecial, Transpos<u>e</u>, and choose OK.

Data Management

The visible result is the same as if you had used the TRANSPOSE function. However, instead of containing links back to the sheet named Fig5.3, cells A1:E4 contain the transposed values in the original source range. This is, of course, because the operation copies and pastes the values from the sheet named Fig5.3.

Suppose that cells A1:E4 in Fig5.3 had themselves contained references of this form

    =A25

in cell A1, for example. Then, Edit, Paste Special, Transpose would return the #REF! error value. Transposing references in this way is more than Excel can handle. Consider, for example, the difficulties involved if the references were to noncontiguous cells—or, worse, to different worksheets.

Should you want to use the Edit menu to transpose a range of cells that themselves contain references, you can also make use of the Values option button in the Paste Special dialog box. In addition to checking the Transpose checkbox, select the Values button. This causes Excel to convert the copied references to values before it transposes them; thus, problems with the #REF! error value are avoided.

Tip

To quickly convert a range of formulas to a range of values, select the range, and then drag it down a row or over a column using the *right* mouse button. Before releasing the mouse button, drag it back to its original location. When you release the mouse button, choose Copy Values from the shortcut menu.

Note, though, that if the copied cells contain references, and if you want to maintain links to the source worksheet, you cannot use Paste Special, Transpose. To maintain the links to cells that themselves contain references, you need to use the TRANSPOSE function.

Managing Data with the Paste Special Options

This chapter has already discussed the use of the Transpose option in the Paste Special dialog box, and the difference between that option and the TRANSPOSE worksheet function. There are several other options in the Paste Special dialog box that can be used to ease and to speed your data management tasks.

If the examples in this section seem a little idiosyncratic, it's because they are. From time to time, you run into situations that call for unusual solutions, and in these cases it's sometimes possible to reach a solution by pasting copied data in an unusual way.

Using Skip Blanks

In some cases, you might want to paste a copied selection into a target area such that blank cells in the copied selection do not overwrite data in the target. Figure 5.4 shows an example.

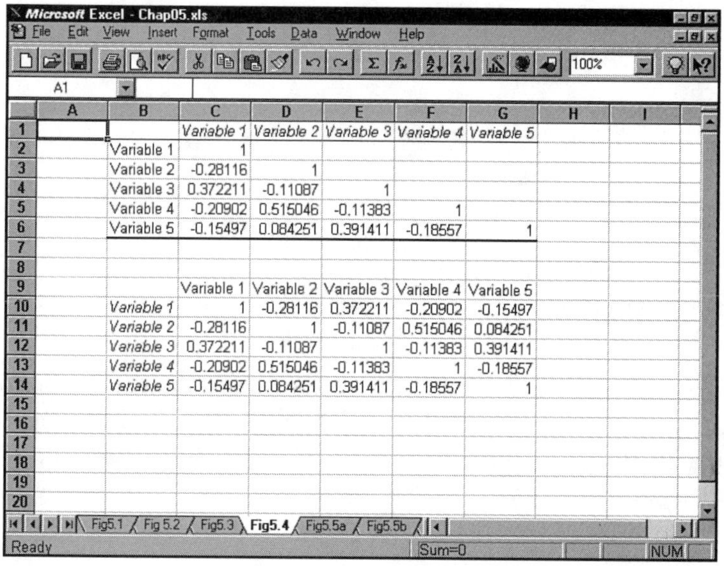

	Variable 1	Variable 2	Variable 3	Variable 4	Variable 5
Variable 1	1				
Variable 2	-0.28116	1			
Variable 3	0.372211	-0.11087	1		
Variable 4	-0.20902	0.515046	-0.11383	1	
Variable 5	-0.15497	0.084251	0.391411	-0.18557	1

	Variable 1	Variable 2	Variable 3	Variable 4	Variable 5
Variable 1	1	-0.28116	0.372211	-0.20902	-0.15497
Variable 2	-0.28116	1	-0.11087	0.515046	0.084251
Variable 3	0.372211	-0.11087	1	-0.11383	0.391411
Variable 4	-0.20902	0.515046	-0.11383	1	-0.18557
Variable 5	-0.15497	0.084251	0.391411	-0.18557	1

Fig. 5.4
The Analysis ToolPak's Correlation tool returns a triangular matrix, but sometimes you want a square matrix.

Cells C2:G6 in figure 5.4 contain a triangular correlation matrix. By definition, the correlation between Variable 1 and Variable 2, for example, is identical to the correlation between Variable 2 and Variable 1. Therefore, it would be redundant to show the correlation between the pairs of variables twice, as is done in cells C10:G14.

> **Note**
>
> If you neither understand correlations nor care to, don't worry. The point of this section is to describe the effects of transposing data and of skipping blanks, not to discuss statistical analysis.

However, sometimes redundancy is desirable. There are some statistical analyses that require the correlation matrix to be square instead of triangular. By using Edit, Paste Special, Transpose and Skip Blanks, it's easy to change the triangular matrix in C2:G6 to the square matrix shown in C10:G14.

To do so, follow these steps:

1. Open the file named Chap05.xls from the companion disk.
2. Select the worksheet named Fig5.4.
3. Select B1:G6, and choose Edit, Copy.
4. Select cell B9, and choose Edit, Paste Special.
5. In the Paste Special dialog box, check the Transpose box, and choose OK.
6. Select B9:G14, and choose Edit, Copy.
7. Select B1, and choose Edit, Paste Special.
8. In the Paste Special dialog box, check the Skip Blanks box, and choose OK.

You now have, in cells C2:G6, the square matrix shown in cells C10:G14 of figure 5.4.

In words, you transposed the original, triangular matrix, and this turned it upside down. In the final step, you also chose to skip blanks. This means that the triangle of *blank* cells was not pasted—if they had been pasted, the original, triangular matrix would have been overwritten with blanks. Try it again, but this time don't check the Skip Blanks box.

Converting Text Values to Numeric Values

Suppose that you have opened a text file into an Excel worksheet, in which some cells that should be numbers have been treated as text values. Where possible—depending on whether Excel *can* interpret the value as a number—you want to convert these text entries to their numeric values.

The fastest way to make this conversion is to use Edit, Paste Special, Multiply. Enter the value 1 in some blank cell. Select that cell, and choose Edit, Copy. Select the cells that you want to convert to numeric values and choose Edit, Paste Special, Multiply. Then, choose OK.

The effect is to multiply each text value by 1. If Excel can interpret the text value as a number, it does so, and converts it to its numeric representation. (You could also copy a zero, and use Edit, Paste Special, Add. In either case, the numeric value of the text entry would be unchanged.)

It is usually better to make judicious use of the Text Wizard to avoid this sort of problem. (See Chapter 21 for detailed information on the Text Wizard). When you open an ASCII file whose extension is .txt or .prn, Excel starts the Text Wizard. This Wizard enables you, among other options, to specify a particular format for each column of data that is brought into the worksheet.

However, some text files are laid out such that any given column can contain both data that should be treated as text and some that should be treated as numeric. It is more difficult to convert a numeric value to text than it is to convert a text value to numeric. In a case like this, then, it's preferable to read the column in as text and subsequently convert text values to their numeric representations.

Tip

If you open a file that has the extension .csv (short for *comma separated values*), Excel does not start the Text Wizard. If you want to use the Text Wizard on such a file, first rename it so that its extension is .txt or .prn.

Tip

To convert a numeric value to text, use the FIXED worksheet function; for example

    =FIXED(A1,2)

where the second argument specifies the number of decimal places to retain. Then, select the cell that contains the FIXED function and use Edit, Copy and Edit, Paste Special, Values.

Using Edit, Go To

If you skipped version 5 of Excel and moved directly from version 4 to version 7, you might initially miss some of the Go To options available in version 4. They're still around in version 7, but you have to look a little farther to find them. Use Edit, Go To, Special to select cells that are precedents, dependents, visible cells, the Last Cell, and so on.

Modifying the Location of the Last Cell

An Excel worksheet has a special cell called the Last Cell. It is defined as the intersection between the lowermost row that has a value (or that had one since the file was last saved), and the rightmost column that has a value (or had one since the last save).

For example, suppose that the only two cells in a worksheet that contain entries are H1 and A100. Then, the worksheet's last cell is H100. If you remove these entries by clearing the cells, the worksheet's last cell is still H100.

To demonstrate this to yourself, follow these steps:

1. Make two entries in a new worksheet, in any two cells that you want.
2. Choose Edit, Go To.
3. In the Go To dialog box, click Special.
4. In the Go To Special dialog box, choose the Last Cell option button, and choose OK.

After you choose OK, the active cell will be the intersection of the row of the lower of the two cells and the column of the rightmost of the two cells. Even if you clear the cells, Edit, Go To, Special, Last Cell takes you to the same cell.

This can be a very handy tool:

- You can use it to check that the worksheet is not larger than it needs to be.
- It's a quick way to select the lower right corner of an area that you want to highlight—to name a range, perhaps, to format a range, or to define a range to be printed.
- You can use it in Visual Basic for Applications (VBA) to make sure that when you write values to a worksheet, your code does not overwrite any existing data. For example

    ```
    Selection.SpecialCells(xlLastCell).Select
    ```

    This is not necessarily the most efficient use of worksheet space, but the next row and column are certain to be clear.

It often happens that you have a worksheet which, over time, uses fewer and fewer rows or columns. This can occur if you are summarizing its information. You might, for example, replace several detail rows of data by totalling them into a new, summary row, and then deleting the detail rows.

In this case, the cell that Excel regards as the Last Cell does not change. For an example, see figure 5.5.

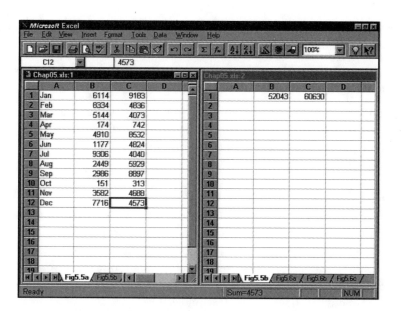

Fig. 5.5
The Last Cell depends on the location of the last-used row and column when the file is saved.

Data Management

The first window in figure 5.5 displays a worksheet that contains data in A1:C12—one row for each month of the year. To best follow this discussion, open the file named Chap05 on the companion disk and activate the sheet named Fig5.5. Then, follow these steps:

On the Disk

1. Select row 1.

2. Choose Insert, Row. The data area shifts down one row.

3. In cell B1, enter

    =SUM(B2:B13)

4. Copy cell B1, and paste it to C1.

5. Select B1:C1 and choose Edit, Copy. Then, choose Edit, Paste Special, Values.

6. Select A2:C13, and choose Edit, Clear, All. Or, select rows 2 through 13 and choose Edit, Delete.

If you now use Edit, Go To, Special, Last Cell, Excel makes C13 the active cell. Clearing the information in A2:C13, or deleting rows 2 through 13, has no effect on the location of the Last Cell.

Now, save the file, close it, and reopen it. Choosing Edit, Go To, Special, Last Cell shows that the Last Cell is now C1.

This demonstrates that you must save a file, close it, and then open it again in order for the change in what is actually the Last Cell to take effect.

The position of the Last Cell has no effect on the space that is occupied by a file on your disk. Other things being equal, a workbook with exactly one entry, in A1, occupies the same amount of disk space as a workbook with one entry in Z1000.

Modifying Visible Cells Only

Another handy usage of Edit, Go To, Special is the Visible Cells Only option button. Suppose that your worksheet contains a report that you want to format so that detail rows use the Regular font, and the summary rows use the Bold font. You could, of course, select the summary rows one by one or as a multiple selection and assign the bold font to them. But selecting all those rows is tedious. See figure 5.6, first window.

Fig. 5.6
Toggling the Hide Detail and Show Detail symbols quickly groups and ungroups detail rows.

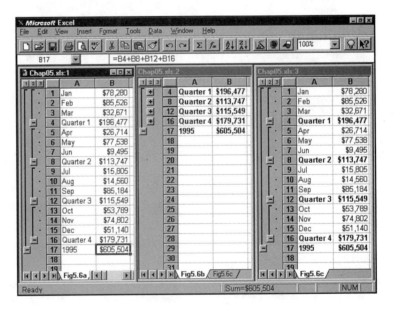

A better way is to hide the detail rows first. If you have created an outline for the worksheet, you can do this very easily with the Outline Symbol's Hide Detail Symbol or its Row or Column Level Symbols (these are described in Chapter 1).

Then, select Edit, Go To, Special, Visible Cells Only. It will appear at first as though the entire worksheet has been selected, but the hidden rows are *not* selected. Choose Format, Cells and click the Font tab. Select Bold from the Font Style list box, and choose OK (see fig. 5.6, second window).

Now, use the Outline Symbol to display the hidden rows. You will find that the detail rows that were hidden retain the Regular font, and the summary rows that were visible are now in Bold. See figure 5.6, third window.

You need not have outlined a worksheet for this approach to work. You can also hide rows or columns by using Format, Rows or Format, Columns and choosing Hide. Edit, Go To, Special, Visible Cells Only still causes an action to apply only to the unhidden cells.

> **Tip**
>
> If you hide rows or columns using Format, Rows, Hide or Format, Columns, Hide, and a cell in one of the hidden rows or columns is active, then Edit, Go To, Special, Visible Cells Only cannot find any visible cells.

Chapter Summary

This chapter described how to use certain worksheet functions and menu commands to satisfy unusual data management requirements. By use of TRANSPOSE, you can reorient a range of data, maintaining links to the original range.

You can also reorient the range, and discard links, by combining Paste Special, Transpose with Paste Special, Values. The OFFSET function extends the capabilities of the INDEX function. Skipping blanks and text conversions are among the other possibilities available from the Paste Special dialog box.

The next chapter, "Protecting Business Data from Tampering," focuses on preventing users from modifying your data. Mentally include yourself among those users against whom your data require protection. It's entirely possible to accidentally delete or overwrite a data set that you have spent hours accumulating.

Protecting Business Data from Tampering

The process of managing data inevitably involves the maintenance of the data's security. Anyone can accidentally lose data that has been placed into an Excel worksheet, and this chapter provides several techniques that you can use to reduce the likelihood of such loss. Furthermore, it describes methods you can use to hide or protect vital workbooks and workbook elements against the possibility of deliberate, malicious tampering.

It's important to understand that the techniques presented in this chapter are specific to a particular file, worksheet, or worksheet element. You cannot set any particular Excel option that always, for example, requires a password to be entered in order to open a workbook. This is, of course, as it should be—setting such a global option would make it hopelessly complicated to use Excel at all. Still, keep in mind that if you want to protect workbooks or their elements, you must arrange for the protection on a workbook-by-workbook basis.

Protecting Files

When you save a file with File, Save As and click the Options button, Excel provides you with several choices for your use in tailoring what users can do with the file. The stricter levels of protection require that a user know passwords before opening or saving the file is possible. The more lenient level simply provides a warning if a user is about to save any changes that might have been made. Figure 6.1 shows the dialog boxes involved in this process.

Fig. 6.1
File, Save As offers options to limit access to the workbook.

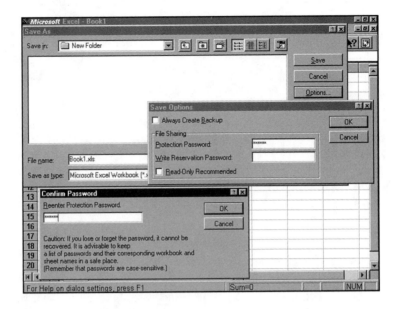

Using the Protection Password

The most inclusive barrier that you can set up for a workbook is the protection password. If you employ this password, no one who does not know it can even open the workbook.

Within Excel, there is no way to break a password. Therefore, when you use this option, be absolutely certain that it's one you will remember—if you forget it, you will have locked yourself out.

> ### Note
>
> Some companies have marketed third-party password breakers. They are touted as tools to help people who have forgotten their own passwords, or to help companies open password-protected workbooks saved by an employee who has subsequently left the firm. These programs work on Excel workbooks.
>
> The reasons cited for using a password breaker might sound disingenuous to you, but by and large they're legitimate. A surprising number of help requests are posted to various bulletin board services, seeking ways to open a protected workbook whose password has been forgotten. Some of those requests are likely from snoopers, but some are doubtless justified. Passwords are easy to forget.
>
> In addition to the normal recommendations about choosing a password (use something more difficult to guess than your date of birth or telephone number; don't write it down where it's easy to find; change it from time to time; don't use the same password for every workbook), be aware that it's possible to purchase software for about $100 that renders the password useless.

To exercise the password protection option, just type a password in the Protection Password edit box in the Save Options dialog box. The characters you type do not appear on the screen: they are represented by asterisks. After you have typed the password, you can exercise other options by filling a checkbox or clicking in the Write Reservation Password edit box.

After you choose OK, a dialog box appears that prompts you to re-enter the password. The Confirm Password dialog box, also shown in figure 6.1, appears, and its Caution statement is well worth noting. In particular, passwords are case-sensitive in Excel. If you supply *Indiscreet* as a password, neither *indiscreet* nor *INDISCREET* nor *InDiScReEt* nor any variation on capitalization other than *Indiscreet* will work.

Once you have retyped the password, Excel checks that the two versions are identical. If they are not, Excel displays an alert message to that effect and returns you to the Save Options dialog box. If the versions are identical, you are returned to the Save As dialog box: if you want to specify additional options, you must click the Options button again.

Once a password has been specified and the workbook saved, a user who attempts to open it sees a dialog box requesting that the password be entered. A user who knows the password can enter it in an edit box; again, the characters that are typed are represented by asterisks. The workbook cannot be opened until the password is entered correctly. There is no limit to the number of times that the user can attempt to type the correct password.

Links to a password-protected file require that the password be entered. If a user enters a link formula into a cell of an open workbook—something like this, for example

```
='C:\My Documents\[Book1.xls]Sheet1'!$A$1
```

Excel requests that the user supply the correct password.

Using the Write Reservation Password and the Read-only Option

The Write Reservation password affords greater access to a workbook than does Password Protection. Unless the Password Protection is also set, a user can open a workbook that has a Write Reservation password. If this password is not known, the user cannot save the file using its original name.

When you open a workbook that has a Write Reservation password, you are prompted by means of the Password dialog box shown in figure 6.2.

Fig. 6.2

You can choose between supplying a workbook's Write Reservation password and opening the workbook as read-only.

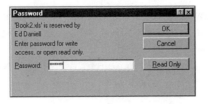

The purpose of this password is to allow other users to open and view the contents of the workbook, but to prevent them from saving any changes they might make, using the current file name.

Suppose that you have spent a considerable amount of time developing a workbook named Budget.xls, and that you want input from colleagues as to how well it works. If you save it with a Write Reservation password (but not a protection password), your colleagues can open it, test it, and even make changes to it. But they will not be able to save it with the name Budget.xls unless they know its write reservation password. They *can* save it if they supply a different file name. In this way, you can be reasonably sure that the workbook is safe from accidental or deliberate tampering.

The user might choose to open the file as read-only. In that event, if the user chooses File, Save, a message that the file is read-only is displayed. Then, the standard Save As dialog box appears. This gives the user an opportunity to save the file under another name. If the user tries to save the workbook under the same name with the Save As dialog box, the message about its read-only status is displayed again. If the user chooses to save the workbook under another name, the password edit boxes are blank—that is, the user can set new passwords for the new file.

Of course, none of this applies if the user knows the Write Reservation password when the file is opened. Supplying the correct Write Reservation password in the Password dialog box enables the user to change and save the file without restriction.

Using the Read-Only Recommended Checkbox

The Read-Only Recommended checkbox option (refer to fig. 6.1) operates similarly to the Write Reservation password, but it is more lenient. No password is needed. If you save a workbook with this box checked, a user who opens it is warned that you recommended that its status be read-only. This warning is shown in figure 6.3.

The user can choose No, to enable a subsequent File, Save under the same file name. Choosing Yes prevents any subsequent saves with the same file name, just as though a Write Reservation password had been required.

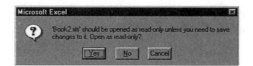

Fig. 6.3
The read-only recommendation is a good way to protect yourself against saving inadvertent changes to a workbook.

The Read-Only Recommended option allows the user to exercise judgment about the file's read-only status, but does not impose the burden of supplying a Write Reservation password. It's particularly useful if you are developing an Excel workbook or application, and are testing it. Suppose that you make some tentative changes to its functionality or appearance during the testing process. Before you save the workbook with the same name—thereby over-writing the existing version—you might want to test those changes more extensively.

If, the last time you saved the workbook, you chose the Read-Only Recom-mended checkbox option, you supply yourself with a reminder *not* to re-save it with the same name. As a bonus, you need not remember a Write Reserva-tion password, and you're free to concentrate on your testing and revising without worrying about making an unwanted change irreversible.

Arranging for Automatic Backups

Another way to protect yourself against unwanted changes to a workbook is to arrange for an automatic backup when you save a workbook. You can do so by checking the Always Create Backup checkbox in the Save Options dia-log box (refer to fig. 6.1).

When you save the workbook under its existing name with this box checked, Excel creates a new file named Backup Of [filename].xlk. For example, if your workbook is named Book1.xls, Excel would create a new file named Backup of Book1.xlk. Notice the use of Windows 95's long file name capability, and also notice the extension .xlk instead of .xls.

The automatic backup option saves the file as it was when it was opened. Suppose that you open Book1.xls, and that it contains only the value *1* in cell A1. You now place a *2* in cell A2, and save the workbook. With Always Create Backup checked, the backup contains only the *1* in A1; Book1.xls, of course, contains the *1* and the *2*.

Now suppose that you open Book1.xls again, place a *3* in cell A3, and save the workbook. The file named Backup of Book1.xlk now contains a *1* in A1 and a *2* in A2: the backup of Book1 reflects that workbook as of the time that it was last opened.

This is a convenience, of course, and it affords some degree of protection against saving unwanted changes to a workbook. But if you want a trail of breadcrumbs, a set of workbooks that shows each version of the workbook as it is modified, you will need to save each version explicitly.

Protecting Workbook Elements

Even if you choose not to protect a workbook by means of a protection password or a Write Reservation password, you can still prevent many workbook elements from changes. You can, alternatively or in addition, prevent a user from viewing certain workbook elements. The distinction to draw is between *protecting* a workbook element and *hiding* it.

For example, suppose that you select rows 2 through 5 and choose Format, Row, Hide. Rows 2 through 5 are now not visible, but you can select rows 1 through 6 and choose Format, Row, Unhide to display them again.

But if you hide rows 2 through 5, then choose Tools, Protection, Protect Sheet and check Contents (see fig. 6.4), you are unable to unhide the rows until you clear the Contents checkbox.

So, hiding a worksheet element operates independently of protecting worksheet elements. You can hide something, but unless you also invoke worksheet or workbook protection from the Tools menu, the element is easily unhidden.

Workbook and Worksheet Protection

The choices involved in protecting a worksheet are shown in figure 6.4.

Fig. 6.4
Worksheet protection is limited to the sheet that is active when you choose Tools, Protection, Protect Sheet.

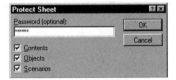

> **Note**
>
> If a module or dialog sheet is active when you choose Tools, Protection, Protect Sheet, you have no choices as to *what* to protect. The entire sheet is protected. There is an edit box where you can enter a password.

Worksheet protection works differently for different worksheet elements. As noted in the previous section, checking Contents in the Protect Sheet dialog box prevents the user from unhiding a hidden row or column. It also prevents the user from hiding a visible row or column.

However, checking Contents has no effect on worksheet cells unless you have formatted them as Locked or Hidden (see the next section for more information on this option). The default status for a worksheet cell is Locked: unless you clear that option, checking Contents prevents a user from modifying the contents of a cell.

The Protect Sheet dialog box also enables you to protect worksheet objects. This represents a broad class of elements, from text boxes to buttons to embedded charts to data maps. No special, additional setting (such as locking cells or hiding rows) is needed to protect a worksheet object. If you check the Objects checkbox, the user is unable to select an object. And if the object cannot be selected, it can't be moved, resized, discarded, edited, or otherwise modified.

On a protected sheet, you cannot change the status of a row or column from hidden to visible or vice versa; nor can you change cells from locked to unlocked or unlocked to locked. Similarly, the protected status of a scenario cannot be changed. When you add a scenario to a worksheet, one of your options is to protect the scenario from editing or deletion (see Chapter 13, "Creating Business Scenarios" for more details on this option).

The option to protect the scenario has no effect unless the worksheet is protected. Merely choosing the protection option in the Scenario Manager dialog box does not by itself prevent someone from editing or deleting it. However, once the worksheet itself is protected, a user cannot modify a protected scenario.

In contrast, if you choose not to protect an individual scenario, protecting the worksheet does not protect the scenario.

Table 6.1 summarizes these worksheet protection choices.

Table 6.1 Protection Choices	
Worksheet Element	**Worksheet Protection On**
Cell locked	Cannot unlock or edit cell
Cell unlocked	Cell editing possible; cannot lock cell
Cell hidden	Cannot view cell's contents in formula bar

(continues)

Table 6.1 Continued	
Worksheet Element	**Worksheet Protection On**
Cell unhidden	Cell's contents visible in formula bar
Row/column hidden	Cannot unhide
Row/column unhidden	Cannot hide
Object	Cannot add, move, change, or delete
Scenario protected	Cannot delete or edit
Scenario unprotected	Editing and deletion possible

With worksheet protection off, the user can freely lock and unlock cells, hide and unhide cells, rows and columns, take any action on an object, and edit and delete scenarios.

In contrast to worksheet protection, workbook protection allows you to prevent changes to the windows and the sheets in the workbook. To protect a workbook, choose Tools, Protection, Protect Workbook. This displays the dialog box shown in figure 6.5.

Fig. 6.5
The Structure checkbox in the Protect Workbook dialog box applies to the structure of the workbook's sheets.

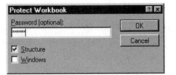

If you check the Structure checkbox, a user is unable to:

- Delete a sheet
- Move a sheet
- Hide a sheet
- Unhide a sheet
- Rename a sheet
- Insert a sheet

This sort of protection is very useful in a workbook that contains or is used by a Visual Basic for Applications (VBA) macro. It often happens that the VBA code expects or requires that specific sheets exist in the workbook. It can also happen that your VBA code needs to use a sheet that is in a particular location in the workbook or that has a particular name.

It's good programming practice to check for sheets' presence, location, hidden status, name, and so on, before beginning the process of manipulating the sheets and their contents. However, rather than subjecting the user to frustrating error messages that, for example, a required sheet cannot be found, you might want to consider protecting the workbook's structure. Doing so prevents the user from creating an error condition related to the structure of the workbook's sheets. If your VBA code needs to modify the structure of the workbook while it is running, you can include statements that unprotect the workbook at the right time and protect it again when processing is complete.

The checkbox option to protect the workbook's windows, shown in figure 6.5, prevents the user from:

- Moving a window
- Resizing a window
- Hiding a window
- Unhiding a window
- Closing a window

Unless your application depends heavily on the actual positioning of windows on the screen, this option is less valuable than the Structure protection option.

Locking and Hiding Cells

As you might expect, locking a cell and then protecting its worksheet makes the cell inaccessible. You can view locked cells' contents, but you cannot delete or change them. Nor can you change their formatting characteristics.

You cannot view in the formula bar the contents of a hidden cell on a protected worksheet. The idea is to conceal from the user any formula in the cell. If you're of a larcenous turn of mind, you might try using Tools, Options and clicking the View tab to fill the Formulas checkbox. Ordinarily, doing so would display formulas instead of values on the worksheet. But if the cells are hidden and the worksheet protected, setting the Formulas option causes cells containing formulas to appear empty.

By default, cells are locked but not hidden on a new worksheet. To change the status of cells that you have selected, choose Format, Cells and click the Protection tab, shown in figure 6.6. Then, fill or clear the Locked and Hidden checkboxes.

Fig. 6.6

By default, all cells are locked. When you protect a worksheet, it's expected that an unlocked cell would be the exception.

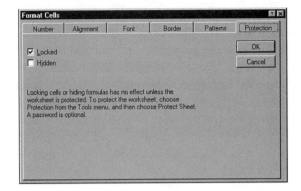

As figure 6.6 shows, you can also supply a password to protect the sheet. The only way to modify a locked cell in a protected sheet is to first unprotect the sheet. You must know the password that was used when the sheet was protected in order to unprotect the sheet.

What if you want to hide a cell's contents, not only in the formula bar but in the cell itself? Format the cell with the ;;; cell format. This is not a built-in format. To use it, follow these steps:

1. Choose Format, Cells, and click the Number tab.
2. Select Custom from the Category list box.
3. In the Type edit box, enter three consecutive semicolons (;;;).
4. Choose OK.

This custom format prevents a cell's contents, whether a value or a formula, from appearing in the cell itself. Combining this format with hiding the cell and protecting the worksheet prevents the user from viewing the cell's contents anywhere on the active sheet.

Tip

We wouldn't leave you without a back door. To view a cell that has been hidden in this fashion, create a link to the cell from another worksheet. Assuming that the cell is F2 on Sheet1 in Book1, switch to another worksheet and enter

```
=[Book1]Sheet1!$F$2
```

What about copying a locked cell's contents? Even if the worksheet is protected, it's entirely possible to copy a locked cell's contents. All you need to do is find an unlocked cell or an unprotected worksheet to paste it to. That's easy enough—just open a new worksheet. The catch is that you cannot copy a formula, just its value. Suppose that cell A1 on Sheet1, which is protected, contains the formula = 5 + 3. If you insert a new sheet and enter in some cell =Sheet1!A1, the formula returns the value, *not* the formula, in cell A1 of Sheet1.

The following case study shows how you might bring all these options into play in a worksheet.

Case Study: Commission Statements

Sales commissions are sensitive matters. Especially where the percentages that apply to commissions differ, and where management overrides (a percentage of each sale that is paid to sales management) exist, it's important to keep the information confidential.

Consider the sales commission worksheet shown in figure 6.7.

	A	B	C	D	E	F	G
	Sales Representative	Jones	Date of hire:	4/5/95			
1	Sales Representative	Jones	Date of hire:	4/5/95			
2	Sales last month	$25,000					
3	Commission	$825					
4	Bonus	$100					
5	Payable:	$925					
6							
7	Projection, next month	$40,000					
8							
9	Manager's name	Manager's override					
10	Thompson	$250					
11	Sales Rep's bonus	$100					

Fig. 6.7
A worksheet that contains sensitive information can make good use of locked and hidden cells.

All the information in the worksheet is displayed in figure 6.7. The work-sheet is prepared by the company's commission accounting group, with one worksheet for each sales representative in a region. Each region has one workbook. The flow of the worksheet through the company is tracked in the paragraphs that follow.

A copy of the workbook is sent to the sales manager for each region. For the worksheet shown in figure 6.7, the sales manager is Thompson and the sales representative is Jones. Thompson adds a discretionary bonus for Jones in cell B11, and forwards a copy of the worksheet to Jones. Jones adds a sales forecast for the following month in cell B7, and sends the worksheet back to Thompson. Thompson, in turn, sends a copy of the workbook back to national headquarters.

When it originally prepares the worksheet, the commission accounting group maintains the integrity of the information by locking and hiding certain cells, and protecting the worksheet's contents using Tools, Protection, Protect Sheet. A Password for sheet protection is supplied, its Contents box checked, and the workbook is sent to Thompson.

Before protecting the worksheet, though, the commission accounting group locks and hides certain cells, as follows:

- Both the sales manager and the sales representative should be able to see the representative's sales for the prior month, $25,000 in cell B2, but neither person should be allowed to change that amount. The cell is locked, but not hidden.

- Although sales representatives know—they know to the *penny*—how much commission they are to be paid, they do not necessarily know all the conditions that might affect their commision rates. This company pays a commission of 3.3% to representatives who have been in its employ for less than two years, and 5.3% to other representatives. The formula in cell B3 is

    ```
    =IF(TODAY()-HireDate < 730,0.033,0.053)*B2
    ```

    Jones has worked for the company for less than two years, and so Jones's commission is 3.3% times his sales. The information about the relationship between tenure and commission rate is considered confidential, so the formula in B3 is locked and hidden. This means that the formula cannot be changed and cannot be viewed in the formula bar. Its result, however, is visible in the cell itself. Jones's date of hire, in cell D1 and named HireDate, is also locked.

- Cell B4 links to cell B11, where Thompson enters the bonus that he wants the company to pay to Jones. Because it's considered neither necessary nor desirable that Jones know the basis for this bonus, cell B4 is locked (it can't be changed) and hidden (its source can't be determined by looking in the formula bar).

- The total commission payable, cell B5, should be locked but visible. It is simply the sum of B3 and B4.

- Cell B7, Jones's sales forecast for the next month which he enters and returns to Thompson, is unlocked (so that Jones can enter it) and visible (so that everyone can see it).

- The range A9:B11 is where commission accounting enters Thompson's override (cell B10) and where Thompson can enter an amount for a bonus for Jones. To prevent Jones from seeing any of this information in the formula bar, the entire range is hidden.

- To prevent Jones from seeing any information in A9:B11 in their cells, the cells' formats are set to the special ;;; format.

- The entire range A9:B11 is also locked, with two exceptions. B11 is unlocked so that Thompson can temporarily change its format to Currency, and enter a bonus amount for Jones. And B10 is unlocked so that Thompson can change its format to Currency and check the override. Then, Thompson changes the format of B10 and B11 back to ;;;, saves the sheet, and forwards it to Jones. Because these cells are unlocked, Thompson is able to change their formats to Currency and back to ;;;.

The result of this protecting, hiding, and formatting is shown in figure 6.8.

Fig. 6.8
By locking, hiding, and formatting the cells properly, employees' access can be limited to the information that they need to know.

	A	B	C	D	E	F	G
1	Salesman	Jones	Date of hire:	4/5/95			
2	Sales last month	$25,000					
3	Commission	$825					
4	Bonus	$100					
5	Payable:	$925					
6							
7	Projection, next month	$40,000					
8							
9							

If you open the file named Chap06.xls on the companion disk, and activate the sheets named Fig6.7 and Fig6.8, you can verify that changes cannot be made to the locked cells, that hidden formulas cannot be viewed in the formula bar, and that cells with the ;;; format cannot be viewed in the cells themselves.

On the Disk

As noted in the previous section (and if Jones has read this book), Jones could open a new worksheet and link cells there to cells A9:B11 in the worksheet shown in figure 6.8. This would defeat the purpose of hiding the cells and formatting them with the ;;; format.

If it is critical to maintain confidentiality of cells like these, you could move the range to some random area well away from the visible range—say, AD125:AE127. It would also be advisable to make an entry in cell IV16384 (the rightmost and lowermost possible cell on a worksheet) so that the sheet's Last Cell property does not provide a clue to the location of the information in AD125:AE127.

Hiding Rows and Columns

There are various ways to hide rows and columns in Excel. Perhaps the simplest is to select rows (or columns) by selecting their headers, and choosing Format, Row, Hide. You unhide them, of course, by choosing Format, Row, Unhide or Format, Column, Unhide.

Rows and columns can also be hidden by using either the AutoFilter or the Advanced Filter to filter a list in place, as described in Chapter 1. You can also hide rows or columns by grouping detail rows or columns in an outline.

Protecting the worksheet with Tools, Protection, Protect Sheet and checking the Contents checkbox prevents the user from unhiding a hidden row or column, and from hiding an unhidden row or column. There is an exception.

Suppose that you have an Excel 7 worksheet with a list in, say, A1:A20. Using a method such as Format, Row, Hide, hide (say) rows 10 through 15.

Now, protect the worksheet with Tools, Protection, Protect Sheet. Of course, you cannot now use Format, Row, Unhide. But you can use the Advanced Filter to display all the rows by using A1:A20 as the List Range, specifying no criteria, and filtering the list in place. If you unlocked a couple of cells before protecting the sheet, you could use them as a criterion, to cause the Advanced Filter to hide any rows whose list entries do not conform to the criterion.

Note that AutoFilter and Show All are disabled for a protected sheet, but Advanced Filter is not.

Hiding Sheets

Hiding a worksheet can be a useful technique if, either for reasons of security or cosmetics, you want to keep a user from changing its contents—or even from knowing that the worksheet exists. For example, suppose that you want to display for the user the results of some complicated calculations and look-ups. You do not want the user to have access to the formulas themselves. In that case, you could put the calculations and lookups on a worksheet and display the results on another worksheet by means of linkages. Then, hide the worksheet that contains the calculations.

To hide a sheet, use Format, Sheet, Hide. Unless you then choose Tools, Protection, Protect Workbook and check the Structure box, a user can unhide the sheet by means of Format, Sheet, Unhide. To add an additional level of security, of course, you can also specify a password in the Protect Workbook dialog box.

At times, you might want to hide a sheet in a workbook but not protect the workbook. For example, one of the sheets might be a VBA module that you want to hide from the user, but you want the user to be able to insert and delete other sheets such as charts and worksheets. If you allow the user to insert and delete other sheets, you have to remove workbook protection. But if that protection is removed, the user can unhide the VBA module.

The solution is to use a special VBA constant called xlVeryHidden. For more information on using this constant, see the final section in this chapter, "Protecting Elements with VBA."

Protecting Workbooks on a Network

If your computer is connected to a local area network, it is likely that from time to time you will want to use a workbook that is in use by another user. In this case, the creator of the workbook has presumably *not* arranged for password protection, so that a password is not needed to open the file, or its creator has shared the password with the intended users of the workbook.

Excel 7 provides for the eventuality that multiple users might need the same workbook simultaneously by means of *shared lists*. A shared list is one that at least two users have access to simultaneously. By setting options in File, Shared Lists, you can prevent changes by another concurrent user, or allow those changes and monitor any conflicts between entries you make and entries the other user makes.

When two users have access to a shared list, each can make new entries, edit entries, sort the list, and save the results. However, neither user can save formulas entered in the list or save formats of its cells.

If the users of a shared list make changes to it that are in conflict—for example, you might enter the name "William Shakespeare" in cell A1, and I might enter the name "Dave Barry" in the same cell—Excel needs a means of resolving the conflict. If I have already saved my version of the workbook when you are ready to save yours, you are notified that a conflict (or conflicts) exists, and you are asked which entry to use.

You can also arrange for a record of such conflicts, including the users and the values involved, the date, the location in the list, and the resolution chosen.

Allowing Multi-User Editing

To set the options for shared lists, select File, Shared Lists. In the Shared Lists dialog box, check Allow Multi-User Editing to permit another user or users to use the workbook simultaneously, or clear the checkbox to deny that permission (see fig. 6.9).

Fig. 6.9
The default choice in the Shared Lists dialog box is to allow multi-user editing.

The dialog box also contains a checkbox labeled Show Conflict History. This checkbox is disabled unless at least one other user has opened the workbook.

To view a list of users who also have the workbook open, click the Status tab.

Suppose that I already have the workbook open at the time that you open it, and that I have chosen to deny access to another user by clearing the Allow Multi-User Editing checkbox. In that case, you will receive the message shown in figure 6.10.

Fig. 6.10
This message means that the user who already has the workbook open has chosen not to share it while it is open.

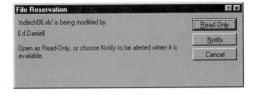

You can choose to be notified when the file is once again available, or you can choose to open the file as read-only. As you learned earlier in this chapter in the section on workbook protection, opening the file as read-only allows you to modify it freely, but if you want to save your changes you must do so under another file name.

On the other hand, I might have accepted the default option to allow multi-user editing. In that case, you are able to open the workbook and edit it. Suppose that you make an entry that conflicts with one that I have made—for example, we make different entries in cell A1. Whichever one of us is the last to save the file sees the dialog box shown in figure 6.11.

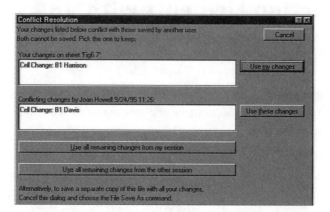

Fig. 6.11
If you save a shared list such that a conflict in data entries would result, this dialog box enables you to resolve the conflict.

You can resolve the conflict in favor of the entry that you made or in favor of the entry that I made. If you have also checked the Show Conflict History checkbox in the Shared Lists dialog box, Excel adds a new worksheet to the workbook before saving it. The worksheet might appear as shown in figure 6.12.

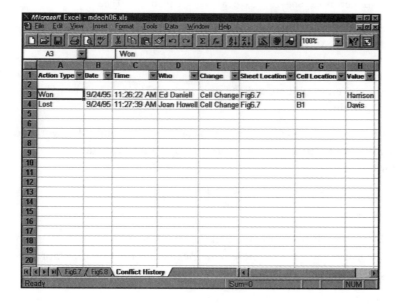

Fig. 6.12
The conflict history summarizes information about data conflicts, the users involved, and the resolution.

You can use this worksheet as a guide to further conflict resolution. You might want to discuss the conflicts and how you chose to resolve them, to ensure that the data in the workbook is accurate or to negotiate which value should be in the saved version.

Protecting Elements with VBA

As noted earlier in the section "Hiding Sheets," you can use VBA to make a workbook object such as a VBA module or a worksheet even more hidden than you can by means of Format, Sheet, Hide.

Suppose that you want to hide a worksheet named CalcValues more completely. In an Auto_Open subroutine of a module in the same workbook, you could include this code

```
ThisWorkbook.Sheets("CalcValues").Visible = xlVeryHidden
```

When this statement executes, it hides the sheet just as though you had hidden it with Format, Sheet, Hide. However, if the user chooses Format, Sheet, the Unhide item is disabled because xlVeryHidden makes the sheet unavailable for unhiding, whether or not the workbook's structure is protected. Or, if the workbook contains another sheet—say, Sheet2—that was hidden via the Format menu, then the Unhide item is available, but only Sheet2 appears as a sheet that can be unhidden.

You can also set the sheet's Visible property to True or False. For example

```
ThisWorkbook.Sheets("CalcValues").Visible = True
```

makes CalcValues visible, regardless of whether it was hidden or xlVeryHidden. And this statement

```
ThisWorkbook.Sheets("CalcValues").Visible = False
```

makes CalcValues hidden, but the user can unhide it by choosing Format, Sheet, Unhide.

The VBA constant xlVeryHidden is not foolproof, of course. If a workbook's structure is not protected, a user can employ a VBA loop such as the following

```
For Each ThisSheet In ThisWorkbook.Sheets
    ThisSheet.Visible = True
Next ThisSheet
```

which sets the Visible property of all sheets in the workbook to True. Note that the use of the For Each statement means that the user does not have to know the names of any hidden or xlVeryHidden sheets.

Chapter Summary

In this chapter, you learned data management techniques that enable you to protect workbooks and their elements against deliberate or accidental changes. Many of these techniques involve the use of passwords. Keep in mind that, even though software is commercially available that will crack Excel passwords, it's important to remember your passwords or to keep them in a safe location.

You have also learned how to protect workbooks that are shared in a network environment, and how to make workbook objects even more inaccessible than is possible by hiding them from Excel's menu structure.

The next chapter, "Understanding Pivot Tables," begins the next section of this book. Pivot tables are a powerful means of analyzing and summarizing data in Excel lists and in external data sources, and are central to the process of managing data in the Excel environment.

Part II

Pivot Tables

Understanding Pivot Tables

With version 5.0, Excel introduced a powerful new means of summarizing data taken from worksheets or from external data sources: the pivot table. *Pivot tables* enable you to display data in a list's column by means of *subtotals* that are defined by another column.

The word subtotals is italicized in the previous paragraph because they are not necessarily simple sums: they can also be averages, counts, percentages, standard deviations and so on.

If you used the crosstabulation capability in a version of Excel that predated version 5.0, you are familiar with some of the reasons to use pivot tables. These reasons include the ability to summarize long lists or databases in a compact format, or to find relationships within the lists that are hidden by all the details.

There are good reasons to switch from crosstabulations to pivot tables, and Excel provides easy ways to convert existing crosstabulations to pivot tables. You will find that pivot tables have many more analysis and display options than crosstabulations do and they are much more tightly integrated with Excel, so you can accomplish the task very quickly.

Why would you want to summarize the data in a list? For an example, see figure 7.1.

It would be tedious, just from viewing columns A and B, to determine that the number of units sold in the Northeast region departs so far from that of the Southwest region. Furthermore, the process of creating a chart is simplified. If you were working with just the lists, it would be necessary to re-structure them to obtain the sum within each region—only then could you identify a range with the totals for the Chart Wizard.

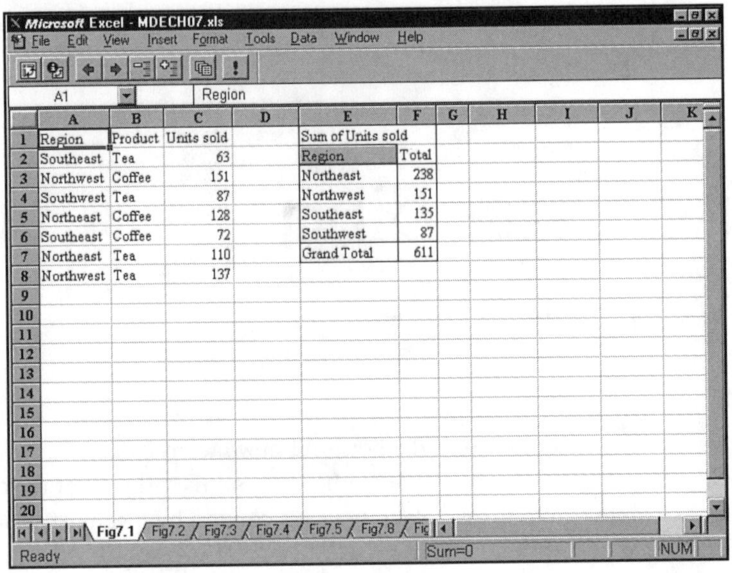

Fig. 7.1

The pivot table enables you to see differences in one variable that are associated with differences in another variable

Using the pivot table capability simplifies this process considerably: it obtains the subtotals automatically and places them in a range that you can immediately use for charting purposes.

To create a pivot table, all you need is a *data field*—the variable that is to be summarized—and a *row* and/or a *column field*—the variable that controls the summary. The next several sections in this chapter discuss these fields in detail.

Understanding Row and Column Fields

A row field in a pivot table is a variable that takes on different values: for example, a row field could be a variable called Manufacturer, whose values are Compaq, Packard-Bell and Apple. For each value of Manufacturer, the pivot table would display a summary of its data field (Annual Sales, perhaps) in a different row.

The same is true of column fields. A column field might be a variable called Year, whose values range from 1990 through 1994. Each column in the pivot table would then represent a different year.

The basic effect of row and column fields on a pivot table is that each value, or *item*, that the field takes on defines a different row or column. So, if a pivot table has a row field that takes on four items and a column field that takes on two items, the pivot table has four rows, two columns, and therefore eight summary cells—exclusive of cells that contain labels, subtotals, and grand totals (see fig. 7.2).

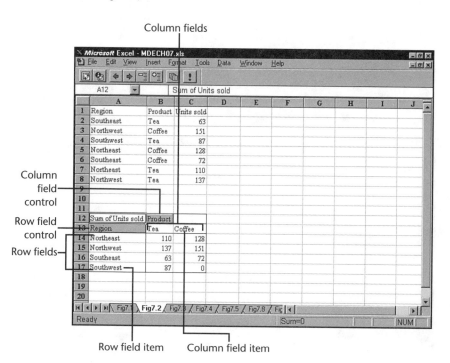

Column fields

Column field control

Row field control

Row fields

Row field item   Column field item

Fig. 7.2
The items of the row and column fields define the structure of a pivot table. A value of zero in the table can indicate the absence of corresponding data in the list.

When you define a pivot table, you *must* specify a data field: that is, a variable on a worksheet that the table is intended to summarize. If you omit a data field, Excel returns an error message.

In contrast, you need not specify either a row or a column field. If you specify neither, you get a table instead of an error message, but you won't get any useful information.

If you specify a row field only, the table returns information about the data field for each value of the row field. It has one column that contains the values of the row field, and another column that contains the corresponding summary values of the data field.

Similarly, a pivot table with a column field only returns two rows: one that contains the values of the column field, and one that contains the corresponding summary values of the data field.

After creating the pivot table, you can use the pivot table toolbar to restructure it (you can also use options under the Data menu, or right-click the mouse button to display a shortcut menu). One way to restructure the table is to redefine a row field as a column field, and vice versa. This is called *pivoting* the table (see fig. 7.3).

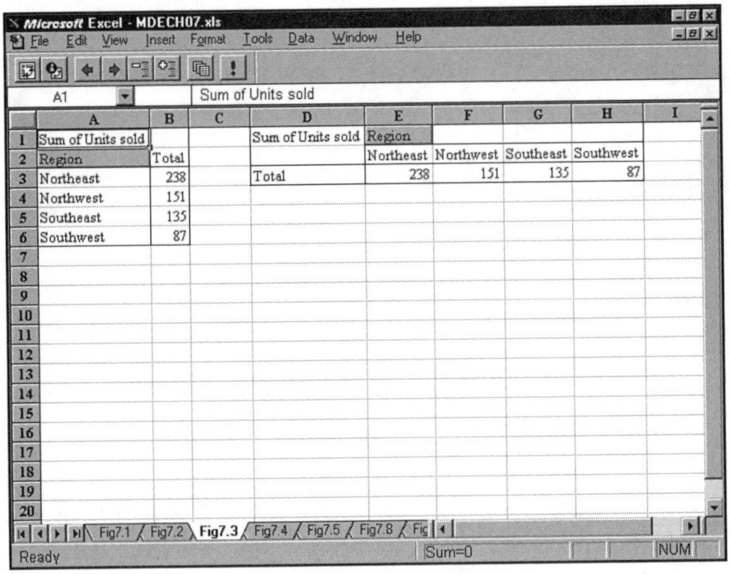

Fig. 7.3

Changing a row field to a column field, or a column field to a row field, is called *pivoting* the table.

Imagine a point at the upper-left corner of the pivot table, and think of it as a pivot point. When you swing a row field up and to the right (making it a column field), the structure of the table pivots; when you swing a column field down and to the left (making it a row field), its structure pivots again.

What if you have more than two variables in your worksheet list that you want to use as row or column fields? In that case, you can define subsidiary, or *inner*, row and column fields. Figure 7.4 shows inner row fields for a table with no column fields, inner column fields for a table with no row fields, and inner fields for a table with both row fields and column fields.

The effect of the inner fields is to add another level of detail to the table. Within one category, or value, of the outer row field, there are several values for the inner field. The data field is summarized first by the value of the outer row field. Within that first-level summary, the data field is further summarized by the corresponding values of the inner row field.

Outer row field

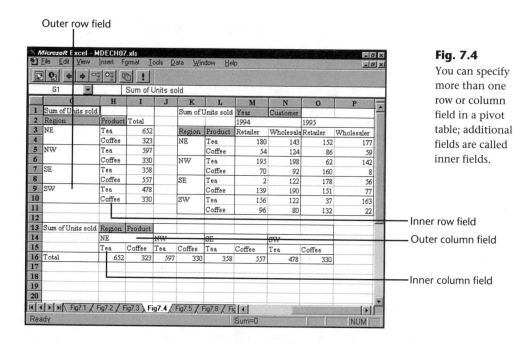

Fig. 7.4
You can specify
more than one
row or column
field in a pivot
table; additional
fields are called
inner fields.

Inner row field
Outer column field
Inner column field

Understanding the Data Field

The data field is the variable that the pivot table summarizes. For each combination of values in the row and column fields, the data field takes on a different value: it's this value that appears in the pivot table's cells.

Most frequently, the way the pivot table summarizes the data field is by its sum: for example, the sum of the revenues for Product A during 1995. Or, if it isn't a variable that can be totaled, the summary statistic might be a count or percentage of the observations in a list. Suppose the data field contained the names of people who work for your company. Names can't be totaled (what, for example, is the sum of "Thelma" and "Louise"?), so you might cause Excel to report the count or percentage of people who work in each department.

Excel provides certain custom calculations that you can apply to the data field. These calculations include options such as running totals, percent of row or column, and so on. The options are limited, however, and if you need a special calculation, such as the future value of a dollar amount, it's necessary to perform that calculation outside the context of the pivot table. Then, you would include the calculated variable in a list when you start the PivotTable Wizard. The section of this chapter titled "Customizing a Data Field" describes the built-in custom calculations, as well as the process of defining your own custom calculations.

Pivot Tables

Understanding the Page Field

The page field operates in a fashion similar to the row and column fields, but there are some crucial differences.

The monitor on your computer has two dimensions: height and width. Therefore, it can represent only two of a pivot table's possible dimensions: rows and columns. One way to get around this limitation, is to use more than one row field or column field by including subsidiary fields.

Sometimes, though, this is not a satisfactory solution. On one hand, you might want to include three fields (besides the data field) in your pivot table, but to make one of them an inner field results in a confusing display, or one that is more complex than necessary.

Suppose, for example, that you want to focus on unit sales for different products, in different sales regions, over several years. You might not be interested in viewing all the information at once: that is, it might not be important to see the unit sales for coffee in the Northwest during 1994, and to compare that with the same result for 1995. Instead, you might want to view Product as the row field and Region as the column field—and yet reserve the option of breaking the data out by year if you wish.

It's this sort of situation that the Page field handles well. If you define Year as a page field, you can display unit sales within Product and Region for all years or for any given year. See figure 7.5 for an example.

Fig. 7.5
A Page field is useful for adding another variable to the pivot table without necessarily viewing all its values at once.

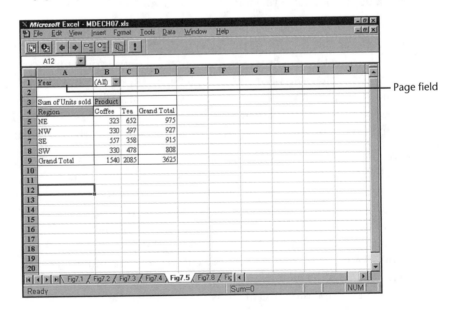

Notice the drop-down box associated with the Page field. By clicking the down arrow next to the drop-down box, you can display all the values the page field takes on. If you click one of those values, the pivot table displays a summary that includes only the values of the data field that correspond to the value of the page field that you selected. Figure 7.6 shows how this works.

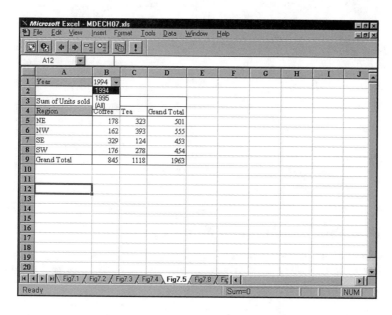

Fig. 7.6
By choosing different values from the page field you can display different subsets of the data in the pivot table.

If you choose the (All) item in the page field's drop-down box, all the observations in the data field are displayed. This option, of course, has the same result as if you specified no page field for the pivot table.

The page field can also show the pivot table on separate worksheets. By choosing Show Pages (see the section titled "Showing Page Items on Separate Worksheets," for more on how to select this option), you can cause Excel to display the pivot table on each of several worksheets: each worksheet contains a pivot table that summarizes the data field for each value of the page field. Each worksheet's name is the value of the page field that it summarizes. This is displayed in figure 7.7.

Pivot Tables

Fig. 7.7
The page field's
Show Pages option
creates new work-
sheets that contain
different subsets of
the full pivot table.

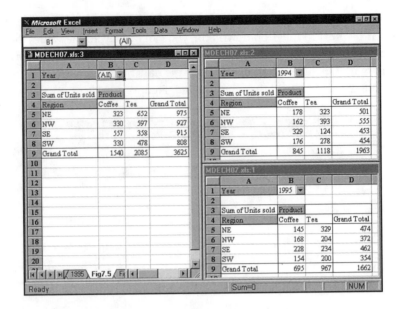

Understanding Data Types

The *kind* of data you use to create a pivot table can have dramatic effects on
the way Excel displays the table. Key to understanding these effects is the
level of measurement used for each variable.

Understanding the Effect of Discrete Variables

A *discrete variable* is one that can have only a few unique values. Typically,
these values are different names: for example, the names of your customers,
the names of different accounts in a general ledger, or the names of different
product lines you manufacture.

The level of measurement of discrete variables is sometimes termed *nominal*,
because each different value represents the name of something. Discrete variables are ideal for use as row and column fields in a pivot table, because you
usually know in advance how many different values each field can take on.

Discrete variables can also be used as data fields in a pivot table. In this case,
though, you are almost always interested in the *count* of the field's values. It
would be meaningless to request Excel to return, say, the average of the values "Accounts Receivable," "Cash Receipts," and "Owner's Equity."

However, it can be very meaningful to request the count of occurrences of
particular, nominal values of a discrete variable. A pollster, for example, is
keenly interested in knowing the number of people who reply that their atti-
tude toward proposed legislation is "Favorable" or "Unfavorable."

If you define a variable that has something other than a number as one of its values, Excel automatically proposes Count as the function to summarize the data field.

Understanding the Effect of Continuous Variables

As distinct from discrete variables, continuous variables can take on a very large range of values. They are termed *continuous* because their values always represent more or less of some quantity. Examples are profit margin, people's ages, and average daily temperatures.

It's seldom a good idea to use a continuous variable as a row or column field in a pivot table. As a purely practical matter, it can happen that a variable such as net income can take on so many different values that the pivot table becomes unmanageably large, or even impossible for Excel to display. Excel worksheets are limited to 256 columns. If you are analyzing, for example, net income for 300 firms and you specify net income as the column field for a pivot table, it's almost certain that the table would require 300 distinct columns to represent the data—and that's not possible on an Excel worksheet.

Normally, you would want to use a continuous variable as the data field in a pivot table, in order to see something such as the sum or average of its values for different levels of other, discrete variables. If you really wanted to examine the relationship between two or more continuous variables, it would be much more sensible to use something such as an XY(Scatter) chart, a worksheet function such as CORREL( ), or one of the Analysis ToolPak's data analysis tools.

However, under some circumstances, it might make sense to use one or more continuous variables as row or column fields in a pivot table. A special kind of continuous variable uses the *ordinal* level of measurement. Such a variable has more or less of some quantity, but how much more or less is usually unspecified. For example, suppose you're a pollster and you frame the possible answers to a question as "Strongly agree," "Agree," "No opinion," "Disagree," and "Strongly disagree." The notion of *agreement* is being measured here, and different people will express more or less of it—it's a continuous variable.

But there is a restricted number of values that the variable can have (therefore, it's possible to create a pivot table using it as a row or column field). It would be typical for the pollster to create a pivot table using one question as a row field and another question as a column field, to view the relationship between the responses to the two questions.

Choosing a Table Structure

Your principal guide to choosing whether to treat a variable as a row field, a column field, or a data field should be, of course, the sort of information or conclusion that you want the pivot table to portray. But given that basic requirement, you have the option of using all row (or column) fields, or mixing row and column fields.

Aside from the appearance of the table, it makes a difference whether you choose to use only row or column fields, or to use both (see fig. 7.8).

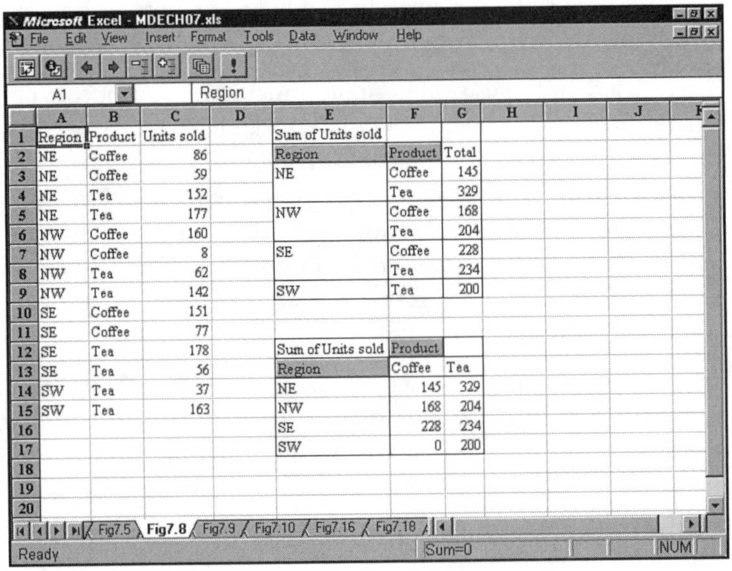

Fig. 7.8

The table with row fields (but no column field) skips empty cells, but the table with both row and column fields accounts for all cells.

Notice in figure 7.8 that the list contains an observation for all combinations of Region and Product, except for the coffee product in the Southwest.

The first table, which uses both Region and Product as row fields, contains no cell for the missing combination. In contrast, the second table, which uses Region as the row field and Product as the column field, does display the one missing cell.

When all control fields are row fields, Excel can simply skip a missing combination. But when one control field is a row field and one a column field, the structure of the table demands that a missing combination be represented somehow: an *intersection* of the values must exist, even if the corresponding *observation* does not exist.

Therefore, if not all combinations are present, and if a concern is to minimize the number of displayed cells, consider making all variables row fields or column fields.

Counting the Possible Cells

In any pivot table, the maximum number of data cells that can exist is the product of the number of unique values in each control field. If row field A can have two values, and column field B three values, the maximum number of cells in a table defined by A and B is six. If A can have two values, B three values and C four values, the table can have a maximum of 24 cells.

This fact can be useful for planning the layout of a table, particularly when you are preparing a very large one. Of course, when not all possible combinations of field values exist in the data source, the number of cells in the actual table will often be smaller than the theoretic maximum.

> **Tip**
>
> You can use Data, Filter, Advanced Filter to find out the number of unique values in each list variable. Fill the Unique Records Only checkbox, and choose the Copy to Another Location option button.

Understanding Display Options

Another effect that the nature of the data in your lists can have on the structure of a pivot table depends on how you choose to display it. You have a variety of options for displaying data fields: in each cell of one table, you can display a data field's sum, average, count, variance, and so on.

If you have chosen a discrete variable as the data field, several display options are sensible. One is Excel's default option, Count. But you can also display the cell's count as a percent of its row, of its column, or of the total Count in the table. See figure 7.9 for an example.

Notice that by displaying the data field in four different ways, it becomes very difficult to interpret the information in the table. The pivot table in figure 7.10 shows the same data, but is limited to percent of total Count as its sole display option. It's much easier to interpret the table if it includes fewer displays.

The same effect occurs with continuous variables: you could choose to display a data field's Sum, Count, Average, Standard Deviation, and so on in each of the table's cells. Again, this can make interpretation difficult.

Fig. 7.9
Combining different display options can make a table difficult to interpret.

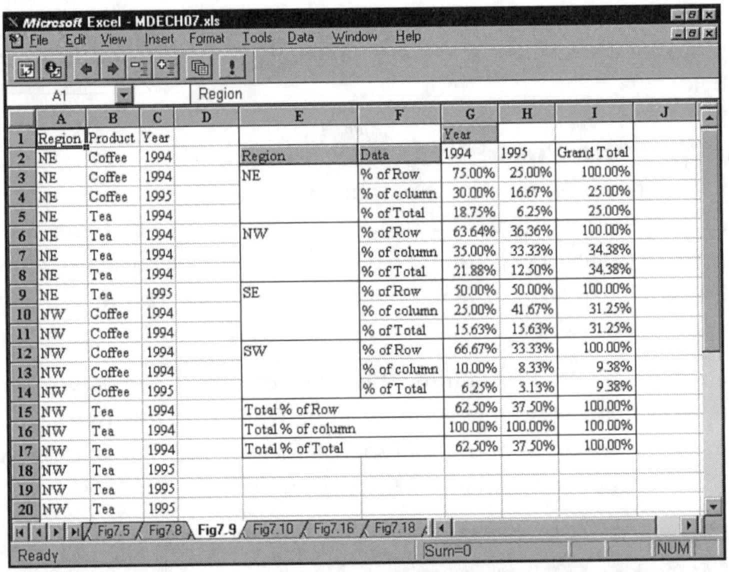

Fig. 7.10
A limited number of display options makes the table much clearer.

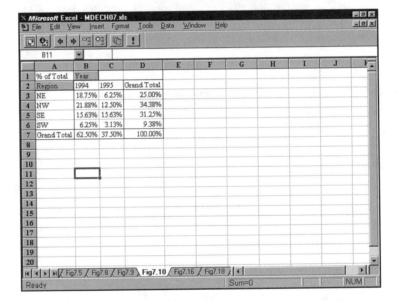

Note

You can display cell counts as percents only if you choose to display the appropriate Grand Totals in the Pivot Table Wizard's final step.

In the past, it was typical for many data management and analysis applications to routinely display all possible ways to summarize a data set. Research has shown that the resulting clutter made things difficult for those who were viewing the table. It's much better, if at all possible, to minimize the number of options you choose for displaying your data field.

Of course, if the pivot table is not intended for visual use (such as in a report) but instead as an intermediate step (perhaps as a source of data for an Excel chart), then the issue of visual clutter is much less important. Keep in mind, though, that you create a new set of cells in your pivot table each time you add a display option for the data field.

Using the Pivot Table Wizard to Create a Table

There are just three ways to create a pivot table: by using the Pivot Table Wizard, by using Visual Basic for Applications (VBA), and by using the Scenario Manager. Creating a pivot table by means of VBA is discussed in Chapter 10, and by means of the Scenario Manager in chapter 15. This section details the choices you have available at each point as you complete the Pivot Table Wizard.

There are two main ways to start the wizard: either by selecting PivotTable from the Data menu, or by using the PivotTable Wizard toolbar button. To install the Pivot Table toolbar, follow these steps:

1. Choose View, Toolbars.
2. Check the Query and Pivot checkbox in the Toolbars list box.
3. Choose OK.

    or

1. Choose View, Toolbars, Customize.
2. Click Data in the Categories list box.
3. Position your mouse pointer over the PivotTable Wizard button in the Buttons area of the Customize dialog box.
4. Hold down the mouse button, and drag the button onto an existing toolbar, into the toolbar area or onto the worksheet (either action creates a new toolbar).

Step 1: Choosing the Type of Data Source

After you have installed the Pivot Table toolbar or toolbar button, simply click it to initiate the PivotTable Wizard. When you do so, the first of the four steps in the wizard appears (see fig. 7.11).

Fig. 7.11
Identify the type of data source you want in Step 1 of the PivotTable Wizard.

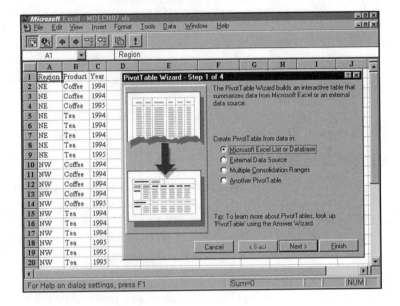

You can build a pivot table using four different types of data source:

- *A worksheet range that contains a list or database.* This is probably the most frequently used source for a pivot table's data.

- *An external data source.* A Microsoft Access database is an example.

- *Multiple consolidation ranges.* These are ranges in worksheets that may or may not belong to the same workbook.

- *Another, existing pivot table.* This option can save you time if you want to display the data you have already put into a table in a different way. It also saves memory. See the section titled "Other Pivot Tables" in Chapter 8.

Depending on the option you choose, the Pivot Table Wizard displays a different dialog box for Step 2.

Step 2: Specifying the Data Source

Suppose you chose Microsoft Excel List or Database in Step 1. In that case, the dialog box shown in figure 7.12 appears.

The reference, if any, that appears in the Range edit box depends on what was highlighted on the worksheet before you started the Wizard:

- If you have highlighted a single cell that is within or immediately adjacent to a range that contains at least ten cells (for example, five rows and two columns) of data, the reference to that range appears in the edit box.

- If you have highlighted a single cell that is neither within or adjacent to such a range, the edit box is empty.

- If you highlighted a range, either fully or partly populated with data, that contains at least ten cells, the reference to that range appears in the edit box.

- If you highlighted a range, either fully or partly populated with data, that is adjacent to another such range, only the reference to the highlighted range appears in the edit box.

Why should you care? Because all of this implies that the fastest way to select a worksheet range as a pivot table's data source is to highlight one cell within the range before you start the Wizard. This allows Excel to choose the range on your behalf.

Your range must be organized as a *list* (see Chapter 1 for further information on lists): that is, one or more columns of data in which the first row contains a label that identifies the data in each column. The columns need not be adjacent, although it is usually more convenient if they are.

After confirming or entering the range that contains the data source, choose OK to proceed to the next step.

Step 3: Designing the Pivot Table

This is the most critical step in creating the table: it's at this point that you determine which variables will act as row, column, page and data fields (see fig. 7.13).

To drag a field button into one of the field areas, move your mouse pointer over the field button, hold down the mouse button, and continue to hold it down as you move the pointer into the proper area. Then, release the mouse button.

Pivot Tables

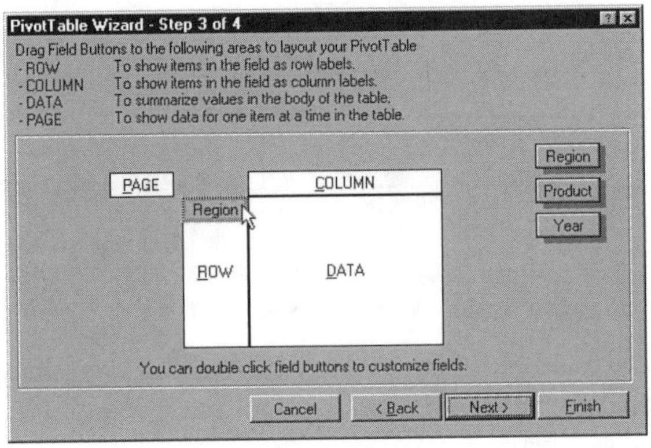

Fig. 7.13

In Step 3 of the Pivot Table Wizard, drag field buttons into the Row, Column, Page, and Data areas.

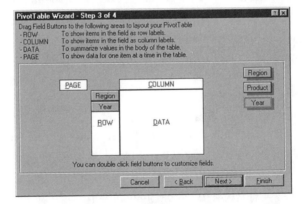

As an alternative to dragging the field buttons with the mouse, you can use the field areas' accelerator keys. For example, to move a field button into the Row area, click on the button to highlight it and then press Alt+R.

You can put more than one field button into a field area to create an *inner* field or fields. Suppose you move field buttons named "Region" and "Year" to the row area. Figure 7.14 shows the appearance of the field areas if you do so.

Fig. 7.14

Dragging more than one field button into a control field area creates at least one outer and one inner field.

Tip

To make one row field the outer field, and another row field the inner field, move the button for the outer field *above* the button for the inner field. To make one of two column fields the inner field, move it to the *right* of an outer column field.

Step 4: Setting the Final Options

This final step in creating a pivot table lets you specify:

- The worksheet cell that will contain the upper-left corner of the pivot table
- A name for the pivot table
- The inclusion or omission of grand totals for rows and columns
- Whether to apply an Autoformat to the table
- Whether to save the data with the pivot table

Leaving the PivotTable Starting Cell box blank causes Excel to begin the pivot table in cell A1 of a new sheet. In most cases, you would accept the default options that Step 4 offers: you will normally want grand totals and an Autoformat, and you will normally want to save the data with the table.

You might want to change the default name of the pivot table: the default name that Excel proposes is just a numeric increment, such as Pivot Table 1, Pivot Table 2, and so on. If you plan to base more pivot tables on the one you are creating, it's useful to provide a more descriptive name. Later, when you base another pivot table on the current one, the PivotTable Wizard will ask you which pivot table to use as a basis. Answering this question is easier if you have provided a descriptive name in Step 4.

Tip

A descriptive name for a pivot table can also prove useful if, subsequently, you use VBA code to access the pivot table. A descriptive name will help make your VBA code more self-documenting.

The dialog box for Step 4 is shown in figure 7.15.

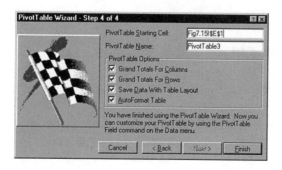

Fig. 7.15
The most important option in Step 4 of the PivotTable Wizard is choosing the table's location.

Pivot Tables

II

A couple of these options are subtle. The AutoFormat Table option applies a built-in format to the table that resembles the "Simple" option in the Format, AutoFormat command. The AutoFormat Table option in the PivotTable Wizard applies borders to the values of the row and column fields, and formats the cells that contain the names of the row and column fields to resemble buttons. If you clear the AutoFormat Table checkbox, you see only the worksheet's normal gridlines to distinguish one pivot table cell from another.

You can also specify whether to Save Data with Table Layout. This option pertains to a hidden structure associated with the pivot table, termed the *cache*. This is a place where the table's source data is stored for fast retrieval when you change some aspect of the table. There will be more to come on the table's cache later in this chapter; for now, understand the following tradeoffs. If you *do* choose to save the cache with the table layout:

- The file size is increased. You are saving two copies of the data source: the source itself and the table's cache.
- It can take longer—perhaps not noticeably, but longer nonetheless—to save the file. It does *not* take longer to open the file because Excel does not access the cache until it is needed (for example, when you modify the table).
- You can base a new pivot table on the existing pivot table. If you choose to do this in Step 1 of the PivotTable Wizard, the new pivot table accesses the same cache as the first one. You save space because you need only one cache instead of two in order to have two different tables that use the same data source.

If you *don't* choose to save the cache with the table layout:

- The file size is not increased. You are saving only the data source itself.
- There is no effect on the length of time it takes to save and open the file.
- You can't base a new pivot table on the existing pivot table.

Tailoring the Pivot Table's Formats

Regardless of any formatting you have applied to your data source, the initial format of the data in a pivot table is General. After the table has been created, you can format its cells by choosing Format, Cells. But if you subsequently make any change to the pivot table (even just refreshing its data from the cache) you will lose the special formatting you applied.

There is a way to make the format of a data field permanent:

1. Select a cell in the pivot table that represents its data field.

2. Either click the Pivot Table Field button on the Query and Pivot toolbar, or choose <u>D</u>ata, Pivot Table F<u>i</u>eld. The Pivot Table Field dialog box appears.

3. Click <u>N</u>umber. The Format Cells dialog box appears.

4. Choose one of the available formats, and choose OK to close the Format Cells dialog box. Choose OK again to close the Pivot Table Field dialog box.

Defined in this way, Excel will keep the format of the data field's cells when you refresh or otherwise customize the pivot table. This approach doesn't work for row, column, or page fields; in fact, the <u>N</u>umber option doesn't appear in the Pivot Table Field dialog box if you have first selected a field other than a data field.

If you choose F<u>o</u>rmat, <u>A</u>utoformat on the pivot table, you have your choice of 17 different predefined formats you can apply to the *entire* table. If you apply one of these autoformats, the format stays with the table whether you refresh its data, pivot the table, remove one of its fields, add a new field, or perform some other operation that affects its display (see fig. 7.16).

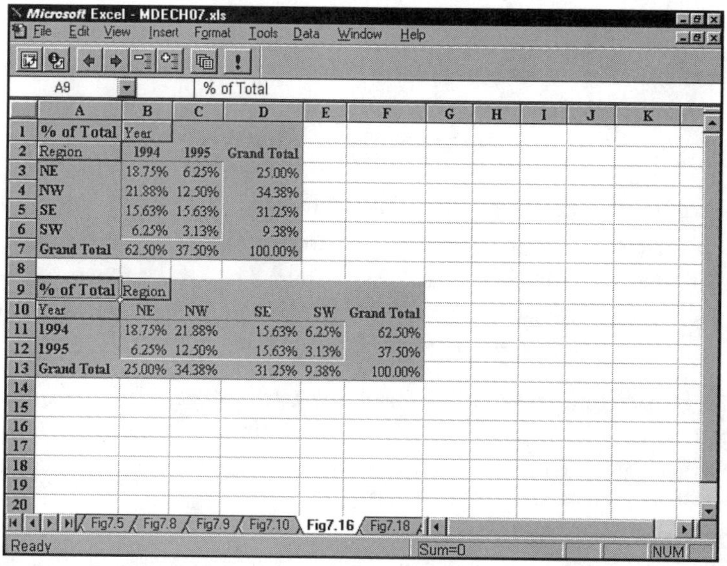

Fig. 7.16
The auto-format remains with the table after it has been pivoted.

But choosing F<u>o</u>rmat, <u>A</u>utoformat doesn't offer you an option to set a particular number format—Currency, for example—for the data field. To set that format, you need to use the PivotTable Field button or <u>D</u>ata menu item.

Pivot Tables

So, to format the table such that all fields have a particular format and that the table retains its formats when you refresh or make some structural change to it:

- Format the data field using the PivotTable Field button or menu item.
- Format the entire table using Format, Autoformat.

Using the Pivot Table Wizard on an Existing Table

Once you have created a pivot table, you can use the PivotTable Wizard to make changes to it. You might find that you prefer a different layout, or you might want to add a field that you did not initially include, or you might decide to apply an autoformat.

One fundamental feature of pivot tables is that they are interactive: you can always go back into the table and change one or more of its attributes. There are different ways to do so—the pivot table toolbar, the Data menu, and mouse shortcuts—but until you become familiar with your different options it's useful to employ the Wizard, because it guides you through your options.

Further, if you use the Wizard to modify the pivot table, you can make several changes in one step, instead of using one button to make one change, another button to make another, and so on.

This chapter discusses using the Query and Pivot toolbar, as well as mouse shortcuts, in subsequent sections. For the moment, and as an introduction to your options, the focus is on the PivotTable Wizard.

Using the Wizard to Modify Fields

When you select a worksheet cell that is part of a pivot table and then click the PivotTable Wizard button, the Wizard starts again, but at Step 3 instead of Step 1. This is because you have already specified its data source type (Step 1) and its data source reference (Step 2).

You *can* go back and revise this information in the Wizard by choosing the Back button in Steps 2, 3, and 4. In most cases, though, your intent is to modify the table's layout and display options, so the Wizard begins at Step 3.

Pivoting the Table

In Step 3, you can change any of the structural aspects of the pivot table by dragging the field buttons to new locations. For example, to change a row field to a column field, just drag the field button from the row area to the column area. Or, suppose you have both a row and a column field. You can change that layout to one with two row fields by dragging the column field button to the row area.

> **Note**
>
> Although you can use accelerator keys to move field buttons *into* the Page, Row, Column, and Data areas from their initial location in the upper-right corner of the dialog box, you can't use them to move a field button from a field area to another field area.

In Step 3, you can also remove any field buttons from the Page, Row, Column, and Data areas. Simply select a button and drag it anywhere out of its area other than into another field area.

Customizing a Control Field: Subtotals

With the Step 3 dialog box active, you can double-click any field button (whether or not you've moved it into a field area) to set certain options for that field (see fig. 7.17).

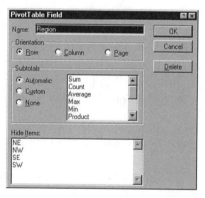

Fig. 7.17
By double-clicking a row, column, or page field button you can specify how you want it to appear in the pivot table.

By default, Excel provides a subtotal for every item in every control field when you first create the pivot table. To suppress or customize a subtotal for outer fields, use the PivotTable Field dialog box. Figure 7.18 shows how this works:

Pivot Tables

II

Fig. 7.18

Specifying a subtotal for a control field changes the structure of the pivot table.

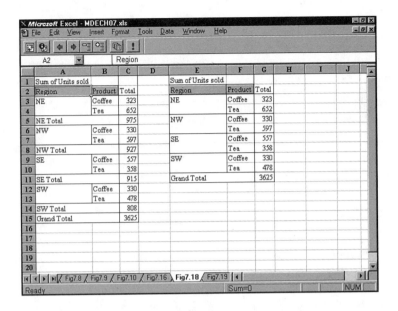

Notice in figure 7.18 that:

- The *structure* of the pivot table is changed by suppressing an outer row field's subtotals. Each subtotal row appears immediately after all the detail rows for the inner fields. Suppressing the subtotal rows reduces the size of the pivot table.

- *With no* outer field subtotals, there is no direct way to determine the data field's values for a particular outer field item. *With* outer field subtotals, you can determine the data field's value for a given outer field item because the subtotal ignores differences due to the inner field items.

Recall that Excel provides the "subtotal" for the innermost field automatically when you first create the pivot table. Therefore, there is no subtotal to modify via Step 3 for the innermost field. But if you invoke the PivotTable Field dialog box by double-clicking an innermost field, you can use it to create a *block total* subtotal. To do so, follow these steps:

1. Bring up the PivotTable Field dialog box by double-clicking the innermost field, by clicking the PivotTable Field button on the Query and Pivot toolbar, or by choosing the PivotTable Field item from the Data menu.

2. In the Subtotals area, choose the Custom option button.

3. Ensure that the summary function you want for the block total is highlighted in the Subtotals list box.

4. Choose OK.

Figure 7.19 shows a pivot table with block totals.

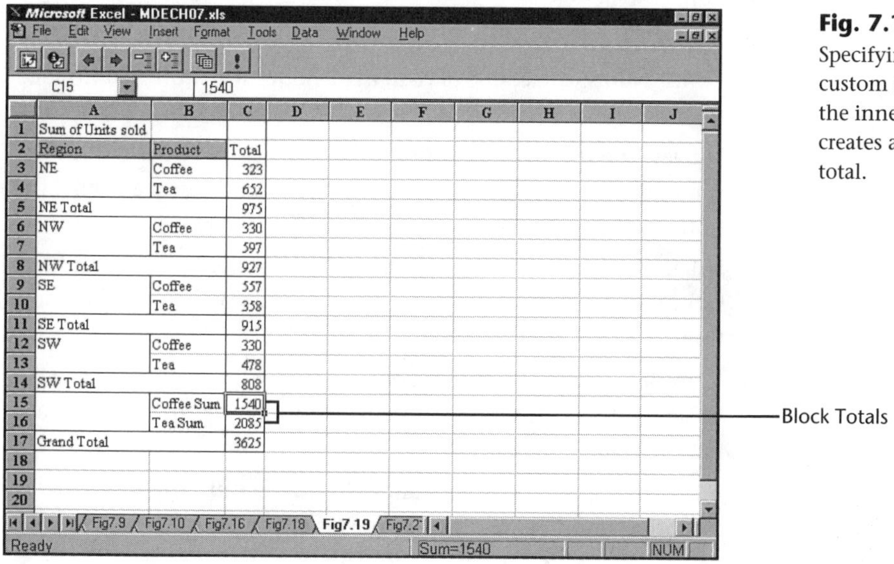

Sum of Units sold		
Region	Product	Total
NE	Coffee	323
	Tea	652
NE Total		975
NW	Coffee	330
	Tea	597
NW Total		927
SE	Coffee	557
	Tea	358
SE Total		915
SW	Coffee	330
	Tea	478
SW Total		808
	Coffee Sum	1540
	Tea Sum	2085
Grand Total		3625

Fig. 7.19
Specifying a custom subtotal for the innermost field creates a block total.

In effect, a block total for an innermost field acts as though the field were the outermost field in the pivot table. You get the summary function for each item in the innermost field without regard to differences in any of the other fields in the table.

Customizing a Control Field: Summary Functions

Another option available to you when you double-click a field button in Step 3 of the PivotTable Wizard is the modification of the summary function. Recall that if the Data field contains numeric values only, the Wizard chooses Sum as the default summary function; if there is any other type of value in the Data field, the Wizard's default choice is Count.

When you create subtotals for a control field, the Wizard's default choice as the summary function for subtotals is the same: Sum for a numeric data field and Count for a data field that is not entirely numeric. You can change the summary function to any one of the following:

- Sum: the default for entirely numeric data fields
- Count: the default for data fields that contain any non-numeric value
- Average: the sum of the data field values within the subtotaled item, divided by the count of the values

- Max: the largest data field value within the subtotaled item
- Min: the smallest data field value within the subtotaled item
- Product: the product of all data field values within the subtotaled item
- Count Nums: the count of data field values within the subtotaled item that are numeric
- StdDev: the standard deviation of the data field values within the subtotaled item, assuming that the values are a sample from a population
- StdDevp: the standard deviation of the data field values within the subtotaled item, assuming that the values compose an entire population
- Var: the variance (the square of the standard deviation) of the data field values within the subtotaled item, assuming that the values are a sample from a population
- Varp: the variance of the data field values within the subtotaled item, assuming that the values compose an entire population

Most often, you are likely to use the default summary function. The main purpose of a subtotal on a field item is to compare the detail information from inner fields with the summary, subtotal information from outer fields.

Occasionally, you might want to use a different summary function for a subtotal than you do for the detailed summaries within the item. You might even want to obtain two or more subtotals for items within the same control field.

Suppose you wanted to see the average *and* the standard deviation for each item within a control field (this can give you a quick, eyeball estimate of whether the data are distributed normally). To do so, you would take these steps:

1. With Step 3 of the PivotTable Wizard active, double-click an outer row or column field.
2. Choose Average from the Custom subtotals list box.
3. Choose StdDev from the Custom subtotals list box. Notice that Average remains highlighted.
4. Choose OK.
5. Choose Finish to close the PivotTable Wizard.

These actions return two subtotals for each item in the control field: its average and its standard deviation.

> **Tip**
>
> To deselect a highlighted, custom summary function in the subtotal list box, click it.

Customizing a Data Field

If you double-click the data field in Step 3, a different version of the PivotTable Field dialog box appears (see fig. 7.20).

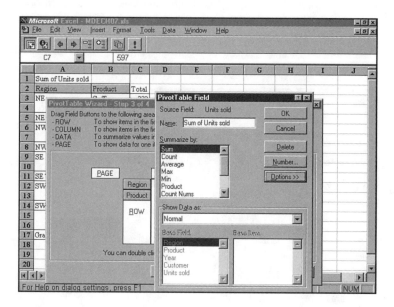

Fig. 7.20
Double-clicking the Data field button lets you specify a summary function and a custom calculation method.

II

Pivot Tables

It's important to understand the difference between a summary function and a custom calculation method. The summary function (Sum, Count, Average, and so on) defines which statistic Excel returns for the data field. The custom calculation (Normal, Difference, % Of, and so on) defines the further calculation that Excel applies to the statistic.

Suppose you want the summary function to be Count, and the custom calculation to be % Of Column. Excel would first count the number of values for each item in the innermost field (the summary function), and then would express that number as a percent of the total number of values in the column (the custom calculation).

A further complication arises when you want the custom calculation to be one of these options:

- Difference From
- % Of
- % Difference From
- Running Total In

For these custom calculations, you need to specify a *base field* as well. Implicit in each calculation is a basis from which a difference will be calculated, a percentage will be found, or a running total will be made. When you choose a base field, you supply that basis to Excel. This is easier to understand by seeing an example, which is shown in figure 7.21.

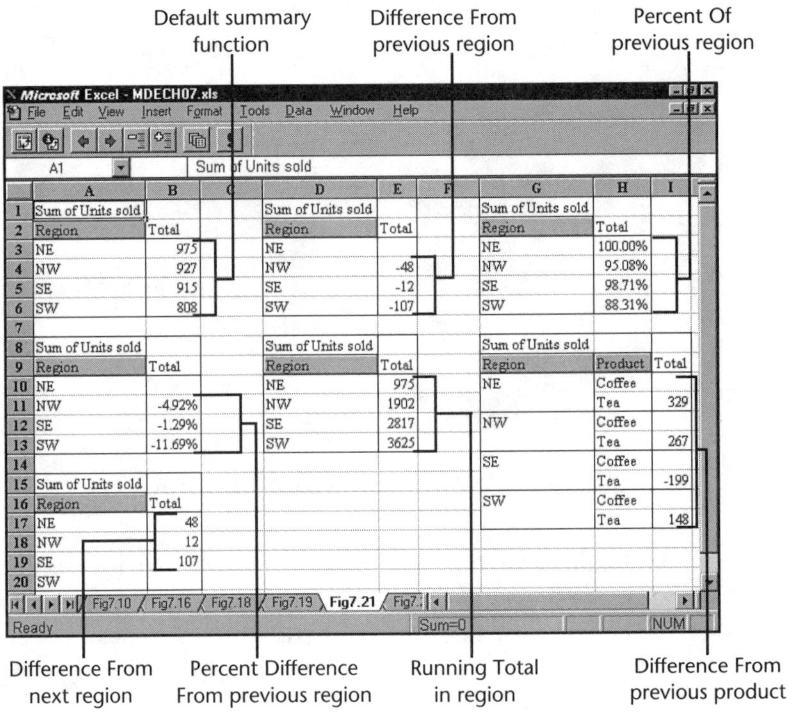

Fig. 7.21
Different custom calculations display the same summary function in different ways.

The first pivot table in figure 7.21 uses the default options: the summary function is Sum and there is no custom calculation.

The second pivot table also uses Sum as the summary function, but uses Difference as the custom calculation. The base field is the innermost field. If you compare the first and second pivot tables, you will notice that the data field value shown for each item in the second table is the difference between the actual Sum in the first pivot table and the *previous* Sum in the first pivot table. To obtain this result, follow these steps:

1. With Step 3 of the PivotTable Wizard active, double-click the data field button. The PivotTable Field dialog box appears.

2. Click the Options button.

3. In the Show Data As drop-down box, select Difference From.

4. In the Base Field list box, select the innermost (in this case, the only) field.

5. In the Base Item list box, select *(previous)*.

6. Choose OK.

7. Choose Finish to close the PivotTable Wizard.

To obtain the results shown in the remaining pivot tables in figure 7.21, you could instead:

- Select % Of in the Show Data as drop-down box to return a percentage of a base field instead of a numeric difference.

- Select % Difference From in the Show Data As drop-down box to return the difference expressed as a percentage.

- Select Running Total In from the Show Data As drop-down box to return the sum of the data field for the current item of the innermost field and any previous items in the innermost field. (In this case, you have no choice of Base Item, because it's always the total of the current and any previous items.)

- Select a different field in the Base Field list box, to base the custom calculation of a difference from, a percentage or a running total on a different field.

> **Tip**
>
> If you choose a different base field, make sure the new base field is a control field in the table. If not, the Data field will contain the #N/A error value.

- Select a different Base Item, to calculate a difference from or a percentage of the *next* (instead of the *previous*) item. You could also select a specific item from which all differences or percentages would be calculated.

Again, all these custom calculations are made on the basis of the summary function that you choose. For example, instead of Sum, you could use Max as the summary function. Then, Difference From would be calculated by subtracting the maximum Data field value in one item from the maximum

Pivot Tables

Data field value in another item; % Of would be calculated by dividing one maximum value by another maximum value, and so on.

None of the remaining custom calculations involve the use of a base field. They are:

- *Normal.* This option is the default; you would actually use it to return to the default if you had previously chosen a different custom calculation.

- *% of Row.* This option shows each data value as a percent of the total of the values in the row. It is informative only if you have at least one column field; else, it returns 100%, because if there is no column field then the custom calculation divides the value by itself.

- *% of Column.* This option shows each data value as a percent of the total of the values in the column. It is informative only if there is at least one row field, in order that there be more than one row to total as a basis for the percentage.

- *% of Total.* This option shows each data value as a percent of the total of the values for the table. It's identical to % of Row if there are no column fields, and to % of Column if there are no row fields.

- *Index.* This option shows the ratio of the observed values to the values that would be expected on the basis of row and column totals. It's useful as a precursor to certain statistical tests, such as the chi-square test for independence in a contingency table. See Chapter 11, "Analyzing Pivot Tables," for more information.

The interaction of fields, summary functions, custom calculations and base fields creates many choices. This section has provided a brief overview of the topic, and Chapter 9, "Applying Special Pivot Tables Options," will provide a more detailed look at the various options and the reasons for selecting them.

Using the Pivot Table Toolbar

When Excel completes the pivot table on a worksheet, it automatically displays the Query and Pivot toolbar. Using that toolbar, you can:

- Choose the PivotTable Wizard button to start the PivotTable Wizard, either to modify an existing pivot table (if the active cell is within the table) or to create a new table (if a cell in an existing pivot table is not active).

- Choose the PivotTable Field button to change the characteristics of an existing pivot table field. This button has an effect only if you first select a cell within the pivot table: then, it displays the PivotTable Field dialog box discussed previously.

- Choose the Ungroup or Group button to expand or collapse a pivot table control field. These options (as well as the remaining options on the Query and Pivot toolbar) are unavailable from the PivotTable Wizard, and are discussed in detail below. They function differently depending on whether or not the active cell is part of an existing pivot table.

- Choose the Hide or Show buttons to display or suppress detail items in a control or data field.

- Choose the Show Pages button to show each item in a Page field on a different worksheet.

- Choose the Refresh Data button to show changes that might have occurred in the underlying data source.

Grouping and Ungrouping Items

At times, you may want to combine (or *group*) certain items in a pivot table's control fields. For example, you might have a row field that initially shows net income for a firm on a monthly basis. If you decide you want the pivot table to display net income on a quarterly basis, you can group the row field so it no longer displays individual months, but instead combines groups of three months into single quarters. This is shown in figure 7.22.

II

Pivot Tables

	A	B	C	D	E	F	G	H	I	J
1	Date	Income		Sum of Income			Sum of Income			
2	1/31/94	$69,433		Date	Total		Date	Total		
3	2/28/94	$29,935		1/31/94	$69,434		Qtr1	$269,340		
4	3/31/94	$21,235		2/28/94	$29,936		Qtr2	$402,726		
5	4/30/94	$76,034		3/31/94	$21,236		Qtr3	$100,217		
6	5/31/94	$53,856		4/30/94	$76,034		Qtr4	$148,659		
7	6/30/94	$47,224		5/31/94	$53,857					
8	7/31/94	$38,235		6/30/94	$47,224		Sum of Income			
9	8/31/94	$40,210		7/31/94	$38,235		Years	Date	Total	
10	9/30/94	$21,771		8/31/94	$40,210		1994	Qtr1	$120,603	
11	10/31/94	$39,504		9/30/94	$21,772			Qtr2	$177,114	
12	11/30/94	$91,181		10/31/94	$39,504			Qtr3	$100,216	
13	12/31/94	$17,972		11/30/94	$91,182			Qtr4	$148,657	
14	1/31/95	$33,646		12/31/94	$17,973		1995	Qtr1	$148,734	
15	2/28/95	$65,322		1/31/95	$33,647			Qtr2	$225,609	
16	3/31/95	$49,766		2/28/95	$65,322					
17	4/30/95	$74,397		3/31/95	$49,766					
18	5/31/95	$83,305		4/30/95	$74,398					
19	6/30/95	$67,907		5/31/95	$83,306					
20				6/30/95	$67,908					

Fig. 7.22
The Group button can automatically combine dates or times into higher-level items.

The first pivot table in figure 7.22 shows a company's net income for each of 18 months. Selecting a cell within the Date column of the pivot table, and then choosing the Group button from the Query and Pivot toolbar, brings up the dialog box shown in figure 7.23.

Fig. 7.23

If Excel recognizes items in a control field as dates or times, it displays a special Grouping dialog box.

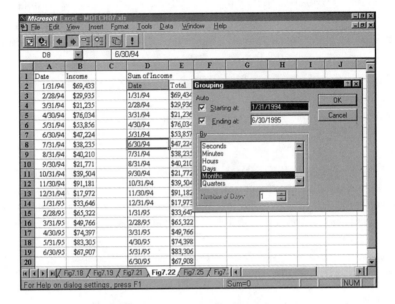

By selecting Quarters in the By list box, you can group each of these months into their respective quarters. This is shown in the second pivot table in figure 7.22. Notice that the second pivot table makes no distinction as to the year in which the quarter occurs: it shows four quarters only. Because *only* Quarters was selected from the By list box, the first three months in 1994 and the first three months of 1995 were grouped into the first quarter. Similarly, the second three months of both 1994 and 1995 were grouped into the second quarter.

To maintain the distinction between quarters in 1994 and 1995, choose *both* Quarters and Years in the By list box. The effect of selecting both grouping options is shown in the third pivot table in figure 7.22.

Refer again to figure 7.23. The Grouping dialog box offers a Starting At and an Ending At option. If you fill either of these checkboxes, Excel uses the full range of dates to establish the groups—whether or not you use the associated edit box to supply a different Starting At or Ending At value.

But if you enter different Starting At or Ending At values, Excel ignores pivot table items that predate the Starting At value or that postdate the Ending At value. You can use these options to restrict the range of values that the pivot table displays.

The final option in the Grouping dialog box is Number of Days. This becomes available if you select Days (only) from the By list box. It enables you to summarize the data field on the basis of weekly, biweekly or other periods defined by a constant number of days.

Note

You can't establish a group for a pivot table's Data field.

The preceding discussion has assumed that the control field you wish to group contains data that Excel can interpret as dates or times. If, instead, the control field items are numbers that are *not* dates or times, a different dialog box appears when you choose the Group button (see fig. 7.24).

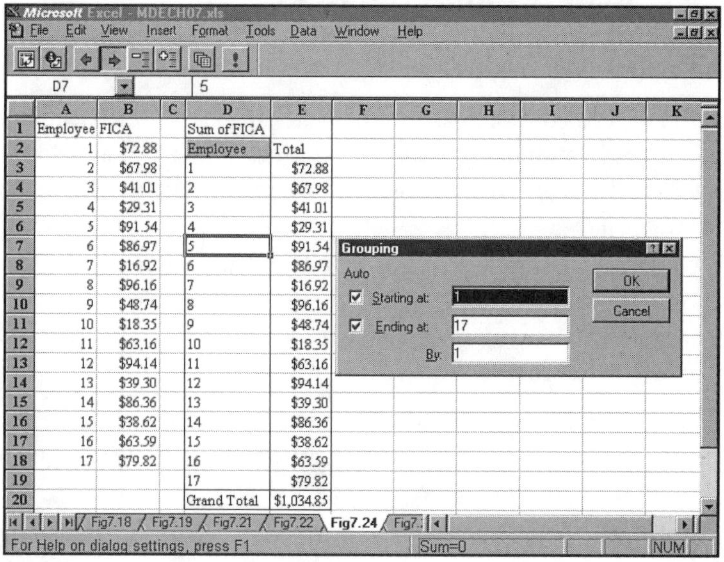

II

Pivot Tables

Fig. 7.24
If the items in a control field are numeric, but Excel can't recognize them as dates or times, it displays this Grouping dialog box.

The dialog box shown in figure 7.24 enables you to specify a Starting At and Ending At value, just as the Grouping dialog box shown in figure 7.23 does. In this case, however, the By edit box allows you to specify the increment that Excel will use when it converts the underlying numbers to groups. The increment that you enter in the <u>B</u>y edit box defines the size of the difference between the lower- and upper-bounds of a group. Excel starts with the minimum item value, uses the increment to establish the upper bound for the first group, and then uses the upper bound for that group to establish the lower bound for the next group.

> **Note**
>
> If there are no underlying data values within a group defined by the prior upper bound and the <u>B</u>y value, the table skips that group.

Finally, if there are data in the control field that are neither numeric nor interpretable as a date or time, Excel displays an error message that it cannot group that selection. If you establish a group on a properly valued field, subsequently change a value to, say, a text value, and then refresh the table (see "Refreshing the Data in a Pivot Table" later in this chapter), Excel ungroups the field.

Hiding and Showing Detail Items

The issue of hiding and showing pivot table details causes some confusion. There are actually two kinds of "hiding" you can choose:

- If you select a control field and then click the PivotTable Field toolbar button, you can hide one or more items belonging to that field by using the Hide <u>I</u>tems list box. The hidden item or items do not appear in the pivot table.

- If you select a control field item, or a data field, and then click the Show Detail or Hide Detail button on the PivotTable toolbar, you can show (or, if visible, suppress) detail information about the items summarized by the chosen item.

Suppose you choose a control field item or items, and then click the Show Detail toolbar button. Excel then displays as new items in the same table, the details within the control field item (see fig. 7.25).

Notice that the second pivot table in figure 7.25 displays the details of the field immediately within the control field. In this case, that field is the Data field, so specific data field values are displayed. Contrast this with the pivot tables shown in figure 7.26.

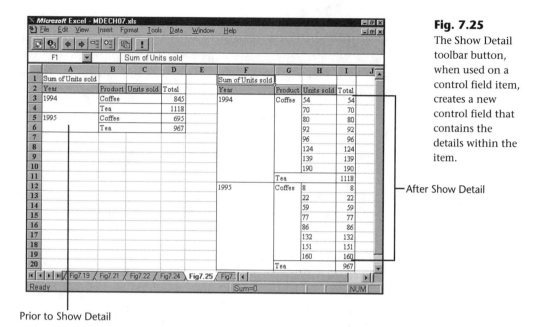

Prior to Show Detail

Fig. 7.25

The Show Detail toolbar button, when used on a control field item, creates a new control field that contains the details within the item.

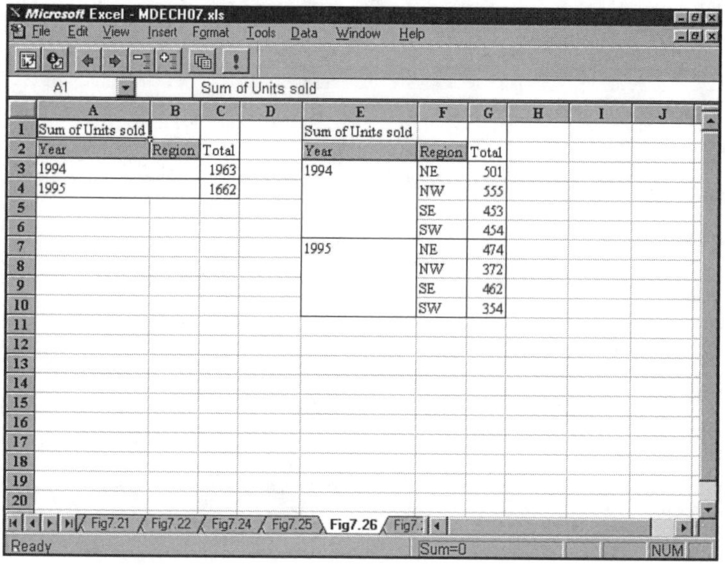

After Show Detail

Fig. 7.26

The Show Detail toolbar button, when used on an *outer* control field, shows the details of an *inner* control field.

In figure 7.26, the first pivot table displays only the items of the outer row field, although the presence of another row field is indicated by its field button. The second pivot table displays the details within the items of the outer row field: these are the inner row field items. This, of course, is the default structure for a pivot table.

But the detail goes no farther: individual data field values that are summarized by the inner field items are not shown in detail. To show the details of *both* the inner field items *and* the data field values, you would have to choose to show the details of both the outer row field and the inner row field.

 To reverse the process of showing item details, select the item whose details are displayed, and click the Hide Detail button on the Query and Pivot toolbar.

 Now, suppose you select a data field cell and then click the Show Detail button on the Query and Pivot toolbar. In this case, Excel opens a new worksheet and displays the detailed values of the data field there (see fig. 7.27).

Fig. 7.27
Using the Show Detail toolbar button on a data field creates a new worksheet that displays the individual data field values and their associated control field items.

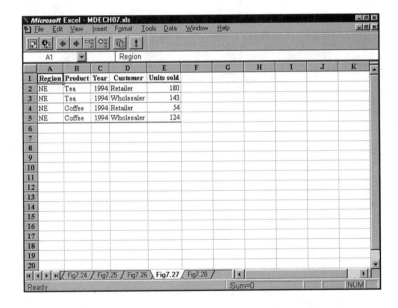

Showing Page Items on Separate Worksheets

As discussed earlier in this chapter in "Understanding the Page Field," you can summarize all the data in the underlying source in a pivot table, or you can restrict the display to data associated with just one page field item.

The Show Pages button on the Query and Pivot toolbar enables you to replicate the pivot table on different worksheets, so that each worksheet's pivot table summarizes the data associated with each item in the page field.

Refreshing the Data in a Pivot Table

Recall that a pivot table is not linked *directly* to its underlying data source: it's linked directly to a hidden cache, which is built from the data source.

If you create a pivot table from, say, a worksheet list, and subsequently change data in that list, the change is not immediately reflected in the pivot table. To update the pivot table to reflect the changes you made in the lists, you have to select a cell within the pivot table and then click the Refresh Data button on the Query and Pivot toolbar. You can also right click the mouse button and choose Refresh Data, or Select Refresh Data from the Data menu.

This process is a little more complicated if, in Step 4 of the PivotTable Wizard, you didn't choose to save the data with the pivot table. Suppose you subsequently saved the file and reopened it. If you then try to create another pivot table using the existing pivot table as its source, you will see an error message when you click the Next button in Step 2 of the PivotTable Wizard that reads `Pivot table saved without underlying data.` Use the `Refresh Data` command to update the pivot table. By "underlying data," Excel means there's no cache because you chose not to Save Data with Table Layout in Step 4 when you originally created the pivot table.

If you receive this message, cancel out of the PivotTable Wizard, select a cell in the original pivot table, and click the Refresh Data toolbar button. So doing rebuilds the cache, and you can now proceed to create a new pivot table based on the existing table.

It's often a bad idea to refresh the data in a pivot table, especially if the table has been built using VBA. This is because you might have set certain options (for example, hiding a control field item) that cause the pivot table to display the data source in an unexpected way. Or, if you changed the header row of a list from, say, *First Quarter* to *Qtr1*, Excel cannot find a column headed *Qtr1*.

In that case, simply changing the data source and then refreshing the table might not result in the display you anticipate, and you could be misled.

Unless you are certain that you know exactly which options have been set for a given pivot table, it's usually better to rebuild the table from scratch when you make changes to its source, rather than simply refreshing an existing table.

Using the Pivot Table Itself to Set Options

Most of the options already discussed in this chapter—pivoting a table, creating subtotals, showing and hiding details, and so on—can be selected without using the Query and Pivot toolbar, the PivotTable Wizard, or the Data menu. Once you have become comfortable with the range of options available to you, it's often faster and more convenient to make the change directly on the pivot table itself.

Figure 7.28 shows the process of pivoting a table by means of moving field buttons in the pivot table.

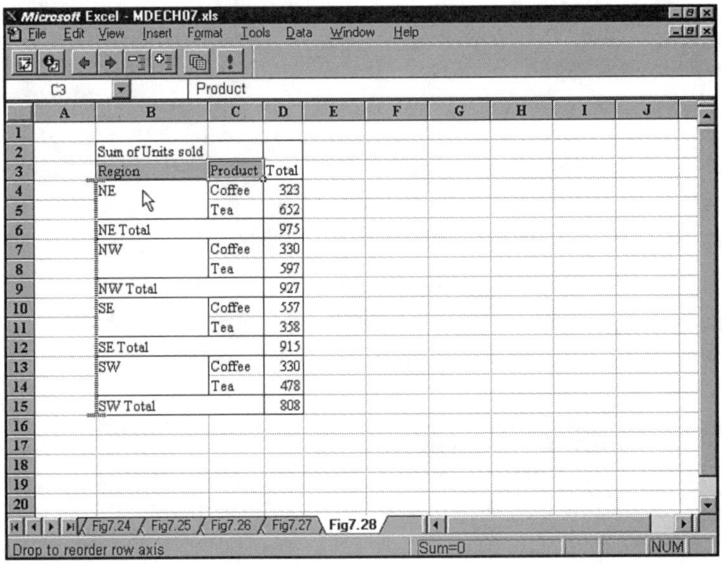

Fig. 7.28
You can pivot a table by dragging field buttons to different areas of the worksheet's pivot table.

To change the inner row field in figure 7.28 to a column field, follow these steps:

1. Place your mouse pointer over the row field button that you want to change to a column field.

2. Hold down the mouse button to select the field button.

3. Drag the field button into the column area. As you begin to drag, an icon that resembles a table with more rows than columns appears by your mouse pointer.

4. As the mouse pointer moves into the column area, the icon changes to one that resembles a table with more columns than rows.

5. Release the mouse button. The table pivots to display the field as a column field instead of a row field.

Of course, the reverse process—changing a column field into a row field—also works. Follow the same series of steps, but drag the column button into the row area.

If you begin to drag a button outside the limits of the pivot table area, the icon beside your mouse pointer changes to a button with a large "X" superimposed. Releasing the mouse button at this point causes the field to be discarded from the pivot table.

Finally, dragging the field button to a point above the pivot table causes the icon to change to one resembling a slanting stack of mailbox slots. Releasing the mouse button at this point causes the field to change to a page field.

To hide and display details within a control field item, double-click on that item. There are three possibilities:

- If the control field currently displays details of an inner field or of the data field, double-clicking it will hide the details.

- If the control field currently summarizes details, double-clicking it will show its details.

- If there is no inner field, Excel shows a dialog box that requests that you select the field you want to show.

If you want to display details of a data field—remember, doing so creates a new worksheet that contains the data field values and their associated control field items—double-click the data field summary.

To change the characteristics of an entire *control field*, double-click the field's button on the pivot table. This will bring up the PivotTable Field dialog box. Recall this dialog box allows you to change the field's orientation, display its subtotals or hide selected items.

You can't display the PivotTable Field dialog box for the data field (which gives you options such as the data field's Number format, summary functions and custom calculations) by double-clicking any part of the pivot table. Instead, if you want a shortcut for the toolbar buttons and the PivotTable Wizard, you can access a shortcut menu by clicking a pivot table cell with the right mouse button. Figure 7.29 shows this shortcut menu.

Fig. 7.29
The pivot table's shortcut menu gives you quick access to options such as the PivotTable Field dialog box for a data field.

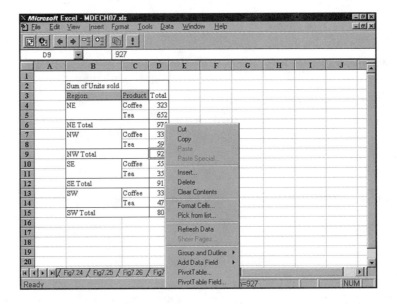

Sorting Pivot Table Fields

While a pivot table is usually displayed with control field items in sorted order (ascending by rows for a row field, ascending by columns for a column field), it can happen that the original sorted order is changed as you work with the table. This is particularly apt to occur when you have multiple row or multiple column fields: it isn't necessarily the case that an inner row field's items are displayed in sorted order when they are summarized within an outer row field's items—even if the outer field's items are sorted.

Sorting Control Field Items

If you want to sort the pivot table by an inner field's items, follow these steps:

1. Click the field's button.
2. Choose Data, Sort.
3. Complete the options in the Sort dialog box (see Chapter 1 for details on sorting). The Labels (Labels) option is required for a control field, because its items are represented as text in the pivot table.
4. Choose OK.

You might find, however, that the data in the control field do not sort as you wish them to. This can occur when the control field's data in the underlying source is numeric. Then, you would want the numbers 11, 12, and 111 to appear in that order in the pivot table. But control field items in a pivot table are displayed as text values, and as text these three numbers would sort as 11, 111, and 12.

To work around this problem, follow these steps:

1. Enter the number **1** in some empty cell, and make that cell active.
2. Choose Edit, Copy.
3. Highlight the control field items that you want to sort.
4. Choose Edit, Paste Special. The Paste Special dialog box appears.
5. Choose the Multiply option button in the Paste Special dialog box.
6. Choose OK.

The effect is to multiply all the text values by 1, which (when their original values are numeric) converts them to numbers. Now you can select the control field and sort it in numeric order.

You can also sort a pivot table by its data field values. To do so, click a *control* field's button, and choose Data, Sort. The Sort By box has the focus when the dialog box appears, so just click in a data field cell. Change any other options as you wish, and choose OK.

Applying Custom Sort Orders

If one of your fields contains items that belong to a custom list, you can specify that the sort order for that field should be the order that the items appear in the custom list. There must, of course, be a custom list whose values correspond to the items in the control field. Given that a custom list exists, you can use it as a sort order by following these steps:

1. Make a cell in the pivot table active, or click the field button whose values you want to sort.

2. Choose Data, Sort.

3. If its reference is not already in the Sort By box, click on a cell in the pivot table that contains one of your custom list values.

4. Click the Options button. The Sort Options dialog box appears.

5. Click the down arrow next to the First Key Sort Order drop-down box.

6. Click the appropriate custom list in the drop-down box.

7. Choose OK in the Sort Options dialog box, and choose OK in the Sort dialog box.

The pivot table will be sorted according to the custom list's order.

Tip

You can export items from a pivot table into a custom list. Choose Tools, Options and select the Custom Lists tab. Click in the Import List from Cells box, and highlight the pivot table cells to compose the list. Click Import, and then choose OK.

Chapter Summary

This (very long) chapter has given you an overview of the different options you can use to create, format and structure a pivot table. Most of these options will be explored more fully in subsequent chapters. The next chapter begins this exploration with a discussion of your options for a pivot table's data sources.

Placing Business Data into Pivot Tables

In Chapter 7, "Understanding Pivot Tables," you saw how a pivot table can be based on a variety of data sources, including a list or database on a worksheet, another pivot table, or an external database. You specify the source that you want in Step 1 of the PivotTable Wizard.

This chapter discusses the structure of the source data in more detail, and provides more information about the considerations and procedures involved with each of the sources.

Using Worksheet Lists

Chapter 1, "Managing Business Data with Lists," goes into some detail about lists and list management. To review:

- A list is the data in one or more columns and in one or more rows of the columns, on a worksheet.

- It is normal and useful, if not absolutely necessary, for the first row in the list to contain the names for the data in the columns: for example, AnnualSalary.

- Each column is termed a *field*, and each row containing data within the field is termed a *record*.

■ Usually, all the data in a field is of the same type, both conceptually and syntactically. For example, you would not tend to put a person's street address in a field named City. Nor would you tend to put a number in a field named CustomerName.

Figure 8.1 shows step 1 of the PivotTable Wizard where you specify a source. Figure 8.2 shows an example of a list that you might use as that data source for a pivot table.

You can choose any or all of the fields to compose the data source for the pivot table.

Fig. 8.1
Step 1 in the PivotTable Wizard lets you choose the type of data source for your pivot table.

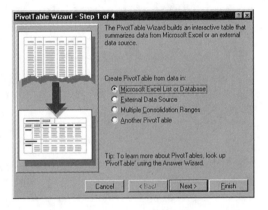

Note

Excel's Help file guidelines for creating lists suggest that you not create more than one list on a worksheet: else, if you filter one list, records in other lists might become hidden.

Creating a Pivot Table from a List

To create the pivot table shown in figure 8.2, follow these steps:

1. Click the PivotTable Wizard button on the Query and Pivot toolbar.

2. Choose the <u>M</u>icrosoft Excel List or Database option button in Step 1 of the PivotTable Wizard (refer to fig. 8.1). Then, choose Next.

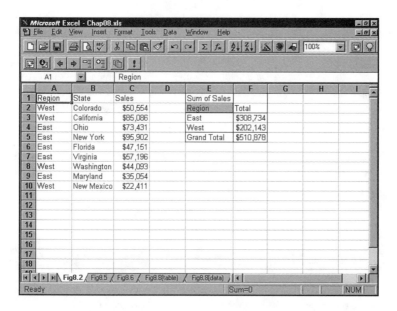

Fig. 8.2
Fields in a list become fields in a pivot table.

3. Step 2 of the PivotTable Wizard appears. Move your mouse pointer over cell A1, and hold down the mouse button. Drag through the range A1:C10 so that each of its cells is highlighted. A moving border, sometimes termed a *marquee*, appears around the range to indicate that it is selected. (If you have selected a cell in or adjacent to the A1:C10 range prior to starting the PivotTable Wizard, the Wizard fills in the range on your behalf.)

4. Release the mouse button.

The Range edit box in Step 2 now contains the addresses of the lists for your pivot table (see fig. 8.3).

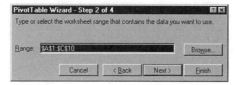

Fig. 8.3
Fill in the Range edit box by using your mouse, or by typing the cell addresses.

> **Note**
>
> The first row of your list should contain the field names. Although the names won't appear in the pivot table's Data field, Excel uses the field's name to designate its corresponding field in the pivot table. Therefore, you should select the cells with the fields' names, as well as the data in the list, in Step 2's Range edit box.

In figure 8.3, notice that the name of the sheet where the list is found does not appear in the Range edit box. The name of the sheet is not strictly necessary, so you can omit it if you type the list address. But if you use a list on a sheet other than the active sheet, the name of the sheet where the list is found is a necessary part of the Range specification.

> **Tip**
>
> To select a list on other than the active sheet by using your mouse, first click that sheet's tab to activate it. Then, drag through the appropriate range or ranges and choose the Next button.

Finally, notice in figure 8.3 that the dialog box contains a Browse button. If you choose it, Excel displays a Browse dialog box that lets you navigate on your disk to the location of another Excel workbook that contains the list you want to use as a data source. However, Excel does not open that file for you, so you must know in advance the full worksheet address (the worksheet name and cell addresses) of the list you want to use for the pivot table.

When you have specified the address of the list in Step 2, choose Next. Step 3 of the PivotTable Wizard appears, as shown in figure 8.4.

Fig. 8.4
Step 3 of the PivotTable Wizard lets you define which fields become Row, Column, Data, or Page fields in the pivot table.

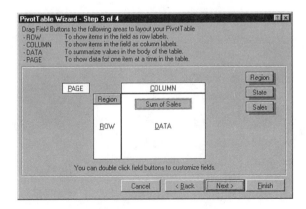

Steps 3 and 4 of the PivotTable Wizard are standard: they don't vary according to the type of data source that you specify in Step 1. Simply drag the field names into the appropriate areas, click Next, fill in any options you wish in Step 4, and choose Finish.

Displaying Computed Fields

Excel users who are new to pivot tables are often confused by this limitation: you can't create a new field in a pivot table. Suppose you have data on the market price of a group of stocks at the beginning of the calendar year and their price at the end of the year. You would like to create a pivot table that shows the difference between the two prices.

In a case such as this, you must specifically create a new field on the worksheet that contains the price difference before you create the pivot table. Then, you would include that field in Step 2 of the PivotTable Wizard, where you specify the range of data to include.

It's true, as noted in Chapter 7, that there are certain specific display formats you can use to show a computed field. For example, you might use the pivot table to compute the price difference as shown in figure 8.5.

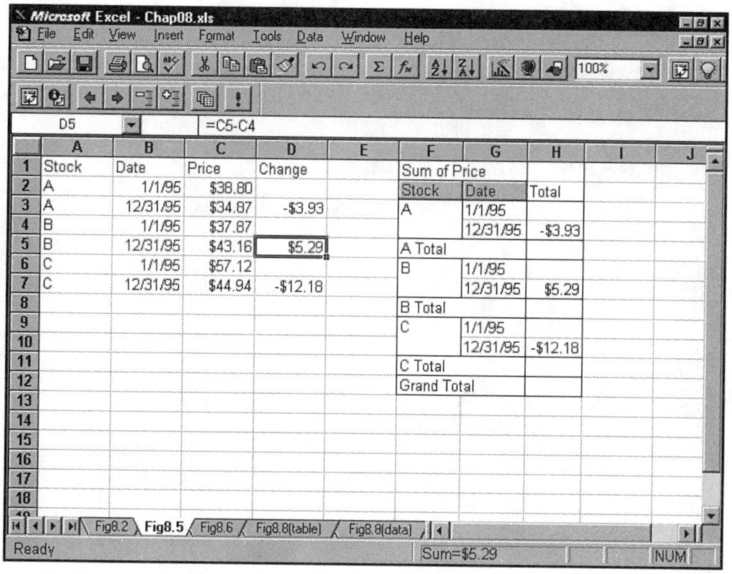

Fig. 8.5
Showing the data as Difference From results in a computed field.

To format the pivot table shown in figure 8.5, take these steps in Step 3 of the PivotTable Wizard:

1. Drag the Price button into the Data area.
2. Double click the Sum of Price button.
3. Click the Options button in the PivotTable Field dialog box.
4. Choose Difference From in the Show Data as list box.
5. Choose Date as the Base Field.
6. Choose *(previous)* as the Base Item.

However, this approach is limited to the values that actually appear in the pivot table. Notice, in figure 8.5, that both the values for Date are visible. If you were to hide either value, 1/1/95 or 12/31/95, the difference between the values would disappear.

Suppose you wanted to display even a slightly more complicated calculation, or that you did not wish to display every value of the base field. For example, you have current prices for several stocks, and the number of shares of each that you own, in lists. If you want a pivot table to display the value (price times shares) for each stock, you must calculate the product explicitly. Figure 8.6 shows this situation.

Fig. 8.6

A more complicated calculation must be made explicit on the worksheet.

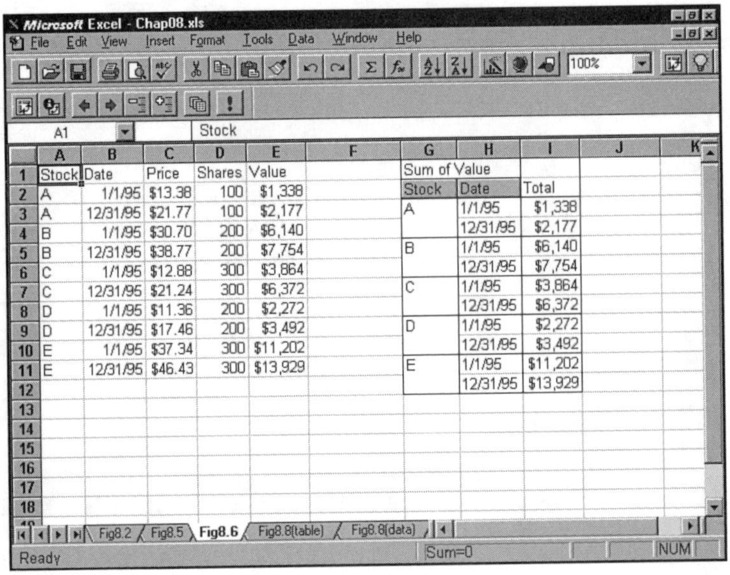

In this situation, you want the pivot table to display a calculation that the PivotTable does not offer. There is no Summarize By or Show Data As option that enables you to multiply the value of one variable by the value of another.

There *is* a Summarize By option, Product, that multiplies values. However, the Product option does not multiply one field by another: it returns the product of all the values of one field that belong to one category of another field. For example, suppose your Price list contains the average stock price for each month in the year. Then, summarizing with the Product option would return the product of all twelve average stock prices for a given stock.

Since there is no pivot table option that enables you to multiply the values of one field by the corresponding values in another field, you must make the multiplication explicitly on the worksheet, and then use the result of that calculation as the Data field in the pivot table.

Using Excel Databases

An Excel database is a special kind of worksheet range, consisting of one or more columns with a header row that you can reference simultaneously.

In versions of Excel prior to version 5, many functions depended on the Database range. Versions 5 and 7 emphasize the use of lists, and de-emphasize the use of worksheet databases. However, the capability still exists and can make the creation of a pivot table just a little more convenient.

Suppose you have several adjacent columns on one worksheet, as shown in figure 8.7.

Pivot Tables

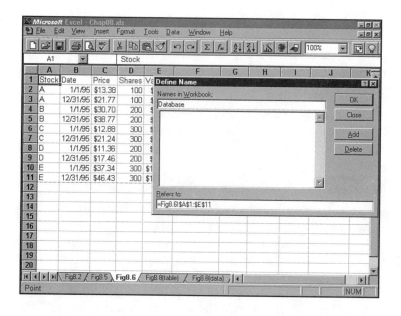

Fig. 8.7
You can combine several columns into an Excel worksheet database.

By giving the name Database to the full range occupied by the columns, you can reference them simultaneously in the PivotTable Wizard. To name the full range, follow these steps:

1. Select the range A1:E11.
2. Click in the Name box, and type **Database**.
3. Press Enter.

    or:

2. Select Insert, Name, Define. The Define Name dialog box appears.
3. In the Names in Workbook edit box, type Database, and choose OK.

Use the Insert, Name, Define method to create more than one range named Database in the same workbook but on different sheets. To do so, type the name of the sheet in the Names in Workbook edit box, followed by an exclamation point and the name Database. For example

Sheet1!Database

This makes the name Database local to Sheet 1, and you can define other Database ranges on other sheets, each local to the sheet where it resides.

With a range named Database defined and accessible to the active sheet, you can start the PivotTable Wizard and in Step 1, choose the Microsoft Excel List or Database option button. Then, in Step 2, the range named Database appears in the Range edit box. When you proceed to Step 3, you find that all the fields contained in the Database range are available to define as fields.

The convenience is that by using the database, you don't need to select a specific range on the worksheet in Step 2. It's automatically made available to the PivotTable Wizard because it belongs to the Database range.

You can, of course, give a name other than Database to the range, and still have the columns contained in the range appear as fields in Step 3. However, using the name Database means that the range name automatically appears in Step 2 in the Range edit box. You would need to type it yourself if the range were named, for example, CombinedColumns.

Chapter 4, "Using Excel Databases To Organize Business Information," discusses some of the other advantages of worksheet databases in detail. One of these advantages is that you can use criteria to cause worksheet functions such as DSUM and DAVERAGE to ignore certain database records. However, establishing a range of criteria has no effect on a pivot table built from a database. Whether or not a criteria range exists for the worksheet database, all database records will be used in the resulting pivot table.

Other Pivot Tables

Using another pivot table as the data source for a new pivot table offers several advantages:

- Creating the new pivot table is slightly quicker, because you do not need to specify the address of the range that contains the source data.

- The new pivot table uses the data cache that Excel created for the existing pivot table. Depending on the amount of source data that the tables represent, this can save a large amount of the space required to store the file.

- If you decide to use the Refresh Data menu option or toolbar button to update the pivot tables, all tables that share the same cache are updated.

Understanding the Data Cache

Chapter 7 made brief reference to the data cache. To fully understand the effect of selecting a data source in Step 1 of the PivotTable Wizard, it's necessary to understand the cache.

Recall from Chapter 7 that a pivot table doesn't link directly to its source data, whether that data is in a list, a worksheet database, another pivot table, or an external data source. When Excel creates a pivot table, it takes the intermediate step of creating a data cache. The cache contains all the data in the data source, but in a format that allows you to make changes to the pivot table more quickly than if the pivot table were directly linked to the source data.

The next two sections discuss the cache in detail.

Saving Data with the Table

In Step 4 of the PivotTable Wizard, one of your options is to check or to clear the Save Data with Table Layout checkbox. As will become clear, it's almost always correct to accept the default value (checked) for this checkbox.

If the checkbox is checked when you choose Finish, Excel creates the data cache for the table *and* saves the cache in the file when it is saved. If the checkbox is not checked when you choose Finish, Excel still creates the cache; however, when you save the workbook, the cache is *not* saved with the workbook. Therefore, when you open the workbook again, there is no data cache associated with the pivot table.

II

Pivot Tables

You can't see the cache directly, nor can you directly determine whether a pivot table was created with a cache.

However, if there is no data cache associated with the pivot table, you can't perform any operation that changes the structure of the pivot table. For example, you wouldn't be able to pivot it (that is, change the orientation of one or more of its control fields), show or hide details, or start the PivotTable Wizard with a pivot table cell selected. If you attempt to do so, the following alert message appears: *Pivot table saved without underlying data. Use the Refresh Data command to update the pivot table.* (The Refresh Data command is discussed in the following section.)

There is no special advantage to clearing the Save Data with Table Layout checkbox in Step 4 of the PivotTable Wizard. And there is the disadvantage that to modify the table, you must first use the Refresh Data command. It's true that the file occupies less space in memory and on your disk if you save it without the cache. But there are better ways to save space. Consider the following benchmark:

A new workbook was opened with a list, consisting of three fields, occupying the range A1:C3000. A pivot table was created with one row field, one column field and one data field, but the cache was not saved. Then, the pivot table was re-created along with the cache. Finally, the source data were deleted.

The file was saved, and its size noted, after each of these operations. These were the results:

- List-only: file size, 129 Kb
- List and pivot table, no cache: file size, 151 Kb
- List, pivot table and cache: file size, 179 Kb
- Pivot table and cache only: file size, 62 Kb

So, yes, saving the cache with the pivot table does increase the file size. But if size is an issue, you can simply delete the list or database from which the pivot table was created. So doing can shrink the size of the file, as shown in the previous list, to less than half its original size.

What if you want the data back? Retrieve it from the cache. Here's how:

1. Create a pivot table using a list or a worksheet Database.
2. In Step 4 of the PivotTable Wizard, make sure that the Save Data with Table Layout checkbox is checked, and choose Finish.

3. Delete the list or database on which the pivot table is based.

4. If you wish, save the file, close it and then reopen it (this is not a necessary step, but it serves to demonstrate that this procedure works even on a file that has been closed).

5. Double-click the cell that contains the Grand Total in the pivot table's Data field.

> **Tip**
>
> If you didn't choose either the Grand Totals For Columns or the Grand Totals For Rows checkboxes in Step 4 of the PivotTable Wizard, you won't see a Grand Totals cell. Select a cell in the pivot table, start the Wizard and check the Totals boxes in Step 4. This will add the Grand Totals cell to the pivot table.

After you double-click the Grand Total cell, Excel opens a new worksheet and copies the data in the cache onto it. The data is unlikely to be in the same row order as the original lists, unless they happened to be sorted in pivot table order. Nevertheless, this is a convenient way to delete data temporarily for the purpose of saving disk and memory resources.

Figure 8.8 shows a pivot table with the Grand Totals cell selected and the sheet that results from double-clicking it.

> **Note**
>
> Because the total of the stock price at the start and the end of the year is meaningless, Stock subtotals were suppressed in the table. Double-click the Stock button in Step 3 of the Wizard, and set the Subtotals to None.

In sum, there are good reasons to save the data cache with the pivot table, by checking the Save Data with Table Layout checkbox in Step 4 of the PivotTable Wizard. If the cache exists, you can modify the pivot table or create another pivot table from it. If the cache does not exist, you will save some file space, but you will have to use the Refresh Data command before you can modify the pivot table. If file size is a real issue, you can always delete the underlying data, and bring it back from the cache by double-clicking the Grand Totals cell.

Fig. 8.8

Recover the original data lists by double-clicking the Grand Totals cell (cell C13 in the pivot table).

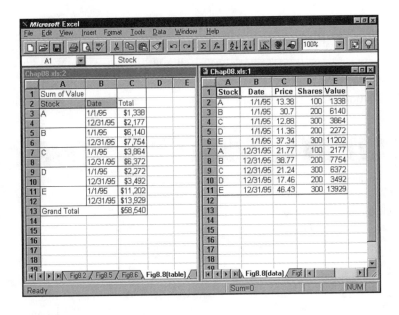

Refreshing the Pivot Table

There is a Refresh Data button on the Query & Pivot toolbar, and a Refresh Data option in the Data menu. There is also a Refresh Data item on the short-cut menu that appears when you select a pivot table cell using the right mouse button. Each of these performs the same two functions. The functions are:

- To build a data cache for a pivot table that was created and saved without one
- To update the information in a pivot table when the source data changes, *after* the pivot table was created

Really, the two functions amount to the same thing. When a pivot table has no cache, the cache must be built before you can make structural changes to the table and before you can base another pivot table on it. When you change the source data values, the cache must be rebuilt so that the pivot table has access to the new values. So, choosing either a menu command or the toolbar button does one thing: it builds a new data cache.

When a pivot table has no cache associated with it, there's no alternative to refreshing the data. The cache must be rebuilt before you can do anything meaningful with the pivot table.

But if you want the pivot table to reflect changes made to the source data values, it's recommended that you rebuild the pivot table from scratch, rather than rebuilding the cache.

Suppose that you create a table with a control field named *Fiscal Year 1992*. To save space, you subsequently name that field *FY92* in the source data. If you now refresh the data, the field disappears from the pivot table, and you will have to build it again from scratch.

If you delete a field from a worksheet list that is the source data for a pivot table, and refresh the data, you receive a message that the Pivot table field name is not valid.

If you have chosen an option other than Normal as a way to show a data field, refreshing the data can in some cases cause the structure of the pivot table to change, returning it to a Normal representation. In other cases, refreshing the data can cause an illegal operation shutdown.

If you have hidden an item within a control field, you might subsequently forget that you have done so. Refreshing the data does not un-hide that item, and if you are unaware that it is hidden then the table's display could cause you to come to an erroneous conclusion.

Problems with refreshing can occasionally arise when you base a pivot table in one sheet on a pivot table in another sheet.

So, unless you are absolutely certain that you know what effect refreshing a pivot table's data will have, don't do it. Instead, rebuild the table from scratch.

Building Pivot Tables from External Sources

Choosing the <u>E</u>xternal Data Source option button in Step 1 of the PivotTable Wizard invokes Microsoft Query. Query is a utility that you can use to build Structured Query Language statements that retrieve data from sources outside Excel through Open Database Connectivity (ODBC) drivers.

There's a lot of meat in that last sentence. The next two sections describe the components involved in more detail.

Understanding External Sources

An external data source can be as complex as a formal database or as simple as a text file. A formal database is one that is created by an application such as dBASE or Access. A text file, of course, is an ASCII file created by any application that can save text to disk, such as Excel, Word, or the Windows Notepad or WordPad. You could even create a text file using the DOS Edlin text editor.

A formal database always has fields and records. Conceptually, a database field is similar to a worksheet list in Excel: it contains values that share a data type (numbers, for example, or text values) and that have the same meanings (Zip codes, for example, or salaries or stock ticker symbols). Each field contains records—similar to the rows in an Excel worksheet list. A field named "Salary" might contain the annual salary earned by each employee in your company. Another field named "Employee" might contain the names of the employees, another named "SSN" might contain their social security numbers, and so on.

In a database such as the one just described, the records in each field need not be in the same order. For example, the Employee field could be sorted alphabetically and the Salary field could be in ascending order, from the lowest to the highest salary paid. A particular employee is associated with a particular salary by means of an *index*: an identifier that uniquely specifies a particular employee and a particular salary. Therefore, if the 100th record in the Employee field has the index "1" and the 500th record in the Salary field has the same index, the database program can pull those two records together in a report that lists salary by employee.

In contrast, a simple text or ASCII file must have two attributes: the first row of text in each field is deemed to be the name of the field, and each field must be in the same order. Suppose that the information in the following table constitutes a text file:

Name	Salary
Smith	$45,853
Jones	$37,221
Williams	$66,792
Roberts	$61,739

Because the first row contains the values "Name" and "Salary," these two values are assumed to be the field names. Each entry in the Name field must be associated with the entry in the same row in the Salary field: it's assumed that Smith, for example, makes $45,853. Compare that information with the following table:

Smith	$45,853
Jones	$37,221
Williams	$66,792
Roberts	$61,739

If you tried to open the file shown in the second table as a pivot table's external data source, the assumption is that the first column is a field named "Smith" and that the second column is a field named "$45,853." This is almost certainly not the intention. If you have a text file you want to treat as an external data source, be certain that the first row in each column contains a meaningful field name.

Using Drivers

A *driver*, in the context of external data sources, is a utility that extracts data from a formal database or from a text file. In order for that extract to occur properly, the driver must take into account the structure of the target database. The internal structure of a dBASE file differs from that of an Access file; both of these are different from the internal structure of a Sybase file, and so on.

These structural differences are conceptually similar to the difference in the internal structure of an Excel workbook and a 1-2-3 file. For example, to open a 1-2-3 file with Excel, you must notify Excel that it is a 1-2-3 file so that Excel can take account of the differences in the file's structure.

You use one driver for a database file created by each different database application. Excel 7 comes with several different drivers:

- Access
- FoxPro
- dBASE
- Paradox
- Text files
- Excel workbooks
- SQL Server (drives Sybase 4.2 as well as other database files)

So, if you have a database structured according to any one of these formats, Excel 7 provides you with a driver that can extract data from it and present the data to Excel to summarize in a pivot table.

Microsoft Query is not a driver, nor is it a database manager. It is a utility that accepts menu-driven commands from you and translates them into Structured Query Language (SQL, often pronounced "sequel") queries. Many different database managers such as Access and Paradox recognize SQL commands. An SQL command includes such specifications as:

- The name of the database to query
- The fields to retrieve from the database, such as Name and Salary

■ Criteria to apply to records within the fields, such as *Name begins with "E" and Salary greater than $50,000*

■ Whether only unique records are to be retrieved

Microsoft Query constructs the SQL command for you, so you don't have to know SQL syntax in order to retrieve the data from the external source.

Once you have defined, by means of your specifications, which fields and records are to be extracted, Query and Excel take over. The database records are retrieved and passed to the PivotTable Wizard, and you continue with Step 3 of the Wizard as usual.

Performing an Extract

This section guides you through creating two pivot tables, one built using data from a text file and one using data from an Access file. Both files can be found on the companion disk, in the folder named *Chapter 8*. The files contain identical data: the only difference is that one is ASCII text (Staff.csv) and the other is in Access format (Staff.mdb).

To retrieve data from the file named Staff.csv (or from any such text file) directly into a pivot table, you need to have the ODBC driver for text files installed. To retrieve data from the file named Staff.mdb (again, from any .mdb file), you need to have the ODBC driver for Access files installed.

To install these drivers, quit all open applications and run Add/Remove Programs from the Windows 95 Control Panel. After Setup has checked for installed components, choose Add/Remove, and select the Converters, Filters, and Data Access component. Then, select the Data Access component. If necessary, check the Microsoft Query, Microsoft Access Driver, and Text Driver component checkboxes. Then, complete Setup and restart Excel.

To obtain the data from the text file, follow these steps.

1. Start the PivotTable Wizard, and choose the External Data Source option button in Step 1. Click Next.

2. In Step 2, click the Get Data button. Microsoft Query starts.

3. The Select Data Source dialog box appears (see fig. 8.9).

4. If you see no entries in the Available Data Sources list box, or if you don't see the data source you want, continue with step 5. Otherwise, continue with step 6.

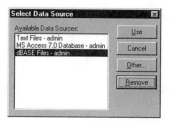

Fig. 8.9
The Select Data
Source dialog box
lists the types of
data sources that
Query has used at
least once on your
computer.

5. Click the Other button. The ODBC Data Sources dialog box appears,
and displays a list of sources for which you have drivers installed. Select
the one you want to add, so that it appears in the Enter Data Source
edit box, and choose OK. See figure 8.10.

Note

There might be ODBC drivers installed on your computer that do not appear
in the ODBC Data Sources dialog box. If you do not see a driver that you
believe to be installed, do the following:

1. Click the New button.

2. The Add Data Source dialog box appears, and displays all the installed
ODBC drivers.

3. Select the driver you want and choose OK.

4. An ODBC setup dialog box appears.

5. Add a name for the new Data source, optionally add a description and
select a directory by clicking the Select Directory button, or a database
by clicking the Select button.

6. Click OK to return to the ODBC Data Sources dialog box.

Fig. 8.10
The ODBC Data
Sources dialog box
lists the types of
data sources for
which you have
drivers installed
on your computer.

Pivot Tables

6. Select one of the available data sources to specify the ODBC driver that Query should use. To open Staff.csv, select Text Files—admin in the Available Data Sources box, and choose Use. To open Staff.mdb, select MS Access 7.0 Database—admin, and choose Use.

7. The Add Tables dialog box appears as shown in figure 8.11. Select a data file from the Table Name box. You can use the Directories list box and the Drives drop-down box to navigate to the location of the file you want to use. Navigate to wherever you chose to install the Staff.csv and Staff.mdb files from the companion disk, and select either Staff.csv or Staff.mdb. Choose Add.

Fig. 8.11
Select the file that contains the external data in the Add Tables dialog box.

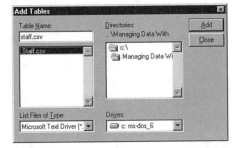

8. If you want to include more data files in the list of external data sources, choose another data file using the Add Tables dialog box. When you have finished, choose Close.

   The Query window appears. See figure 8.12, which shows the different panes in the Query window.

9. You have already selected a data file, whose fields appear in the Table pane. If you do not see the Table pane, click the Show/Hide Tables button. If you do not see the Criteria pane, click the Show/Hide Criteria button.

10. It's necessary to move at least one field from the Table pane to the Data pane. You can do this by double-clicking a field name in the Table pane, dragging a field name from the Table pane to the Data pane, or by clicking the down-arrow on the drop-down box in the Data pane and selecting a field name. To add all the fields in the table simultaneously, double-click the asterisk at the top of the list.

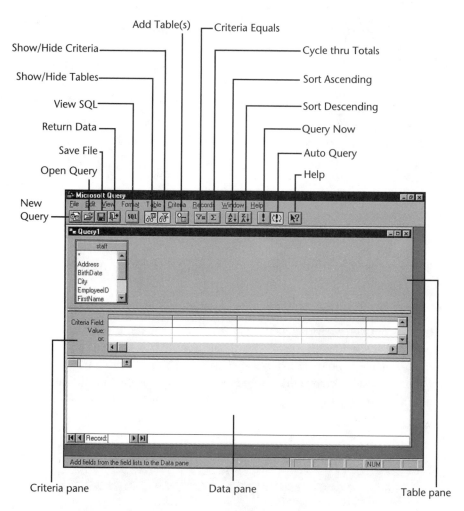

Add Table(s)
Criteria Equals
Show/Hide Criteria
Cycle thru Totals
Show/Hide Tables
Sort Ascending
View SQL
Sort Descending
Return Data
Query Now
Save File
Auto Query
Open Query
Help
New Query

Criteria pane
Data pane
Table pane

Fig. 8.12
The Query window displays the external data sources currently available in the Table pane, any existing record selection criteria in the Criteria pane, and records that meet the criteria in the Data pane.

Pivot Tables

11. To restrict the records that Query returns to the Excel pivot table, use the Criteria pane. Select Criteria, Add Criteria. The Add Criteria dialog box appears as shown in figure 8.13.

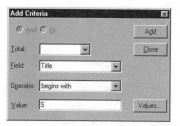

Fig. 8.13
The Add Criteria dialog box helps you create the SQL statement that Query will send to the ODBC driver.

12. Click the down-arrow on the Field drop-down box to select a field. Scroll down the Field drop-down box and select Title.

13. Click the down-arrow on the Operator drop-down box to select a method for comparing a particular record with a particular value. Scroll down the Operator drop-down box and select Begins With.

14. Click in the Value edit box to enter a criterion value against which the chosen field in each record will be compared, to determine whether to return the record to Excel. Click in the Value edit box and enter **S**. This criterion will cause Query to return all records for which the Title field begins with an "S"—in this case, titles that begin with the word "Sales."

15. Choose Add to enter the criterion to the Criteria pane. You can now continue by entering another criterion, or you can choose Close to enter the criterion and return to the Query window. Choose Add, then choose Close. Notice in figure 8.14 that only records for which the Title field begins with an "S" are now visible in the Data pane.

16. Select File, Return Data to Microsoft Excel.

When you complete step 16, Query sends an SQL command to the ODBC driver that you specified in step 6. The driver uses the SQL command to query the database you specified in step 7, and returns the fields and records from the database to Excel. Only those fields that you specified in the Query window's Data pane, and only those records that you specified in the Criteria pane, are returned to Excel.

Fig. 8.14
Once you have added a criterion, the Data pane shows only those records that meet the criterion.

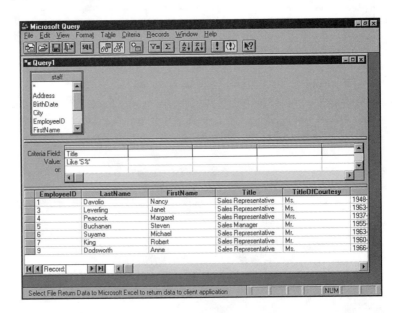

At this point, you are returned to Step 2 of the PivotTable Wizard. The driver uses the SQL command to query the database you specified in step 7, and returns the fields and records from the database to Excel. After choosing Next to proceed to Step 3 of the PivotTable Wizard, you can continue creating the pivot table just as though you were using data from an Excel worksheet.

Figure 8.15 shows the Step 3 dialog box after the data have been returned from the text file.

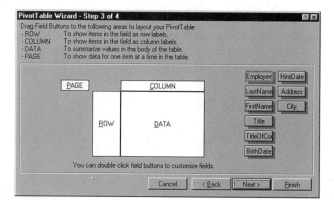

Fig. 8.15
After Query returns the data from the external data source, you can use Step 3 to define the pivot table's structure.

Pivot Tables

Using Multiple Consolidation Ranges

At the beginning of this chapter, it was noted that a worksheet list used in a pivot table must ordinarily reside on the same worksheet. However, Step 1 of the PivotTable Wizard offers the Multiple Consolidation Ranges option, which lets you specify lists on different worksheets.

This option is most useful when you store similar data in different worksheets. For example, you might have a workbook that contains sales data for each of several salespeople. Each month's sales data are kept on a different worksheet. For an example, see figure 8.16.

Notice in figure 8.16 that the field in column B on each worksheet has the same label: Sales. Because Sales will be the Data field in the pivot table, it's necessary to provide that list with an identical name on all worksheets. If, for example, the worksheet named January in figure 8.16 used the label *January Sales*, and the other worksheets used the label *Sales*, Excel would assume that there were two data fields: one named January Sales and another named Sales.

Fig. 8.16
The Multiple Consolidation Ranges option lets you combine data from different worksheets into one pivot table.

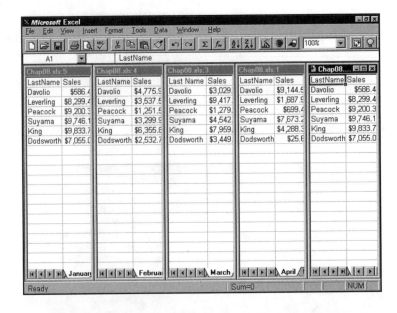

Figure 8.17 shows the pivot table that results from using the consolidation ranges in figure 8.16.

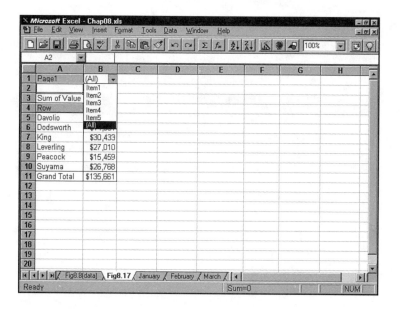

Fig. 8.17
This pivot table
is built using the
ranges shown in
fig. 8.16. Notice
the default field
names assigned
by Excel.

To create the pivot table in fig. 8.17, use the data file on the companion disk
for Chapter 8 as follows:

1. Open the file named Chap08.xls and insert a new worksheet.

2. Start the PivotTable Wizard, and in Step 1 choose the Multiple Consolidation Ranges option button.

3. In Step 2a, leave the Create a Single Page Field for Me option button selected. Click Next.

4. In Step 2b, with the insertion point in the Range edit box, click the January sheet tab. This makes the January worksheet active.

5. Highlight cells A1:B7 on the January worksheet, and click the Add button in the Step 2b dialog box. The reference appears in the All Ranges list box (see fig. 8.18).

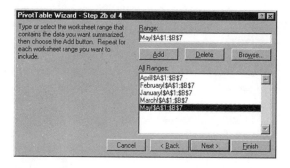

Fig. 8.18
Use Step 2b of
the PivotTable
Wizard to iden-
tify multiple
worksheet ranges
as data sources for
the pivot table.

6. Click the February sheet tab to make that worksheet active. Notice the Range edit box now contains both the name of the worksheet (February) and the address of the range used for the January worksheet. Click Add.

> **Tip**
>
> If possible, format your worksheets so the data on each worksheet occupies the same range. If you do, you can let Excel fill in the cell references for you. If you do not, you will have to re-establish the cell reference for each worksheet in the Range edit box.

7. Repeat step 6 for the remaining worksheets: March through May. When you have finished, click Next.

When, at the end of step 7, you click Next, Step 3 of the PivotTable Wizard appears, as shown in figure 8.19.

Fig. 8.19

When the data source is multiple ranges, Excel uses default field labels (Page, Row, Column, and Value) instead of the list headers.

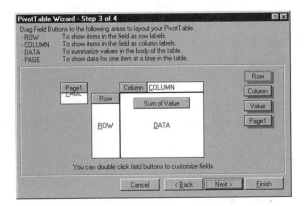

Notice in figure 8.19 that Excel uses default field labels. You can change the labels to some other name by double-clicking them, and typing a new name in the Name edit box of the PivotTable Field dialog box. Or, if you wish, you can supply custom names later, after the pivot table has been created on the sheet.

At this point, you can finish creating the pivot table as usual by completing PivotTable Wizard Steps 3 and 4.

Creating Your Own Page Fields

The PivotTable Wizard enables you to customize up to four different Page fields when you use multiple consolidation ranges as your data source. Each Page field can represent one or more of the consolidation ranges. So, in the example used in the previous section, you could arrange for Page Field 1 to represent sales for January *and* sales for February—or, it could represent January sales and March sales, or any combination of the five worksheet ranges in the example.

Using this option, you can control the names of the items in the Page field of the resulting pivot table, instead of settling for the default names of Item1, Item2, and so on.

You can create up to four such Page fields. Each Page field can represent a different combination of the data source ranges.

> **Note**
>
> This option can easily and quickly become confusing. You are *not* limited to four worksheet ranges as Page fields, because each Page field can represent any number of worksheet ranges. You *are* limited to four Page fields.

The process of creating a Page field and its items is shown in figure 8.20.

For example, to create one custom Page field using the example in the previous section, and representing sales for January and for March, follow these steps:

1. Start the PivotTable Wizard, and choose Multiple Consolidation Ranges as your data source. Click Next.

2. In Step 2a, select I Will Create the Page Fields option button. Click Next.

3. In Step 2b, after identifying the worksheet ranges by using the Range edit box and the Add button, select the 1 option button below the All Ranges list box.

4. In the All Ranges list box, click the range that represents January sales (January!$A$1:$B$7).

5. In the Field One drop-drown edit box, type **January Sales**.

6. In the All Ranges list box, click the range that represents March sales (March!$A$1:$B$7).

Pivot Tables

Fig. 8.20
If you create your own Page fields, you can control how the individual items are named.

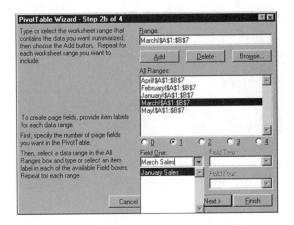

7. In the Field Qne edit box, type **March Sales**. Click Next.

8. In Step 3, drag the Page 1 field button into the PAGE area. Click Next, and complete Step 4 as usual.

Now, when you click the Page button on the completed pivot table, you can choose to view January Sales, March Sales, or All sales. Note that the All option represents the sum of all ranges, not just January plus March.

Chapter Summary

In this chapter, you have learned how to create pivot tables from worksheet lists and databases, and under what circumstances you must compute a field explicitly on the worksheet. You have also learned how to use external databases and text files as data sources for pivot tables, and how to use more than one worksheet as a data source. Chapter 9, "Applying Special Pivot Table Options," describes how to set options for different fields to obtain custom results in your pivot tables.

9

Applying Special Pivot Table Options

Chapter 7, "Understanding Pivot Tables," touched on several methods of customizing pivot tables, including subtotals, summary functions, and the use of page fields. This chapter goes into greater depth on how to use these capabilities, which differ depending on whether you choose to customize a control field or a data field. You will also learn about some of the side effects of using subtotals in control fields and of specifying multiple page fields in a pivot table.

Customizing Row and Column Fields

There are five ways that you can arrange to set all the special options for row and column fields:

- Double-click the field's button in Step 3 of the PivotTable Wizard.

- Select any cell in the field—whether a field control or a cell containing a field value—and click the PivotTable Field button on the Query and Pivot toolbar.

- Select any cell in the field—again, a field control or a field value—and choose PivotTable Field from the Data menu.

■ Double-click the field control. Do not double-click a field value: This action displays or hides details within that value.

■ Right-click any cell in the field. This brings up a shortcut menu with a variety of items, including PivotTable Field.

Any one of these actions displays the PivotTable Field dialog box, shown in figure 9.1.

Fig. 9.1
The PivotTable Field dialog box provides you with ways to alter the display of a row or column field.

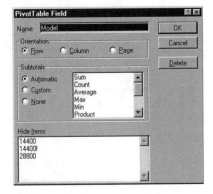

The available options are described in the next section.

Using the PivotTable Field Dialog Box for Row and Column Fields

By means of this dialog box, you can pivot the table. Just choose a different location for the selected field in the Orientation area. For example, a row field can be changed to a column or a page field by clicking either the Column or the Page option button.

> **Tip**
>
> It's usually faster to change a control field's orientation by dragging its control, either directly on the pivot table or in Step 3 of the PivotTable Wizard. But if you want to make several different changes to a field, using the PivotTable Field dialog box is quicker.

The PivotTable Field dialog box also lets you set the type of calculation used for totals and subtotals in the pivot table.

Do not be misled by the terms "total" and "subtotal." These terms imply that the values are summed. It is true that the usual method of summarizing the values that compose a control field's category is to sum them, but there are other ways to do this. You can specify that the values be represented by their average, instead of their sum; or, you can choose to summarize them by their product, standard deviation, count, and so on. Therefore, these are really "summaries" and "sub-summaries" rather than totals and subtotals. However, for consistency with Excel's usage, this book refers to them as totals and subtotals.

By choosing one or more items in the Subtotals list box in the PivotTable Field dialog box, you can display the summary values as:

- *Sum (the default if the data field is entirely numeric).* The total of the data field values in the row or column category.

- *Count (the default if the data field contains at least one non-numeric value).* The number of values in the data field.

- *Average.* The mean data field value.

- *Max.* The maximum data field value.

- *Min.* The minimum data field value.

- *Product.* The result of multiplying all the data field values in the row or column category.

- *Count Nums.* The number of numeric data field values.

- *StdDev.* The standard deviation of the data field values, assuming that they represent a sample from a population.

- *StdDevp.* The standard deviation of the data field values, assuming that they represent a population.

- *Var.* The variance of the data field values, assuming that they represent a sample from a population.

- *Varp.* The variance of the data field values, assuming that they represent a population.

You can choose one or more of these options from the Subtotals list box by clicking the ones you want. To remove one that you have selected, just click it again. Choosing at least one of the list box options clears the Automatic option button (the default), and selects the Custom option button. If you want to suppress all subtotals, choose the None option button.

Pivot Tables

If you have only one row field or column field, these options have no effect. The assumption is that the subtotal for each item in a row field (for example) is already available in the data field, and therefore adding a subtotal cell to the control field would be redundant. See figure 9.2 for an example.

Fig. 9.2
When there is only one row or column field, the subtotal is assumed to exist in the data field.

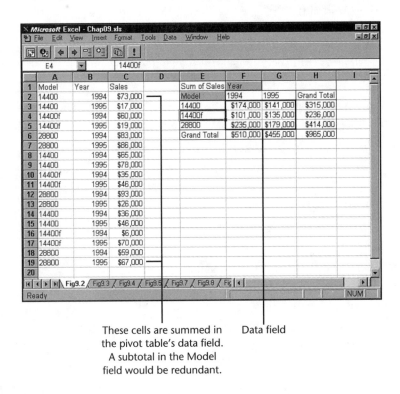

These cells are summed in the pivot table's data field. A subtotal in the Model field would be redundant.

Data field

What if you have only one row field and want to display, say, both the sum and the average for each row field category? The solution is to use two data fields in the pivot table. For example, you could use Sum of data and Average of data. See the next section for a description of how to do this.

If you have more than one row or column field, the Subtotals options do have an effect on the appearance of the pivot table (see fig. 9.3).

Notice in figure 9.3 how the subtotals are calculated. Cells G5:G7 are the sum, the count, and the average of the values for the 14400 value of the Model variable, used as an outer row field. Similarly, cells G16:G18 are the sum, the count, and the average, of values for the 28800 Model. The subtotals are *not* the sum, average, and count of their corresponding fields in the pivot table itself. The pivot table always goes to the underlying data to calculate its totals and subtotals.

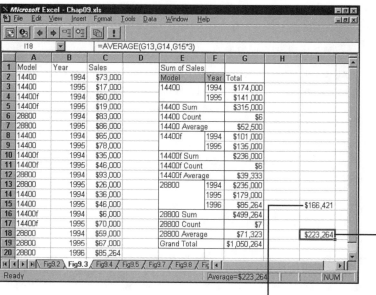

Fig. 9.3
Subtotals appear
in the pivot table
when there is more
than one row or
column field.

1 =AVERAGE(G13:G15)   2 =AVERAGE(G13/3,G14/3,G15)

For example, the value in cell G18 is $71,323. This is the average of cells
C6:C7, C12:C13, and C18:C20. If the value in cell G18 were the average of
cells G13:G15 *in the pivot table*, its value would be $166,421 (see cell I15). The
latter can be a useful way to obtain, say, an unweighted average when the
categories contain different numbers of values, but the pivot table does not
offer this as an option. It's necessary to make that calculation explicitly on
the worksheet. You also might want to calculate a weighted average (see cell
I18 in figure 9.3, for example).

What do these different averages mean? The average shown in cell G18, the
average returned by the pivot table, is the total of the Model 28800 Sales divided by the number of Model 28800 records in the worksheet list. If the
records were contributed by different sales regions, for example, $71,323 in
G18 would represent the average regional sale of this model in each year.
Each sale in each region has an equal weight in the average.

If the three values in G13:G15 were averaged, the result of $166,421 would be
the annual average total sales of the 28800 model. Each year's total sales has
an equal weight in the average.

But the average of the values in the pivot table, $166,421, does not take into
account the fact that the list contains only one record for Model 28800 sales
in 1996. You might consider it more realistic to adjust the annual average

total sales to take into account the unequal number of records per year. The formula in cell I18

```
=AVERAGE(G13,G14,G15*3)
```

steps up the value of the 1996 Model 28800 sales so that it receives the same weight as an individual record for 1994 or 1995. In effect, it assumes that three records for 1996 would have the same average as the one actually reported. This *weighted average* might be a more accurate estimate of average total sales than the simple average of cells G13:G15.

> **Note**
>
> If you want the overall count and average of all the underlying values in the same pivot table that shows subtotals for row or column fields, you would use block subtotals, as described in Chapter 7.

An error exists in the Product subtotal option. Suppose that you create a pivot table with exactly one row field and one or more column fields, and that you choose the Product option for the row field's subtotal. The Grand Total cell for the full table (that is, the intersection of the row Grand Totals and the column Grand Totals) is *not* the product of all the underlying values. Instead, it is the Grand Total for the table's first row (see fig. 9.4).

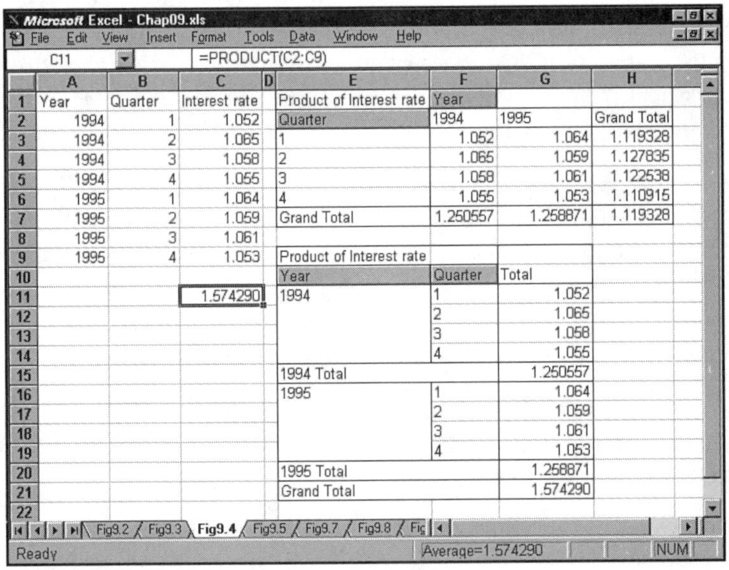

Fig. 9.4

A pivot table with one row field and one or more column fields returns the wrong Grand Total for Product subtotals.

Notice that the Grand Total cell, H7, displays 1.119328. It should display 1.574290. However, a pivot table with more than one row field returns the proper value (see cell G21 in fig. 9.4). Therefore, be careful if you choose to create a pivot table with one row field whose subtotal option you set to Product.

The final option in the PivotTable Field dialog box for row and column fields allows you to hide one or more categories of the field (refer to fig.9.1): if you selected the 28800 category in the Hide Items list box, that category would not appear in the pivot table.

Customizing the Data Field

You'll recall from the previous section that if you specify a subtotal for a row or column field, Excel provides subtotals only if that row or column field is an outer field. If the field is the only row or column field, there is no outer field. In that case, if you want to view custom subtotals, you must arrange for them by customizing the data field. See figure 9.5 for an example.

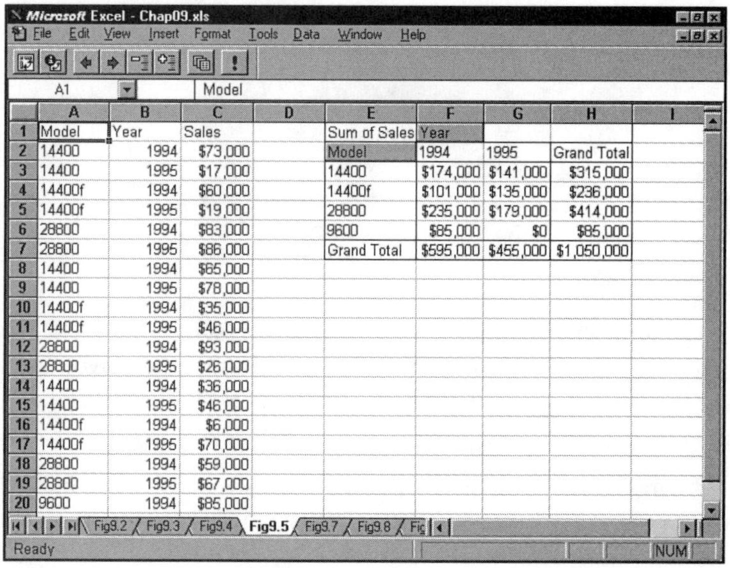

	A	B	C	D	E	F	G	H	I
1	Model	Year	Sales		Sum of Sales	Year			
2	14400	1994	$73,000		Model	1994	1995	Grand Total	
3	14400	1995	$17,000		14400	$174,000	$141,000	$315,000	
4	14400f	1994	$60,000		14400f	$101,000	$135,000	$236,000	
5	14400f	1995	$19,000		28800	$235,000	$179,000	$414,000	
6	28800	1994	$83,000		9600	$85,000	$0	$85,000	
7	28800	1995	$86,000		Grand Total	$595,000	$455,000	$1,050,000	
8	14400	1994	$65,000						
9	14400	1995	$78,000						
10	14400f	1994	$35,000						
11	14400f	1995	$46,000						
12	28800	1994	$93,000						
13	28800	1995	$26,000						
14	14400	1994	$36,000						
15	14400	1995	$46,000						
16	14400f	1994	$6,000						
17	14400f	1995	$70,000						
18	28800	1994	$59,000						
19	28800	1995	$67,000						
20	9600	1994	$85,000						

Fig. 9.5
This pivot table has no outer row or column field, so custom subtotals must be specified for the data field.

To obtain the subtotals for the data shown in figure 9.5, follow these steps:

1. Complete the PivotTable Wizard through Step 2, then choose Next.

2. Drag the row field button (Model) into the ROW area, the column field button (Year) into the COLUMN area, and the data field button (Sales) into the DATA area. Double-click the Sales button in the DATA area, and use the Number button to set its format to Currency.

3. Drag the data field button into the DATA area once again. The DATA area now has two buttons: one labeled Sum of Sales, and one labeled Sum of Sales2.

4. Double-click the button labeled Sum of Sales2. The PivotTable Field dialog box appears, as shown in figure 9.6.

5. Select Average in the Summarize By list box. The entry in the Name box changes to Average of Sales2.

6. Click in the Name box and edit the name to read Average of Sales. Click the Number button to set its format to Currency.

7. Choose OK to close the Pivot Table Field dialog box.

Fig. 9.6

Use the PivotTable Field dialog box with a data field selected to create custom subtotals for an inner row or column field.

After you choose OK, complete Step 4 of the PivotTable Wizard. The resulting pivot table appears as shown in figure 9.7. Compare the first pivot table, without the Average subtotal, to the second pivot table, which contains both the Sum and the Average subtotals.

Also compare figure 9.7 to figure 9.3. Pivot tables in both figures have sub-totals, but note the difference in their layouts, which depends on whether the subtotals are assigned to an outer row field (see fig. 9.3), or to the data field (see fig. 9.7).

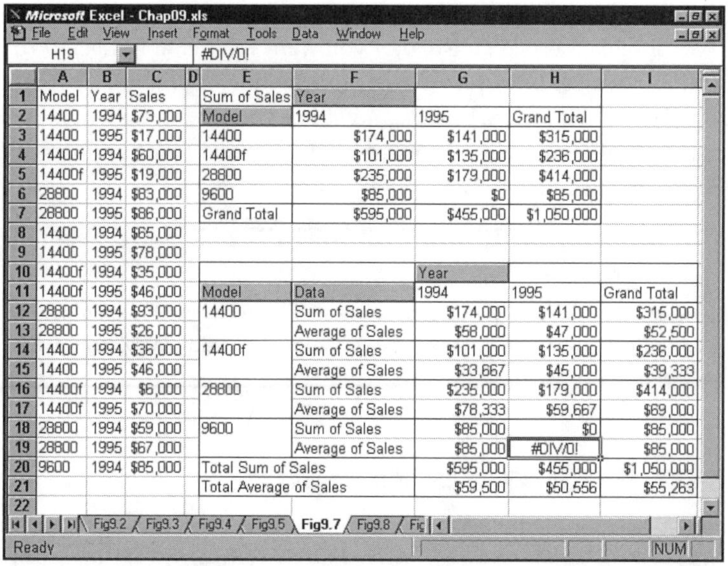

	A	B	C	D	E	F	G	H	I
1	Model	Year	Sales		Sum of Sales	Year			
2	14400	1994	$73,000		Model	1994	1995	Grand Total	
3	14400	1995	$17,000		14400	$174,000	$141,000	$315,000	
4	14400f	1994	$60,000		14400f	$101,000	$135,000	$236,000	
5	14400f	1995	$19,000		28800	$235,000	$179,000	$414,000	
6	28800	1994	$83,000		9600	$85,000	$0	$85,000	
7	28800	1995	$86,000		Grand Total	$595,000	$455,000	$1,050,000	
8	14400	1994	$65,000						
9	14400	1995	$78,000						
10	14400f	1994	$35,000				Year		
11	14400f	1995	$46,000		Model	Data	1994	1995	Grand Total
12	28800	1994	$93,000		14400	Sum of Sales	$174,000	$141,000	$315,000
13	28800	1995	$26,000			Average of Sales	$58,000	$47,000	$52,500
14	14400	1994	$36,000		14400f	Sum of Sales	$101,000	$135,000	$236,000
15	14400	1995	$46,000			Average of Sales	$33,667	$45,000	$39,333
16	14400f	1994	$6,000		28800	Sum of Sales	$235,000	$179,000	$414,000
17	14400f	1995	$70,000			Average of Sales	$78,333	$59,667	$69,000
18	28800	1994	$59,000		9600	Sum of Sales	$85,000	$0	$85,000
19	28800	1995	$67,000			Average of Sales	$85,000	#DIV/0!	$85,000
20	9600	1994	$85,000		Total Sum of Sales		$595,000	$455,000	$1,050,000
21					Total Average of Sales		$59,500	$50,556	$55,263
22									

Fig. 9.7
Specifying custom subtotals for the data field adds a data field control on the pivot table.

Tip

There is an error value, `#DIV/0!`, in cell H19 of figure 9.7, which contains the value for the average sales of the 9600 model during 1995. Because there are no values in the underlying data for that model during that year, the denominator of the average is zero, and this results in the error value.

You cannot hide an error value with the ";;;" custom format, and you cannot delete values from a data field.

You can, however, avoid the error value in the pivot table by adding an extra record in the underlying data, in which the year is 1995, the model is the 9600, and the sales value is $0. In most cases this will not cause any misleading conclusions.

Figure 9.7 contains an object not yet encountered. Notice the control labeled Data in cell F11. This indicates that the subtotals are based on the data field, not on a row or column field.

Although the data field control looks much like the row and column controls—apart from its label—it does not function in the same way. Recall from the prior section that you can double-click a row or column control to access the PivotTable Field dialog box; or, with the row or column control selected, you can select PivotTable Field from the Data menu.

You cannot take either of these actions with a data field control selected. After the pivot table has been created, if you want to alter an aspect of the data field, you must select one of its *values*. For example, in figure 9.7, you could select any cell in the G12:I21 range and either choose Data, PivotTable Field, or click the PivotTable Field button on the Query and Pivot toolbar, or right-click PivotTable Field from the shortcut menu.

Note

Remember, do not double-click a data field value. This does not bring up the PivotTable Field dialog box—instead, it displays the data field's individual values.

Customizing Page Fields

Chapter 7 discussed one of the ways you can customize the page field, by showing each page field value on a separate worksheet. To do so, select the page field control, and click the Show Pages button on the Query and Pivot toolbar. As an alternative, you can right-click a cell in a pivot table that has a page field, and click Show Pages on the shortcut menu.

You can also customize a page field just as you do a row or a column field, either by double-clicking the page field's control, or by selecting it and choosing Data, PivotTable Field.

Using Multiple Page Fields

Just as you can create more than one row or column field, you can create more than one page field. See figure 9.8 for an example.

The pivot table in cells F1:G9 of figure 9.8 has one page field. Notice that there is one row between the page field and the remainder of the table. If you create a new pivot table with two page fields, its first row contains the control for the first page field, the second row contains the control for the second page field, the third row is blank and Excel builds the table down from that row.

But suppose you use the PivotTable Wizard to add a page field, or that you drag a field control on the worksheet to change it to a page field. In that case, Excel leaves the pivot table in place and adds the new page field above it, unless the pivot table already occupies row 1 of the worksheet. This is shown by the layout of the pivot table in cells I1:J10 of figure 9.8.

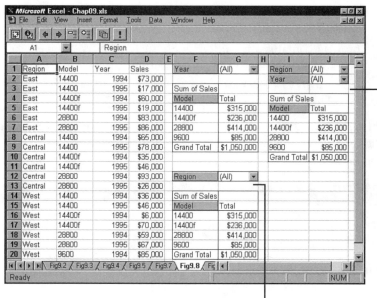

Fig. 9.8
Multiple page fields are stacked on the worksheet.

Blank row between page field and pivot table

This row would be overwritten if Year were added as a page field

However, suppose that the body of a pivot table begins in row 14, as is the case for the pivot table in cells F12:G20 of figure 9.8. If you now add Year as a page field, it builds up to row 11—row 11 would contain Region as a page field, row 12 would contain Year as another page field, and row 13 would be the usual, blank row between the page field and the body of the table. If row 11 is empty, there is no problem. But if there is already information in row 11, several different things can happen, depending on what row 11 contains:

- If row 11 contains part of another pivot table, you will receive the error message *Pivot table cannot overlap another pivot table.* You will have to move one of the two pivot tables and restart the PivotTable Wizard. Therefore, to avoid having to complete the PivotTable Wizard twice, make sure that the rows above the pivot table's location are clear before you start the Wizard.

- If row 11 contains an array formula extending across at least three columns, you will receive the error message *Cannot change part of an array.* The new page field requires two columns, one for the page field control and one for the drop-down box. You cannot overwrite two columns of an array formula that occupies more than two columns, and you will have to move either the array formula or the pivot table.

Again, make sure that the rows above the pivot table are clear before you start the Wizard.

■ If row 11 contains other information, such as labels, numbers, or non-array formulas, you will receive the warning message *Replace contents of destination cells?*. You can choose OK to replace the contents, or Cancel to stop the operation.

If there is information in row 13, however, you receive no message because it is the "extra" row between the page field and the body of the pivot table (an exception would be an array formula that occupies both row 12 *and* row 13).

Tip

If you use the PivotTable Wizard to add the page field, a cell in the table's new first row is highlighted by a *marquee* (Microsoft's terminology, also described as a moving border) when you reach Step 4 of the Wizard. This indicates where the new page field will be located in case you are about to overwrite existing information.

When a pivot table has two or more page fields, they interact to determine what information is displayed in the body of the table. See figure 9.9 for an example.

Fig. 9.9
Multiple page fields have different effects, depending on which pages are selected.

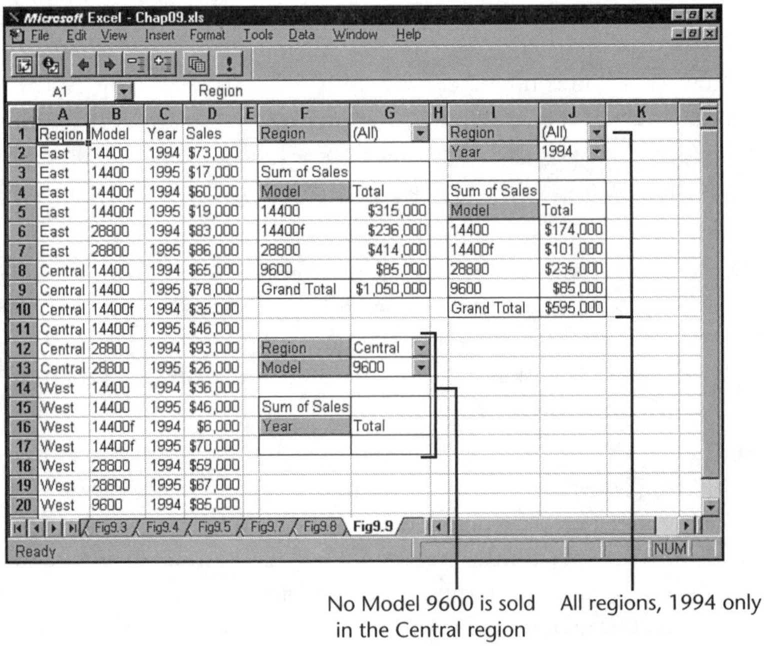

No Model 9600 is sold in the Central region

All regions, 1994 only

The pivot table in cells F1:G9 in figure 9.9 has one page field. The page that is showing is All—that is, all the field's pages are displayed in the pivot table.

The pivot table in cells I1:J10 has two page fields. The first page field is set to All, and the second page field is set to 1994. The pivot table itself displays a summary of the underlying values that have any value on the Region page field, and that have a value of 1994 on the Year page field.

The pivot table in cells F12:G17 also has two page fields, but both are set to a specific page. If you examine the underlying data, you will see that there are no records from the Central region *and* a value of 9600 as the model. Therefore, the pivot table's display is empty.

In other words, multiple page fields are connected by logical ANDs. Any record displayed in the pivot table must be associated with the chosen value for the first page field and the chosen value for the second page field.

> **Note**
>
> You can show the data that corresponds to each page field value when you have defined multiple page fields. However, you can select only one page field at a time. That is, you can show all pages of Page Field A, and subsequently you can show all pages of Page Field B, but you cannot choose both Field A and Field B in the Show Pages dialog box.

Chapter Summary

In this chapter, you have learned more about the choices available to you if you wish to customize a row, column, page, or data field in a pivot table. In particular:

- There are different ways to create subtotals, depending on whether the pivot table has more than one row or column field.

- You can stack page fields in a pivot table; however, the behavior of the Show Pages option differs according to whether one page field or multiple page fields exist.

- If you are adding another page field to an existing pivot table, the table builds up from its original starting row, rather than down from its original ending row.

The next chapter describes how to use Visual Basic for Applications (VBA) to create and customize pivot tables. These techniques can save you a considerable amount of effort if you build pivot tables repetitively, as their underlying data changes over time.

10

Using VBA To Create Pivot Tables

Pivot tables are interactive. That is, the PivotTable Wizard makes it easy to create them, to pivot their fields, and to change the way they display data. Why would you ever want to use Visual Basic for Applications (VBA) to perform any of those tasks?

There are several reasons to do so. Just because you've taken the time and effort to understand how pivot tables work and how to use the PivotTable Wizard doesn't mean people you work with have also. You can use VBA to make it easier for them to manage data with pivot tables.

Or, suppose you need to create a report that uses pivot tables on some regular, recurring basis. If it's an annual report, then it might not be too troublesome to re-create its pivot tables manually. But if it's a monthly or even a weekly report, then it makes good sense to automate the creation of the pivot tables.

This chapter describes how you can use VBA code to accomplish the repetitive tasks involved with creating pivot tables. It also describes how you can automate queries to external data sources, and how you can use VBA to make it easier for other users, who might not yet understand the PivotTable Wizard, to create their own pivot tables.

Of course, you don't have to be an experienced VBA programmer to generate the needed code. You can activate Excel's macro recorder and then carry out whatever actions are required to create the pivot table. Excel records the corresponding VBA code for you, and you can subsequently edit the code to bring about different results. In this chapter you will also find examples of how to understand the code, how to edit it, and how to run it.

Using VBA to Create or Modify Pivot Tables

If you've never used VBA to control Excel, you might find it difficult to fully understand the material in this chapter. Even if you feel perfectly comfortable with pivot tables, and even if you've used a version of Basic in the past, keep in mind that pivot tables can be complicated beasts, and VBA structures are different from those you may have learned and used previously. (See Que's *Special Edition Using Excel Visual Basic for Applications*, 2nd Edition for more on VBA and Excel.)

If you've already experimented with VBA in Excel, and have a feel for concepts such as objects, methods, and properties, it's likely that you will recognize much of the following material, and feel comfortable with it.

The first example we cited for using VBA with pivot tables was the recurring report. When you want to summarize regularly updated data to obtain a current picture of the data, VBA can save time (so you don't need to answer interactively all the questions posed by the PivotTable Wizard) and help ensure that the report is created in the same way, time after time.

Case Study: Creating a Recurring Inventory Analysis

Suppose you're tracking your company's inventory value each month. The results of a sample query from your mainframe database are shown in figure 10.1.

Some of the inventory records shown in figure 10.1 are full, stand-alone units, and others are bits of systems—available for special circumstances when a customer's setup requires them. Because the routine that downloads the data is a full report, rather than a database query with selection criteria, all records must appear in the data set. However, you would prefer that your monthly pivot table report not include them.

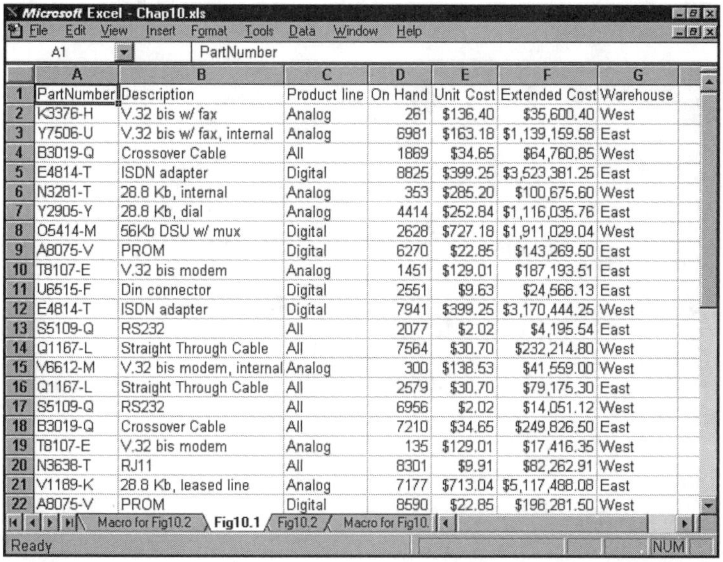

	A	B	C	D	E	F	G
1	PartNumber	Description	Product line	On Hand	Unit Cost	Extended Cost	Warehouse
2	K3376-H	V.32 bis w/ fax	Analog	261	$136.40	$35,600.40	West
3	Y7506-U	V.32 bis w/ fax, internal	Analog	6981	$163.18	$1,139,159.58	East
4	B3019-Q	Crossover Cable	All	1869	$34.65	$64,760.85	West
5	E4814-T	ISDN adapter	Digital	8825	$399.25	$3,523,381.25	East
6	N3281-T	28.8 Kb, internal	Analog	353	$285.20	$100,675.60	West
7	Y2905-Y	28.8 Kb, dial	Analog	4414	$252.84	$1,116,035.76	East
8	O5414-M	56Kb DSU w/ mux	Digital	2628	$727.18	$1,911,029.04	West
9	A8075-V	PROM	Digital	6270	$22.85	$143,269.50	East
10	T8107-E	V.32 bis modem	Analog	1451	$129.01	$187,193.51	East
11	U6515-F	Din connector	Digital	2551	$9.63	$24,566.13	East
12	E4814-T	ISDN adapter	Digital	7941	$399.25	$3,170,444.25	West
13	S5109-Q	RS232	All	2077	$2.02	$4,195.54	East
14	Q1167-L	Straight Through Cable	All	7564	$30.70	$232,214.80	West
15	V6612-M	V.32 bis modem, internal	Analog	300	$138.53	$41,559.00	West
16	Q1167-L	Straight Through Cable	All	2579	$30.70	$79,175.30	East
17	S5109-Q	RS232	All	6956	$2.02	$14,051.12	West
18	B3019-Q	Crossover Cable	All	7210	$34.65	$249,826.50	East
19	T8107-E	V.32 bis modem	Analog	135	$129.01	$17,416.35	West
20	N3638-T	RJ11	All	8301	$9.91	$82,262.91	West
21	V1189-K	28.8 Kb, leased line	Analog	7177	$713.04	$5,117,488.08	East
22	A8075-V	PROM	Digital	8590	$22.85	$196,281.50	West

Fig. 10.1
The term "Extended Cost" is normally used to mean the number of items in stock, times their unit cost.

Note

In inventory management, these stand-alone "piece-parts" can be critical equipment. They are often service spares, and might be valued differently depending on whether they are new or used, so you might want an additional field that defines that status. It's also wise to establish minimum and maximum levels for these parts in yet another field. Just because this example hides them in the pivot table does not mean that they're unimportant.

Tip

Consider a pivot table with a Date variable as the row field and Description as both the column field and the data field. This is a convenient way to help establish minimum and maximum inventory levels for different types of inventory stock.

You can create a pivot table manually, hiding the items you don't want to show up in the table, which is shown in figure 10.2.

Fig. 10.2

Hiding certain
items in the
Description field
makes this pivot
table easier to
interpret.

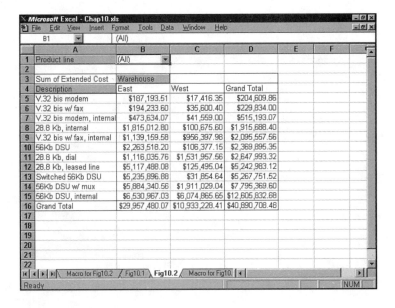

It's a useful exercise to create the pivot table shown in figure 10.2 manually,
from the data shown in figure 10.1. If you do, you'll realize how convenient
it is to let VBA do it for you. Follow these steps:

1. Open the file on the companion disk named Chap10.xls, and activate
   the sheet named Fig10.1.

2. Select any cell in the range A1:G41.

3. Choose Data, PivotTable. Or, if you have the Query and Pivot toolbar
   visible, click the PivotTable Wizard button.

4. Accept the default option of Microsoft Excel List or Database in Step 1.
   Choose Next.

5. Accept the default Range of A1:G41 in Step 2. Choose Next.

6. In Step 3, drag the Product Line button to the Page area, and the Warehouse button to the Column area.

7. Drag the Extended Cost button into the Data area. Double-click the
   Extended Cost button to open the PivotTable Field dialog box, and
   click the Number button. Format the field as Currency, with two
   decimal places. Choose OK, and then choose OK in the PivotTable Field
   dialog box.

8. Drag the Description button into the Row area. Double-click the Description button to see the PivotTable Field dialog box. In the Hide
   Items list box, select these items in order to prevent them from being

displayed in the pivot table: Crossover Cable, Din connector, DROM, ISDN adapter, Power supply, PROM, RJ11, RS232, and Straight Through Cable. Choose OK to return to Step 3 of the PivotTable Wizard.

9. Choose Finish in Step 3 to bypass Step 4 (to open a new worksheet) and to create the pivot table.

10. With the pivot table visible, select any cell within its Grand Total column. Choose <u>D</u>ata, <u>S</u>ort, make sure that the <u>A</u>scending option button is selected, and choose OK.

By taking these ten steps, you will have created the pivot table shown in figure 10.2. To create the same pivot table using VBA, follow these steps:

1. Activate the sheet named Fig10.2, and delete the pivot table.

2. Activate the sheet named Fig10.1, and select any cell in the data range.

3. Choose <u>T</u>ools, <u>M</u>acro, select Fig2Macro from the list box, and choose <u>R</u>un.

Do you see how much more quickly the pivot table is created? No matter how much more data there might be in the sheet named Fig10.1, the pivot table adjusts to capture it. The individual columns can be in any order, so long as they are contiguous. Given that the raw data range has columns named Warehouse, Description, Product Line, and Extended Cost, the pivot table will be created in exactly the same way every time the macro is run.

Tip

Inventory levels can get out of control surprisingly quickly. It's not unusual to perform this sort of analysis several times a month, and that makes it particularly important to arrange for the easy, fast creation of the pivot table. You can't do it more easily or faster than by using a VBA subroutine.

The VBA macro named Fig2Macro is discussed line by line in the next section.

Using VBA to Build a Pivot Table

The VBA code used to create the inventory pivot table in the previous section is shown here, along with explanations of selected VBA statements

```
Option Explicit
```

This statement requires that any variables (such as InRange, in the code after the next tip) be declared specifically in the VBA code. If Option Explicit were omitted, VBA would enable you to declare variables on the fly—that is, you could suddenly refer to a new variable in the middle of the code, without formally declaring it first. In a sense, Option Explicit imposes an inconvenience on you, because it requires you to declare all variables that your code uses.

Suppose that you want to use a variable named *Chrysanthemum*. It is just barely possible that at some point in your code, you might misspell this variable name as *Chrysanthamum*. Without the presence of the Option Explicit statement, VBA would assume that the misspelled version of the name constitutes a new variable. Then, you would be working with two variables, not just one, and the results of your code would almost certainly be wrong.

Then, the subroutine itself is declared

```
Sub Fig2Macro()
```

and the screen is frozen, to make execution faster

```
Application.ScreenUpdating = False
Dim InRange As Range
```

> **Tip**
>
> `Application.ScreenUpdating` is the equivalent of =ECHO() in the Excel version 4 macro language.

InRange is declared as an object: specifically, a range object that will serve as the input data for the pivot table

```
Selection.CurrentRegion.Select
Set InRange = Selection
```

These two statements first direct Excel to expand the current selection from one cell within the range of input data to all contiguous and filled rows and columns. Then, the variable InRange is assigned, with the Set statement, to represent the selection. This makes the coding easier: it's both quicker and more easily traced and debugged to refer to the worksheet range as InRange than as, for example, [Chap10.xls]Fig10.1!A1:G41.

> **Tip**
>
> Notice the use of the := operator in the ActiveSheet.PivotTableWizard statement. In VBA, this is used to assign a value to a named argument, such as SourceType. Do not confuse it with Pascal's assignment operator or with VBA's normal equals-sign assignment operator.

```
ActiveSheet.PivotTableWizard SourceType:=xlDatabase, SourceData:= _
    InRange, TableDestination:="[Chap10.xls]Fig10.2!R3C1", _
    TableName:="PivotTable1"
```

This statement establishes the pivot table. By specifying that the SourceType is an xlDatabase, it in effect completes Step 1 of the PivotTable Wizard. By specifying that the SourceData is InRange, it completes Step 2 of the Wizard.

The specification of the TableDestination includes the name of the destination workbook (Chap10.xls), the name of the sheet that the table is to occupy (Fig10.2), and the cell where the table is to start (R3C1, or row 3 and column 1).

Recall from Chapter 7, "Understanding Pivot Tables," that a Page field requires two additional rows at the top of a pivot table. This example employs a Page field. Notice that the TableDestination specification calls for the table to begin in row 3. This leaves room for the Page field above it. However, Excel is capable of shifting the table down two rows, if necessary to make room for the Page field, if the specification had instead been R1C1.

Tip

Establishing a Page field that represents different product lines makes it easier to see what's happening to your inventory levels.

The TableName specification provides a name for the table, just as you can name it in Step 4 of the PivotTable Wizard. This name is particularly useful if you intend to display more pivot tables whose sources are this pivot table. As VBA subsequently builds the remaining tables, you can use this name as their data source

```
With ActiveSheet.PivotTables("PivotTable1")
```

The With statement establishes an object for subsequent references to methods or properties. By using the statement immediately above, you can use a subsidiary object, or method or property, without having to repeat what the object belongs to. For example, one way to make False the Visible property of three pivot field items would be to use these three statements

```
ActiveSheet.PivotTables("PivotTable1").PivotFields("Description")
➡.PivotItems("Crossover Cable").Visible = False
ActiveSheet.PivotTables("PivotTable1").PivotFields("Description")
➡.PivotItems("Din connector").Visible = False
ActiveSheet.PivotTables("PivotTable1").PivotFields("Description")
➡.PivotItems("DROM").Visible = False
```

But by using the With statement, you can imply that subsequent objects, methods or properties belong to the object cited in the With statement. For example, these statements accomplish the same tasks as the above three statements

```
With ActiveSheet.PivotTables("PivotTable1")
    With .PivotFields("Description")
        .PivotItems("Crossover Cable").Visible = False
        .PivotItems("Din connector").Visible = False
        .PivotItems("DROM").Visible = False
```

It requires an additional two statements to do the same thing, but the five statements are much more legible and actually execute faster than the three fully qualified statements. Because there are actually nine, not just three, items to hide, the code will be briefer using the With syntax.

Notice, by the way, the use of the nested With statements. The PivotItems objects belong to the PivotFields object, which in turn belongs to the PivotTables object. Why not use just one With statement, instead of nesting them? Because this With statement

```
With ActiveSheet.PivotTables("PivotTable1").PivotFields("Description")
```

requires that all objects, methods, and properties inside the With block must belong to the PivotFields object. By using the nested With statements, the code can refer first to the inner With's PivotFields object; then, the inner With can be terminated and the outer With continues with statements that refer to its PivotTables object.

To continue with the VBA code

```
With ActiveSheet.PivotTables("PivotTable1")
    With .PivotFields("Description")
        .PivotItems("Crossover Cable").Visible = False
        .PivotItems("Din connector").Visible = False
        .PivotItems("DROM").Visible = False
        .PivotItems("ISDN adapter").Visible = False
        .PivotItems("Power supply").Visible = False
        .PivotItems("PROM").Visible = False
        .PivotItems("RJ11").Visible = False
        .PivotItems("RS232").Visible = False
        .PivotItems("Straight Through Cable").Visible = False
    End With
```

This block of statements hides all the specified items in the row field, just as you did by setting the field's options when you created the pivot table manually. Notice the End With statement, which terminates the inner instance of the two nested With statements. The outer With is still in effect, as shown by the next statement

```
    .AddFields RowFields:="Description", ColumnFields:="Warehouse",
    PageFields:="Product line"
```

The AddFields specification is a method that belongs to the PivotTables object. Because the outer With, which specifies the PivotTables object, is still in effect, AddFields is taken to refer to that object. The statement specifies that the Description variable is to be the Row field, the Warehouse variable is to be the Column field, and the Product Line is to be the Page field.

The next With block, which is again nested within the outer With block for the PivotTables object establishes Extended Cost as the pivot table's data field. It also sets the data field's number format to currency, using a dollar sign, a thousands separator, and two decimals

```
With .PivotFields("Extended Cost")
     .Orientation = xlDataField
     .NumberFormat = "$#,##0.00"
End With
```

Tip

If you use Last In, First Out (LIFO) or First In, First Out (FIFO) as your method of inventory valuation, you should certainly create pivot tables that show not only extended cost but unit cost as well. See Que's *Business Analysis with Excel* for information on how to use Excel to calculate both LIFO and FIFO.

The next statement, End With, finally terminates the outer With statement. Then, the pivot table is sorted by means of these two statements

```
Cells(5, 4).Select
Selection.Sort Key1:="R5C4", Order1:=xlAscending, Type:= _
     xlSortValues, OrderCustom:=1, Orientation:=xlTopToBottom
```

The cell defined by the intersection of the fifth row and the fourth column is selected, so that the Sort method can find the appropriate range to sort.

Lastly, the screen updates are turned on again

```
Application.ScreenUpdating = True
End Sub
```

Pivot Tables

II

Bypassing Query

Many of the same considerations apply when you create a pivot table using an external data source. But here the issues have twice the impact, because when you manually create a pivot table that's based on an external source, you must set both your pivot table options and your Query options (see Chapter 8, "Placing Business Data into Pivot Tables").

When you use the PivotTable Wizard to create a pivot table from an external source, you have no choice: you must use Microsoft Query to set up the database tables, define the selection criteria, and specify which fields you want to return to Excel. Further, you need to choose the ODBC driver to use for the database you want to query.

Using VBA, you can bypass all this. VBA provides a way to set up the SQL queries directly, so that you need not go through Query to access and return the data.

Case Study: Employee Location

As the Sales Manager of a small firm, you want to keep tabs on what cities your sales staff are located in, as well as how many staff are located in each city. You routinely query your firm's Access database, which contains information on all its employees—including, among other information, the city where the employee is located and the employee's title. From this data, you build a pivot table with a row field with one item for each city, and a data field that shows the count of employees in the city.

> **Tip**
>
> If your database contained information on market size in a given city, you might want to follow this analysis by creating an XY chart using market size as one variable and number of employees in the city as the other variable. This would help you to determine whether your staff is deployed to best advantage.

It happens that all sales staff have titles that begin with the letter "S," such as Sales Representative and Sales Manager. No other employee's title begins with an "S," so when you retrieve the data from the Access database you specify that only records whose value on the Title field begins with an "S" are to be returned.

Rather than querying the database and creating the pivot table manually each time you want to view where your sales staff are located, you create a VBA macro that automatically extracts the data and displays it in a pivot table.

The following is an example of VBA code that shows how this analysis might be done

```
Sub Fig3Macro()
ActiveSheet.PivotTableWizard SourceType:=xlExternal, SourceData:= _
    Array("DSN=MS Access 7.0
➡Database;DBQ=C:\staff.mdb;DefaultDir=C:\;DriverId=25;FIL=MS
Access;UID=admin;", _
    "SELECT Employees.Title, Employees.City " _
    & "FROM Employees WHERE (Employees.Title Like 'S%')"), _
    TableDestination:="R1C1", TableName:="PivotTable1"
ActiveSheet.PivotTables("PivotTable1").AddFields RowFields:="City"
ActiveSheet.PivotTables("PivotTable1").PivotFields("Title").Orientation
➡= xlDataField
End Sub
```

This simple subroutine speeds things up considerably. It results in the pivot table shown in figure 10.3.

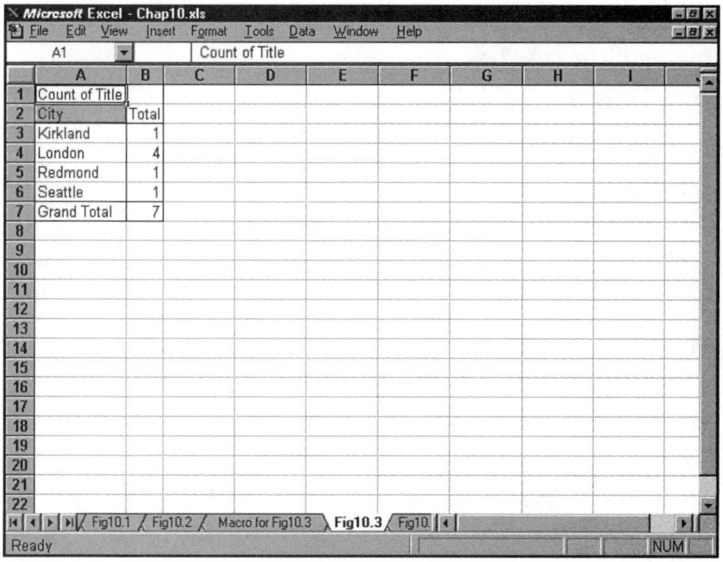

Fig. 10.3
A convenient way of counting observations in a control field is to specify a non-numeric variable as the data field.

> **Note**
>
> The counts of employees per city, in the pivot table shown in figure 10.3, are created by the PivotTable Wizard, not by the SQL query to the database.

Once you have created the macro, you can repeat exactly the same database query and create a pivot table that differs only in its data—not in its structure—whenever you want to repeat the analysis. Merely open the workbook that contains the macro, select or insert a fresh worksheet, and use <u>T</u>ools, <u>M</u>acros to choose and run the VBA code.

From the point of view of obtaining the data from an external source, the second line in the previous code is the critical statement. The SourceData argument consists of an array of two strings, a connecting string and a query string. The first string is

```
"DSN=MS Access 7.0
Database;DBQ=C:\staff.mdb;DefaultDir=C:\;DriverId=25;FIL=MS
Access;UID=admin;",
```

This connecting string defines such items as the data source name (DSN: here, it's an Access 7.0 database) and the user ID (UID: here, admin, or the database administrator).

The second, or query, string in the array defines which fields to use and the criterion that returned records must meet

```
"SELECT Employees.Title, Employees.City FROM Employees Employees
➥WHERE (Employees.Title Like 'S%')"),
```

This string defines the query that is submitted to the database. The query defines:

- Which fields to return to Excel, by means of the SELECT; here, these are the employee's Title and the City where the employee is located.
- Which table in the database to retrieve records from, by means of the FROM; here, the table is named Employees.
- Which records to retrieve, by means of the WHERE; here, only those records where the Title begins with the letter "S."

When you extract the information from the database manually, Microsoft Query constructs these strings on your behalf. It uses your responses to the dialog boxes that appear when you specify an external data source to the PivotTable Wizard. As you saw in Chapter 8, Query displays the names of the fields in the database, any selection criteria that you include, and the actual values in the fields. This relieves you of the need to know the field names and the values that the selection criteria apply to.

The trade-off is that you must start Query to get that information on your screen. But if you are familiar with the structure of the external database then you can name the fields in the query string, and set the criteria properly. For example, suppose you wanted to return the employee's first name, last name and date of birth, and to obtain only those records where the employee is not located in London; you could modify the query string as follows

```
"SELECT Employees.BirthDate, Employees.FirstName,
➥Employees.LastName FROM `C:\staff`.Employees " _
    & "Employees WHERE (Employees.City<>'London')"
```

Of course, to use VBA to bypass the Query screen, you need to know that these fields in the Employee table of the staff database are named BirthDate, FirstName, LastName, and City, and that one of the possible values for City is "London."

To take advantage of VBA in returning data to a pivot table, it's best to record a VBA macro as you go through the PivotTable Wizard and Query. This way, Excel records the VBA statements that will reproduce the actions you take, and you can subsequently edit those statements to achieve a different result more quickly.

You will seldom want to edit the first, connecting string in the array, because that is the one that establishes the connection between Excel and a particular database. The database type and its disk location are not invariant, but neither do they change frequently. You could, of course, edit the name of the database and its location if necessary.

To record a VBA macro that creates a pivot table from external data, and that you can subsequently edit, follow these steps:

1. Activate a worksheet where you want the table to appear.

2. Choose <u>T</u>ools, <u>R</u>ecord Macro, and select <u>R</u>ecord New Macro from the cascading menu.

3. Modify the default macro name if you wish, and choose OK. A new module sheet is added to the active workbook, and the Stop Recording toolbar button appears in the toolbar area.

4. Create the pivot table, choosing an external data source and using Query as described in Chapter 8.

5. When the pivot table is complete, click the Stop Recording button. The button is removed from the toolbar area.

6. Activate the new module sheet. It will contain the VBA code needed to replicate the pivot table that you just created. You can edit the code to make changes that will create a pivot table with different fields, based on different record selection criteria, located in a different range or worksheet, or representing any other modification that you wish to make.

Bypassing the PivotTable Wizard

As easy as it is to use the PivotTable Wizard, you can make it even easier by anticipating and restricting what the user is able to do.

Suppose you want to make it possible for a colleague who is unfamiliar with pivot tables to create one. You want to automate the creation of the pivot table enough so that it's not necessary to use the PivotTable Wizard or Query. But you also want to enable the user to control which fields are shown, as well as their orientation in the pivot table. Figures 10.4 and 10.5 show an example of how you might go about doing this.

Fig. 10.4
Clicking the Show Field Names worksheet button places the list boxes on the worksheet.

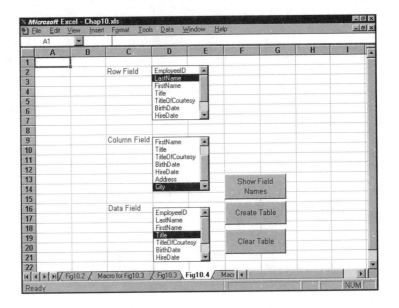

When the user first activates the sheet named Fig10.4 in the file named Chap10.xls on the companion disk, the sheet contains only the three worksheet buttons. Clicking the Show Field Names button causes the VBA macro named CreateListBoxes to run. This macro, detailed in proceeding paragraphs, places three list boxes on the worksheet: one for the user to identify a row field, one for a column field, and one for a data field.

The user highlights one field in each list box and then clicks the Create Table button. This causes the VBA macro named CreatePivotTable to run, taking the user's specifications as to fields and using them to create the pivot table. Figure 10.5 shows the result.

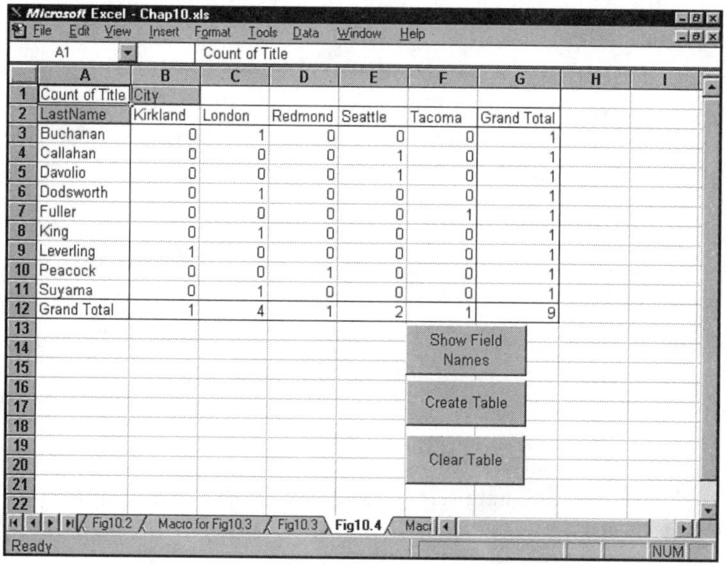

Fig. 10.5
Clicking the Create Table button removes the list boxes and creates the pivot table.

After viewing the pivot table, the user can click the Clear Table button to remove the pivot table from the sheet.

Here is the VBA code for the CreateListBoxes macro

```
Option Base 1
```

The first statement, Option Base 1, is actually not part of the subroutine itself. It establishes 1 as the base of any array declared on the module sheet. Without this statement, the base of arrays would be zero. It's much easier to understand the code if the first element in an array is referred to as, for example, ArrayName(1) than as ArrayName(0)

```
Sub CreateListBoxes()
Dim FieldArray As Variant
Dim i As Integer, j As Integer
```

These three statements declare the subroutine itself, and declare the existence of three variables: FieldArray, i, and j. The latter two variables are just counters that are used to control the initiation and termination of For-Next loops. FieldArray is used as an array that contains all the field names that will be accessible to the pivot table

```
Application.ScreenUpdating = False
ActiveSheet.ListBoxes.Add(144, 13.2, 76, 69).Select
ActiveSheet.ListBoxes.Add(144, 106.2, 76, 69).Select
ActiveSheet.ListBoxes.Add(144, 198, 76, 69).Select
```

The first of these four statements simply freezes the screen, to cause the macro to execute faster. The latter three statements each create a list box. The four numeric arguments in each statement establish the list box's distance from the left side of the cell A1 (144 in each case), its distance from the top of cell A1 (13.2, 106.2 and 198), its width (76) and its height (69). These numbers all represent 72nds of an inch (one *point*).

The next statement

```
FieldArray = Array("EmployeeID", "LastName", "FirstName", "Title",
➡ "TitleOfCourtesy", "BirthDate", "HireDate", "Address", "City")
```

assigns nine values to the variant FieldArray. These values are the names of the fields found in the data source. The field names will be placed in the list boxes, for the user to choose from.

Three list boxes have been placed on the worksheet, and FieldArray has been populated with the nine field names. The next block of code cycles through the three list boxes by means of the control variable j in a For-Next loop

```
For j = 1 To 3

   For i = 1 To 9
      ActiveSheet.ListBoxes(j).AddItem Text:=FieldArray(i)
   Next i

Next j
```

Each time the outer loop executes, the inner loop adds nine items to the current list box from the FieldArray variable. This populates the list boxes.

Next, labels are added to the list boxes

```
ActiveSheet.ListBoxes(1).TopLeftCell.Offset(0, -1).Value =
➡"Row Field"
ActiveSheet.ListBoxes(2).TopLeftCell.Offset(0, -1).Value =
➡"Column Field"
ActiveSheet.ListBoxes(3).TopLeftCell.Offset(0, -1).Value =
➡"Data Field"
```

Each ListBox object has a TopLeftCell property, which identifies the worksheet cell that is under the upper-left corner of the list box. The first of the preceding three statements puts the label "Row Field" in the cell that is offset by zero rows and one column left of the first list box's top-left cell. The second and third statements add labels to the second and third list boxes.

These labels might not fit in their columns, so the next statement auto-fits the column width in order that each label fully appear within the column

```
ActiveSheet.Columns(ActiveSheet.ListBoxes(3).TopLeftCell.Offset
➡(0, -1).Column).AutoFit
```

Finally, cell A1 is selected, the screen is unfrozen, and the subroutine is terminated

```
Cells(1, 1).Select
Application.ScreenUpdating = True
End Sub
```

The worksheet now appears as was shown earlier in figure 10.4. The user selects a field name from the first list box; this field will be the pivot table's row field. Field names are also selected from the second and third list boxes to establish a column field and a data field for the pivot table.

To create a worksheet button and assign VBA code to it, follow these steps:

1. Enter the VBA code on a module sheet, or choose Tools, Record Macro, Record New Macro to establish the VBA code.

2. Activate the worksheet where you want the button to appear.

3. Choose View, Toolbars. In the Toolbars list box, check the Drawing toolbar item, and choose OK.

4. The Drawing toolbar appears. Click the Create Button button. Your mouse pointer changes to crosshairs. Hold the mouse button down and drag in the worksheet to establish the button's size and location. Release the mouse button.

5. The Assign Macro dialog box appears as shown in figure 10.6.

6. Choose the name of the macro that you want to assign to the button in the Macro Name/Reference list box, and choose OK.

7. To label the button, drag across its default label to highlight it, type a new label, and click somewhere on the worksheet outside the button.

Fig. 10.6

You can also start by creating the worksheet button and then recording a new macro from the Assign Macro dialog box.

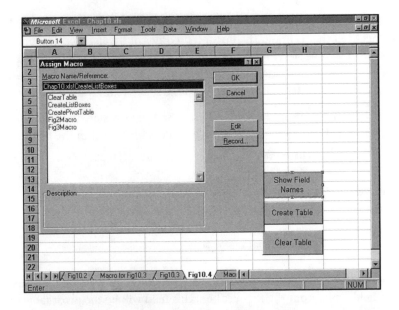

After putting the list boxes on the worksheet, the user clicks the Create Table button, which causes the CreatePivotTable macro to execute.

The code for the CreatePivotTable macro is shown in the following example. The first five statements are similar to statements at the beginning of the CreateListBoxes macro

```
Sub CreatePivotTable()
Dim RowField As String, ColumnField As String, DataField As String
Dim FieldArray As Variant
Dim i As Integer
Application.ScreenUpdating = False
FieldArray = Array("EmployeeID", "LastName", "FirstName", "Title",
➥ "TitleOfCourtesy", "BirthDate", "HireDate", "Address", "City")
```

The subroutine is declared, as are some necessary variables, the screen is frozen, and the variant FieldArray is populated.

The next block of code checks to make sure the user has chosen a field name in each list box. For each list box, the code checks if the list box's value is zero, which indicates that no choice has been made. If a list box value is zero, a message is displayed, requesting that a choice be made from each list box, and the subroutine is terminated. Otherwise, if a list box value is nonzero, processing continues normally

```
For i = 1 To 3
   If ActiveSheet.ListBoxes(i).Value = 0 Then
      MsgBox Prompt:="Please select one field from each list box",
➥Buttons:=vbOKOnly, Title:="Missing field"
      End
   End If
Next i
```

Then, the new variables RowField, ColumnField, and DataField are assigned their values according to which field name the user has chosen from each list box

```
RowField = FieldArray(ActiveSheet.ListBoxes(1).Value)
ColumnField = FieldArray(ActiveSheet.ListBoxes(2).Value)
DataField = FieldArray(ActiveSheet.ListBoxes(3).Value)
```

Consider the first of these three statements. The user's choice in the first list box on the worksheet identifies the pivot table's row field. The list box has a value: the number of the item in the list box that the user chooses. The list box was populated with the values of FieldArray. So, if the user chooses the second item in the list box, that is the same field name as the second item in FieldArray. The second item in FieldArray is "LastName," so the variable RowField takes on the value "LastName." The values of ColumnField and DataField are assigned in the same fashion.

Then, the code clears the label, such as "Row Field," that was placed next to each list box

```
ActiveSheet.ListBoxes(1).TopLeftCell.Offset(0, -1).Clear
ActiveSheet.ListBoxes(2).TopLeftCell.Offset(0, -1).Clear
ActiveSheet.ListBoxes(3).TopLeftCell.Offset(0, -1).Clear
```

A For-Next loop deletes the list boxes from the worksheet

```
For i = 1 To 3
   ActiveSheet.ListBoxes(1).Delete
Next i
```

Notice that the index of the ListBoxes is constant. Each time the loop executes, a list box is deleted, and what had been the second list box becomes the first list box. Therefore, each time the loop executes, it deletes what is currently the first list box on the active sheet.

Now, the code makes use of the values in the variables RowField, ColumnField, and DataField. In the two-string array used by the PivotTableWizard method, the actual variable names are replaced by the

Pivot Tables

variables that contain the names. Notice that the only fields retrieved from
the database are the ones specified by the user by means of the list boxes

```
ActiveSheet.PivotTableWizard SourceType:=xlExternal, SourceData:= _
    Array("DSN=MS Access 7.0
Database;DBQ=C:\staff.mdb;DefaultDir=C:\;DriverId=25;FIL=MS
Access;UID=admin;", _
    "SELECT    Employees." & RowField & ", Employees." & ColumnField
& ", Employees." & DataField & " " _
    & "FROM Employees Employees "), _
    TableDestination:="R1C1", TableName:="PivotTable1"
```

Then, the pivot table's control fields are assigned

```
ActiveSheet.PivotTables("PivotTable1").AddFields
RowFields:=RowField, ColumnFields:=ColumnField
```

and the data field is assigned

```
ActiveSheet.PivotTables("PivotTable1").PivotFields(DataField).Orientation
➡= xlDataField
```

The pivot table has now been created on the worksheet. It remains to un-
freeze the screen, and end the subroutine

```
Application.ScreenUpdating = True
End Sub
```

The worksheet's third button, Clear Table, is assigned to this code

```
Sub ClearTable()
Application.ScreenUpdating = False
ActiveSheet.PivotTables(1).TableRange2.Columns.ColumnWidth =
➡ActiveSheet.StandardWidth
ActiveSheet.PivotTables(1).TableRange2.Clear
Application.ScreenUpdating = True
End Sub
```

There are two statements in this subroutine that might as yet be unfamiliar.
Its third statement makes use of the TableRange2 property of a pivot table.
This property is the range occupied by a pivot table, including cells that are
occupied by any page fields. (There is another property, TableRange1, that returns the range occupied by a table exclusive of any page fields.) The statement identifies the columns occupied by TableRange2, and sets their width
to the active sheet's standard column width. The statement is necessary because the columns might have been widened by the pivot table, moving the
worksheet buttons off the screen.

The fourth statement in the subroutine merely clears the range occupied by
the pivot table.

The chapters in this book on pivot tables have repeatedly mentioned the
drawbacks to refreshing pivot tables. Code such as the subroutines described

just now can also be used to rebuild pivot tables quickly from scratch. In this way, you can avoid the problems associated with refreshing pivot tables, and yet retain the convenience of recalculating a pivot table by just clicking a button.

> **Note**
>
> The three macros described in this section are intended as *examples* of how you can use VBA code to ease the creation of pivot tables for a user. They are not intended as production versions, and various checks would have to be included to protect against runtime errors.
>
> For example, you would want to check that the user did not choose the same variable as both the row field and the column field. You might want to disable the second and third worksheet buttons until the first one is pressed, and the first and third buttons until the second is pressed. You would want to check that a pivot table did not already exist on the worksheet at the time that CreatePivotTable is run. There are many more such error checks that you would want to build into the code, most of them dependent on the particular approach that you want to use.

Chapter Summary

This chapter has explored the use of VBA to make the creation of pivot tables quicker, and easier for those new to the PivotTable Wizard. You have learned how to bypass the Wizard entirely by selecting its options through VBA statements, and how to bypass Microsoft Query by creating the necessary connecting string and query string. You have also learned how to use VBA to populate list boxes to give the user some control over what is otherwise a completely automatic process.

The next chapter, "Analyzing Pivot Tables," concludes the section on pivot tables. An entire branch of statistical analysis pertains to the use of contingency tables—the statistical term for pivot tables. You will learn how to make inferences about the relationships among a pivot table's fields.

Pivot Tables

11

Analyzing Pivot Tables

This book concerns itself principally with the management of data by means of Excel, so a chapter on analyzing pivot tables—as distinct from managing them—may seem out of place at first.

But there's little reason to manage data in the first place if you're not going to do anything with it. And pivot tables offer some unique methods of analysis that business enterprises use far too seldom, mostly because they don't realize that the tools are at their disposal. The intent of this chapter is to draw them to your attention.

As discussed in Chapter 7, "Understanding Pivot Tables," it's normal for the control fields in a pivot table to be discrete variables. Examples include variables such as region, product, terms of sale, and attributes such as defective versus non-defective. In contrast, data fields are often continuous variables such as revenue, profit, and product preference measures.

But there are many instances when two or more discrete control variables combine in a pivot table to describe a discrete data field. Excel offers many methods to analyze the relationships between and among continuous variables. Examples include functions that support regression analysis such as CORREL, LINEST and TREND, chart types such as XY (Scatter), and Analysis ToolPak add-ins such as ANOVA and Regression.

But suppose you're a sales director who is monitoring the success versus the failure of sales proposals. You have a count of the number of successful and unsuccessful proposals in each of your four sales territories. Is there a way you can determine whether the differences in success rates in the territories are reliable?

You can't use, for example, CORREL or LINEST. What are the two numeric variables that you would use as arguments to CORREL? What are the numeric variables that constitute the x-values or the y-values required by LINEST?

You could graph the results on a bar or column chart, where the x-axis represented territory and the y-axis represented the number or percent of successful sales proposals. But, while useful and informative, such a chart tells you nothing about the *reliability* of the differences in success rate. Put differently, the chart tells you nothing about whether the sales territories have some characteristic—the quality and experience of their sales managers, perhaps, or the demographics of the territories—that is associated with differences in sales success.

Tip

Particularly from a cost standpoint, the analysis of success rates (or "hit rates"), is an important management activity. Virtually every sales proposal entails both staff and material costs. Serious attempts to target sales efforts at high-probability prospects are usually well rewarded.

To put this problem in context, suppose you also have information about the amount of revenue earned from each successful sale in the same four territories. In this case, you could compute the average revenue earned by each territory, and compare the territories on that basis. Excel tools such as the ANOVA add-in would return information about the reliability of differences among the territories as measured by average sales revenue.

But average sales revenue addresses a different issue than sales proposal hit rate. A territory might have a relatively high average revenue, due perhaps to one hugely successful sales representative or one customer with very deep pockets, but a relatively low success rate for its sales proposals.

How can you analyze proposal success as a function of sales territory? Read on.

Understanding Contingency Analysis

The first approach that might occur to you when confronted with a situation similar to the success rate problem is to create a pivot table. Figure 11.1 shows data on proposal success by territory, along with a table that summarizes the information.

Fig. 11.1
Glancing at the simple counts reported in the pivot table tells you that you might have a problem in the Northwest region.

	A	B	C	D	E	F	G
1	**Region**	**Proposal**		Count of Proposal	Proposal		
2	Southeast	Successful		Region	Successful	Unsuccessful	Grand Total
3	Northwest	Unsuccessful		Northeast	5	8	13
4	Northwest	Unsuccessful		Northwest	17	46	63
5	Southeast	Unsuccessful		Southeast	20	15	35
6	Northwest	Unsuccessful		Southwest	20	19	39
7	Northwest	Unsuccessful		Grand Total	62	88	150
8	Southeast	Unsuccessful					
9	Northwest	Unsuccessful					
10	Southeast	Successful					
11	Northwest	Unsuccessful					
12	Southwest	Unsuccessful					
13	Southeast	Unsuccessful					
14	Northeast	Successful					
15	Southwest	Successful					
16	Northwest	Unsuccessful					
17	Southwest	Unsuccessful					
18	Southwest	Unsuccessful					
19	Northeast	Successful					
20	Northwest	Unsuccessful					
21	Southwest	Unsuccessful					
22	Southwest	Successful					

You create this table by following these steps:

1. Activate the sheet named Fig11.1,2,3 in the file Chap11.xls from the companion disk.

On the Disk

2. Select any cell in the range A1:B151.

3. Choose Data, PivotTable. The PivotTable Wizard starts.

4. In the Wizard's first Step, choose Microsoft Excel List or Database.

5. In the second Step, accept the default worksheet range.

6. In the third Step, drag the Proposal button into the Column area and into the Data area. Drag the Region button into the Row area.

7. In the fourth Step, enter **D1** as the Pivot Table Starting Cell, and choose Finish.

Tip

In Step 3 of the Wizard, dragging the same discrete variable into a control area and into the Data area is a simple way to get a count of observations for each cell in the pivot table.

The Northwest is a sore thumb. That region has generated more proposals than any of the other three (63), but it seems to have relatively few successes. It's easier to see this with percentages, so you change the representation of the Data area from Count to Percent of Total, by means of these steps:

II

Pivot Tables

1. Highlight any cell in the Data area of the pivot table.

2. Choose Data, PivotTable Field, and click Options in the PivotTable Field dialog box.

3. In the Show Data As drop-down list, choose % of Row, and choose OK.

This converts the raw counts in each table cell to percent of the total row count. The results are shown in figure 11.2.

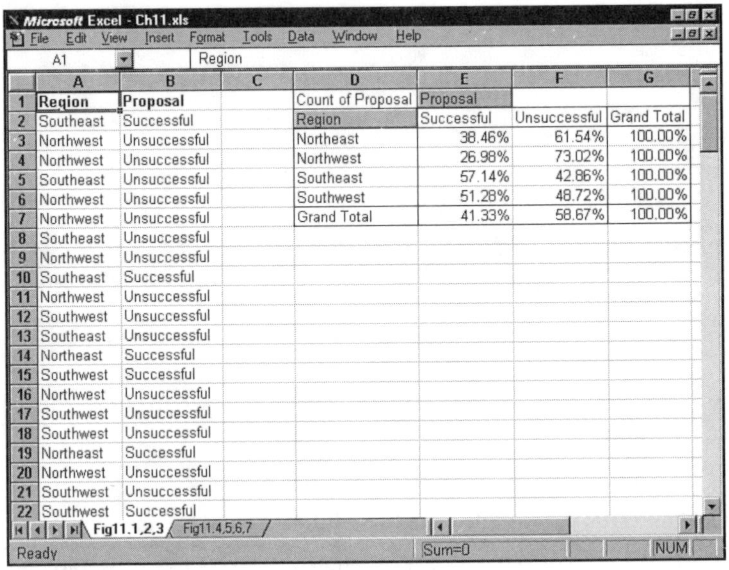

Fig. 11.2
Representing the pivot table's data area as percent of each row confirms your initial impression that the Northwest is in trouble.

It's illuminating to see that in the Northwest, over 73% of proposals have been unsuccessful. The largest percent of unsuccessful proposals in other regions is less than 62%, in the Northeast.

This kind of analysis is sometimes termed *contingency analysis*, and the layout of the pivot table, whether it contains counts or percents, is referred to as a *contingency table*. The question that it addresses is whether the counts of one variable are contingent on another variable. In this example, it appears that success rate is contingent on which region a sales representative belongs to. If you were in sales for this company, you'd much rather stay out of Oregon.

But should you really reach this conclusion? Isn't it possible that the observations in the pivot table are just a random event—that the Northwest region just had a bad month or quarter? Surely it's possible, and you should want to test the notion that there's some degree of association, or contingency, between the region and the success rate of proposals.

At its heart, this is a question of whether the observed cell counts depart very far from the expected cell counts, and it's in calculating the expected cell counts that the pivot table's Index item comes into play (see fig. 11.3).

Original data set

Pivot table showing index of proposals

Pivot table showing count of proposals

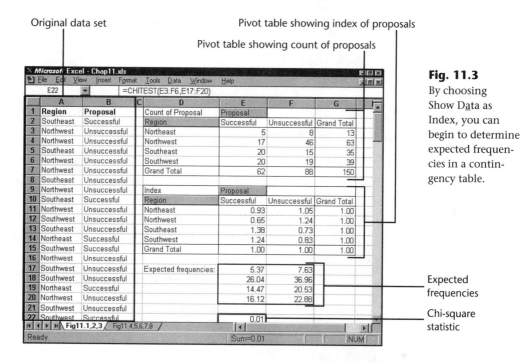

Fig. 11.3
By choosing Show Data as Index, you can begin to determine expected frequencies in a contingency table.

Expected frequencies

Chi-square statistic

To create the pivot table shown in cells D9:G15 of figure 11.3, follow these steps:

1. Change the pivot table shown in figures 11.1 and 11.2 from % of Row back to a Normal representation in its data field.

2. Create a new pivot table as described for figure 11.1, but, in Step 3 of the PivotTable Wizard, choose to Show Data as Index.

Each entry in the second pivot table, shown in cells D9:G15 of figure 11.3, is identical to the result of this formula

```
Index = (Cell Frequency × Total Frequency) / (Row Frequency ×
Column Frequency)
```

In the case of the first row, first column, where Region equals Northeast and Proposal equals Successful, this is

```
.93 = (5 × 150) / (13 × 62)
```

Not very informative as yet, but examine cells E17:F20 in figure 11.3. These cells contain this array formula

```
=E3:F6/E11:F14
```

So, the value in cell E17 is the result of dividing the value in cell E3 by the value in cell E11

```
5.37 = 5 / .93
```

5.37 is the *expected* cell frequency for successful proposals in the Northeast region. It is how you would allocate the total number of proposals for the Northeast region according to how all proposals divide in terms of success versus failure. Described in numbers

```
5.37 = 13 × (62 / 150)
```

Described in words, take the ratio of all successful proposals to all proposals, 62/150, and apply it to the number of proposals in the Northeast region. The result is the number of successful proposals you would expect in the Northeast, if their distribution across all regions applied to the Northeast.

The ratio of all successful proposals to all unsuccessful proposals is 62/88, or 70.5%. This is also the result of dividing the expected number of successful proposals in any region by the expected number of unsuccessful proposals for that region. For example, this formula

```
5.37 / 7.63 = 70.5%
```

is for the Northeast, and this

```
26.04 / 36.96 = 70.5%
```

is for the Northwest, and similarly for the Southeast and Southwest regions.

If the division of all proposals between successful and unsuccessful applied regardless of region, then there would be *no* relationship—no association, no contingency—between region and proposal success. This is what is meant by *expected* frequency.

Excel provides a worksheet function, CHITEST, that takes two ranges as arguments: a range of actual, observed frequencies and a range of expected frequencies. CHITEST returns the probability of observing the actual frequencies under the assumption that the expected frequencies represents the true state of nature. In this case, the value shown in cell E22 of figure 11.3 is returned by

```
=CHITEST(E3:F6,E26:F29)
```

The result of the function is .01. Suppose there is no relationship between sales region and proposal success rate. Further, assume that you gathered information on sales proposals—the region in which they originated, and their eventual success or lack thereof—100 times. The value returned by CHITEST, .01 in this case, means that only once in those 100 occasions would you see a difference between observed and expected frequencies as large as this one.

> **Tip**
>
> If you want to know the actual value of the chi-square test statistic in addition to it's probability level, use the CHIINV function. If the CHIDIST function is in cell A1, use =CHIINV(A1,df) where df is (Rows in table – 1) × (Columns in table – 1).

There are two possibilities:

- You have, by chance, observed the one time in 100 that you would see a difference between observed and expected frequencies this large, when there is no relationship between region and success rate.

- There *is* a relationship between region and success rate, in which case the data you obtained might be typical rather than atypical.

It's more rational to assume that there *is* a relationship than it is to assume that you have observed a highly unlikely event. And, reasoning back to the beginning of this discussion, it follows that there is something special about the regions that is associated with differences in success rates.

But be careful: It does not necessarily follow that it's your regional sales management that causes the observed differences among the regions (although that's one possibility). Nor does it necessarily follow that the relationship between region and success rate is a causal one. It's conceivable that you could change sales management in the Northwest to no effect. Perhaps the Northwest has considerably more competition for your potential customers than other regions. Perhaps you have one particularly persistent sales representative in that region who keeps hearing "No" from a prospect but won't take it for an answer.

Whatever the reason, this kind of analysis suggests that there's probably something dependable going on between region and success rate for proposals. If, as sales director, you believe that it bears further investigation, you can investigate confidently, instead of worrying that what you observed is a random phenomenon.

II

Pivot Tables

Understanding Log-Linear Basics

The analysis discussed in the previous section is the traditional way of analyzing contingency tables, has a long and honorable history, and is quite useful. However, it doesn't provide as much information as one would wish.

A more recent technique ("recent" is relative: the method became popular in the mid- to late-1970s) is *log-linear* analysis. The intent of this method is to extend ideas about regression analysis to contingency tables.

If you are familiar with regression analysis, you know that the approach involves developing an equation that best describes the relationship between one or more predictor variables and a predicted variable. The equation is often written in this form

$$y = mx + b$$

where y is the predicted variable, x is the predictor variable, m is a coefficient for the predictor variable (you can think of it as the slope of the line on a chart that graphs the x-values against the y-values), and b is a constant that describes the overall elevation of that regression line. If there is more than one predictor variable, the equation would be written as

$$y = m_1 x_1 + m_2 x_2 + b$$

Note

You may be more familiar with these forms of the equation

$$y = a + bx$$

for a single predictor, or

$$y = a + b_1 x_1 + b_2 x_2 ...$$

for multiple predictors. Excel manuals and help files employ the convention that *b* represents the intercept, *m* represents the coefficient, and *x*, as usual, represents the predictor variable.

So, if you were trying to predict revenue earned by knowledge of advertising expenditures (x_1) and unit price (x_2), you might use regression analysis to solve for m_1, m_2 and b. This might enable you to maximize revenues by optimizing advertising expenses and unit price.

Often, in regression analysis, there is no relationship between a predictor variable and a predicted variable. In that case, the coefficient of the predictor variable is not significantly different from zero: changes in the predictor itself have no, or little, impact on the predicted variable.

The idea behind log-linear analysis is to apply this way of thinking to situations where the predicted variable is not a continuous one such as revenue, but a discrete one such as the count of events or things in a contingency table.

By using log-linear analysis, you develop an equation that is analogous to a regression equation. The predictor variables (in Excel's terminology, the "x" variables) are membership in one level or another of a row or column variable. The size of each predictor variable's coefficient gives you a sense of its influence on the count of observations in a contingency table.

Suppose you are analyzing the results of a market trial, during which you have placed an advertisement both in a magazine and a newspaper. You want to know whether one medium—magazine or newspaper—was more effective than another in catching consumers' eyes.

You arrange for several focus groups, where subscribers to either the magazine or the newspaper, but not both, are asked whether they recognize the advertisement. The results of these interviews are shown in figure 11.4.

If you were to perform a traditional chi-square analysis on these findings, as was done in the previous section, you would obtain the results shown in figure 11.5.

The value returned by the CHITEST function, .10, is not statistically significant according to conventional criteria. Fully 10 times out of a hundred you would expect differences between observed and expected observations as large as this one, even if there's no relationship between the control variables. But a different picture emerges from a log-linear analysis.

Fig. 11.4
Your advertisement was apparently more effective in magazines than in newspapers.

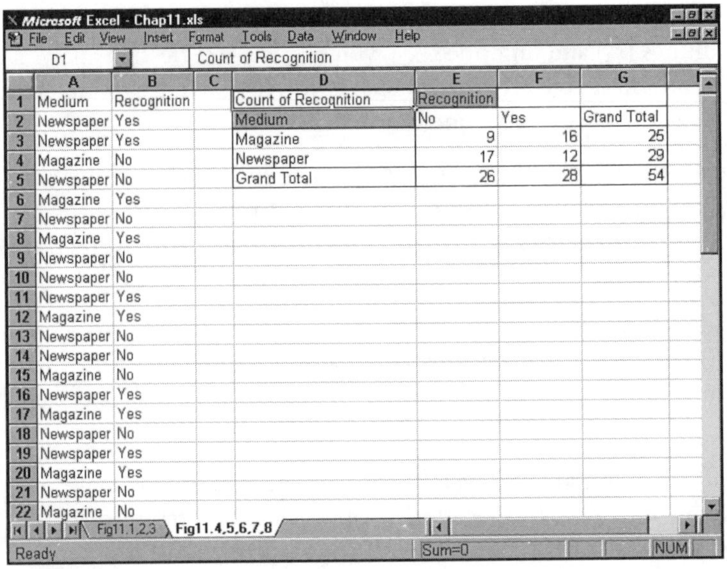

Fig. 11.5
The difference between observed and expected frequencies is not significant at conventional levels.

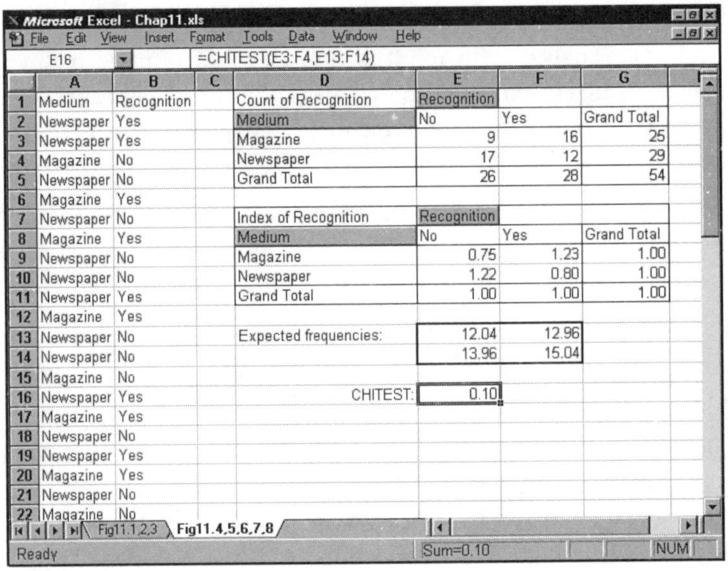

There are some basic calculations, not too intuitive, that form the basis of log-linear analysis. Six values are required in this case:

- The geometric mean of the table. The geometric mean is the root of the product of the frequencies in the table's cells. The geometric mean of a six-cell table is the sixth root of the product of the six frequencies. This value is analogous to the constant in a regression equation.

- A factor for each level of each control variable: thus, in this case, four factors. In log-linear analysis these are termed *taus*. They are analogous to the coefficients of the variables in a regression equation.

- A factor for the interaction, or the combined effect, of the two control variables. This is also termed a tau.

Excel provides a worksheet function, GEOMEAN, that returns the geometric mean. The remaining values must be calculated with formulas, shown in figure 11.6.

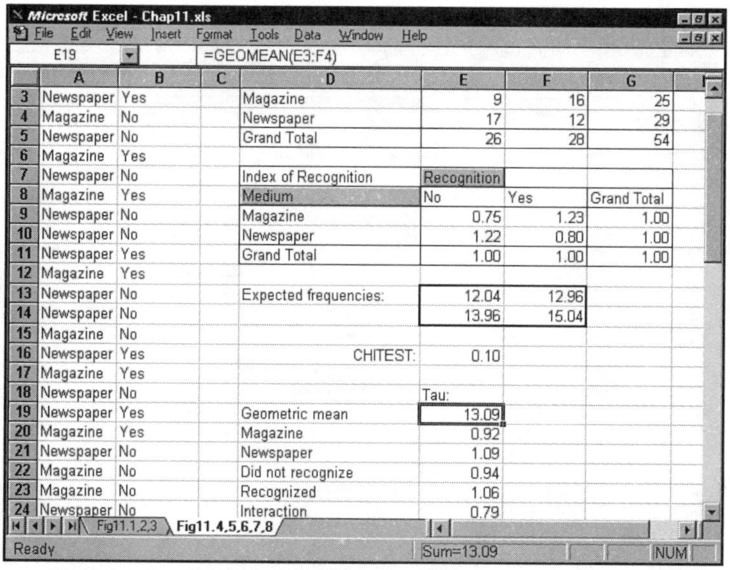

Fig. 11.6
Each level of a control variable in a pivot table has a tau associated with it.

The geometric mean in cell E19 of figure 11.6 is returned by

```
=GEOMEAN(E3:F4)
```

The tau for the Magazine value of Medium, in cell E20, is

```
=SQRT(E3*F3)/E19
```

That is, the square root of the product of those who did not recognize the magazine advertisement and those who did, divided by the geometric mean.

The tau for the Newspaper value of Medium, in cell E21, is

```
=1/E20
```

This is simply the reciprocal of the tau for Magazine.

The tau for those who did not recognize the advertisement, in cell E22, is

```
=SQRT(E3*E4)/E19
```

and for those who did recognize it

```
=1/E22
```

Finally, the tau for the interaction of Medium and Recognition is

```
=((E3*F4)/(F3*E4))^0.25
```

That is, the fourth root of the ratio of the cross-products of the frequencies.

It's worth noting that you can use the geometric mean with the taus to perfectly replicate the original cell frequencies. The calculations are shown in cells E26:F27 of figure 11.7.

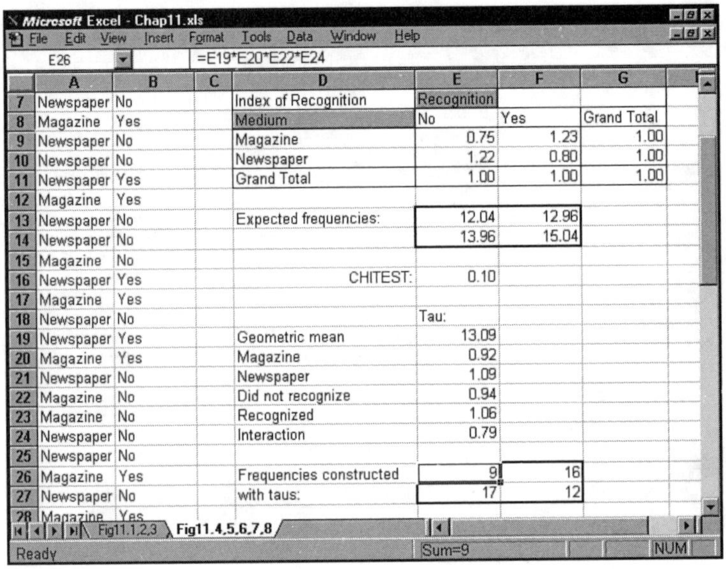

	A	B	C	D	E	F	G
7	Newspaper	No		Index of Recognition	Recognition		
8	Magazine	Yes		Medium	No	Yes	Grand Total
9	Newspaper	No		Magazine	0.75	1.23	1.00
10	Newspaper	No		Newspaper	1.22	0.80	1.00
11	Newspaper	Yes		Grand Total	1.00	1.00	1.00
12	Magazine	Yes					
13	Newspaper	No		Expected frequencies:	12.04	12.96	
14	Newspaper	No			13.96	15.04	
15	Magazine	No					
16	Newspaper	Yes		CHITEST:	0.10		
17	Magazine	Yes					
18	Newspaper	No			Tau:		
19	Newspaper	Yes		Geometric mean	13.09		
20	Magazine	Yes		Magazine	0.92		
21	Newspaper	No		Newspaper	1.09		
22	Magazine	No		Did not recognize	0.94		
23	Magazine	No		Recognized	1.06		
24	Newspaper	No		Interaction	0.79		
25	Newspaper	No					
26	Magazine	Yes		Frequencies constructed	9	16	
27	Newspaper	No		with taus:	17	12	
28	Magazine	Yes					

Fig. 11.7
The products of the geometric mean and the appropriate taus replicate the original cell frequencies.

The formula in cell E26 of figure 11.7, for example, is

```
=E19*E20*E22*E24
```

That is, the geometric mean, times the tau for Magazine, times the tau for No Recognition, times the tau for the interaction, returns the exact frequency of those who read the magazine and did not recognize the advertisement.

As it happens, it's more convenient to work with the logarithms of the geometric mean and the taus. Converting these values to logarithms means that they can be added rather than multiplied, and a standard error can be derived for each of them. (The standard errors are analogous to the standard errors of regression coefficients and intercepts.) This is the basis for the term *log-linear*: the logs are added to produce a linear equation.

The logs of the geometric mean and of the taus and are shown in cells E37:E42 of figure 11.8. Each is just the natural logarithm of the original value. For example, cell E37 contains

```
=LN(E19)
```

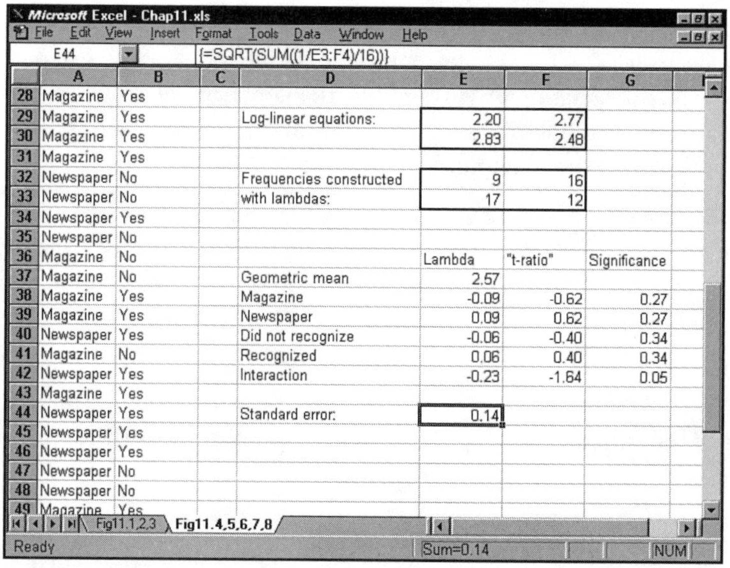

Fig. 11.8

Converting taus to lambdas by taking logarithms results in a regression-like equation to predict cell frequencies.

When they are converted to logarithms, the taus are referred to as *lambdas*— the Greek letter "L," standing for logarithm.

Once converted to lambdas, they can be summed in this manner

```
=E37+E38+E40+E42
```

which is the formula shown in cell E29 of figure 11.8. It is analogous to a regression equation: The sum of the log associated with the geometric mean, the log of the tau for Magazine, the log of the tau for No recognition, and the log of the tau for the interaction.

Taking the anti-log of that sum

```
=EXP(E29)
```

returns 9 in cell E32. And 9 is the number of respondents who did not recognize the advertisement from the magazine.

Now, compute the standard error of the lambdas. In contrast to standard regression analysis, there is only one standard error for all the lambdas. It is returned by this formula, shown in cell E44 of figure 11.8

```
=SQRT(SUM((1/E3:F4)/16))
```

It's entered as an array formula. E3:F4 contain the original cell frequencies, and the divisor, 16, is the square of the number of cells in the table. In other words, the standard error is the square root of the sum of the reciprocals of the frequencies, divided by the square of the number of cells.

At last, you're in a position to analyze the individual and joint effects of the medium for the advertisement and whether or not people recognize it. If a lambda is truly zero, it has a nearly normal distribution, with a mean of zero and a standard deviation of 1. Therefore, the lambdas can be divided by their standard error to return a statistic that is similar to a t-ratio. This statistic can then be tested by the Excel function NORMSDIST.

In figure 11.8, the ratios are shown in cells F38:F42, and their statistical significance levels are shown in G38:G42. It's not usual to test the log of the geometric mean, since it's just a representation of the overall count, and ordinarily not of interest.

What is of interest is the significance of the lambdas, since they express how far a level of a control variable departs from its expected value. The significance of the lambda in cell E38, for example, is returned by this formula in cell G38

```
=1-NORMSDIST(ABS(F38))
```

The value in F38 is the ratio of the lambda to its standard error. The ABS function, which returns the absolute value of its argument, is used because some ratios are negative, due to the effect of obtaining the logarithm of a fraction. NORMSDIST returns the cumulative probability of a standardized value. Because it returns the cumulative density of the normal curve, rather than a point estimate, it is subtracted from 1.

The result is the likelihood of observing a lambda this large under the assumption that its value in the population is zero. Of course, a lambda of zero would mean that the associated category has no effect on the cell frequency beyond its expected value. Recall that the lambdas are added together in the log-linear equation, so a lambda of zero implies that there is no effect associated with that category.

The lambdas for the individual control variables are not significantly different from zero. However, the lambda for the interaction is significant at the .05 level, a conventional criterion for deciding that an effect is significant. This means that although the individual effects of medium and recognition are not significant, their *joint* effect is.

If you plan an advertising campaign subsequent to the market trial, you can assume with some confidence that your advertisements should go into the magazine rather than the newspaper, because your focus group participants disproportionately recognized the advertisement from the magazine rather than from the newspaper. The log-linear analysis suggests that this is a dependable finding.

Notice, by the way, that the log-linear analysis returned a statistically significant result, while the traditional chi-square test did not. This is because the log-linear tests are more sensitive than the chi-square test—in statistical parlance, the chi-square test is less powerful.

Keep the title of this section, "Understanding Log-Linear Basics," firmly in mind. Only the very fundamental aspects of this sort of analysis have been discussed here. You can use the procedures outlined above on a two-by-two table, but things start to get much more complex when you have a table with more dimensions, or when there are more than two levels to your control variables. And things become extremely complex when you start to deal with log-linear models that drop some terms out of the log-linear equation. Nevertheless, the basic principles remain the same, and Excel provides the capabilities to deal with these more complex models.

Chapter Summary

In this chapter you have learned how to apply techniques of statistical inference to situations where the dependent variable is a count of cases. Pivot tables are an ideal tool for developing contingency tables, which can be further analyzed by means of traditional chi-square tests, and the more recently developed family of log-linear techniques.

This chapter concludes the section on Excel's pivot tables. The next section on scenario management describes how you can create and use a completely different approach to retrieving and summarizing data—one in which you can arrange for other users to participate.

Pivot Tables

Part III

Scenario Management

12

Understanding Business Scenarios

The Scenario Manager is a tool that supports data management by storing, retrieving, and displaying different assumptions about inputs to a model. The model often describes marketing, financial, or budgeting processes, but it need not be restricted to business applications. Any model that employs data and formulas to return results can be built, tested, and tuned by means of the Scenario Manager.

Scenario management can be complex, although once you understand how its tools work it is remarkably easy. This chapter provides an introduction to scenarios and guides you through examples of their use. Chapters 13 through 16 detail the options available to you at each step.

Using Scenarios

You use scenarios to describe the effect of changing different input assumptions on outcomes that you're interested in. The input assumptions are related to the outcomes by formulas that you create. The inputs, and their results, are stored by Excel so that you can easily display them and cycle through different assumptions to view their effects.

Each set of assumptions and outcomes is termed a *scenario*. Figures 12.1 and 12.2 show an example.

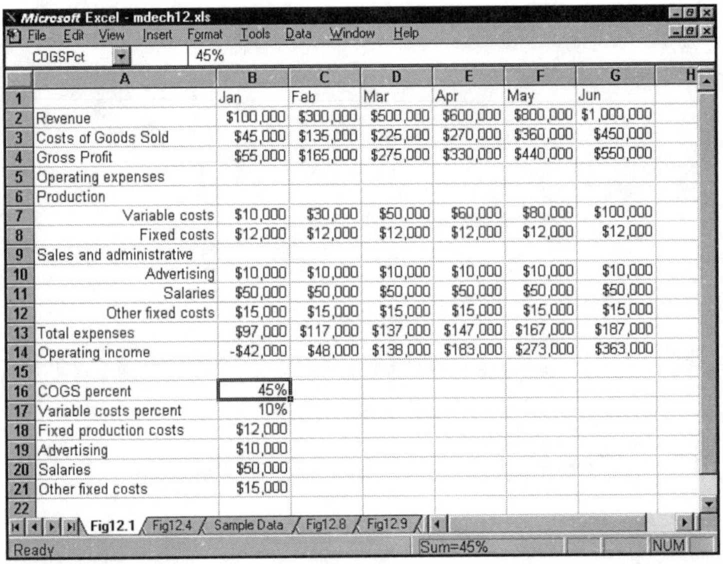

Fig. 12.1

This scenario shows optimistic assumptions as to Revenue for a marketing program.

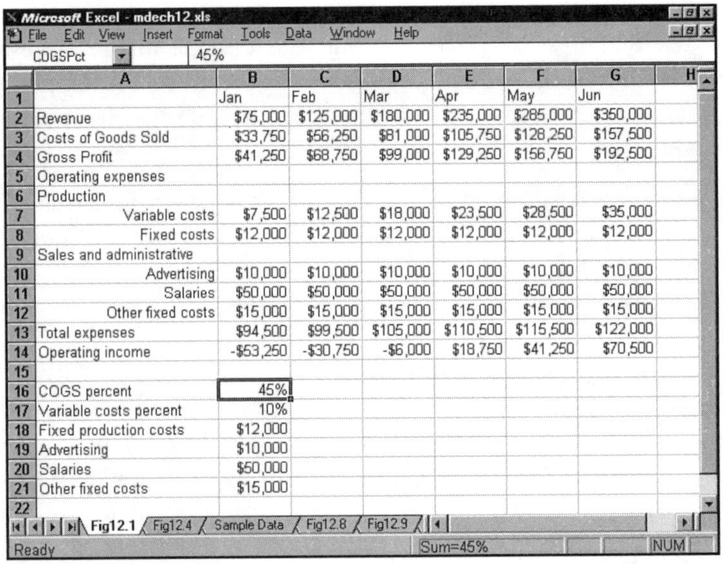

	A	B	C	D	E	F	G	H
		Jan	Feb	Mar	Apr	May	Jun	
1		Jan	Feb	Mar	Apr	May	Jun	
2	Revenue	$100,000	$300,000	$500,000	$600,000	$800,000	$1,000,000	
3	Costs of Goods Sold	$45,000	$135,000	$225,000	$270,000	$360,000	$450,000	
4	Gross Profit	$55,000	$165,000	$275,000	$330,000	$440,000	$550,000	
5	Operating expenses							
6	Production							
7	Variable costs	$10,000	$30,000	$50,000	$60,000	$80,000	$100,000	
8	Fixed costs	$12,000	$12,000	$12,000	$12,000	$12,000	$12,000	
9	Sales and administrative							
10	Advertising	$10,000	$10,000	$10,000	$10,000	$10,000	$10,000	
11	Salaries	$50,000	$50,000	$50,000	$50,000	$50,000	$50,000	
12	Other fixed costs	$15,000	$15,000	$15,000	$15,000	$15,000	$15,000	
13	Total expenses	$97,000	$117,000	$137,000	$147,000	$167,000	$187,000	
14	Operating income	-$42,000	$48,000	$138,000	$183,000	$273,000	$363,000	
15								
16	COGS percent	45%						
17	Variable costs percent	10%						
18	Fixed production costs	$12,000						
19	Advertising	$10,000						
20	Salaries	$50,000						
21	Other fixed costs	$15,000						
22								

COGSPct   45%

Fig12.1 / Fig12.4 / Sample Data / Fig12.8 / Fig12.9

Ready   Sum=45%   NUM

Fig. 12.2

This scenario shows best guess assumptions as to Revenue for the same marketing program.

	A	B	C	D	E	F	G	H
		Jan	Feb	Mar	Apr	May	Jun	
1		Jan	Feb	Mar	Apr	May	Jun	
2	Revenue	$75,000	$125,000	$180,000	$235,000	$285,000	$350,000	
3	Costs of Goods Sold	$33,750	$56,250	$81,000	$105,750	$128,250	$157,500	
4	Gross Profit	$41,250	$68,750	$99,000	$129,250	$156,750	$192,500	
5	Operating expenses							
6	Production							
7	Variable costs	$7,500	$12,500	$18,000	$23,500	$28,500	$35,000	
8	Fixed costs	$12,000	$12,000	$12,000	$12,000	$12,000	$12,000	
9	Sales and administrative							
10	Advertising	$10,000	$10,000	$10,000	$10,000	$10,000	$10,000	
11	Salaries	$50,000	$50,000	$50,000	$50,000	$50,000	$50,000	
12	Other fixed costs	$15,000	$15,000	$15,000	$15,000	$15,000	$15,000	
13	Total expenses	$94,500	$99,500	$105,000	$110,500	$115,500	$122,000	
14	Operating income	-$53,250	-$30,750	-$6,000	$18,750	$41,250	$70,500	
15								
16	COGS percent	45%						
17	Variable costs percent	10%						
18	Fixed production costs	$12,000						
19	Advertising	$10,000						
20	Salaries	$50,000						
21	Other fixed costs	$15,000						
22								

COGSPct   45%

Fig12.1 / Fig12.4 / Sample Data / Fig12.8 / Fig12.9

Ready   Sum=45%   NUM

On the Disk

You can find these scenarios in the file named Chap12.xls on the companion disk, on the worksheet named Fig12.1. The scenario shown in figure 12.1 is named *Revenue: Optimistic,* and the scenario shown in figure 12.2 is named *Revenue: Best Guess.*

To view the scenarios, follow these steps:

1. Open the file Chap12.xls, and make sure that sheet Fig12.1 is active.

2. Select Tools, Scenarios. The Scenario Manager dialog box appears. See figure 12.3. Because two scenarios have already been defined for this worksheet, you see their names in the Scenarios list box.

3. In the Scenario Manager dialog box, select one of the scenario names in the Scenarios list box. The name that is highlighted when you start the Scenario Manager is the one whose data is displayed when you activate the sheet named Fig12.1.

4. Choose Show to display the scenario's values on the worksheet.

5. Choose Close.

Fig. 12.3

The Scenario Manager dialog box lets you choose a scenario, and manage other options for that scenario.

Notice how easy it is to view the results of different assumptions about revenue. As you toggle between the two scenarios, optimistic and best guess revenue assumptions are placed in cells B2:G2 of the worksheet. The formulas in the worksheet that depend on B2:G2 change accordingly, resulting in higher or lower operating income for the January through June periods.

Because certain cells in a scenario contain different values in different scenarios, they are termed *changing cells*—they have the same designation in other Excel tools, such as Goal Seek and the Solver. The chapters on scenario management in this book use the terms *input assumptions* (which better describes the purpose that the user has for them) and *changing cells* (which better describes how Excel treats them) synonymously.

Using the Scenario Manager, you do not need to store the different assumptions about revenue in worksheet cells. They are stored in the Scenario Manager, out of the way of the worksheet and its calculations.

III

Scenario Management

Modifying Assumptions

You can change or add to the assumptions that form the basis of a scenario. For example, to change the value of January's revenue in the Revenue: Best Guess scenario from $75,000 to $80,000, follow these steps:

1. Select Tools, Scenarios.

2. Choose Revenue: Best Guess from the Scenario Manager's list box.

3. Click Edit.

4. In the Edit Scenario dialog box, choose OK.

5. In the Scenario Values dialog box, type 80000 in edit box 1 (labeled $B$2).

6. Choose Show in the Scenario Manager dialog box, and choose Close.

Notice that a line is added in the Comment box in the Scenario Manager dialog box, indicating that you modified the scenario on today's date. This helps you track changes that have been made to the scenario.

As a result of changing the revenue assumption for January from $75,000 to $80,000, the operating income for January changes from a negative $53,250 to a negative $51,000.

Summarizing Scenarios

Although toggling back and forth between different scenarios is a handy way to manage different sets of input assumptions, it's not ideal for viewing the effects of different inputs simultaneously.

The Scenario Manager provides two different ways of summarizing all the scenarios that you have created: a summary report and a pivot table. Chapter 13 describes these options in greater detail; for now, follow these steps to create a summary report:

1. Choose Tools, Scenarios.

2. Click Summary. The Scenario Summary dialog box appears.

3. Choose the Scenario Summary option button.

4. Click in the Result Cells edit box and on the worksheet highlight cells B14:G14.

5. Choose OK.

When the Scenario Manager finishes processing the summary, a new worksheet that appears as shown in figure 12.4 is added to your workbook. By default, Excel names this new worksheet Scenario Summary. For convenience in reference, the worksheet name has been changed to Fig 12.4.

	A	B	C	D	E	F
1	Scenario Summary					
2			Current Values:	Revenue: Optimistic	Revenue: Best Guess	
4	Changing Cells:					
5		$B$2	$75,000	$100,000	$75,000	
6		$C$2	$125,000	$300,000	$125,000	
7		$D$2	$180,000	$500,000	$180,000	
8		$E$2	$235,000	$600,000	$235,000	
9		$F$2	$285,000	$800,000	$285,000	
10		$G$2	$350,000	$1,000,000	$350,000	
11		COGSPct	45%	45%	45%	
12		VarCosts	10%	10%	10%	
13		FixedCosts	$12,000	$12,000	$12,000	
14		AdvExpense	$10,000	$10,000	$10,000	
15		Salaries	$50,000	$50,000	$50,000	
16		OtherFixed	$15,000	$15,000	$15,000	
17	Result Cells:					
18		$B$14	-$53,250	-$42,000	-$53,250	
19		$C$14	-$30,750	$48,000	-$30,750	
20		$D$14	-$6,000	$138,000	-$6,000	
21		$E$14	$18,750	$183,000	$18,750	

Fig. 12.4

The Scenario Summary displays information about the changing cells and result cells for each scenario in the worksheet.

This summary worksheet details the input assumptions for each scenario (labeled "Changing Cells" on the worksheet) as well as the scenario's result cells.

By using both the Scenario Manager dialog box and the Scenario Summary, you can view the details of the scenario in your preferred format for the worksheet model, as well as the differences among the scenarios in a summary format.

Tip

If you prefer not to deal with the outline symbols above and to the left of the worksheet area, choose Tools, Options and click the View tab. Then, clear the Outline Symbols checkbox.

Creating Scenarios

There are many ways of creating a new scenario (see chapters 13 and 14 for details), but the most straightforward is to create it from existing worksheet cells. Here's how to create the scenarios shown in figure 12.1 and 12.2. Begin by opening the file on the companion disk named Chap12.xls, if you haven't done so already, and activating the worksheet named Sample Data. Then, follow these steps:

On the Disk

III

Scenario Management

1. Choose <u>T</u>ools, S<u>c</u>enarios. The Scenario Manager dialog box appears, as shown in figure 12.5.

Tip

Scenarios belong to worksheets, not directly to workbooks. The worksheet named Sample Data initially has no scenarios defined. Therefore, the Scenarios list box contains no scenario names, even though the workbook has several scenarios saved with it.

Fig. 12.5
Preparing to add a scenario to a worksheet.

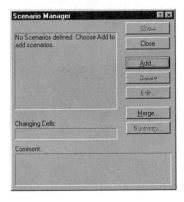

2. In the Scenario Manager dialog box, click <u>A</u>dd. The Add Scenario dialog box appears as shown in figure 12.6.

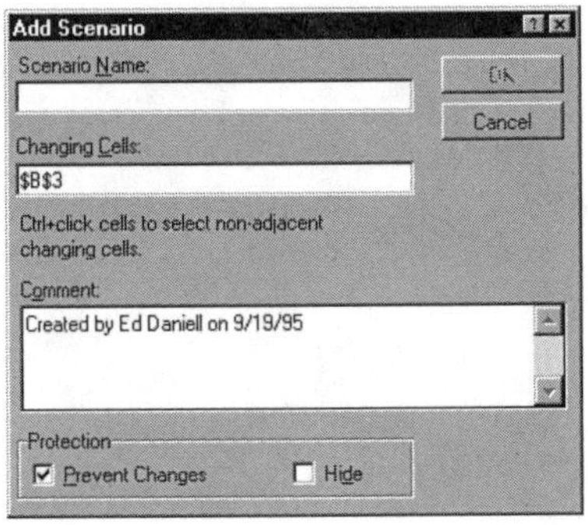

Fig. 12.6
The OK button in the Add Scenario dialog box is disabled until you enter a name for the scenario.

3. Type a name for the scenario in the Scenario <u>N</u>ame edit box.

4. Click in the Changing <u>C</u>ells edit box, and drag across whatever address is showing there. Then, highlight cells B2:G2 on the worksheet. You

will see the address of this range of cells, as an absolute reference, in the Changing Cells edit box.

Tip

You can move a dialog box around the screen so that it doesn't hide cells that you need to see. Using your mouse pointer, drag the dialog box by its title bar.

---

5. Hold down the Ctrl key. While you are holding it down, highlight cells B16:B21. The address of this range, again as an absolute reference, appears in the Changing Cells edit box after the reference to B2:G2. The two range addresses are separated by a comma, indicating that you have made a multiple selection.

6. Set the scenario's Protection properties as you wish. These properties are discussed in Chapter 13. To set them as they are for the scenarios shown in figures 12.1 and 12.2, clear both checkboxes.

7. Click OK. The Scenario Values dialog box appears as shown in figure 12.7. Because the Scenario Manager uses values that are already in the worksheet for the initial values of the changing cells, you do not need to modify or enter any values in these boxes—although you can do so if you wish.

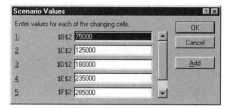

Fig. 12.7
Use the scroll bar to the right of the changing cell edit boxes to display more changing cells.

8. Choose OK. When you do so, the Scenario Manager dialog box appears again. At this point, you can add another scenario, show the scenario, select another option such as editing or deleting a scenario, or end the scenario management process for the time being.

9. To end the process, choose Close.

You can now retrieve the data in the scenario you just added at any time. Choose Tools, Scenarios, select the name of the scenario in the Scenario Manager's Scenarios list box, and choose Show.

III

Scenario Management

When you close the Scenario Manager, the data that appear on your worksheet might or might not conform to the data in the scenario that you added. Unless you chose Show before closing the Scenario Manager, the data on your worksheet is *not* the scenario's data, although it might be identical to the scenario.

This distinction is easiest to make if, while the Scenario Values dialog box is active in step 7, previously, you modify the value of one of the changing cells. Then, when the Scenario Manager dialog box reappears in step 8:

- If you click Show, the changed value of the cell you modified appears on the worksheet.

- If you do not click Show, the changed value of the cell you modified does not appear in the worksheet, but it is part of the scenario all the same.

Changing Cells

The main point of creating a scenario is to modify its input assumptions—its changing cells—to determine and document the effect of changing the inputs on the results of the model. There are many reasons for doing this sort of analysis. Among them:

- To quantify the result of one particularly critical assumption.

- To quantify the *range* of likely outcomes, given a range of values for a critical assumption (this is often termed *sensitivity analysis*).

- To determine which assumptions have the greatest impact on the result.

- To group changing cells into categories of inputs: for example, so as to give different individuals on a planning team responsibility for different portions of the model.

Case Study: A Marketing Model

For example, consider the marketing model presented in this chapter, and repeated for convenience in figure 12.8.

The model uses the *percentage of sales* approach to building a business model: that is, many of the variables in the model are expressed as a percentage of the sales revenue for each month. The Cost of Goods Sold, for example, is calculated in cells B3:G3 by means of this formula:

```
=COGSPct*Revenue
```

COGSPct (short for Cost of Goods Sold Percentage) is the name of cell B16. *Revenue* is the name of the range B2:G2. The formula takes advantage of

Excel's implicit intersection. In cell B2, COGSPct is multiplied by the value of the Revenue range in column B. Similarly, in cell C2, COGSPct is multiplied by the value of the Revenue range in column C. The intersection between the column where the formula exists (column B, C, D and so on) and the row where the range named Revenue exists (row 2) is *implicit* in the formula.

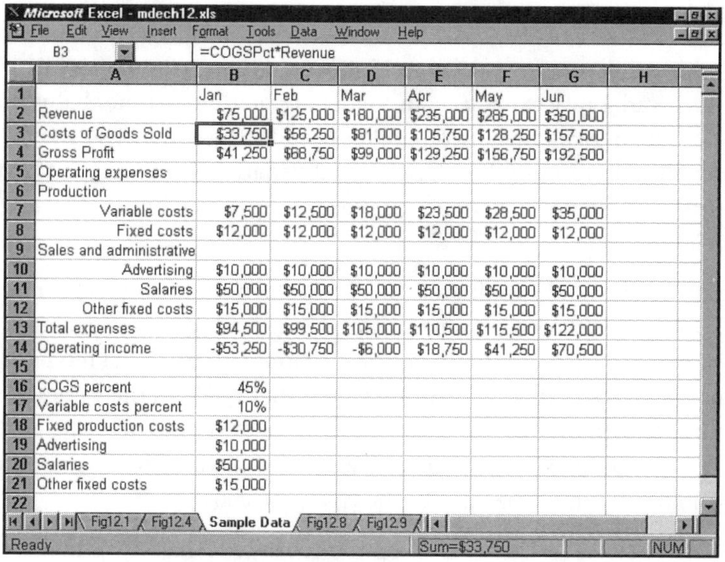

	A	B	C	D	E	F	G	H
1		Jan	Feb	Mar	Apr	May	Jun	
2	Revenue	$75,000	$125,000	$180,000	$235,000	$285,000	$350,000	
3	Costs of Goods Sold	$33,750	$56,250	$81,000	$105,750	$128,250	$157,500	
4	Gross Profit	$41,250	$68,750	$99,000	$129,250	$156,750	$192,500	
5	Operating expenses							
6	Production							
7	Variable costs	$7,500	$12,500	$18,000	$23,500	$28,500	$35,000	
8	Fixed costs	$12,000	$12,000	$12,000	$12,000	$12,000	$12,000	
9	Sales and administrative							
10	Advertising	$10,000	$10,000	$10,000	$10,000	$10,000	$10,000	
11	Salaries	$50,000	$50,000	$50,000	$50,000	$50,000	$50,000	
12	Other fixed costs	$15,000	$15,000	$15,000	$15,000	$15,000	$15,000	
13	Total expenses	$94,500	$99,500	$105,000	$110,500	$115,500	$122,000	
14	Operating income	-$53,250	-$30,750	-$6,000	$18,750	$41,250	$70,500	
15								
16	COGS percent	45%						
17	Variable costs percent	10%						
18	Fixed production costs	$12,000						
19	Advertising	$10,000						
20	Salaries	$50,000						
21	Other fixed costs	$15,000						
22								

Fig. 12.8
Variables such as Cost of Goods Sold depend both on monthly revenue and on the percentages in cells B16:B17.

In figure 12.8, the value of COGSPct is a particularly critical assumption. No matter the month, and no matter the amount of revenue, COGSPct takes its toll on the company's Gross Profit, and eventually on its operating income. Whatever percent is entered in cell B16 causes a reduction in its Gross Profit, and therefore B16 can be considered critical in this model.

In contrast, consider the fixed costs of production in cells B8:G8. These costs—items such as factory overhead—are constant regardless of how many product units are produced and sold. Their relative influence on operating income becomes weaker and weaker as more and more revenue is created. Although significant during the early months of the plan, fixed production costs become less so by June.

Therefore, in considering which cells constitute the most critical assumptions for the model, you would certainly include COGSPct, and you would tend to discount the fixed production costs. In terms of managing the scenario's changing cells, you would probably give more attention to the effect of modifying COGSPct and less to modifying the fixed production costs.

How would you go about managing COGSPct? Recall that cell B16 is one of the changing cells in the scenarios. You might survey different suppliers of the materials used in the production of your finished goods, and determine how much each would charge you to purchase a given amount of material. You would then create at least two scenarios: one that included the cost quoted by the least expensive supplier and one that included the quote from the most expensive supplier.

A scenario summary (refer to figure 12.4) would then conveniently display how much variability exists in your model's operating income that is due to choice of supplier. Significant variability would suggest that you should pay considerable attention to this choice; slight variation would suggest that you can focus your attention elsewhere in your effort to maximize operating income.

It might be that responsibility for the development of this model is not yours alone; rather, it is shared by a production manager and a sales manager. The three of you can each contribute to the development of a final model. The production manager might create a scenario that specifies the values for variable and fixed production costs; the sales manager might create another scenario that specifies the anticipated revenue; and you would retain the responsibility for the remainder of the changing cells.

The Scenario Manager provides an option to *merge* scenarios, so that your combined efforts can be presented in one scenario that is, presumably, the best-informed that can be created. Chapter 13, "Creating Business Scenarios," discusses this option in detail.

Viewing Scenarios

There are several ways to view scenarios, either those in the active worksheet or in another worksheet or workbook. Among the methods are:

- In the Scenario Manager dialog box, select a scenario from the Scenarios list box and choose Show.

- In the Scenario Manager dialog box, choose Summary to create a new worksheet with all scenarios displayed in report form, or to display result cells in pivot table form.

- From the WorkGroup toolbar, click the down arrow next to the scenarios drop-down box to display the available scenarios, and select one of them.

- In the Scenario Manager dialog box, choose Merge.

The first three of these four methods limit the available scenarios to those in the active *worksheet*. The fourth, making use of Merge, makes available all the scenarios in all active *workbooks*. You have already seen how to use the Show button on the Scenario Manager to display scenarios sequentially, and how to use the Summary button to combine scenarios in report form. The remainder of this chapter describes how to convert a scenario to a pivot table, how to use the WorkGroup toolbar and how to merge scenarios into the active worksheet.

Displaying a Scenario as a Pivot Table

A summary report of the scenarios in a worksheet is not interactive in the sense that a pivot table is. You can edit it, and if you choose to leave its outline symbols in place you can easily hide and display its details. However, you cannot drag controls or otherwise redefine it as you can a pivot table.

The Scenario Manager enables you to create pivot tables based on the scenarios on the active worksheet. They do not display as much information about the scenarios as does the summary report, but they are manipulated more easily. There are some special aspects to pivot tables created by means of the Scenario Manager that it's necessary to know:

- You cannot refresh the pivot table other than by rebuilding it. As was discussed in Chapter 7, this is hardly a drawback. It is almost always preferable to rebuild a pivot table and not to refresh it.

- If you select the pivot table and then invoke the PivotTable Wizard, you cannot back up before Step 3 of the Wizard.

- You define the pivot table's data field or fields by selecting them before creating the pivot table.

- The pivot table's row field consists of the names of the scenarios on the active sheet.

- The pivot table's page field consists of the names of users who have created scenarios on the active sheet.

These distinctions will become more clear in the remainder of this section.

To begin the process of creating a pivot table from scenarios, have active a worksheet that contains at least two scenarios. (It's possible but pointless to create a pivot table from one scenario only.) You could use the worksheet named Fig12.9 in the Chap12.xls file on the companion disk. Then, follow these steps:

On the Disk

1. Choose Tools, Scenarios. The Scenario Manager dialog box appears.

2. Choose Summary. The Scenario Summary dialog box appears. See figure 12.9.

Fig. 12.9
Use the Scenario Summary dialog box to choose the result cells that you want to display in either a summary report or in a pivot table.

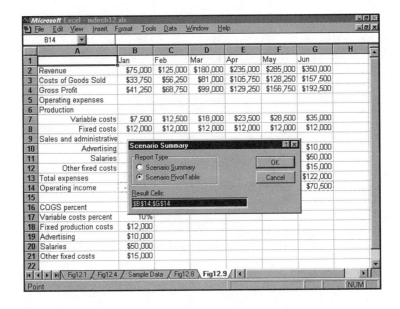

3. Select the Scenario <u>P</u>ivot Table option button.

4. Click in the <u>R</u>esult Cells edit box. Then, highlight cells B14:G14 on the worksheet.

5. Choose OK.

The pivot table shown in figure 12.10 appears on a new worksheet, named Scenario Pivot Table.

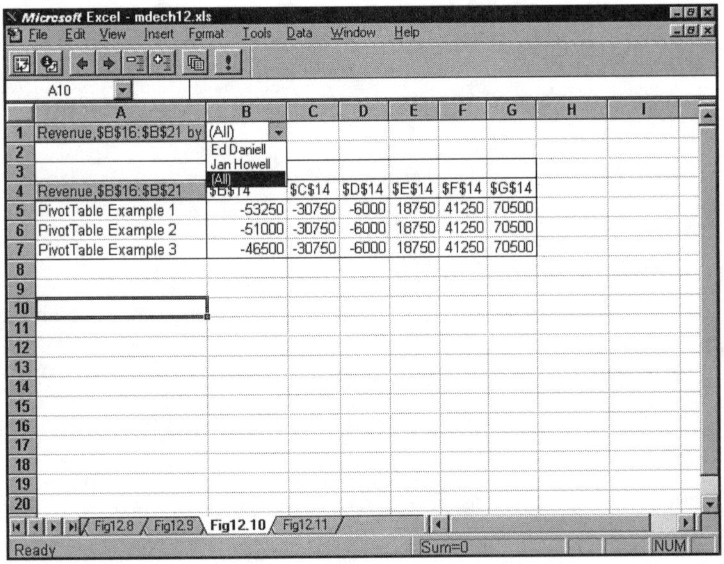

Fig. 12.10
By default, a scenario pivot table has a page field, a row field and at least one data field.

If, to create the pivot table, you used the worksheet Fig12.9 from the companion disk, you can find three different values in its page field. (They are shown in figure 12.10.) The values are Ed Daniell, Jan Howell and (All).

Recall that when you create or modify a scenario, the Scenario Manager stores your user name along with the scenario's values. For example, the Comment box in the Scenario Manager dialog box automatically adds comments such as "Created 9/15/95 by John Smith". When you create a pivot table based on the worksheet's scenarios, the Scenario Manager employs the user names that are associated with each scenario as values for the table's Page field.

If yours is the only user name associated with the scenarios on a given worksheet, then the Page field has only two values: your user name and (All). The usual way that other user names enter the scenarios on a worksheet is by means of the Merge button on the Scenario Manager dialog box.

> ### Tip
>
> You can change your user name by selecting Tools, Options and typing a new name in the User Name edit box on the General tab.

Also notice in figure 12.10 that the pivot table's row field consists of the scenarios on the worksheet, and is labeled by the names you assign them in the Scenario Manager.

The Data field, in cells B5:G7 of figure 12.10 consists of the values in cells B14:G14 for each scenario on the worksheet. These are the values in the result cells that you identified in step 4, above.

If, with a cell in the pivot table active, you select the Data menu, you will see that the Refresh Data option is disabled. This option (as well as the Refresh Data button on the Query and Pivot toolbar) is not available when the pivot table has been created by the Scenario Manager. Even if you modify the value of a changing cell via the Scenario Manager, you cannot refresh the table: you must rebuild it.

Notice also that if you start the PivotTable Wizard with a blank cell active, the Another PivotTable option is disabled. A new pivot table cannot be built using a data cache associated with the Scenario Manager's pivot table.

And if, with a cell in the pivot table active, you start the PivotTable Wizard, you will find that you cannot use the Back button to move the Wizard to Steps 1 or 2.

You can find more detailed information on these and related issues in Chapter 14, "Solving Business Scenarios."

Using the WorkGroup Toolbar

Especially if you have many scenarios defined for a worksheet, it can be inconvenient to have to use Tools, Scenarios to switch back and forth among scenarios so as to view them on the worksheet. A simpler approach involves using the WorkGroup toolbar.

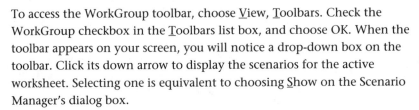

To access the WorkGroup toolbar, choose View, Toolbars. Check the WorkGroup checkbox in the Toolbars list box, and choose OK. When the toolbar appears on your screen, you will notice a drop-down box on the toolbar. Click its down arrow to display the scenarios for the active worksheet. Selecting one is equivalent to choosing Show on the Scenario Manager's dialog box.

If your computer is not connected to a local area network, the other buttons on the WorkGroup toolbar are of minimal value, and you might want to move the Scenarios drop-down box—rather than the entire toolbar—into your workspace. To do so, follow these steps:

1. Choose View, Toolbars, and click Customize. Or, right-click on a toolbar and choose Customize from the shortcut menu.

2. In the Customize dialog box, choose Utility from the Categories list box.

3. Drag the Scenario drop-down box from the Buttons section of the Customize dialog box onto a toolbar, into the toolbar area, or onto the worksheet.

4. In the Customize dialog box, choose Close.

You can use this box, termed the Scenarios box, to switch among defined scenarios, to add a new scenario, or to edit defined scenarios. For more information on these capabilities, see Chapter 13, "Creating Business Scenarios."

> **Caution**
>
> The Scenarios box makes it very easy inadvertently to alter the values of a scenario's changing cells. If a scenario name is visible in the box, and if you select the same name from its drop-down, Excel assumes that you want to use the current worksheet values in that scenario's changing cells. Unless this is your intent, respond No to the warning message.

Merging Scenarios

As noted in the section above, titled "Viewing Scenarios," the only way that you can view or manipulate a scenario that exists on another worksheet, or in another workbook, is to merge it into the active worksheet.

To review briefly, you can merge a scenario from another worksheet by means of these steps:

1. With the workbook that you want to merge a scenario from open but not active, choose <u>T</u>ools, S<u>c</u>enarios.

2. On the Scenario Manager dialog box, choose <u>M</u>erge.

3. In the Merge Scenarios dialog box, select the <u>B</u>ook and the <u>S</u>heet that you want to merge scenarios from.

4. Choose OK.

Any scenarios on the chosen worksheet are copied to the active worksheet.

You might try this with a completely blank worksheet active at the time that you start the Scenario Manager. Doing so can make it easier to understand exactly what a scenario is. While a scenario has other attributes, such as the name of the user who created it, a scenario fundamentally consists of cell addresses and values.

When you choose <u>S</u>how after merging scenarios to a blank worksheet—or if you create a scenario for a worksheet, and then clear the worksheet and <u>S</u>how the scenario—you will see that the values associated with the changing cells are placed into the addresses associated with the changing cells.

The really interesting part of a worksheet model consists of the formulas that depend on the values of the changing cells. It's those formulas that create the results that you're interested in, but they are not part of the scenario itself.

Figures 12.11 and 12.12 make this explicit. They display scenarios that you can find on the companion disk, as described in the next set of instructions.

To reproduce the sheet as displayed in figures 12.11 and 12.12, follow these steps:

1. Open the workbook named Chap12.xls on the companion disk.

2. Open a new workbook.

3. Choose <u>T</u>ools, S<u>c</u>enarios, and click <u>M</u>erge.

4. In the <u>B</u>ook list box on the Merge Scenarios dialog box, choose Chap12.

5. In the <u>S</u>heet list box, click on Fig12.11, and choose OK.

6. In the Scenario Manager dialog box, click Show. The values for the changing cells in John's Scenario appear in the active worksheet. Click Merge.

7. In the Book list box on the Merge Scenarios dialog box, choose Chap12.

8. In the Sheet list box, click on Fig12.11, and choose OK.

9. In the Scenario Manager dialog box, click Show. The values for the changing cells in Judy's Scenario appear in the active worksheet.

10. Choose Close.

Fig. 12.11

This worksheet shows a scenario that has been merged from *John's Scenario*

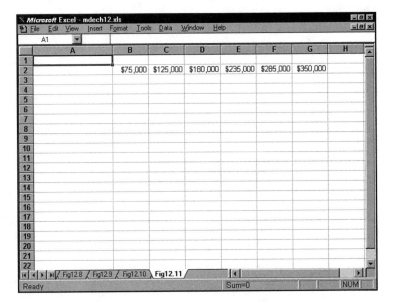

If you now use the Scenario Manager to edit either John's or Judy's scenario, you will see that the changing cells in John's scenario consist of B2:G2, while the changing cells in Judy's scenario consist of B16:B21. This brief exercise demonstrates that:

- It can be useful for different scenarios to have different changing cells. To revisit the scenarios described at the beginning of this chapter, it may be that John has responsibility to estimate sales revenues, and that Judy has the responsibility to estimate the costs and expenses.

- If you merge two scenarios that have different addresses for their changing cells—as is the case in this example—it's necessary to keep track of what the values in these cells mean, and where in the merged model they should be placed. For example, if John's responsibility was to estimate Revenues, it could be disastrous if their values were shown in the row intended for Cost of Goods Sold.

■ Judy's Scenario did not include cells B2:G2 in its changing cells. But these cells, populated by showing John's Scenario, are not cleared when you show Judy's Scenario. Only the values in the addresses of changing cells in a scenario are changed when you show it.

Scenario merged
from John's Scenario

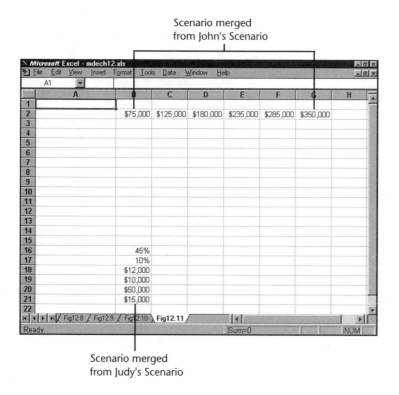

Scenario merged
from Judy's Scenario

Fig. 12.12
This worksheet shows two scenarios: *John's Scenario* as displayed in figure 12.11, and a scenario that has been merged from *Judy's Scenario.*

Chapter Summary

This chapter has provided an overview of several of the basic aspects of creating, showing, summarizing, and merging scenarios. With this overview, you are prepared to deal with the details and options involved in each of these actions, and with additional capabilities such as editing scenarios, protecting and hiding them, creating scenarios by using the Solver, and using VBA to manage them. Each of these topics is treated in detail in the next four chapters.

III

Scenario Management

13

Creating Business Scenarios

Excel offers several methods for managing scenarios, from creating them to editing their changing cells to merging scenarios from different worksheets and workbooks into the active sheet. Chapter 12 provided an overview of these activities; this chapter goes into greater detail on each one.

Adding a Scenario

Chapter 12 mentioned, without elaboration, that there are several ways to add a new scenario to a worksheet. They are:

- *Directly from the worksheet, using Tools, Scenarios.* Chapter 12 gives an example of using this method.

- *By means of the Solver.* When the Solver has reached a solution to a problem that you pose, one of your options is to save the solution values as a scenario. This process is discussed in detail in Chapter 14.

- *By using Visual Basic for Applications (VBA).* This method is discussed in this chapter.

- *From the Scenario box.* This method is also discussed in this chapter.

Let's briefly review the standard method of creating a scenario. Have active the worksheet that contains the cells that will become the changing cells or input assumptions. Choose Tools, Scenarios and click Add in the Scenario Manager dialog box. Provide a name for the new scenario, and define the addresses of the changing cells by highlighting them on the worksheet. The Scenario Manager then gives you an opportunity to adjust the values of the changing cells by means of the Scenario Values dialog box. Finally, exit the Scenario Manager by choosing OK. A new scenario then becomes a part of the active worksheet.

Adding a Scenario from the Scenario Box

The quickest way to add a scenario is with the Scenario box. This box is found on the Workgroup toolbar, but you can also place it on its own toolbar by following the steps described in the "Using the Workgroup toolbar" section in chapter 12.

Adding a scenario in this way involves just three steps:

1. Highlight the cells you want the scenario to treat as changing cells.

2. Click in the Scenario box.

3. Type a name for the scenario.

This method is faster than using the Scenario Manager, because you don't have to deal with a series of dialog boxes (the Scenario Manager itself, the Add Scenario dialog box and the Scenario Values dialog box).

Case Study: Using VBA to Create a Sales Quota Scenario

In most cases, it's best to create scenarios directly from the worksheet, as summarized above. There are some cases, however, when you're better off letting VBA do the work for you.

For example, suppose you are a sales representative with an annual quota. From time to time during the quota year, you want to check your progress against the quota. You can set up some worksheet formulas as shown in figure 13.1.

The formula used in cell B5 of figure 13.1 is

```
=(B1-B3)/((DATEVALUE("12/31/95")-TODAY())/7)
```

This formula finds the difference between the annual quota and year to date sales (B1 – B3), and divides by the number of weeks remaining in the year. The number of remaining weeks is returned by subtracting the serial number of today's date from the serial number of the final day in the year, and dividing the result by 7.

But this isn't quite enough for your purposes. As an experienced sales representative, you plan which sales you hope to make during the year as well as when you hope to close those sales. You want a means of determining what your progress toward quota *should* be at the start of any given week during the year.

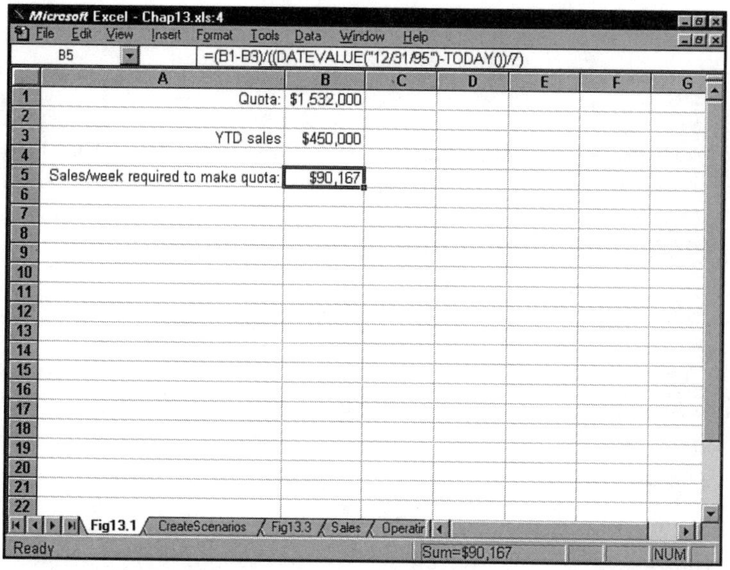

Fig. 13.1
You can keep track
of your progress
toward an annual
goal by using the
TODAY( ) function
in a formula.

One good way to make that determination is by means of a scenario that displays a particular date and the amount you need to have sold by that date. But if you want to be able to show that scenario for any week during the year, you would have to manually enter 52 different scenarios, plus the two changing cells (date and accumulated sales) for each scenario. This is too much work.

You can, however, use VBA to do the work on your behalf. Shown below is code that creates the scenarios for you

```
Sub CreateScenarios()
Dim Week As Integer
Dim DateNumber As Date
Dim DateName As String
Dim Quota As Single
Dim SalesPerWeek As Single
Dim SalesNeeded As Single
```

The seven lines of code shown above declare the VBA subroutine and the variables that are required by the main code. Then, three variables are initialized. The variable Quota is set to the annual quota, 1532000. The amount of sales required per week to meet that quota is set to the quota, divided by 52. And the variable DateNumber, which contains the serial number that corresponds to a particular date, is initialized to the end of the first week in 1995

```
Quota = 1532000
SalesPerWeek = Quota / 52
DateNumber = DateValue("January 7, 1995")
```

Then the main body of the subroutine is entered. This consists of a loop that executes once for each of the 52 weeks in the year

```
For Week = 1 To 52
```

A string variable is needed to represent the date that is current each time the loop executes. This string variable, DateName, is assigned the text representation of DateNumber. Also, the variable named SalesNeeded is incremented by the average sales required each week

```
DateName = Str(DateNumber)
SalesNeeded = SalesNeeded + SalesPerWeek
```

Then, a new scenario is created for the active sheet. Its name is set to the current value of DateName—for example, the first time through the loop DateName equals "1/7/95", and that is the value used for the name of the new scenario.

The changing cells are defined as B7:B8 on the active worksheet. When a scenario is shown, these cells will contain, respectively, the date associated with the scenario and the sales needed by that date. It's not necessary, but it's convenient, to add a comment to the scenario that contains the string representation of the current date

```
ActiveSheet.Scenarios.Add Name:=DateName,
ChangingCells:=Range("B7:B8"), _
    Values:=Array(DateName, SalesNeeded), Comment:= _
    "Sales required through " & DateName, Locked:=True,
Hidden:=False
```

Then, DateNumber is incremented by 7, so that its value will be correct for the next week, when the loop is next executed

```
DateNumber = DateNumber + 7
```

Finally, the loop terminates and returns to its top. This process continues until the control variable Week reaches its final value, 52. Then, the subroutine is terminated

```
Next Week

End Sub
```

The result is a set of 52 scenarios, one for each week of the year. You can choose Tools, Scenarios and show the scenario for the particular week that you're interested in. In this way, you can view on the worksheet how much you should have sold by that week in order to be on track to meet your annual quota.

For example, if you chose the scenario for 8/26/95, the worksheet would appear as shown in figure 13.2.

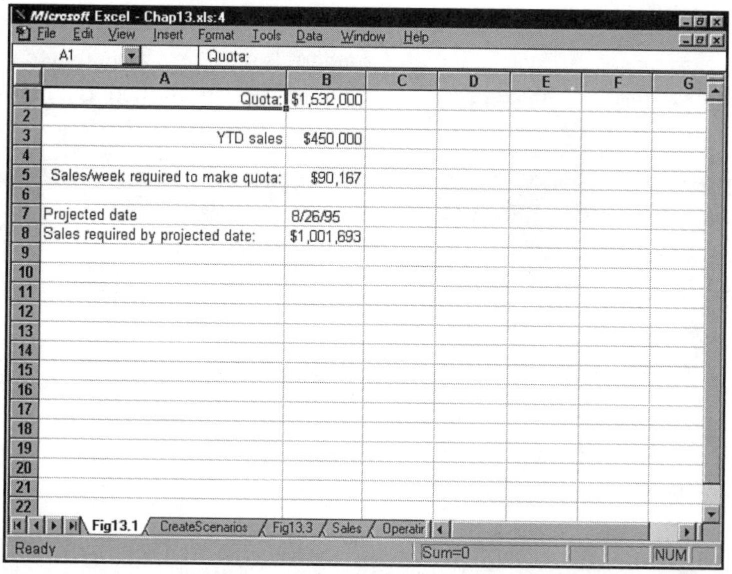

Fig. 13.2
With your weekly
scenarios defined,
you can quickly
call up information
specific to a partic-
ular week.

Tip

If you are in sales or sales management, you might consider complicating this example slightly to carry information about the amount of revenue you anticipate from
different accounts throughout the year.

Dealing with Limitations to Scenarios

There are some limits to scenarios. One, the maximum number of scenarios
that can belong to a worksheet, is a function of the amount of memory installed in your computer: obviously, the more memory available the more
scenarios you can define. But there is no prespecified upper limit to the number of scenarios you can add to a worksheet.

Another limitation to scenarios is the number of changing cells. No scenario
can be defined as having more than 32 changing cells, regardless of the
amount of memory installed in your computer. There is no workaround to
this limit—but you'll find that in most cases 32 changing cells is plenty.

When you create a summary report of the scenarios in a worksheet, you are
limited to 251 scenarios. You'll find more on this in Chapter 15, but the brief
reason is that a scenario summary report (as distinct from a scenario pivot
table) reports each scenario in a different column.

III

Scenario Management

An Excel worksheet has a maximum of 256 columns. In a scenario summary report, several columns are reserved for labels, leaving 251 available to contain information on the worksheet's scenarios. Therefore, there is a maximum of 251 scenarios that can be summarized in a report.

Caution

If you use VBA to create a scenario summary report, and there are more than 251 scenarios defined for the worksheet, Excel terminates with an illegal operation error message and shuts itself down.

You can't create more than one scenario with the same name on the same worksheet. If you attempt to do so, you receive a warning message that scenario names must be unique.

It's possible that merging scenarios from other worksheets or workbooks would result in duplicate scenario names. Suppose several sales managers are working on revenue projections for 1997. When you merge their scenarios from other workbooks into a single worksheet, you find that more than one manager has chosen the scenario name "Make Quota". The duplicate scenario names create a conflict, which the Scenario Manager handles by adding information about the scenario's source and creation date.

For example, suppose two sales managers have the Excel user names George Carlton and James West (use Tools, Options and click the General tab in the Options dialog box). Both Carlton and West provide you with workbooks created on September 30, 1996. Each workbook contains a revenue projection scenario, and in each case the scenario is named "Make Quota".

When you merge George's scenario into a new workbook on one worksheet, it is named "Make Quota". When you merge James' scenario into the same worksheet, it is named "Make Quota James West 9/30/96". Finally, if you merge more than one scenario with the same name, the same user name and the same date, Excel adds a numeral (1, 2, etc.) after the date: "Make Quota James West 9/30/96 1".

The same rules are followed if you merge scenarios that you created. Suppose that your Excel user name is Joan Howell, and that you create a scenario in Book1 named "BestGuess". You create another scenario in Book2, also named "BestGuess". If you now merge the scenario from Book1 into Book2, its name will be "BestGuess" plus the date it was created. The user name Joan Howell is omitted from the merged scenario.

Changing Cells with Formulas

You can't create a scenario on one worksheet with changing cells that are found on another worksheet. For example, suppose Sheet2 is the active sheet, and Sheet1 contains the cells you want to use as changing cells. You can start the Scenario Manager, and, in the Add Scenario dialog box, name the scenario and then enter a reference such as Sheet1!$B$20:$E$20 in the Changing Cells edit box. But if you do so, you receive a message that the reference must be on the active sheet.

You can get around this by using cell links. In this example, with Sheet2 active, you could select cell B20 and enter

    =Sheet1!B20

This creates a link to the value in cell B20 on Sheet1. Copy and paste that formula into C20:E20. Then, start the Scenario Manager and specify cells $B$20:$E$20 on Sheet1 as the changing cells for the scenario.

Caution

Early releases of Excel version 7 contained a bug in the cell linking mechanism. In a new workbook, you could link (say) cell S20 in Sheet2 to cell S20 in Sheet1. However, if and when the value in cell S20 on Sheet1 changed, the linkage between the two cells did not update automatically and consistently. It was necessary to press Ctrl+Alt+F9 to recalculate Sheet2.

This bug had an effect only when the two cells or ranges had identical addresses on the two sheets, as described in the prior example. A patch for this problem has been provided on various online services.

This approach does not maintain the formulas themselves in the scenario. Any formula, whether a link as above or a formula such as =1/20 or a worksheet function such as =PI(), is converted to a value in the changing cell. This is true both of the changing cell's value as displayed by the Scenario Values dialog box, and of the actual cell entry when you choose <u>S</u>how in the Scenario Manager dialog box.

In case you have formulas in changing cells, Excel displays a warning message that formulas in changing cells will be replaced by constant values when you show a scenario.

> **Caution**
>
> This is the only warning that you receive. If you have a formula in a changing cell
> prior to creating the scenario, that formula will be overwritten when you choose to
> show the scenario. Therefore, you should be very careful that you don't overwrite
> any formulas that you are unwilling to lose.

Editing Scenarios

The process of editing a scenario is quite simple. Start the Scenario Manager
and choose Edit in the Scenario Manager dialog box. Excel displays the Scenario Values dialog box. This dialog box contains a vertical scroll bar you
can use to display more changing cells if the scenario has more than can be
shown simultaneously. Select a cell and change the value you want it to contain when you show the scenario on the worksheet.

Protecting Scenarios

There's one circumstance under which you cannot edit the changing cells
in a scenario: if the scenario is protected, *and* if its worksheet is protected
by choosing Tools, Protection, Protect Sheet, and selecting the Scenarios
checkbox. If the worksheet is protected in this fashion, you can add a new
scenario to it, but you can't delete or edit any scenarios that are themselves
protected.

There are two ways to protect a scenario: fill either the Prevent Changes or
the Hide checkbox in the Add Scenario dialog box—or, of course, you can fill
both checkboxes. If the Prevent Changes box is filled, the scenario can't be
edited or deleted. If the Hide box is checked, the scenario doesn't appear in
the list of available scenarios, and thus it can be neither edited nor deleted.

Remember, neither the Prevent Changes nor the Hide option has any effect
unless the worksheet is protected, with the Scenarios checkbox filled.

If a scenario is both protected and shown on the worksheet, you could check
the effect of changing cells on result cells by modifying the changing cells directly on the worksheet. However, you can't even do this if the changing cells
are locked, and the worksheet protected with the Contents checkbox is filled.

When you make a change to a scenario, Excel adds information to the comments that describe the scenario in the Edit Scenario dialog box. Recall that
when you first create the scenario, Excel creates the comment, "Created by
[user name] on [creation date]". When the scenario is edited, Excel adds another comment, "Modified by [user name] on [modification date]".

This is particularly useful if more than one user has access to the scenario. Although Excel does not maintain a history of the actual editing changes that might have been made, it creates a trail of bread crumbs through the scenario's editing history. If an unexpected modification to the scenario has been made, you are in a position to check with the users who might have made the change, with the knowledge of the date on which the change was made.

Unless the scenario is protected as described above, a user who edits a scenario can delete the comment by clicking on it in the Comment list box in the Edit Scenario dialog box, and pressing the Delete key. So, the edit trail is hardly foolproof. If you want to ensure that a scenario is not tampered with, check Prevent Changes or Hide in the Add Scenario or Edit Scenario dialog boxes. Then, when the worksheet itself is active once again, choose Tools, Protection, Protect Sheet, fill the Scenarios checkbox in the Protect Sheet dialog box, and enter a password.

Merging Scenarios

As mentioned earlier in the "Dealing With Limitations to Scenarios" section, merging scenarios created by different users can be a useful way to divide the labor involved in creating a worksheet model. This is particularly so when different staff bear responsibility for different parts of the model.

Figure 13.3 shows a worksheet, adapted from the Business Planner template that accompanies Excel 7, that is used to create financial forecasts in an income statement, balance sheet, and cash flow sheet.

The Business Planner actually uses scenarios to display sample data that accompanies it. With a workbook based on the Business Planner template open, if you use the Planner toolbar to enter or remove sample data, a VBA macro shows a scenario with sample data or sets the changing cells' values to zero.

Tip

The use of a worksheet or toolbar button with an assigned macro that shows or removes sample data by means of a scenario is a useful means of demonstrating a worksheet's functionality to its users.

The income statement, balance sheet and cash flow sheet are linked by formulas to the data sheet in figure 13.3. As different values are entered into the data sheet, the impact of the different input assumptions is reflected in the projected financials on the linked sheets.

Fig. 13.3

The data sheet is divided into sections that specify operational information, expense information, and financing information.

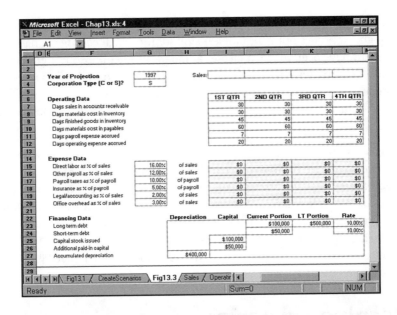

How might you use a sheet like the one shown in figure 13.3 to involve others in the development of a model?

Case Study: Projecting Financial Outcomes

You are responsible for creating financial projections for the next fiscal year for your company, and decide to use the Business Planner to assist in their creation. In order to base the projections on the best possible information, you get the company's operations manager, sales director, cost accountant and chief financial officer to provide you with Best Case, Best Guess, and Worst Case scenarios for the information in the Planner's data sheet.

The sales director will supply estimates of revenue for cells I3:L3 of the worksheet shown in figure 13.3. The operations manager will supply information for cells I7:I12. It's assumed that the operating data will not change across quarters, so only I7:I12 are needed. The cost accountant will take care of cells G15:G20, and the chief financial officer will provide information about debt, capital, and depreciation in the Financing Data range.

To keep things manageable—and to prevent any one of your colleagues from changing someone else's cells—you divide the sheet up into four segments, copy each segment to a different workbook, and distribute one to each participant. These separate segments are shown in figure 13.4.

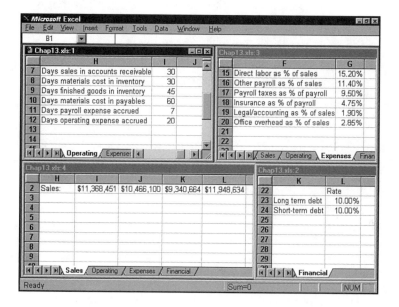

Fig. 13.4
Each participant creates three scenarios—Best Case, Best Guess, and Worst Case—on each worksheet.

Notice that the changing cells in each distributed worksheet are the same as the changing cells in the main data sheet. This is to ensure that when you merge the scenarios into the main data sheet, they will be shown in the proper location.

For example, your main sheet uses cell I3 to contain projected first quarter sales. Suppose the Sales worksheet you distributed to the sales manager had first quarter sales in cell B1. When the time comes to merge the sales manager's scenarios back into your main sheet, you want the changing cell for first quarter sales to appear in cell I3. But if that changing cell is identified as B1 instead of I3, its value would be merged into B1.

Your colleagues each create a Best Guess, Best Case, and Worst Case scenario on the worksheets you gave them, and return the worksheets to you.

To merge the scenarios from one of the returned worksheets, follow these steps:

On the Disk

1. Open the file named Chap13.xls from the companion disk.

2. Activate the sheet named Fig13.3. This sheet is the main worksheet for collecting the various scenarios.

3. Choose Tools, Scenarios, and click Merge to access the scenarios on the Sales, Operations, Expense and Financial worksheets. The Merge Scenarios dialog box appears. Take the next three steps within this dialog box.

4. In the Book drop-down list, make sure Chap13.xls is selected.

5. In the Sheet list box, choose Sales, and choose OK. This merges all the scenarios in the Sales worksheet into the main data sheet.

6. Select Best Guess in the Scenarios list box. Click Show, and then choose Close.

Because the changing cells for the Best Guess scenario for sales are in I3:L3 of the Sales worksheet, they are shown in cells I3:L3 on the main worksheet.

To merge all the scenarios from the separate worksheets into the main worksheet, choose each worksheet in turn, in the Sheet list box in the Merge Scenarios dialog box. After you select each worksheet, click OK and again choose Merge to proceed to the next sheet. When you have finished, the Scenarios list box in the Scenario Manager dialog box appears as shown in figure 13.5.

You are now in a position to create different sets of outcomes, based on the combination of scenarios you choose to show on the main worksheet. For example, you could use the four Best Guess scenarios (one for Sales, one for Operations, one for Expenses and one for Finance) to create the most likely outcome. Or, to display an overall Best Case, you would choose to show the Best Case for each area of the data sheet. Or, you could project the outcome if revenues turn out to be high—by showing the Best Case Sales scenario—and the operating, expense and financial situation is poor—by showing their respective Worst Case scenarios.

Naming Changing Cells

Naming the changing cells makes it easier to edit a scenario. Activate the Sales worksheet, start the Scenario Manager again, and edit the Best Guess scenario. Notice, as shown in figure 13.6, that the changing cells are identified not by their cell addresses, but by their cell names.

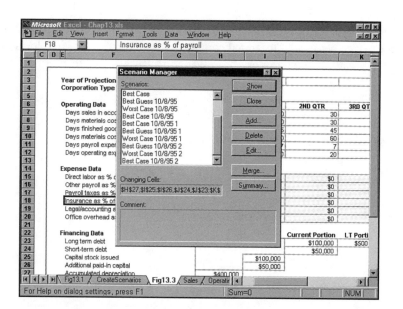

Fig. 13.5
With the various scenarios available to you in the main worksheet, you can mix-and-match different sets of input assumptions to derive different outcomes.

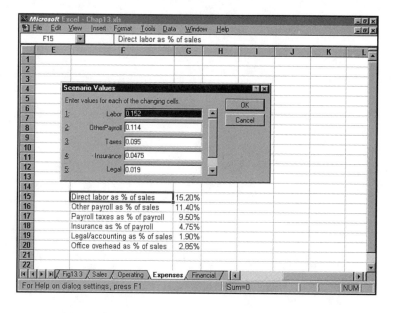

Fig. 13.6
Using cell names for changing cells helps you keep track of which input assumption you are modifying.

Chapter Summary

In this chapter, you have learned the details involved in creating scenarios via different methods, including the use of VBA. You have also learned more about editing existing scenarios, protecting them, and merging them.

III

Scenario Management

One method of creating scenarios is by means of the Solver. This method has been deferred because of its added complexity. The next chapter explores in detail the relationship between the Solver and a worksheet's scenarios.

14

Solving Business Scenarios

Excel's Solver is an add-in that solves complex relationships among variables. It is, in a sense, a sophisticated type of Goal Seek menu item. Instead of asking you to identify a target cell and one changing cell, as Goal Seek does, Solver enables you to identify many changing cells that, together, result in a target cell value that you specify.

This is by no means the only difference between the Solver and the Goal Seek item. There are many other options that you can set in the Solver, some of them fairly abstruse. While this chapter details some of the options within the Solver, it does not go deeply into the complex mathematics that underlie its other options.

Once the Solver has reached a solution that conforms to your specifications, you can save that solution as a scenario. The changing cells that you identify for the Solver become the changing cells in the new scenario. Often, the values that the Solver assigns to the changing cells bring about an optimal result in the target cell. This solution might be the only scenario that you want to keep in the worksheet.

Or, because you can run the Solver repeatedly under different sets of input assumptions, you might want to save several scenarios created by the Solver. All the scenario options that were discussed in Chapters 12 and 13 are available to you when you save a scenario created by the Solver.

Understanding the Solver

The Solver is a sophisticated optimization tool. There is a wide variety of problems that you can solve with it, including models that involve both linear and nonlinear relationships among the variables. Excel 7 supplies a workbook, Solvsamp.xls, with several examples of using the Solver to arrive at solutions to problems that range from optimum product mix to staff scheduling to portfolio analysis. If you are interested in exploring different Solver applications, you should open this file and use the Solver on its various problems.

This chapter presents two relatively simple situations in order to focus on the relationship between the Solver and the Scenario Manager. You will find that the ability to create scenarios using the Solver can streamline the task of data management when different sets of input assumptions are involved in a model.

Understanding Goal Seek

Before tackling the Solver, you'll find it helpful to make sure that you understand Excel's Goal Seek menu item. This item is found in the Tools menu.

When you select Tools, Goal Seek, the dialog box shown in figure 14.1 appears.

Fig. 14.1
Goal Seek changes the value in one cell in order to converge on a value for the target cell.

Case Study: Determining a Salary

Suppose that you manage a marketing group, and have authorization to hire a new employee, including the budget to offer up to $30,000 as a starting salary. Your company's human resources director has informed you that your group's average salary, $39,160, is a little high, and that you should try to offer the new employee a salary that would help to bring the average down to $38,000. What offer should you make, in order to meet that goal?

Use the Goal Seek command. You would have one changing cell (the new employee's salary) and a target cell (the average of all salaries in your group). To do so, see figure 14.2 and follow these steps:

Fig. 14.2
Using Goal Seek to find a new salary that satisfies a specified average salary.

1. Enter this formula as shown in cell E2 of figure 14.2
   =AVERAGE(C3:C11)

2. Select Tools, Goal Seek. The Goal Seek dialog box appears as shown in figure 14.2.

3. In the Set Cell edit box, enter **$E$2** or click that worksheet cell, if it is not already shown in the edit box. This is the cell whose value Goal Seek attempts to set.

4. In the To Value edit box, enter **38000**. This is the goal—the value—that Goal Seek attempts to assign to cell $E$2.

5. In the By Changing cell edit box, enter **$C$11**, or just select the edit box and click in worksheet cell C11. This is the cell whose value Goal Seek will change in order to cause cell $E$2 to have a value of 38000.

6. Choose OK.

Goal Seek returns a value of $28,721 in cell C11. This value causes the average of the values in cells C3:C11 to equal $38,000.

Notice that the value in cell E2 depends on the value in cell C11, because E2's formula refers to C11. This kind of dependency is a prerequisite for Goal Seek to work properly, although the dependency need not be direct.

For example, suppose a new employee's total compensation is to be $38,000. The compensation comprises a commission on sales, plus a base salary. It's assumed that the base salary will be $30,000 and the commission rate 3%. Then, you could use Goal Seek to determine what level of sales is required to return a total compensation of $38,000.

Generalizing from Goal Seek to the Solver

It's a short step from understanding Goal Seek to understanding the purpose of the Solver. Consider the situation shown in figure 14.3.

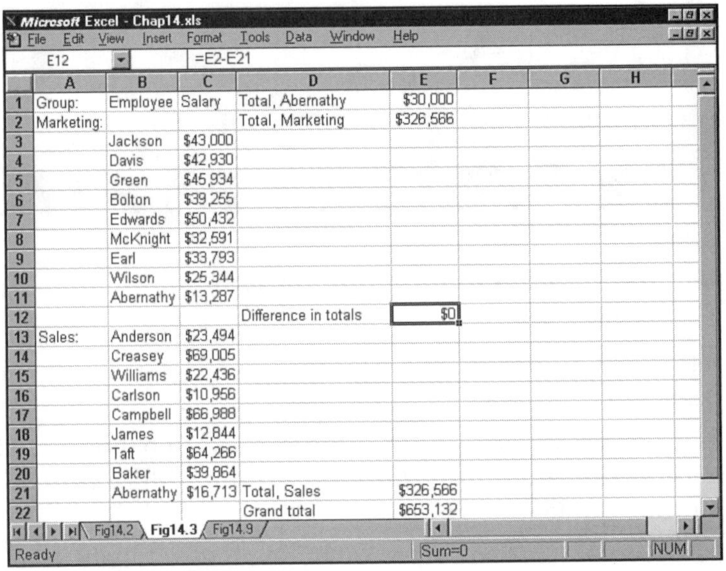

Fig. 14.3
Considerable trial-and-error is needed to equalize the total salaries of the Marketing and Sales groups.

Suppose that a new employee, Abernathy, has been hired to support both the Marketing and Sales groups. You want to allocate Abernathy's salary responsibility between the two groups in order to equalize their total payrolls.

Do you see why this is not an appropriate problem for Goal Seek? It's because the situation involves not one but two changing cells, C11 and C21. These two cells should contain the portion of Abernathy's salary that should be allocated to each group such that the two total group payrolls are equal.

Therefore, use the Solver instead of Goal Seek. As noted at the beginning of this chapter, the Solver is an add-in, and you must make sure that it is available and installed before you can use it. To check, look in the Tools menu. If you see the Sol<u>v</u>er item there, you can proceed. Otherwise, choose <u>T</u>ools, Add-<u>I</u>ns. If you see the Solver in the list of available add-ins, fill its checkbox and choose OK. If it is not in the list of available add-ins, you will need to re-run Setup for Excel; when you do so, be sure that the Solver option is checked as a component to add.

To use the Solver on the problem shown in figure 14.3, take the following steps:

1. Open the file on the companion disk named Chap14.xls, and activate the worksheet named Fig14.3.

2. Select <u>T</u>ools, Sol<u>v</u>er. The dialog box shown in figure 14.4 appears.

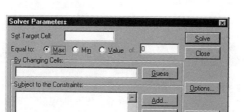

Fig. 14.4
You can provide all the specifications needed for most Solver problems without using its Options button.

3. In the S<u>e</u>t Target Cell edit box, enter **E12**. Cell E12 compares the total payroll of each group by means of this formula:

    =E2-E21

4. Choose the <u>V</u>alue radio button, and enter **0** (zero) in the Value edit box. By doing so, you specify that 0 is the goal value for cell E12 that the Solver will attempt to return.

5. Click in the <u>B</u>y Changing Cells edit box, and then click in worksheet cell C11. Hold down the Ctrl key and click in cell C21. The Ctrl key enables a multiple selection. C11 and C21 are the cells that will contain the portion of Abernathy's salary that is allocated to each group.

6. The Solver needs some constraints so that its solution will be acceptable. You do not want a negative amount—that is, a negative salary—in either cell C11 or C21. Click the <u>A</u>dd button to add a constraint. The Add Constraint dialog box appears, as shown in figure 14.5.

Fig. 14.5
You can use constraints to force the Solver to return a result within a range of possibilities that you find acceptable.

7. Click in the Cell Reference edit box, and then click in worksheet cell C11. The address is added as an absolute reference. (If, instead, you type the address, the Solver converts it to the absolute reference format.)

8. Set the operator to the >= sign.

9. Enter **0** in the Constraint edit box, and click Add. This sequence prevents the Solver from trying to enter a negative salary amount in cell C11.

10. Repeat steps 7 through 9 for cell C21.

> ### Tip
>
> Generally, do not identify a changing cell as a constraint that is to take on a specific value. So doing can cause the Solver to assign that value to the changing cell as a constant, and the result is that what you intend to be a changing cell does not change.

11. Cell E1 sums the values in C11 and C21. Abernathy's salary should not exceed $30,000, so enter **E1** in the Cell Reference edit box, use <= as the operator, and enter **30000** in the Constraint edit box. Click Add.

12. Abernathy's salary should be at least $25,000, so enter **E1** in the Cell Reference edit box, use >= as the operator, and enter **25000** in the Constraint edit box. Choose OK.

13. The Solver Parameters dialog box appears again, and its entries should be as shown in figure 14.6. Choose Solve.

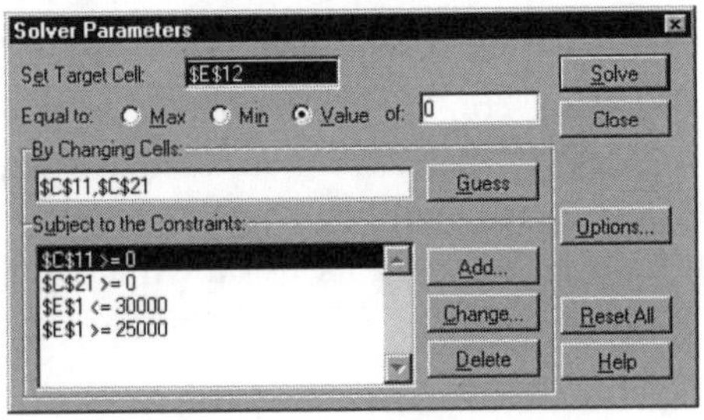

Fig. 14.6
The Subject to the Constraints list box summarizes the constraints that you have placed on the Solver's solution.

When the Solver has finished processing, it displays the Solver Results dialog box, as shown in figure 14.7.

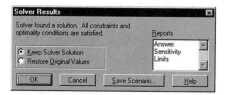

Fig. 14.7
The Solver Results
dialog box appears
when Solver is
finished.

Choose the Save Scenario button, and in the Save Scenario dialog box type a name for the scenario in the Scenario Name edit box. Then, choose OK. The Solver Results dialog box reappears. Choose OK to terminate the Solver.

The worksheet should now appear as in figure 14.8.

	A	B	C	D	E	F	G	H
1	Group:	Employee	Salary	Total, Abernathy	$30,000			
2	Marketing:			Total, Marketing	$326,566			
3		Jackson	$43,000					
4		Davis	$42,930					
5		Green	$45,934					
6		Bolton	$39,255					
7		Edwards	$50,432					
8		McKnight	$32,591					
9		Earl	$33,793					
10		Wilson	$25,344					
11		Abernathy	$13,287					
12				Difference in totals	$0			
13	Sales:	Anderson	$23,494					
14		Creasey	$69,005					
15		Williams	$22,436					
16		Carlson	$10,956					
17		Campbell	$66,988					
18		James	$12,844					
19		Taft	$64,266					
20		Baker	$39,864					
21		Abernathy	$16,713	Total, Sales	$326,566			
22				Grand total	$653,132			

E12 =E2-E21

Fig. 14.8
The Solver returns
values for cells
C11 and C21 that
equalize the pay-
rolls, and that
place Abernathy's
total salary
between $25,000
and $30,000.

Notice that the solution you specified—for cell E12 to equal zero—has been found. Further, the amounts in cells C11 and C21 are both greater than zero, per your first two constraints, and that Abernathy's total salary in cell E1 is between $25,000 and $30,000, per your third constraint.

There are many possible solutions to this problem, because the total salary was constrained to be between $25,000 and $30,000. The Solver returns the first solution it finds that meets both the target and the constraints that you specify. It is likely that, if you duplicate this problem on your computer, the Solver will return a total salary of $30,000. Slightly different inputs can result in a different solution, and the options that are set for the Solver exert an influence on the Solver's solution.

If the first solution that the Solver returns does not seem quite right to you— perhaps you'd prefer that Abernathy's salary not be set to the very top of its possible range—you can run the Solver again, modifying some of the constraints, or you might experiment with changing some of its options.

Now, verify that the scenario you added conforms to the changing cell values that the Solver returned. Choose Tools, Scenarios, and in the Scenario Manager's dialog box select the scenario name you applied. Then, choose Edit. Click OK in the Edit Scenario dialog box to view the changing cells and their values. You can modify them if you wish, but unless you're very careful about doing so you will throw the equality of the two groups' payrolls out of balance.

When you have finished, choose OK or Cancel in the Scenario Values dialog box, and choose Close in the Scenario Manager dialog box to return to the worksheet.

Creating Multiple Scenarios with the Solver

A much more complicated situation is shown in figure 14.9.

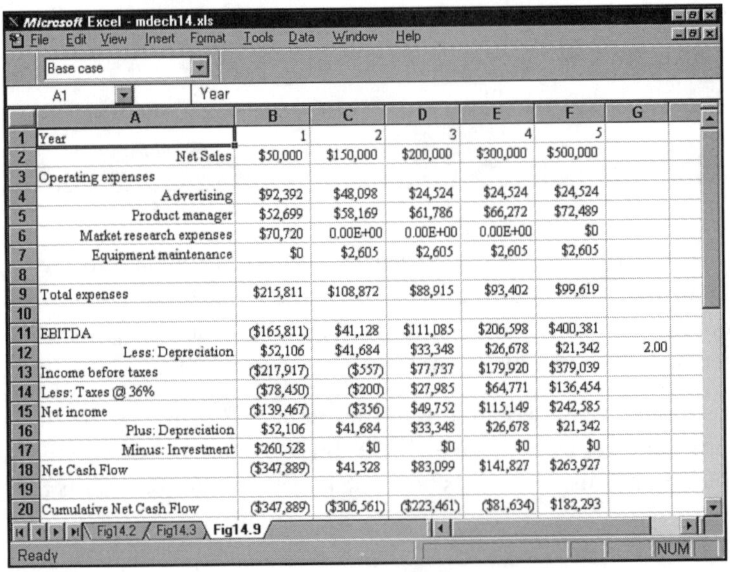

Fig. 14.9
The Solver can optimize the assumptions that form the basis for a product plan.

A	B	C	D	E	F	G
1 Year	1	2	3	4	5	
2 Net Sales	$50,000	$150,000	$200,000	$300,000	$500,000	
3 Operating expenses						
4 Advertising	$92,392	$48,098	$24,524	$24,524	$24,524	
5 Product manager	$52,699	$58,169	$61,786	$66,272	$72,489	
6 Market research expenses	$70,720	0.00E+00	0.00E+00	0.00E+00	$0	
7 Equipment maintenance	$0	$2,605	$2,605	$2,605	$2,605	
8						
9 Total expenses	$215,811	$108,872	$88,915	$93,402	$99,619	
10						
11 EBITDA	($165,811)	$41,128	$111,085	$206,598	$400,381	
12 Less: Depreciation	$52,106	$41,684	$33,348	$26,678	$21,342	2.00
13 Income before taxes	($217,917)	($557)	$77,737	$179,920	$379,039	
14 Less: Taxes @ 36%	($78,450)	($200)	$27,985	$64,771	$136,454	
15 Net income	($139,467)	($356)	$49,752	$115,149	$242,585	
16 Plus: Depreciation	$52,106	$41,684	$33,348	$26,678	$21,342	
17 Minus: Investment	$260,528	$0	$0	$0	$0	
18 Net Cash Flow	($347,889)	$41,328	$83,099	$141,827	$263,927	
19						
20 Cumulative Net Cash Flow	($347,889)	($306,561)	($223,461)	($81,634)	$182,293	

Figure 14.9 shows a five-year budget for a new product. The values shown in the figure are for a scenario titled Base Case. Besides information about product revenue (Net Sales) and expenses directly associated with the product, the plan shows other costs such as depreciation, taxes, and the cost of the equipment required to manufacture the product.

The budget analyzes the costs and expenses to arrive at the payback period: that is, the length of time it will take the new product to break even. In the Base Case, the payback period ends during the fourth year. Notice that the Cumulative Net Cash Flow (row 20 in the model) is still negative at the end of year 4, and is positive at the end of year 5.

Cells B12:F12 and B16:F16 contain the depreciation amounts that apply each year to the new equipment. They are calculated with the double declining balance method

    =DDB($B$17,0,10,B1,$G$12)

The reference to cell G12 in this formula establishes the factor used by the DDB function. In the Base Case, this is 2.00, which is also the default factor for DDB.

How much leeway exists in this model? Suppose that you need to shorten the payback period to four years. Holding the revenues constant, and assuming a minimum cost of new equipment of $250,000, what do the expenses and costs associated with the new product look like if management needs to break even at the end of year 4?

The Solver is an ideal tool to answer this question. To set up the analysis, open the file named Chap14.xls on the companion disk and activate the worksheet named Fig14.9. Then, follow these steps:

On the Disk

1. Choose Solver from the Tools menu.

2. In the Set Target Cell box, enter E20.

3. Choose the Value option button, and enter 0 in the Value edit box. This establishes the outcome—a break even point at the end of year 4, when the Cumulative Net Cash Flow equals zero.

4. Click in the By Changing Cells edit box, and on the worksheet select cells B4:F6. Hold down the Ctrl key, and select cell B17, and then select cell G12. This establishes the operating expenses, the double declining balance factor and the cost of the new equipment as the changing cells.

5. Click the Add button, and in the Add Constraint dialog box, enter B17 as the Cell Reference. Use >= as the operator, and enter **250000** as the Constraint. Choose OK. This establishes $250,000 as the minimum cost of the new equipment.

III

Scenario Management

> **Note**
>
> The Solver encounters a difficulty when a constraint is a cell that has been named with the Name box, with Insert, Name, Define, or with Insert, Name, Create. If you subsequently try to change or delete the constraint (which will be identified by its name, rather than its address, in the Subject to the Constraints list box), the Solver terminates with an error message. The message states that an unexpected internal error occurred or available memory was exhausted.
>
> To avoid encountering this problem, do not use named cells as constraints. If you do encounter the problem, use Insert, Name, Define, choose the offending name in the Names in Workbook list box, choose Delete, and then choose OK. This removes the name from the workbook, and you should be able to use the cell as a constraint, because it is no longer named.

6. Choose Solve. The Solver returns values for the changing cells that result in a payback period of four years. Click the Save Scenario button, and save the scenario under the name BreakEven = 4.
7. In the Solver Results dialog box, choose OK.

One possible set of results that conform to a payback period of four years is shown in figure 14.10.

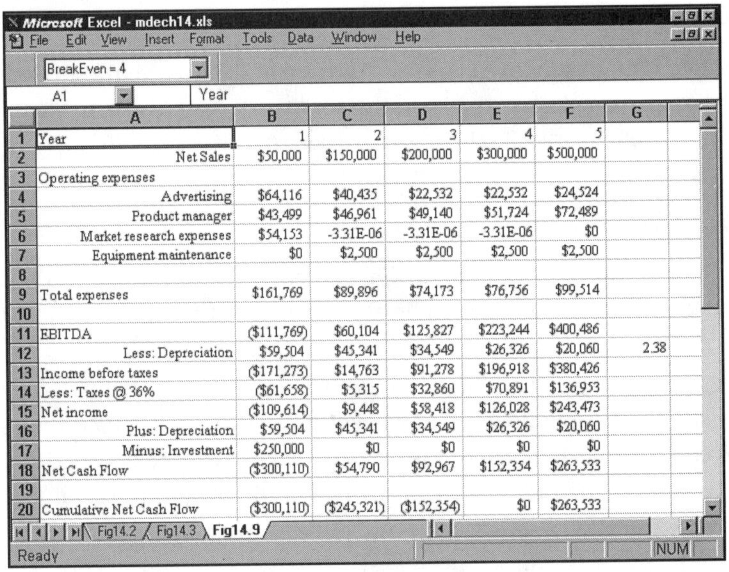

	A	B	C	D	E	F	G
1	Year	1	2	3	4	5	
2	Net Sales	$50,000	$150,000	$200,000	$300,000	$500,000	
3	Operating expenses						
4	Advertising	$64,116	$40,435	$22,532	$22,532	$24,524	
5	Product manager	$43,499	$46,961	$49,140	$51,724	$72,489	
6	Market research expenses	$54,153	-3.31E-06	-3.31E-06	-3.31E-06	$0	
7	Equipment maintenance	$0	$2,500	$2,500	$2,500	$2,500	
8							
9	Total expenses	$161,769	$89,896	$74,173	$76,756	$99,514	
10							
11	EBITDA	($111,769)	$60,104	$125,827	$223,244	$400,486	
12	Less: Depreciation	$59,504	$45,341	$34,549	$26,326	$20,060	2.38
13	Income before taxes	($171,273)	$14,763	$91,278	$196,918	$380,426	
14	Less: Taxes @ 36%	($61,658)	$5,315	$32,860	$70,891	$136,953	
15	Net income	($109,614)	$9,448	$58,418	$126,028	$243,473	
16	Plus: Depreciation	$59,504	$45,341	$34,549	$26,326	$20,060	
17	Minus: Investment	$250,000	$0	$0	$0	$0	
18	Net Cash Flow	($300,110)	$54,790	$92,967	$152,354	$263,533	
19							
20	Cumulative Net Cash Flow	($300,110)	($245,321)	($152,354)	$0	$263,533	

Fig. 14.10 With an extended payback period, the product budget has room for higher expenses and cost of equipment than under the Base Case.

These values are, of course, those associated with the scenario that you saved with the name BreakEven = 4. You must spend less in operating expenses and in purchasing the new equipment, and the depreciation amounts are lower, than under the base case.

Notice also that the factor used for the DDB function, found in cell G12, has increased. This accelerates the rate that depreciation takes, and increases the annual net cash flow.

As you can tell from figure 14.10, the Solver might change the formatting that you have applied to some of the changing cells. In this case, you will need to change the format of those cells back to their original format.

You also might want to put brackets around the possible values of other changing cells, such as requiring that cells B4:F6 must be greater than zero.

Chapter Summary

In this chapter, you have learned some of the basics of Goal Seek and the Solver tool. Both Goal Seek and the Solver arrive at goals, or target values, for a cell that contains a formula by changing the values of other cells. While Goal Seek is a quick means of arriving at a goal value by changing another value, you cannot set any options, such as constraints.

It takes more time to run the Solver, but you can use it to specify a wide range of options. In particular, you can use the Solver to create scenarios. A scenario created by the Solver can be based on the optimum values of the changing cells. It can be based on constraints that you specify, such as the minimum value of a cost component.

The ability to create scenarios by using the Solver means that you can retain its results under different sets of input assumptions without running the Solver repeatedly, each time that you want to duplicate those assumptions. And, when you have more than one person involved in developing a set of scenarios, each contributor might use the Solver on a different portion of a model. Then, you are in a position to merge all the resulting scenarios into one worksheet, where you can combine them to your best advantage.

The next chapter examines the different ways that you can create reports based on multiple scenarios in your workbook.

III

Scenario Management

15

Reporting Scenarios

When you have created several scenarios on a worksheet, it often happens that you want to overcome the main purpose of a scenario: to show, one by one, the result of showing a particular scenario. Instead, you want to view the results of each scenario in one place.

This is the purpose of the S<u>u</u>mmary option in the Scenario Manager. By choosing it, you can arrange to create a new worksheet in the active workbook that summarizes the results of the scenarios that you have defined in the active worksheet. The summary might display the changing cells of each defined scenario or its result cells or both. By viewing the scenario summary, you can quickly determine the results associated with each scenario's changing cells.

This chapter describes the options available for scenario summaries and the effects of choosing each option.

Scenario Summaries

A scenario summary is a worksheet that contains information about the values of each scenario's changing cells. When you create the summary, you have the option of including or omitting result cells in the summary worksheet. The worksheet is outlined, so that you can choose to display or to hide the values of the changing cells, the result cells, or both.

Figure 15.1 shows an example of a scenario summary worksheet.

Notice the outline symbols at the left of the summary itself. By clicking a "+" symbol, you can display any hidden rows, and by clicking a "−" symbol, you can hide the rows within its scope.

Fig. 15.1

You can choose to show or hide the changing cells on a scenario summary worksheet.

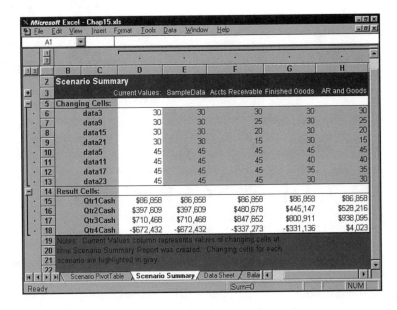

		Current Values:	SampleData	Accts Receivable	Finished Goods	AR and Goods
Scenario Summary						
Changing Cells:						
	data3	30	30	30	30	30
	data9	30	30	25	30	25
	data15	30	30	20	30	20
	data21	30	30	15	30	15
	data5	45	45	45	45	45
	data11	45	45	45	40	40
	data17	45	45	45	35	35
	data23	45	45	45	30	30
Result Cells:						
	Qtr1Cash	$86,858	$86,858	$86,858	$86,858	$86,858
	Qtr2Cash	$397,609	$397,609	$480,678	$445,147	$528,216
	Qtr3Cash	$710,468	$710,468	$847,652	$800,911	$938,095
	Qtr4Cash	-$672,432	-$672,432	-$337,273	-$331,136	$4,023

Notes: Current Values column represents values of changing cells at time Scenario Summary Report was created. Changing cells for each scenario are highlighted in gray.

All scenarios in the worksheet that is active when you create the scenario summary are included. There is no option, whether from a menu, a dialog box, or from Visual Basic for Applications (VBA), to limit the summary to a subset of the existing scenarios.

To create the summary scenario in figure 15.1, follow these steps:

On the Disk

1. Open the file named Chap15.xls from the companion disk.
2. Activate the worksheet named Data Sheet.
3. Choose Tools, Scenarios and click the Summary button.
4. In the Scenario Summary dialog box, shown in figure 15.2, choose the Scenario Summary option button.
5. Click in the Result Cells edit box, and either type the address **I24:L25** or, using your mouse pointer, highlight that range on the Data Sheet.
6. Choose OK.

> **Note**
>
> The worksheets in the workbook Chap15.xls are adapted from a workbook created by using the Business Planner template. The charts, the VBA macros, worksheet objects and cell notes that normally accompany a workbook based on that template have been removed to save space and processing time.

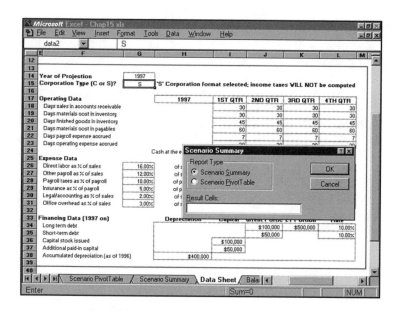

Fig. 15.2
You can specify
that different
result cells are to
be shown in
different scenario
summaries.

When Excel has finished processing, you will see a new worksheet named
Scenario Summary in the active workbook. If you repeat this process, subsequent scenario summary worksheets will be named Scenario Summary 2,
Scenario Summary 3, and so on.

The scenario summary shown in figure 15.1 is the result of the following
case study.

Case Study: Improving Cash Flow

As the owner of a small business, you begin each fiscal year by creating financial projections that incorporate both historical information about your expenses, operations and financial basis, and forecasts of the revenue that you
expect to generate during each of the next four quarters. To assist you in creating these projections, you employ the Business Planner template that accompanies Excel version 7.

You open a new workbook based on the Business Planner template and
switch to the worksheet named Data Sheet. The Planner toolbar contains a
Display example/Remove example toolbar button that populates the worksheet with default values. You click that button to display the values as
shown in figure 15.3.

An amazing coincidence occurs—all of the data in the Business Planner's
Data Sheet example data set conforms precisely to your own business. Therefore, you accept the Planner's example values for the Data Sheet. (Should you

III

Scenario Management

not be so lucky, you can certainly enter values that describe your business's financials instead. For convenience, this case study assumes the example values that accompany the Business Planner.)

Fig. 15.3

The Business Planner's Data Sheet is where you enter operational, expense, and financial information about a business enterprise.

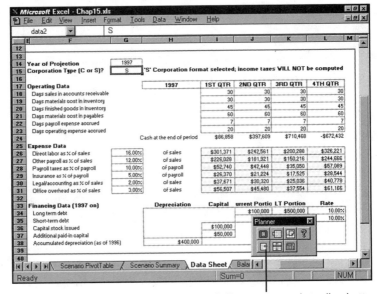

Display example/Remove example toolbar button

However, your forecasted quarterly sales differ from those supplied by the example data, so you switch to the worksheet named Income Statement. In cells H16:K16 of the income statement, you enter the values of your sales forecasts, as shown in figure 15.4.

Tip

To cause Excel to display row and column headings in Business Planner (or any other) worksheets, choose Tools, Options and click the View tab. In the Options dialog box, fill the Row and Column Headers checkbox, and choose OK.

After the workbook recalculates its formulas based on the quarterly sales information that you add, you glance at the bottom of the Income Statement to see the effect on your company's net income (see figure 15.5).

Due mainly to a large cost of sales that you expect to incur in the fourth quarter (see cell K54 in figure 15.5), your net income for the fourth quarter projects to a negative value. However, you are profitable enough during the first three quarters that you can afford this extraordinary expense, and your company should be profitable for the fiscal year.

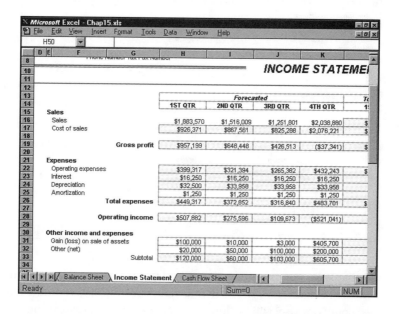

Fig. 15.4
Values shown in the Business Planner's Income Statement, Balance Sheet, and Cash Flow Sheet are driven principally by the sales dollars entered on the Income Statement and the information entered on the Data Sheet.

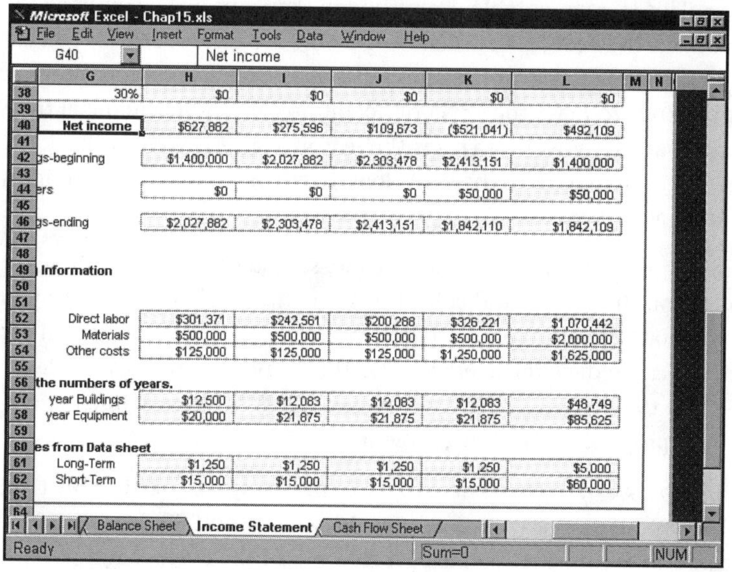

Fig. 15.5
Net income for the year is positive, even though net income for the fourth quarter is negative.

You also check the Cash Flow Sheet to make sure that your projected revenues and expenses during each quarter leave you with enough cash to continue operations (see fig. 15.6).

III

Scenario Management

Fig. 15.6

Your cash flow situation is such that the fourth quarter cost of sales will create a negative cash situation at the end of the year.

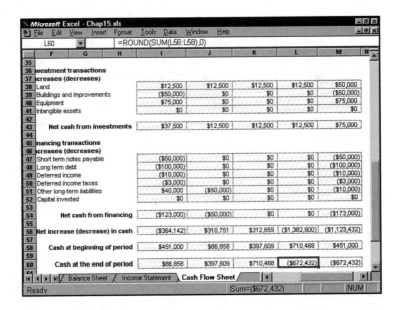

You find that your cash position will not be a healthy one at the end of the year. Cell L60 in figure 15.6 shows that, given your projected revenues and expenses, your company will be down by over $672,000 in cash at the end of the year. This is unacceptable. Even though you expect the company to be profitable for the year (the annual net income is positive, recall), you cannot stand to be without cash at the end of the year. The accrual method of accounting tends to mask the effect of operations and other financial transactions on your *cash* position. This is the reason that it is wise to check both the income statement and the cash flow sheet when you are projecting your company's activities.

Your sales estimates are already optimistic, so you decide to see what you can do about your inventory and collections situations. If you can move your finished goods out of inventory faster, you will convert them to cash earlier. And if you can reduce the average collection period for non-cash sales, you will be able to put cash in the bank earlier. Either of these actions might resolve your projected cash flow problem.

Switching back to the Data Sheet (refer to fig. 15.3), you see in cells I18:L18 that the Days sales in accounts receivable is a constant 30 days throughout the year. This means that you expect to wait, on the average non-cash sale, 30 days to receive payment. And cells I20:L20 each contain the number 45, which means that you expect your finished goods to remain in inventory for 45 days. This is 45 days during which you are not converting material and labor into cash.

You decide to check the result of reducing the average collection period throughout the year, and of reducing the average length of time those finished goods remain in inventory. You take the following steps:

> **Tip**
>
> These steps have already been performed on your behalf in the Data Sheet in the Chap15.xls file on the companion disk.

On the Disk

1. With the Data Sheet active, highlight cells I18:L18. Hold down Ctrl, and highlight cells I20:L20. If you have the Scenario box visible on a toolbar, click in it and enter the name **SampleData**. Otherwise, choose Tools, Scenarios and click Add. Add a scenario named SampleData, making no changes to the values of the changing cells. This establishes a baseline scenario against which you evaluate the results of other scenarios. Choose OK to add the scenario, choose OK again to leave the Scenario Values dialog box, and choose OK once again to leave the Scenario Manager.

2. With the Data Sheet active, enter **25**, **20**, and **15** for Days sales in accounts receivable, for quarters 2 through 4 in cells J18:L18. This projects that you will be able to reduce the average collection period from 30 to 15 days over the course of a year.

3. Highlight cells I18:L18. Hold down Ctrl, and highlight cells I20:L20.

4. Choose Tools, Scenarios, and click Add. Enter **Accts Receivable** as a scenario name. You already have the changing cells highlighted, so make no change in the Changing Cells edit box. Enter a comment if you wish, and choose OK.

5. The Scenario Values dialog box appears. Because you have already entered the values you want for cells I18:L18 and because for this scenario you are retaining the original values for cells I20:L20, you can simply choose OK. Choose OK again to leave the Scenario Manager.

6. On the worksheet, change the values in J18:L18 back to 30. Change the values in J20:L20 to 40, 35 and 30, respectively. This creates the input assumption that you will be able to move finished goods out of inventory more quickly throughout the year.

7. Highlight I18:L18, hold down Ctrl, and highlight I20:L20. Choose Tools, Scenarios, and click Add.

III

Scenario Management

8. The Add Scenario dialog box appears again. As a scenario name, enter **Finished Goods**. The addresses of the changing cells will be the same as for the Accts Receivable scenario, so make no change to the Changing Cells edit box. Add a comment if you wish and choose OK.

9. The Scenario Values dialog box appears again. Since the changing cells already have the values you want, just choose OK, and then choose OK again to leave the Scenario Manager.

10. Repeat steps 6 through 9 to create another Scenario, named **AR and Goods**. This scenario should use the same changing cells as the Accts Receivable scenario and the Finished Goods scenario, but I18:L18 should contain 30, 25, 20 and 15, and I20:L20 should contain 45, 40, 35 and 30.

The result will be four scenarios on the DataSheet: SampleData (the original values), Accts Receivable (in which the days sales in accounts receivable drops during the year), Finished Goods (in which the days finished goods in inventory drops during the year), and AR and Goods (both days accounts receivable and days finished goods drop during the year).

> **Note**
>
> You might have wondered why you were advised to use OK to return to the Scenario Manager and then OK again to return to the active worksheet, instead of using the Add button in the Scenario Values dialog box. The reason is that the Business Planner template makes extensive use of cell names such as Data3. These names have little mnemonic value, but they are integral parts of the workbook's formulas, so they have been retained.
>
> The Scenario Manager uses a cell name, if available, rather than a cell address to identify changing cells in the Scenario Values dialog box. Because it is difficult to determine what, for example, Data3 refers to, you were advised to enter the changing cell values on the worksheet instead of in the Scenario Values dialog box. Choosing OK, rather than Add, in that dialog box lets you return eventually to the worksheet to modify more changing cells.
>
> This book has generally refrained from comments about the Excel product and its associated components such as the Business Planner template. But the use of names such as Data3 and CDB in the Planner is so egregious that it can't pass without comment. If you are going to take the trouble to use names—strongly recommended—in workbooks, you might as well use names that are conceptually rich. It's much easier to deal with a name like AnnualSales than with a name like Data109.

There is one more step necessary before you can create a report that summarizes the four scenarios on the Data Sheet. In Data Sheet cell H24, enter this formula

```
='Cash Flow Sheet'!H58
```

Then, with H24 selected, copy-and-paste it into cells I24:L24. This establishes a link to the cells on the Cash Flow Sheet that show your company's cash at the end of each period. The reason for doing this is that a scenario summary's result cells must be on the same sheet as the scenario itself. As Excel cycles through the four defined scenarios to create the Scenario Summary, the Cash Flow Sheet is recalculated. The information you are interested in is on the Cash Flow Sheet, and it must also be represented on the Data Sheet—the one that contains the scenarios that are being summarized.

Using either the Name box or Insert, Name, Define, name cell I24 as Qtr1Cash, J24 as Qtr2Cash, K24 as Qtr3Cash and L24 as Qtr4Cash. These names will appear as labels in the Scenario Summary.

To create the Scenario Summary, follow these steps:

1. With the Data Sheet active, choose Tools, Scenarios, and click Summary.

2. The Scenario Summary dialog box appears. Choose the Scenario Summary option button.

3. Click in the Result Cells edit box, and either type **I24:L24** or use your mouse to highlight that range on the worksheet.

4. Choose OK.

> **Tip**
>
> You can have a maximum of 251 scenarios defined for a worksheet in order to show them in a Scenario Summary. The worksheet itself can contain more than 251 scenarios, but the Scenario Manager terminates with an error message if you try to put them in a Scenario Summary.

Excel creates the Scenario Summary worksheet shown in figure 15.1 and is repeated for convenience in figure 15.7.

The result cells show that only the scenario that reduces both days sales in accounts receivable and days finished goods in inventory succeeds in bringing about a positive cash position at the end of the year. You decide that you will have to take action both to reduce your average collection period and to accelerate selling your finished goods from your inventory.

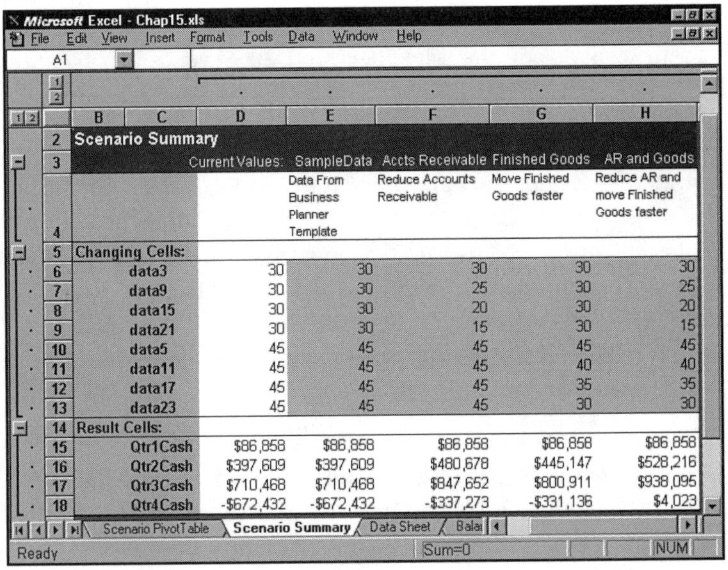

Fig. 15.7
Toggling the first outline symbol on a scenario summary alternately displays and hides the comments associated with each scenario.

	B	C	D	E	F	G	H
2	Scenario Summary						
3			Current Values:	SampleData	Accts Receivable	Finished Goods	AR and Goods
4				Data From Business Planner Template	Reduce Accounts Receivable	Move Finished Goods faster	Reduce AR and move Finished Goods faster
5	Changing Cells:						
6		data3	30	30	30	30	30
7		data9	30	30	25	30	25
8		data15	30	30	20	30	20
9		data21	30	30	15	30	15
10		data5	45	45	45	45	45
11		data11	45	45	45	40	40
12		data17	45	45	45	35	35
13		data23	45	45	45	30	30
14	Result Cells:						
15		Qtr1Cash	$86,858	$86,858	$86,858	$86,858	$86,858
16		Qtr2Cash	$397,609	$397,609	$480,678	$445,147	$528,216
17		Qtr3Cash	$710,468	$710,468	$847,652	$800,911	$938,095
18		Qtr4Cash	-$672,432	-$672,432	-$337,273	-$331,136	$4,023

Deciding to Create the Summary Report

The prior case study probably seemed like a lot of work to go through just to return 16 different result values (four in each of four scenarios), especially when there are other methods available in Excel to perform a what-if analysis. But actually creating the scenario summary requires only one step—most of the work involved is in setting up the scenarios themselves.

After you have created the scenarios, you have a permanent structure you can use to do further what-if analysis. Each scenario is associated with a particular group of input assumptions, and you can modify the input assumptions as you see fit at a later time. You can also examine the effect of the assumptions on different sets of result cells. And you have a permanent record in the form of the scenario summary to refer to in the future.

This record is particularly useful when several colleagues contribute to the scenarios under consideration. The comments associated with their scenarios can contain the name of the contributor and the date that the scenario was created, so by showing those comments on the scenario summary it's easy to tell whose assumptions are contained in each scenario.

Displaying Changing Cells

At the beginning of this chapter, it was stated that including result cells is optional for a Scenario Summary. Changing cells are always included in the summary report, and you cannot suppress this. When you have several scenarios in the same worksheet and when the scenarios include different sets of changing cells, the report can become very long. This is because the report includes a row for each cell in the worksheet that is a changing cell in any scenario.

Thus, if Scenario A uses cells A1:J1 as changing cells and Scenario B uses A2:J2 as changing cells, the Scenario Summary will include twenty rows for changing cells. This can make a summary report lengthier than you might wish.

Fortunately, you can use the outline symbols to hide and display the rows that show the values of the changing cells in each scenario. If you choose to include result cells as well, the outline symbols will hide the rows that display the result cell values.

Pivot Table Summaries

The other option, besides the Scenario Summary, is the Scenario PivotTable. If you select this option, you must identify result cells. Therefore, make sure that you have meaningful result cells available on the worksheet that contains the scenarios (recall that result cells cannot be on a different worksheet than the scenarios).

If you create a pivot table summary based on the same scenarios as were used for the Scenario Summary in the prior section of this chapter, it appears as shown in figure 15.8.

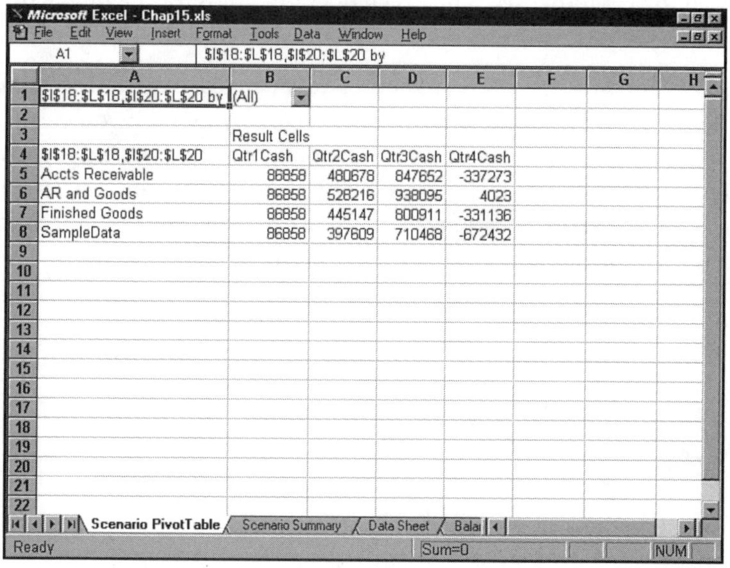

Fig. 15.8
The PivotTable summary shows result cells as items in the Data field and scenarios as items in its Row field.

The formatting is not as attractive as in the Scenario Summary, but the pivot table is interactive, and you can reorient the fields as you do in a pivot table that you create from scratch.

There are limitations to a pivot table created by the Scenario Manager, however. You cannot use the PivotTable Wizard on the Scenario PivotTable to respecify the original data range, and you cannot use Data, Refresh Data on the pivot table (as this book stresses, the latter is hardly a limitation). But the other options available in Steps 3 and 4 of the PivotTable Wizard are available as usual.

Chapter Summary

This chapter guided you through the creation of summary reports by using the Scenario Manager. Such reports are useful ways to display in one place the different results associated with different scenarios. Especially if you have defined many scenarios on one worksheet, it is much easier to view the results associated with each scenario by placing them on one worksheet than it is to cycle through each scenario in turn and note the outcomes visually.

The two types of summary reports available to you are the Scenario Summary and the Scenario PivotTable. Both reports appear in new worksheets. The Scenario Summary displays the values of the changing (and, optionally, the result) cells in a worksheet outline. It usually contains more information than the Scenario PivotTable, which does not display as much information and may need to be reformatted, but which does offer most of the interactive capabilities of pivot tables created by the PivotTable Wizard.

The next chapter explores ways to automate the management of scenarios by using VBA. You will find these techniques especially useful if you create the same scenario structures repetitively, as you might with monthly reports. Chapter 16 also discusses ways to use VBA to move information from multiple scenarios into one location, so that you can avoid the limitations imposed by Scenario Summaries and Scenario Pivot Tables.

16

Using VBA To Create and Manage Scenarios

Just as it's convenient, in the long run, to use Visual Basic for Applications (VBA) code to create and manage pivot tables, it's useful to use VBA code to create, manage, and summarize scenarios. This might seem like overkill—after all, what is there to do with a scenario other than to view it, and occasionally to edit its changing cells?

It turns out that you can use scenarios for a great deal more than "what if" analysis. By using them judiciously, you can manage a lot of data efficiently. The problem is that all that data and scenario management often results in so much keyboard and mouse work that whatever you gain in efficiency is lost.

The solution is to use VBA to do the hard work. As with pivot table management, the key is repetition: if you have reports or analyses that are needed on a regular basis, you will eventually save a significant amount of time by turning over as much as possible to VBA.

This chapter teaches you how to use VBA to collect data from many sources, merge it into one location, summarize it with a summary pivot table, and extract important units from the summary.

Collecting the Information

Suppose you have several worksheets in a workbook, each with a similar layout of data that's been obtained from a different source. As you've seen in Chapter 13, "Creating Business Scenarios," you can create a scenario on each worksheet and subsequently merge the scenarios into one worksheet. This is necessary before you can summarize the scenarios in either a summary report or a pivot table.

This is a typical situation faced by sales management, particularly when the sales representatives are geographically disperse. Consider the problem faced by a sales manager who must direct and support too many sales representatives, located in too many territories, as described in the following case study.

Case Study: Finding the Top Opportunities

As the sales manager of 16 sales representatives, you have arranged for each of them to submit an opportunity analysis report to you each month. They are scattered all over a multi-state area, and at the end of the month they each send you a small, one-sheet Excel workbook to you via file transfer. One such sheet is shown in figure 16.1.

Fig. 16.1
Each month, each of your sales representatives sends you a worksheet laid out like this one.

	A	B	C	D
1	Sales Rep	McHenry		
2	Territory	1		
3	Customer	Lanham Fire District	Fairfax Supply Company	Emphasis Services
4	Product			
5	Revenue	$53,342	$57,952	$28,956
6	Lease/Purchase	Lease	Lease	Purchase
7	Lease term	36	12	
8	Lease Factor	1.02	1.05	
9	Book Date	5/28/96	3/6/96	4/5/96
10	Probability	Low	Medium	Medium

Sheet tabs: McHenry / O'Brien / Lee / Sommars / Jackson / Wagr

Tip

You can use the Template Wizard to create a template for data entry, and to arrange for a routing slip to automatically send worksheets to you as they are completed. See Chapter 22, "Sending Data to External Sources," for a complete description.

You collect all 16 worksheets, one from each sales representative, into a single workbook. (You can view an example of the workbook by opening the file named OAR.xls from the companion disk.)

Each worksheet contains information on the sales representative's three most important current opportunities. These are defined as the opportunities that carry the greatest potential revenue during the next three months. The representative is asked to identify, among other information, the customer name, the revenue potential, and when the sale is expected to be made (the projected book or closure date).

> **Tip**
>
> An opportunity analysis report described here is a useful planning tool. However, it should not request so much data that the sales representative comes to resent the time needed to complete it.

Your purpose in collecting this information is partly to make revenue projections for the next three months to the vice-president of sales, but mainly to determine where you should focus your efforts to assist the sales representatives in closing their most important opportunities. Because you need to prioritize your efforts, each month you would like to find the three opportunities that:

- Carry the greatest amount of potential revenue
- Have the greatest likelihood of turning into an actual sale
- Are the most urgent, as defined by the amount of time you have until the projected book date

You have written VBA code that finds these three opportunities for you, from the 48 (three opportunities times sixteen sales representatives) reported to you each month. This code can be found in the module named Top3Accounts in OAR.xls on the companion disk, and is repeated and discussed below.

Creating the Initial Scenarios

The first block of code declares the subroutine GetTop3, declares a control variable *i* that is used in For-Next loops, and freezes the screen to cause the code to execute faster

```
Sub GetTop3()
Dim i As Integer
Application.ScreenUpdating = False
```

III

Scenario Management

The next line of code places a message on the status bar that tells the user what task is being accomplished at present

```
Application.StatusBar = "Please wait, creating scenarios . . ."
```

Then, a For-Next loop is executed sixteen times—once for each of the sixteen worksheets. These worksheets are the first sixteen in the workbook, so the statement With Sheets(i) establishes a reference to each worksheet in turn. Then, a scenario is added to the currently referenced worksheet. The scenario is given a name taken from the value of that worksheet's cell B1, or Cells(1,2). That cell contains the sales representative's name, so the scenario is named after the sales representative who provided the information.

The changing cells are defined as those within the range B1:D10, and the scenario is defined as locked but not hidden.

Notice that the object .Scenarios belongs to Sheets(i), as does the object .Cells and the object .Range. The With statement, identifying the currently referenced sheet, makes it unnecessary to use expressions such as Sheets(i).Cells(1,2)

```
For i = 1 To 16
    With Sheets(i)
        .Scenarios.Add Name:=.Cells(1, 2).Value,
ChangingCells:=.Range("B1:D10"), Locked:=True, Hidden:=False
    End With
Next i
```

Merging the Scenarios and Calculating Result Cells

After the loop terminates, each of the sixteen worksheets has a scenario associated with it. This makes it possible to merge all the scenarios into one sheet, which is the task of the next five statements

```
Application.StatusBar = "Please wait, merging scenarios . . ."

For i = 1 To 16
    Sheets("MergeScenarios").Scenarios.Merge Source:=Sheets(i)
Next i
```

The first of the five statements updates the user as to the macro's progress. Then, another For-Next loop is entered. Each time the loop executes, the scenario that has been created for each of the first sixteen worksheets is merged into the worksheet named MergeScenarios, which is shown in figure 16.2.

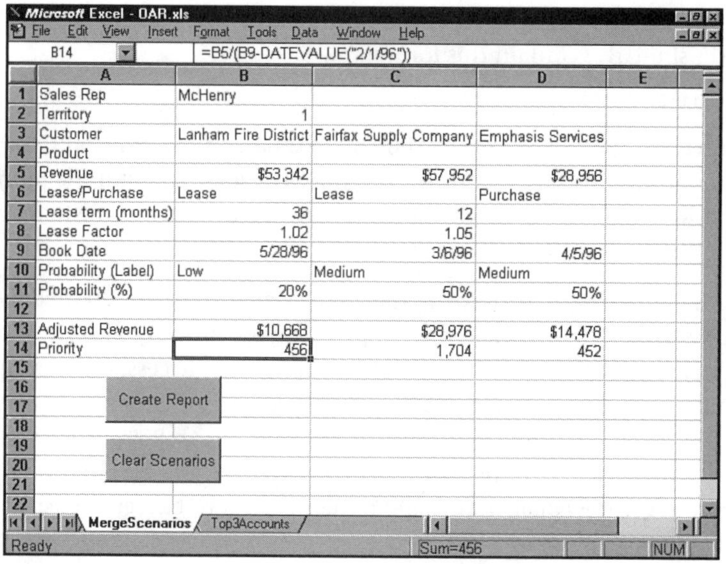

	A	B	C	D	E
1	Sales Rep	McHenry			
2	Territory	1			
3	Customer	Lanham Fire District	Fairfax Supply Company	Emphasis Services	
4	Product				
5	Revenue	$53,342	$57,952	$28,956	
6	Lease/Purchase	Lease	Lease	Purchase	
7	Lease term (months)	36	12		
8	Lease Factor	1.02	1.05		
9	Book Date	5/28/96	3/6/96	4/5/96	
10	Probability (Label)	Low	Medium	Medium	
11	Probability (%)	20%	50%	50%	
12					
13	Adjusted Revenue	$10,668	$28,976	$14,478	
14	Priority	456	1,704	452	

Fig. 16.2
This worksheet collects the 16 individual sales scenarios; shown is the scenario that belongs to McHenry.

The Create Report worksheet button executes the VBA subroutine GetTop3, currently being described. The Clear Scenarios button executes another subroutine, discussed at the end of this section.

Cell B11 of figure 16.2 contains this formula

```
=IF(B10="Low",0.2,IF(B10="Medium",0.5,IF(B10="High",0.8,0)))
```

So, if McHenry reports that the probability of closing this sale is Low, the formula assigns a numeric value of .2, or 20%. If not, the formula checks whether it reports Medium: in that case, it assigns a numeric probability of 50%. If not, the formula checks whether the value in B10 is High, and if so it assigns a numeric probability of 80%. If none of these possibilities exist, the formula assigns a value of zero. You're experienced enough to know that if a representative does not provide an estimate of the likelihood of closing a sale, your competition almost certainly already has a stranglehold on the prospect.

Tip

From time to time, it's useful to validate the probabilities reported by sales representatives against what actually happens with a given opportunity. For example, you might find that you must assign a numeric probability of 50% when a particularly optimistic sales representative reports a high probability of closing a sale.

The formula in B11 is replicated in cells C11 and D11. Cell B13 (and cells C13 and D13 similarly) contain this formula

```
=B11*B5
```

which returns the product of the numeric estimate of the probability of closing the sale and the sale's projected revenue. The logic is that if the probability of closing a selection of sales opportunities is, say, 80%, you will realize 80% of their potential revenue in the long run.

This is the first step in prioritizing the 48 sales opportunities reported by your sales representatives. For example, suppose one opportunity has a revenue projection of $100,000, but only a 20% likelihood of success. Opportunities like this will yield an average of $20,000 in revenue in the long run. Another opportunity has a revenue projection of $50,000, but an 80% likelihood of success. Similar opportunities will yield an average of $40,000 in revenue. Other things being equal, you would rather focus your energies on supporting $40,000 sales than on $20,000 sales.

Cell B14 in figure 16.2 contains this formula

```
=B5/(B9-DATEVALUE("2/1/96"))
```

The denominator of this ratio subtracts the date serial number for February 1, 1996 from the date serial number of the estimated book date for the sales opportunity. The assumption is that the analysis is being performed on February 1, and the denominator is therefore the number of days between the analysis date and the estimated book date.

Note

A more apt formula is

```
=B5/(B9-TODAY())
```

But if the day that you're actually reading this is sometime subsequent to March 1, 1996, that formulation would begin to return negative values, so the 2/1/96 value has been hard-coded into the formula.

The ratio's numerator is the anticipated revenue, as adjusted by the estimated probability of closure. The nearer the estimated book date, the smaller the denominator and, therefore, the larger the ratio. The formula combines the projected value of the sale with a measure of how soon it might occur, to give an estimate of its priority. The greater the revenue opportunity, and the sooner the sales representative hopes to close it, the more it deserves your attention.

Summarizing the Scenarios

At this point, you could terminate the analysis. The sixteen individual scenarios have all been merged into the sheet named MergeScenarios. You could activate the Scenario Manager manually, and step through each scenario, looking for the three opportunities with the greatest priority measure in cells B14:D14. However, it's much more convenient to let the VBA code continue to coalesce the analysis into one range of information. The code continues with a new status bar message

```
Application.StatusBar = "Please wait, creating pivot table summary
of scenarios . . ."
```

and then causes a pivot table summary to be created, by means of this statement

```
Sheets("MergeScenarios").Scenarios.CreateSummaryReportType:=xlPivotTable,
➥ResultCells:=Range("B5:D5,B9:D9,B14:D14")
```

The result cells are B5:D5 (revenue estimates), B9:D9 (estimated book dates) and B14:D14 (estimated priorities). These are the cells that become the Data fields in the summary pivot table. Because the Data field cells represent three different types of information (currency, dates, and the priority combination), they are formatted by means of the following With block

```
With ActiveSheet.PivotTables(1)
    .PivotFields("$B$5").NumberFormat = "$#,##0"
    .PivotFields("$C$5").NumberFormat = "$#,##0"
    .PivotFields("$D$5").NumberFormat = "$#,##0"
    .PivotFields("$B$9").NumberFormat = "m/d/yy"
    .PivotFields("$C$9").NumberFormat = "m/d/yy"
    .PivotFields("$D$9").NumberFormat = "m/d/yy"
    .PivotFields("$B$14").NumberFormat = "0"
    .PivotFields("$C$14").NumberFormat = "0"
    .PivotFields("$D$14").NumberFormat = "0"
End With
```

Notice that the With's object is `ActiveSheet.PivotTables(1)`. When a summary pivot table is created, it is placed on a new worksheet—which of course becomes the active worksheet. The summary pivot table is the first and only one on the new worksheet, so it is identified by its item number, 1. The resulting pivot table is shown in figure 16.3.

Extracting Information from the Summary

Again, you could stop at this point and search through the range B5:J20 for the opportunity with the largest priority value, find the name of the sales representative, return to the MergeScenarios worksheet, activate the Scenario Manager, show that representative's scenario, and find the opportunity associated with the largest priority. Then, you could repeat that process for the second- and third-largest priority values. As you might expect, there is an easier way.

This statement places an array formula in cells E22:E24

```
Range("E22:E24").FormulaArray = "=LARGE(R5C8:R20C10,{1;2;3})"
```

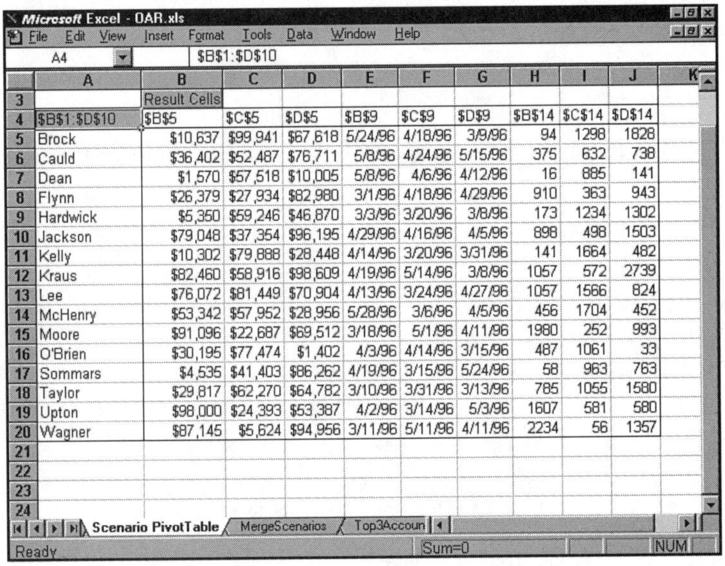

	A	B	C	D	E	F	G	H	I	J
3		Result Cells								
4	$B$1:$D$10	$B$5	$C$5	$D$5	$B$9	$C$9	$D$9	$B$14	$C$14	$D$14
5	Brock	$10,637	$99,941	$67,618	5/24/96	4/18/96	3/9/96	94	1298	1828
6	Cauld	$36,402	$52,487	$76,711	5/8/96	4/24/96	5/15/96	375	632	738
7	Dean	$1,570	$57,518	$10,005	5/8/96	4/6/96	4/12/96	16	885	141
8	Flynn	$26,379	$27,934	$82,980	3/1/96	4/18/96	4/29/96	910	363	943
9	Hardwick	$5,350	$59,246	$46,870	3/3/96	3/20/96	3/8/96	173	1234	1302
10	Jackson	$79,048	$37,354	$96,195	4/29/96	4/16/96	4/5/96	898	498	1503
11	Kelly	$10,302	$79,888	$28,448	4/14/96	3/20/96	3/31/96	141	1664	482
12	Kraus	$82,460	$58,916	$98,609	4/19/96	5/14/96	3/8/96	1057	572	2739
13	Lee	$76,072	$81,449	$70,904	4/13/96	3/24/96	4/27/96	1057	1566	824
14	McHenry	$53,342	$57,952	$28,956	5/28/96	3/6/96	4/5/96	456	1704	452
15	Moore	$91,096	$22,687	$69,512	3/18/96	5/1/96	4/11/96	1980	252	993
16	O'Brien	$30,195	$77,474	$1,402	4/3/96	4/14/96	3/15/96	487	1061	33
17	Sommars	$4,535	$41,403	$86,262	4/19/96	3/15/96	5/24/96	58	963	763
18	Taylor	$29,817	$62,270	$64,782	3/10/96	3/31/96	3/13/96	785	1055	1580
19	Upton	$98,000	$24,393	$53,387	4/2/96	3/14/96	5/3/96	1607	581	580
20	Wagner	$87,145	$5,624	$94,956	3/11/96	5/11/96	4/11/96	2234	56	1357

Fig. 16.3
The pivot table summarizes each of 48 scenarios: revenue in B5:D20, book dates in E5:G20, and priority in H5:J20.

Note

You can use two different reference styles in Excel: R1C1 and A1. Using the R1C1 style, you would identify the intersection of the third *Row* and the fourth *Column* as R3C4. Using the A1 style, you would identify the same cell as D3. To select the style you prefer, select Tools, Options, click the General tab, and choose either the A1 or the R1C1 option button.

The range in the array formula shown above is identified in R1C1 style notation, rather than A1 notation. This style is a requirement for the string that defines the array formula; it isn't a requirement if you are entering a regular worksheet formula.

The array formula finds the first, second, and third largest values in the range R5C8:R20C10—in A1 notation, H5:J20—which contains the calculated priority values. Note the array {1;2;3} as the second argument to the LARGE function, which specifies the first, second, and third largest values. The individual elements of the array are separated by semicolons. Using semicolons instead of commas creates an array consisting of one column and three rows, whereas {1,2,3} would create an array of one row and three columns. Because the array formula occupies one column and three rows (E22:E24), this argument must match the orientation of the range in which it's entered. In this way, the three largest priority estimates are found and placed in E22:E24.

The next statement places another array formula on the worksheet

```
Range("F22").FormulaArray =
"=SUM((RC5=R5C[2]:R20C[2])*ROW(R5C[2]:R20C[2]))"
```

The formula string uses a mix of absolute and relative referencing. For example, the expression R5C[2] means row 5, two columns to the right of the cell in which the formula is entered.

It will help to see this formula as it is represented on the worksheet

```
{=SUM(($E22=H$5:H$20)*ROW(H$5:H$20))}
```

This fragment

```
($E22=H$5:H$20)
```

returns an array of TRUE or FALSE values, depending on whether the value in E22 equals a value in H5:H20. E22 contains the largest priority value, and if that value is found in H5:H20 the array contains a TRUE. However, the value in E22 is not found in H5:H20, so the array contains 16 FALSE values.

This fragment

```
ROW(H$5:H$20)
```

returns the array {5;6;7;...20}, the row numbers that correspond to the range H5:H20. The array of FALSE values is multiplied by the row numbers. Because a FALSE value, when used in an arithmetic expression, is treated as a zero, the result of the multiplication is an array of zeroes. Finally, the full formula sums the values and returns, in F22, a value of zero.

That seems like a lot of work to return a zero. Bear with it: it will become clear shortly.

The next statement

```
Range("F22").AutoFill Destination:=Range("F22:H22"),
➥Type:=xlFillDefault
```

copies and pastes the formula in F22 into the range F22:H22 by means of an autofill—the formula is copied over itself and into the next two cells to its right. Here's the formula as it appears on the worksheet when pasted into cell H22

```
=SUM(($E22=J$5:J$20)*ROW(J$5:J$20))
```

All that differs in this formula, contrasted with the formula as it appears in F22, is that the range of values tested is J5:J20 instead of H5:H20. As it happens, the value in E22 (the largest priority estimate) exists in J5:J20. Therefore, this fragment

```
($E22=J$5:J$20)
```

returns this array

```
{FALSE;FALSE;FALSE;FALSE;FALSE;FALSE;FALSE;TRUE;FALSE;FALSE;
➥FALSE;FALSE;FALSE;FALSE;FALSE;FALSE}
```

The formula then multiplies the TRUE/FALSE array by the array of row numbers, to return this array

```
{0;0;0;0;0;0;0;12;0;0;0;0;0;0;0;0}
```

Finally, the formula takes the sum of the latter array, to return the single value 12—not surprisingly, 12 is the row in which the largest priority value is found: 2739.1 is found in cell J12.

The next statement

```
Range("F22:H22").AutoFill Destination:=Range("F22:H24"),
Type:=xlFillDefault
```

simply autofills the array formulas in F22:H22 so they appear in F22:H24. So doing accounts for the second and third largest priority values.

The worksheet now appears as shown in figure 16.4.

Next, the position of the largest value—the actual row number where the priority value is to be found—in the range F22:H22 is placed in cell I22

```
Range("I22").FormulaR1C1 = "=MATCH(MAX(RC[-3]:RC[-1]),RC[-3]:RC[-
➥1],0)"
```

and the formula is autofilled into the range I22:I24. This results in a 3-cell range containing the row numbers where the first-, second-, and third largest priority numbers are located in the pivot table

```
Range("I22").AutoFill Destination:=Range("I22:I24"),
➥Type:=xlFillDefault
```

Now, there is sufficient information on the worksheet to find the name of the sales representative associated with the largest priority value. This is just a matter of looking in the cell that is 12 rows down from cell A1

```
Range("A22").FormulaR1C1 = "=OFFSET(R1C1,MAX(RC[5]:RC[7])-1,0)"
```

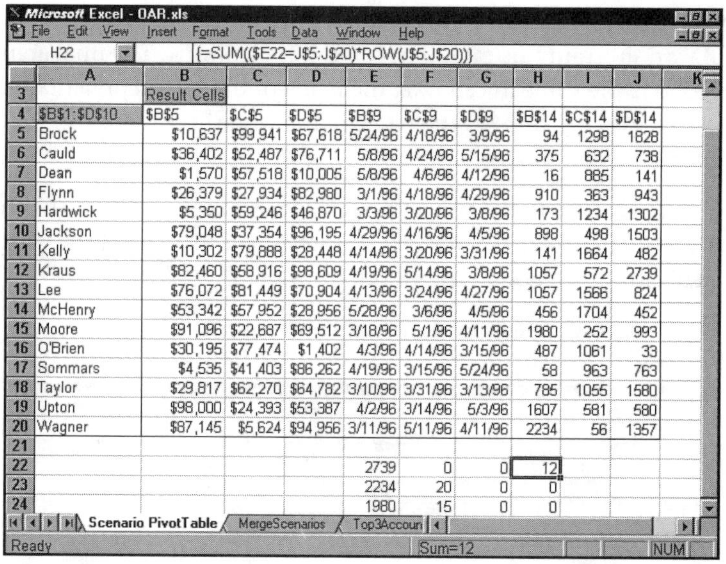

Fig. 16.4

Cells E22:E24 contain the three largest priority values. Cells F22:H24 contain the rows in the pivot table where those three priority values are located.

In words, this places in cell A22 the value of the cell that is offset from A1 (or R1C1) by the maximum value in the range F22:H22—or 12 rows, minus 1— and zero columns. That cell is A12, which contains "Kraus," the name of the sales representative who reports the opportunity with the largest priority value. The formula is autofilled into A22:A24, to return the names of the sales representatives who report the opportunities with the second- and third-largest priority values

```
Range("A22").AutoFill Destination:=Range("A22:A24"),
➥Type:=xlFillDefault
```

Now you know which sales representatives you should call to discuss any support that your office can offer in the process of closing the sales. When you make the phone calls, it would be convenient to know the names of the prospective customers as well as the estimated revenue associated with each opportunity and the anticipated book date. The VBA code arranges for the display of the customers' names as follows

```
Range("B22").FormulaR1C1 = "=INDIRECT(ADDRESS(3,RC[7]+1,,,RC[-1]))"
```

The formula as placed in cell B22 on the worksheet appears as

```
=INDIRECT(ADDRESS(3,I22+1,,,A22))
```

The first argument to the ADDRESS function is a row number: the customer's name is always in row 3 of the original 16 worksheets. The second argument makes use of the MATCH function that was placed in I22. It defines whether

III

Scenario Management

the customer is to be found in the second, third, or fourth column of the original worksheet; in this case, that column is column 4. The final argument to ADDRESS is the value in cell A22: the name of the sales representative. This argument to ADDRESS is the name of the worksheet to look in for the value in row 3, column 4.

So, the formula refers to the value in cell D3 (row 3, column 4) of the sheet named Kraus. That value is ServCo Office Services: the name of the customer associated with the largest of the 48 priority values.

The worksheet now appears as shown in figure 16.5.

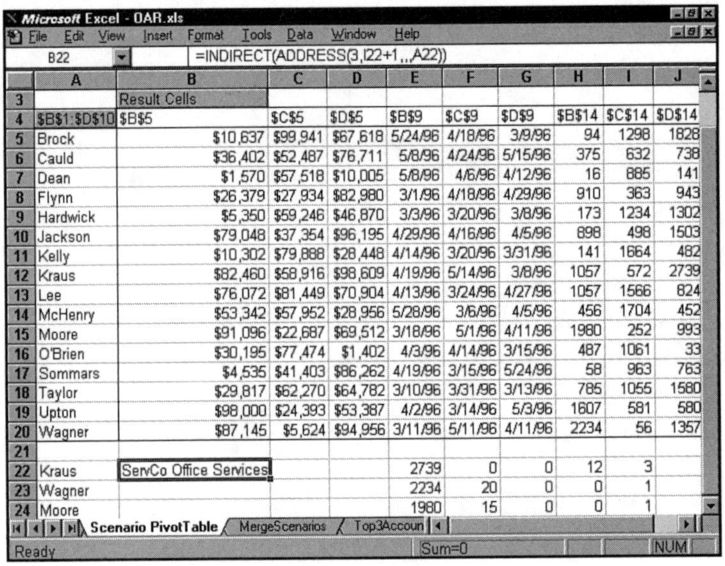

Fig. 16.5

Cells I22:I24 contain the column in the range F22:F24 that contains the row number of the three largest priority values. The formula bar shows how Excel interprets the formula in cell B22 to return the customer's name.

Microsoft Excel - OAR.xls

B22 =INDIRECT(ADDRESS(3,I22+1,,,A22))

	A	B	C	D	E	F	G	H	I	J
3		Result Cells								
4	$B$1:$D$10	$B$5	$C$5	$D$5	$B$9	$C$9	$D$9	$B$14	$C$14	$D$14
5	Brock		$10,637	$99,941	$67,618	5/24/96	4/18/96	3/9/96	94	1298	1828
6	Cauld		$36,402	$52,487	$76,711	5/8/96	4/24/96	5/15/96	375	632	738
7	Dean		$1,570	$57,518	$10,005	5/6/96	4/6/96	4/12/96	16	885	141
8	Flynn		$26,379	$27,934	$82,980	3/1/96	4/18/96	4/29/96	910	363	943
9	Hardwick		$5,350	$59,246	$46,870	3/3/96	3/20/96	3/8/96	173	1234	1302
10	Jackson		$79,048	$37,354	$96,195	4/29/96	4/16/96	4/5/96	898	498	1503
11	Kelly		$10,302	$79,888	$28,448	4/14/96	3/20/96	3/31/96	141	1664	482
12	Kraus		$82,460	$58,916	$98,609	4/19/96	5/14/96	3/8/96	1057	572	2739
13	Lee		$76,072	$81,449	$70,904	4/13/96	3/24/96	4/27/96	1057	1566	824
14	McHenry		$53,342	$57,952	$28,956	5/28/96	3/6/96	4/5/96	456	1704	452
15	Moore		$91,096	$22,687	$69,512	3/18/96	5/1/96	4/11/96	1980	252	993
16	O'Brien		$30,195	$77,474	$1,402	4/3/96	4/14/96	3/15/96	487	1061	33
17	Sommars		$4,535	$41,403	$86,262	4/19/96	3/15/96	5/24/96	58	963	763
18	Taylor		$29,817	$62,270	$64,782	3/10/96	3/31/96	3/13/96	785	1055	1580
19	Upton		$98,000	$24,393	$53,387	4/2/96	3/14/96	5/3/96	1607	581	580
20	Wagner		$87,145	$5,624	$94,956	3/11/96	5/11/96	4/11/96	2234	56	1357
21											
22	Kraus	ServCo Office Services			2739	0	0	12	3	
23	Wagner				2234	20	0	0	1	
24	Moore				1980	15	0	0	1	

Scenario PivotTable / MergeScenarios / Top3Accoun

Ready Sum=0 NUM

Again, the formula is autofilled into cells B22:B24, to return the names of all three customers

```
Range("B22").AutoFill Destination:=Range("B22:B24"),
➡Type:=xlFillDefault
```

The next three statements perform the same operation to obtain the original, estimated revenue amounts and book dates reported by Kraus, Wagner, and Moore. The only difference is in the rows (row 5 for the revenue and row 9 for the book dates) to look in on the three worksheets. Then, the range C22:D22 is autofilled into C22:D24

```
Range("C22").FormulaR1C1 = "=INDIRECT(ADDRESS(5,RC9+1,,,RC1))"
Range("D22").FormulaR1C1 = "=INDIRECT(ADDRESS(9,RC9+1,,,RC1))"
Range("C22:D22").AutoFill Destination:=Range("C22:D24"),
Type:=xlFillDefault
```

The revenues and book dates are given appropriate currency and date formats

```
Range("C22:C24").NumberFormat = "$#,##0"
Range("D22:D24").NumberFormat = "m/d/yy"
```

and, to avoid visual clutter, the results of the intermediate calculations in E22:I24 are hidden in their respective cells

```
Range("E22:I24").NumberFormat = ";;;"
```

The width of columns B through D are autofit to the size needed to display the values

```
Columns("B:D").EntireColumn.AutoFit
```

and the status bar is changed back to the "Ready" message, the screen is unfrozen, and the subroutine is ended

```
Application.StatusBar = False
Application.ScreenUpdating = True
End Sub
```

The final result of this processing is shown in figure 16.6.

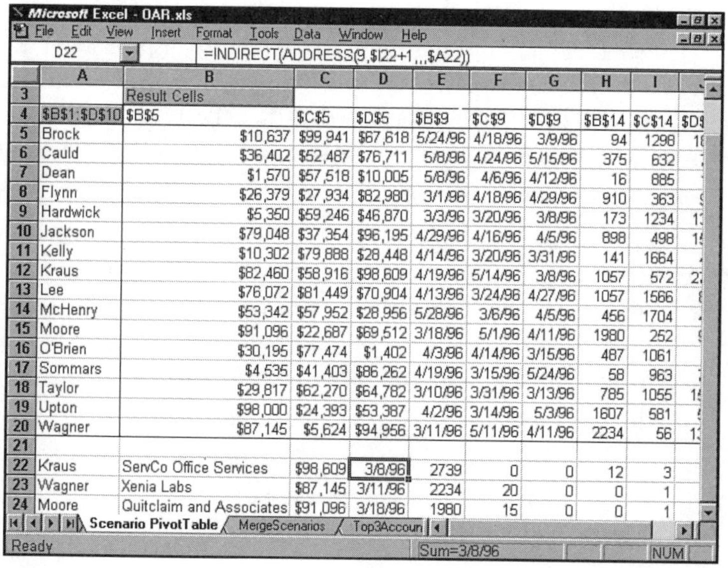

Fig. 16.6
The collection of the data from 16 worksheets and the identification of the three opportunities with the highest priorities would take at least several minutes if done by hand. Using VBA, it takes a few seconds at most.

It might be necessary to revise some of the information supplied by the sales representatives. For example, when you contact Kraus, you might learn that the opportunity does not carry quite as high a likelihood of success as was reported. In that case, you should activate Kraus's worksheet and modify the reported probability level. Having done so, it's necessary to perform the process of scenario creation, merging, and summarizing—but you should clear the scenarios first. Clicking the Clear Scenarios button on the MergeScenarios worksheet accomplishes this (refer to figure 16.2). You are then once again in a position to create, merge, and summarize the scenarios, which will probably result in a different set of three highest-priority opportunities.

> **Tip**
>
> This technique is useful whenever you receive Excel workbooks that are laid out identically. Use it to check physical inventory counts from different warehouses (identify stock that moves too slowly), time sheets that claim too many billable hours, and invoices with unusually small amounts due. The technique combines beautifully with the Template Wizard, which provides identical worksheet layouts and automatic workbook routing.

Chapter Summary

In this chapter, you have learned how to apply VBA to the process of scenario management. When you must manage many scenarios, especially on a repetitive basis, VBA can speed and ease the task dramatically. With a little care, you can create VBA code that will ensure that the reports and analyses based on scenarios are executed in precisely the same fashion time after time; this results, of course, in consistent analysis from report to report.

You have also seen how you can use VBA to enter into the worksheet formulas of both the array and the single-cell varieties. You can use these formulas to extract information from a scenario summary and to refer back to the original worksheets. In this fashion, you can summarize scenarios so you have access to all the information in one place, and then identify detail information that has some particular importance to you.

This chapter concludes the section on scenario management. The next section of the book examines an alternative to scenarios: consolidations. It also discusses the situations in which you might prefer consolidations to scenarios.

Part IV

Consolidations, Views, and Reports

17

Consolidating Business Information

All too often, data as simple as expense-account reporting and as complex as company-wide budgeting arrives on your desk not in a single, neat list, but in a fistful of independent—but related—worksheets or workbooks. Fortunately, Excel provides superior tools for imposing some structure on such data disorder.

The most obvious data consolidation tool is that everyday workhorse, the workbook formula. Excel's multi-dimensional workbooks make it easy to envision and implement this kind of consolidation, and many people are now comfortable enough with the three-dimensional metaphor to take advantage of it. Typically, the "3-D" approach to consolidation involves setting up a series of identical data worksheets within a workbook, then creating a summary worksheet at the front of the workbook that adds (or performs a similar statistical operation) all the corresponding cells in the data worksheets.

For more complex consolidations, a formulaic approach isn't always the answer. The quickest way to resolve such problems usually lies with Excel's Data, Consolidate command. The Data, Consolidate command allows you to consolidate ranges that don't reside in identical areas of the worksheet—an operation that's easy to botch when using formulas. It also allows you to generate accurate consolidations from tables of data that aren't even structurally identical.

Consolidations can be glamorous as well. Microsoft has integrated Excel's table-consolidation feature with the pivot table feature discussed in earlier chapters. You can thus use Excel's Data, PivotTable command to consolidate several ranges into a pivot table that performs just like a pivot table created from a single list. This feature can give you insights into relationships within your data that wouldn't necessarily be evident if you were to use only simple consolidation techniques.

This chapter discusses all of these data consolidation options. Although data consolidation isn't one of the simplest tasks you'll attempt in Excel, the results can be remarkable—and essential for anyone whose responsibilities include intensive data management.

Consolidating with Formulas

With the advent of 3-D spreadsheets, budget planners everywhere quickly latched onto the idea of "roll-up" workbooks. If every sheet in a workbook contained data arranged in an identical structure, it would be a simple matter to insert a single summary sheet whose formulas calculate statistics (such as sum, average, or standard deviation) for all of the data sheets.

Figure 17.1 shows such a summary sheet. Although you can't see it in the figure, this workbook contains four additional nonblank sheets—one for each department in this hypothetical company—in addition to the summary sheet. Each of the departmental sheets has a structure identical to the summary sheet.

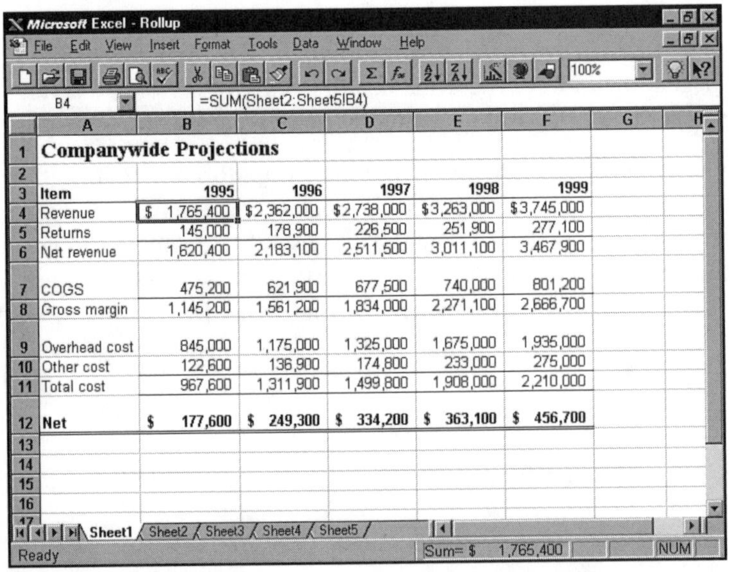

	A	B	C	D	E	F
1	Companywide Projections					
2						
3	Item	1995	1996	1997	1998	1999
4	Revenue	$ 1,765,400	$2,362,000	$2,738,000	$3,263,000	$3,745,000
5	Returns	145,000	178,900	226,500	251,900	277,100
6	Net revenue	1,620,400	2,183,100	2,511,500	3,011,100	3,467,900
7	COGS	475,200	621,900	677,500	740,000	801,200
8	Gross margin	1,145,200	1,561,200	1,834,000	2,271,100	2,666,700
9	Overhead cost	845,000	1,175,000	1,325,000	1,675,000	1,935,000
10	Other cost	122,600	136,900	174,800	233,000	275,000
11	Total cost	967,600	1,311,900	1,499,800	1,908,000	2,210,000
12	Net	$ 177,600	$ 249,300	$ 334,200	$ 363,100	$ 456,700

Fig. 17.1
The simplest form of data consolidation is a "roll-up" in which data from several identical sheets are combined onto a single summary sheet.

Creating Formulaic Consolidations

Excel includes some advanced tools which make it almost effortless to create such a workbook. For example, to make sure all the sheets in the workbook have an identical structure, you can use Excel's Group mode to create them simultaneously.

Select the first sheet in the group, then Shift+click the tab of the last sheet in the group to employ Group mode. Now, everything you enter in one sheet in the group automatically gets entered in the corresponding cells in all the other sheets. When we typed the word Revenue in cell A4 of Sheet1, it simultaneously appeared in cell A4 of Sheet2, Sheet3, Sheet4, and Sheet5, because we had grouped those sheets.

> **Tip**
>
> When in Group mode, Excel automatically applies any changes you make to one sheet in the group to the other sheets. This includes formatting, row widths, and column heights, as well as the entries you place in the cells.

Using Group mode, we quickly created the five identical sheets we need for our consolidation. Although Group mode is so handy that it seems we might want to use it all the time, it's necessary to turn it off once we enter and format the basic structure of our worksheets (the row and column headings in ranges A3:A12 and B3:F3). Only when the sheets are ungrouped can we enter text, data, formulas, and formatting that are unique to the individual sheets. To end Group mode, right-click the sheet tab of a grouped sheet, then select Ungroup Sheets from the shortcut menu.

Once the workbook is set up and the data entered in the four departmental worksheets (Sheet2 through Sheet5), it's time to create the consolidation formulas in Sheet1. To do this quickly and accurately, use Excel's Point mode to create the first three-dimensional formula, then copy that formula to the other cells in the summary sheet.

Point mode allows you to construct a formula by pointing and clicking on cells, rather than typing cell references into a formula. This is especially helpful when creating formulas that span more than one worksheet, since the syntax can be a little confusing.

To create the first 3-D formula in the summary worksheet, we entered

```
=SUM(
```

in cell B4. We clicked Sheet2's sheet tab to display that sheet, then clicked cell B4 to enter it into the formula. Finally, to extend the selection from Sheet2 to Sheet5, we Shift+clicked Sheet5's sheet tab and pressed Enter. The completed formula

```
=SUM(Sheet2:Sheet5!B4)
```

uses the SUM function to consolidate the contents of cell B4 in sheets 2 through 5.

From here, completing the summary sheet is simple. Just copy the existing 3-D formula, such as the one we just created in cell B4 of Sheet1, to the rest of the relevant cells in the summary sheet. In the example, we copied the formula in cell B4 to range B4:F12.

When creating your own consolidations, it may be easier to follow the generic step-by-step list provided below. (These steps assume that your consolidation will take place on multiple sheets within the same workbook, and that all the sheets have the same structure—the optimal circumstances for a formulaic consolidation.)

1. Group the sheets that will contain the data and the consolidation summary. Select the first sheet in the group, then Shift+click the tab of the last sheet. If the tab of the last sheet is not initially available, use the tab-scrolling arrows to scroll to it.

2. Enter the row and column headings in one of the grouped sheets. The text you type appears in all the sheets. Apply the necessary formatting to the headings, along with the cells that will contain data and formulas.

3. Right-click the sheet tab of one of the grouped sheets, then select Ungroup Sheets from the pop-up menu.

4. Enter data in the appropriate sheets.

5. Enter text specific to each sheet (such as a heading in cell A1). Change the names on the sheet tabs if you desire.

6. Enter the consolidation formulas in the summary sheet. Begin by creating one summary formula with a 3-D reference. Type the first part of the formula, such as

   ```
   =SUM(
   ```

   then click on the same cell in the first data sheet. (For example, if you are entering the formula in cell B4 of Sheet1, click cell B4 of Sheet2.)

Finally, Shift+Click the tab of the last data sheet, type a right parenthesis, and press Enter.

7. Copy the formula to all relevant cells in the summary sheet. Choose Edit, Copy, select all the cells that will contain summary formulas, and choose Edit, Paste.

Note

You can use some of these techniques to create formulas that consolidate data from ranges in other workbooks, as long as those workbooks are open. You can use Point mode, for example, by choosing the Window command, displaying the appropriate workbook, and pointing to the desired cell.

After creating such a formula, you can copy it to generate an entire summary table, the same way you can with single-workbook formulas. However, be aware that when you use Point mode to create a reference to another workbook, the reference is absolute, rather than relative. You must change all absolute references to relative references before you can create the summary consolidation table. (See Chapter 1 for a complete discussion of absolute and relative references.)

There are other caveats to consider when you use formulaic consolidations with multiple notebooks. The process of creating the initial formula can be tedious, because you must point to the outside notebooks one by one. It's important to make sure you point correctly, because erroneous references in outside notebooks are notoriously difficult to detect.

Evaluating the Advantages of Formulaic Consolidations

The formulaic method of consolidating data described in the previous section is an obvious choice for many consolidation operations. The smaller and more specialized the consolidation you want to perform, the more likely it is that the formulaic approach is best. The following points summarize the advantages of consolidating data with formulas:

- The consolidation is dynamic. Whenever data changes, the formulas in the summary update automatically.

- The consolidation is flexible. The consolidation formulas in the summary sheet can comprise any calculations that can be performed by an Excel formula. If necessary, you can create a consolidation far more complex than the simple SUM formulas in the example. In addition, it's easy to insert additional data sheets between existing sheets; the consolidation updates automatically.

However, formulaic consolidation isn't for every occasion. Depending on the size of a worksheet, it can be a real resource drain. It's also fairly easy for mistakes to creep in when the data being consolidated is in tables that aren't identical to the consolidation summary. Here is a summary of the disadvantages of consolidating data with formulas:

- Formulas require more memory. In a small worksheet, this is a minor consideration. When resources are scarce, however, a large formulaic consolidation can have a noticeable impact on performance.

- Getting the consolidation right becomes tricky when the consolidation summary isn't located in the same part of the worksheet as all of the data ranges that comprise it. For example, suppose you're trying to consolidate the following three ranges: Sheet2!B4:C13, Sheet3!R26:S35, Sheet4!G21:H30. Even if you're using Point mode, you can botch one or more of these references in the consolidation, and the mistake may not be readily evident.

Using the Data, Consolidate Command

The results produced by Excel's Data, Consolidate command are, in general, almost exactly like those described for formulaic consolidations in the previous section. After you issue the command, you get a summary table that represents the combined values of several source ranges.

In terms of advantages and disadvantages, however, the Data, Consolidate command is pretty much a mirror image of the formulaic consolidation method. By default, the command creates a static table that does not update automatically (although you can specify live links). It also requires you to list the sources of your consolidation on a range-by-range basis, rather than by creating and copying formulas that refer to the source ranges. This reduces the chance for error when the source tables are located in different parts of a sheet than the summary table or come from different files.

Finally, the Data, Consolidate command offers a special feature not available when you use formulas: the ability to consolidate source ranges based on the column and row labels for those ranges. This option can be a real time-saver if your source ranges all contain the same data, but in a different order. As long as the column and row labels are spelled identically in all the tables, Excel will be able to consolidate the information correctly.

In a nutshell, the Data, Consolidate command is preferable to formulaic consolidation under the following circumstances:

■ You are consolidating a large amount of data that would require a large number of formulas.

■ The source ranges for the consolidation are located in different parts of each sheet of the workbook, or in different workbooks.

■ The source ranges for the consolidation contain compatible data, but the data is organized differently in some or all of the source tables.

■ The source ranges for the consolidation contain compatible data that is organized identically, but the row and column labels of the source tables are different.

Consolidating Ranges with the Same Structure

To illustrate the process of consolidating ranges with the same structure, we'll use the three small tables shown in figure 17.2. Normally, of course, consolidations take place on a much larger scale, and comprise source ranges in multiple sheets or workbooks. However, the process works equally well in a single sheet (with one key exception, discussed in this section), so we'll keep things simple for the sake of illustration.

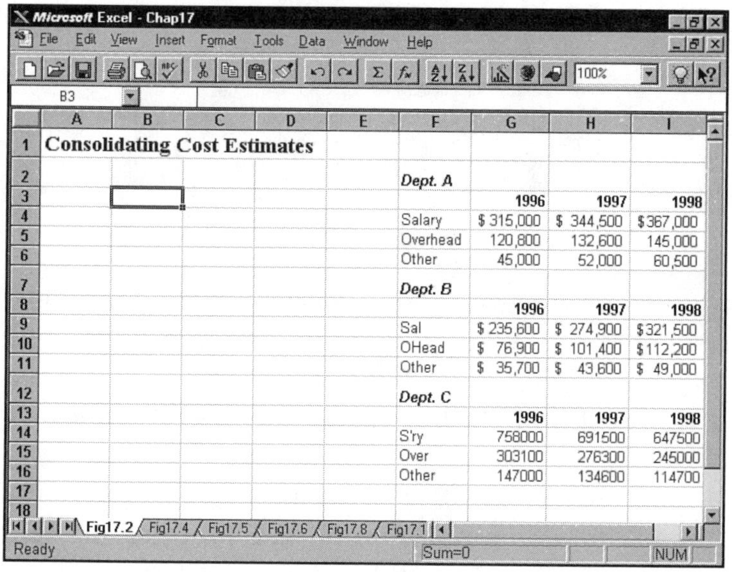

Fig. 17.2
The Data, Consolidate command can quickly combine these three tables into a single, company-wide cost estimate.

Each small source table comprises a single department's projected operating cost over three years. Note that the structure of the three tables is the same— the rows (Salary, Overhead, Other) appear in the same order in each table, as do the columns (1996, 1997, 1998). However, the tables use different abbreviations for the terms *salary* and *overhead*. The example below shows how to overcome these small discrepancies.

To get a company-wide estimate of operating costs, you need to consolidate these three source tables in range A3:D6. This kind of consolidation is a prime candidate for the Data, Consolidate command. You could also use a formulaic consolidation, but it would be a rather tedious matter to create these formulas because the source ranges are not arranged neatly one behind the other on separate sheets of the workbook. With the Data, Consolidate command, you'll be able to identify the entire source ranges, one by one, rather than relying on copies of a single formula.

When you choose Data, Consolidate, the Consolidate dialog box opens as shown in figure 17.3.

Fig. 17.3

The Consolidate dialog box lists the ranges to be consolidated and the function used to perform the consolidation.

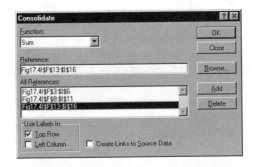

You use this dialog box to specify two key elements of the consolidation: the ranges that contain the source tables, and the statistical operation that will take place in the consolidation (sum, average, standard deviation, and so forth). The process can be summarized as follows:

1. Place the cell pointer in the first cell of the consolidation summary table.

2. Choose Data, Consolidate. The Consolidate dialog box appears.

3. Select the function for the consolidation. In most cases, the default, SUM, is appropriate. Click the drop-down arrow to see all the available consolidation options.

4. With the cursor in the <u>R</u>eference edit box, type or point to the range containing the first source range for the consolidation. If the source range is in a different workbook that is currently open, you can choose <u>W</u>indow, select the name of the workbook to display it, then point to the range. If the source range is in a different workbook that is not currently open, you can use the <u>B</u>rowse button to identify the workbook file. You must then add a range name or address after the workbook file name.

5. Choose <u>A</u>dd to add the table reference in the <u>R</u>eference edit box to the All R<u>e</u>ferences scroll list.

6. Repeat steps 4 and 5 for each source range that you want to include in the consolidation table.

7. Make the appropriate checkbox selections (discussed in the next few paragraphs).

8. Choose OK.

Caution

When you create a consolidation summary table, Excel will overwrite existing data if necessary. To create a consolidation summary table with a specific number of columns and rows, select the range that contains those columns and rows. To create a consolidation summary table with a specific number of columns and an unlimited number of rows, select the cells in the first row of the consolidation summary table. To create a consolidation table with a specific number of rows and unlimited columns, select the cells in the first column of the consolidation summary table.

Excel uses the settings shown earlier in figure 17.3 to create the consolidation summary table shown in range B3:D6 of figure 17.4. In figure 17.3, the source ranges shown in the All R<u>e</u>ferences list box are identified by cell references to help illustrate the consolidation process. In real life, it's generally best to use carefully chosen range names; these make the consolidation much easier to interpret when you return to the Consolidate dialog box.

Fig. 17.4

The consolidation settings shown in figure 17.3 produced this consolidation table. Because the Left Column checkbox was deselected, we placed the cell pointer in cell B3 rather than cell A3 before choosing Data, Consolidate.

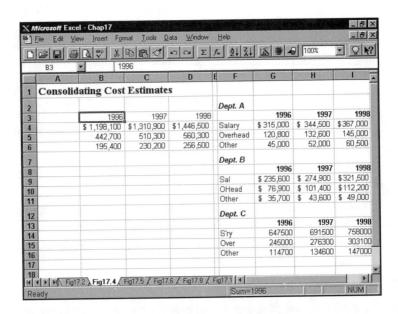

There are a couple of things to note about the completed consolidation table. First, the consolidation table does not have any row headings, because we left the Left Column checkbox in the Consolidate dialog box blank. This was necessary because the source tables used different labeling for the terms *salary* and *overhead*. When these checkboxes are selected, Excel uses the row and column headings to determine which rows and columns in the source tables should be consolidated. This is a useful feature when rows and columns are out of order, as we'll see in the next example. However, in this example, Excel would have treated *Salary, Sal,* and *S'ry* as three different entities, and would have created a separate row for each in the summary consolidation table. Therefore, we must type in the row headings that we prefer in the left column of the summary consolidation table, range A4:A6.

> **Note**
>
> When you deselect the Left Column or Top Row checkboxes in the Consolidate dialog box, you must manually create the omitted headings in the summary consolidation table.

The second thing to notice about the summary consolidation table is the formatting. Each of the three source tables uses different formatting—one with all currency, one with some currency, and one mixed. When you perform a consolidation, Excel applies the formatting from the first source table listed in the All References scroll list to the consolidation summary table.

Figure 17.5 shows the flip side of the previous example. In this example, we have the same three source tables, and this time the spellings of the row and column headings are identical. That's fortunate, because the placement of the rows and columns themselves varies from table to table.

> ### Caution
>
> When you use row and column headings to perform a consolidation of source tables that are arranged differently, be sure the column and row labels within each source table are unique. For example, if each source table has four rows labeled *Subtotal*, the four subtotals will be consolidated into one—probably not what you intended. To prevent this, change the identical headings to make them unique—Subtotal1, Subtotal2, and so forth.

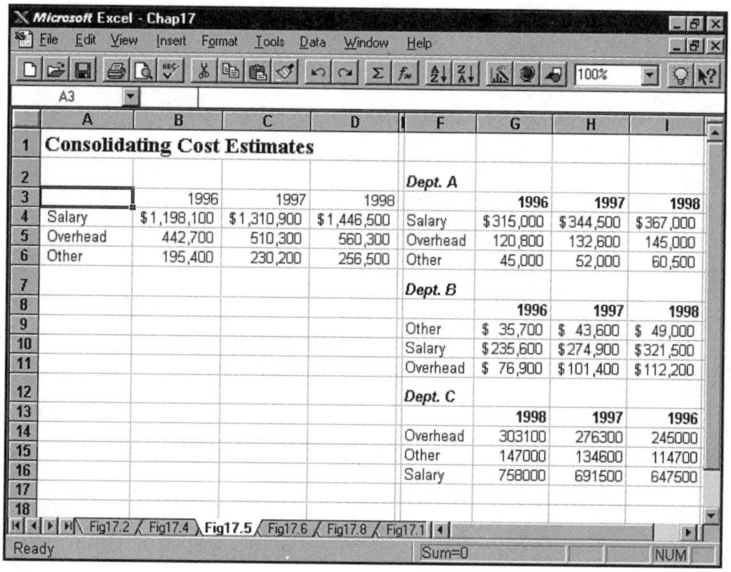

Fig. 17.5

When source tables contain the same information but are structured differently, you can still perform a successful consolidation by using the Left Column and Top Row settings in the Consolidate dialog box.

IV

Consolidations and Views

In this case, we can perform a successful consolidation by selecting both the Left Column and Top Row checkboxes in the Consolidate dialog box. With these settings activated, Excel uses the row and column headings, rather than the structure of the table, to perform the consolidation. Salary data is combined with salary data, 1996 data is combined with 1996 data, and so on. No matter where the data fall in the source tables, the consolidation will always be correct, as long as the row and column headings are all entered correctly.

> **Note**
>
> When you consolidate source tables with different structures, Excel may not arrange the summary consolidation table in the order you want. To prevent this, enter the row and column headings for the summary consolidation table before you perform the consolidation. The row and column headings you use must match those in each of the source tables for the consolidation to be successful.

Linking and Updating Consolidation Tables

In addition to the many options discussed in the previous section, the Consolidate dialog box also gives you the ability to create a *linked* consolidation summary table—one that updates dynamically, just like the formulaic consolidation summary tables discussed at the beginning of this chapter. In fact, when you select the Create Links to Source Data checkbox in the Consolidate dialog box, Excel places formulas *within* the consolidation summary table, then hides the rows where those formulas reside.

Choosing the Create Links to Source Data checkbox in the Consolidate dialog box is very much like entering your own formulas, only faster. The wide range of consolidation functions offered by the Consolidate dialog box cover the functionality most often used in consolidations. A further advantage is the All References list box in the Consolidate dialog box, which clearly spells out the source tables used in a consolidation.

However, there are a few structural reasons *not* to use a linked consolidation summary table instead of formulas that you create yourself:

- Excel limits you to one consolidation summary table per sheet.
- A linked consolidation summary table cannot reside on the same sheet as one of its source tables. (It would be impossible, therefore, to create the summary consolidation tables in figs. 17.4 and 17.5 as linked tables.)

- Excel hides rows when it creates a linked consolidation summary table, so any other data that resides in the same rows as the summary table may also be hidden.

In addition, linked tables require additional system resources, the same way formulas you create yourself do. However, for most small consolidations that would be difficult to generate with formulas, a linked consolidation summary table created with the Consolidate dialog box is optimal.

> **Tip**
>
> Linked consolidation summary tables are optimal for small consolidations whose source ranges reside in a different place on each sheet of a workbook or in different workbooks.

When you choose not to create links to the source ranges, a consolidation summary table remains static, even if the data in the source ranges changes. Fortunately, it's easy to update the table: simply choose Data, Consolidate, then choose OK in the Consolidate dialog box. Because Excel allows only one consolidation summary table per sheet, you don't have to worry about identifying which consolidation you want to update.

Because the Data, Consolidate command opens the Consolidate dialog box, you can also edit a consolidation before updating it. You can add or delete source ranges in the All References list box, choose different settings for the Top Row, Left Column, and Create Links to Source Data checkboxes, and even choose a different summary function.

Consolidating with Pivot Tables

One of the most advanced aspects of Excel's powerful pivot table feature is its ability to consolidate data from several source ranges into a single pivot table. Along the way, you can choose to create up to four filters for the consolidated pivot table.

Figure 17.6 shows four small source ranges that we'll consolidate into a single pivot table. Of course, most consolidations involve several source ranges on different sheets or in different workbooks, but a single-sheet example makes it easier to conceptualize this somewhat complicated process.

Fig. 17.6

These four source ranges can be consolidated into a single pivot table, complete with up to four custom filters.

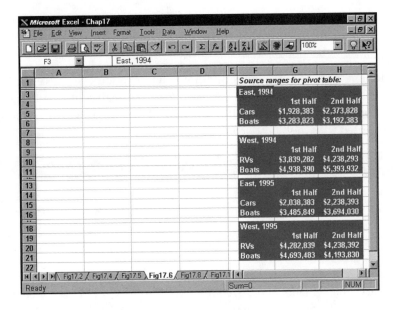

What's the advantage of consolidating source ranges such as these into a single pivot table? First, you can view combined sales for both regions and product lines, the way you can with a normal consolidation table. More important, by creating the proper page filters you can immediately update your consolidated data to show, for example, total sales for 1995, or total sales for a particular region, or sales for a specific region in a specific year.

The following is a list of the steps you use to create a consolidated pivot table, complete with custom page filters. Before attempting to create a consolidated pivot table, you may want to familiarize yourself with step 2b of the Pivot-Table Wizard (shown in fig. 17.7), because this is where most of the action takes place. As you can see, step 2b can politely be described as a chink in Excel's "user-friendly" armor; for the uninitiated, there's little clue what to do here.

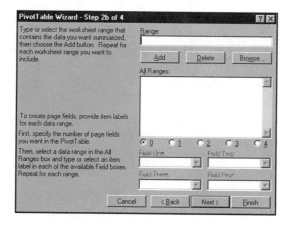

Fig. 17.7
Step 2b of the
PivotTable wizard
takes some getting
used to, but the
results are worth it.

But even though this dialog box is somewhat involved, the step-by-step
method makes creating a consolidation pivot table almost foolproof. Once
you see how we generated the completed pivot table (shown in fig. 17.8),
you'll have a better appreciation of the additional data management capabilities you get when you add the page filters.

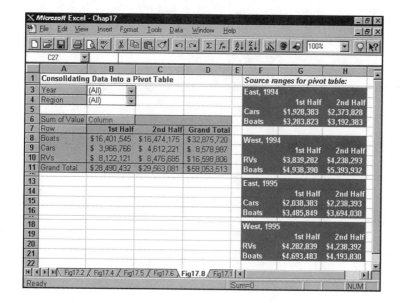

Fig. 17.8
The completed
consolidation
pivot table
includes two page
filters, which allow
you to display data
for specific years
and regions.

Here are the steps required to consolidate a pivot table from several source tables:

1. Choose Data, PivotTable.

2. In step 1 of the PivotTable Wizard, select the Multiple Consolidation Ranges option button, then choose Next.

3. In step 2a of the PivotTable Wizard, select the I Will Create Page Fields option button, then choose Next.

4. In step 2b of the PivotTable Wizard, identify the first source range in the Range edit box. You can point to the range, enter a cell reference, or choose the Browse command button to specify a different workbook file. In the latter case, you must add the range name or cell references of the source table to the file name. In the example, the first source range is located in range F4:H6.

5. When the reference in the Range edit box is complete, choose the Add command button to add it to the All Ranges scroll list.

6. Repeat steps 4 and 5 until all source tables are listed in the All Ranges scroll list. In the example, we added the three other source ranges shown in figure 17.6—ranges F9:H11, F14:H16, and F19:H21. Figure 17.9 shows these ranges listed in the All Ranges scroll list of the dialog box.

Fig. 17.9
Step 2b of the PivotTable wizard with settings appropriate for the example in figure 17.9. Here, the Field One and Field Two drop-down lists display field settings for the first source range, which is highlighted.

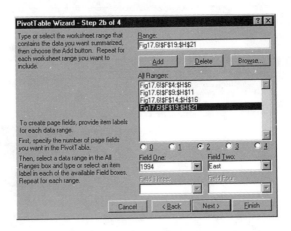

7. Select one of the numbered option buttons (numbered 0 through 4) to specify the number of page fields you want to create in the pivot table. In the example, we have selected 2. This means we have two ways to filter the data in the completed table.

8. Select the first source range in the A<u>l</u>l Ranges scroll list.

9. Create the page filters. As shown previously in figure 17.8, we want to be able to filter the completed pivot table two ways, by year and by region, so we selected option button 2. At this point, the drop-down list boxes for Field <u>O</u>ne and Field <u>T</u>wo became available.

You use these list boxes to specify how a source range relates to the filters you want to create. In this example, the first filter relates to the year; the second relates to the region. Therefore, to specify that the data in range F4:H6 relate to 1994, type **1994** in the Field <u>O</u>ne drop-down list. To specify that the data in this range relate to the East region, type **East** in the Field <u>T</u>wo drop-down list. Figure 17.9 shows how these entries appear in the dialog box.

10. Repeat steps 8 and 9 for each of the source ranges in the A<u>l</u>l Ranges list box. In the example, the second source range was identified as 1994 in the Field <u>O</u>ne drop-down list and West in the Field <u>T</u>wo drop-down list. The third source range was identified as 1995 and East; the fourth source range was identified as 1995 and West.

> ### Tip
>
> Do not press Enter as you repeat steps 9 and 10. To identify the data for a different source range, select that source range in the A<u>l</u>l Ranges list box. If you accidentally press Enter, use the PivotTable Wizard's Back command button to return to step 2b and enter the field information for all source ranges that are listed in the A<u>l</u>l Ranges list box.

11. When you have finished entering field information, choose Next.

12. In step 3 of the PivotTable wizard, reconfigure the fields if necessary. In the example, no reconfiguration was needed, as shown in figure 17.10. Excel will create a consolidated summary table with the same row and column structure as the four source tables. The data within the tables will be summed. Choose Next.

13. In step 4 of the PivotTable wizard, specify a location and name for the pivot table. You can also use the checkboxes to control various pivot table options, as described in other chapters of this book.

14. Choose Finish to create the pivot table.

Fig. 17.10

Once you get
past step 2b, the
PivotTable wizard
returns to familiar
ground. In step 3,
we accept the
defaults (shown
in the figure) to
create a pivot
table with the
same structure as
the source tables.

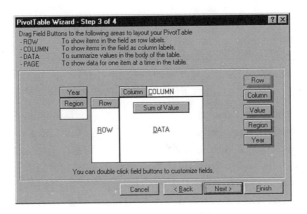

As the preceding steps indicate, the tricky part of creating a consolidation
pivot table is indicating how each source table should be identified in the
Field drop-down lists. The important thing to remember is that Excel doesn't
select the filter that each drop-down list will represent—you do. In the example, we decided that the Field One drop-down list would represent the
year, and the Field Two drop-down list would represent the region. If we had
decided that a regional filter was unnecessary, we could have skipped the
Field Two drop-down list.

It may be tempting to skip the drop-down lists altogether, due to the effort
involved, but this deprives you of a great deal of the power of the pivot table.
Figure 17.8 showed the completed consolidation pivot table with both filters
set to All, and the pivot table shows basically the same information as if there
were no filters at all—it's simply a summation of all sales by product line and
method of sales.

However, by selecting a specific region from the second filter, as shown in figure 17.11, you can immediately view the sales for that region only. This information came from the source ranges, but isn't readily available because it's
fragmented between those ranges. With the consolidation pivot table, you
can ask almost any conceivable question of the data—an option that becomes
enormously powerful if you have more than a few source ranges and create
the appropriate page filters.

If creating such page filters in step 2b of the PivotTable Wizard just seems like
too much trouble, there is a way to avoid it while still creating a powerful
consolidation pivot table. The trick is to select the Create a Single Page Field
For Me option button in step 2a of the PivotTable wizard, instead of the I
Will Create the Page Fields option button specified in step 3 of the numbered
steps listed earlier in this section.

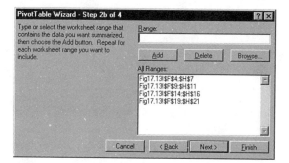

X Microsoft Excel - Chap17							
File Edit View Insert Format Tools Data Window Help							
		B9		3966766			
	A	B	C	D	E	F	G	H
1	Consolidating Data Into a Pivot Table					Source ranges for pivot table:		
3	Year	(All)				East, 1994		
4	Region	East					1st Half	2nd Half
5						Cars	$1,928,383	$2,373,828
6	Sum of Value	Column				Boats	$3,283,823	$3,192,383
7	Row	1st Half	2nd Half	Grand Total				
8	Boats	$ 6,769,672	$ 6,886,413	$ 13,656,085		West, 1994		
9	Cars	$ 3,966,766	$ 4,612,221	$ 8,578,987			1st Half	2nd Half
10	Grand Total	$ 10,736,438	$ 11,498,634	$ 22,235,072		RVs	$3,839,282	$4,238,293
11						Boats	$4,938,390	$5,393,932
13						East, 1995		
14							1st Half	2nd Half
15						Cars	$2,038,383	$2,238,393
16						Boats	$3,485,849	$3,694,030
18						West, 1995		
19							1st Half	2nd Half
20						RVs	$4,282,839	$4,238,392
21						Boats	$4,693,483	$4,193,830

Fig17.4 / Fig17.5 / Fig17.6 / Fig17.8 \ Fig17.11 / Fig17

Ready   Sum= $ 3,966,766   NUM

Fig. 17.11
The page filters
you create in
step 2b of the
PivotTable wizard
allow you to ask
questions of the
data that aren't
readily answered
in the individual
source ranges.
Here, the pivot
table displays
consolidated sales
over the two-year
period, but only
for the eastern
region.

When you tell Excel to create a single page field for you, step 2b of the
PivotTable wizard is easier to manage, as shown in figure 17.12. All you have
to do is identify the source ranges you want to consolidate, using the Add
button to add them, one by one, to the All Ranges scroll list.

```
PivotTable Wizard - Step 2b of 4                              ? X
Type or select the worksheet range that    Range:
contains the data you want summarized,     [                        ]
then choose the Add button. Repeat for
each worksheet range you want to              Add      Delete     Browse...
include.
                                           All Ranges:
                                           Fig17.13!$F$4:$H$7
                                           Fig17.13!$F$9:$H$11
                                           Fig17.13!$F$14:$H$16
                                           Fig17.13!$F$19:$H$21



                         Cancel    < Back    Next >    Finish
```

Fig. 17.12
When you let
Excel create the
page field for you,
step 2b of the
PivotTable wizard
seems a little more
manageable.

However, you get what you pay for. The resulting pivot table contains only a
single filter, as shown in figure 17.13. What's more, the filter corresponds to
the source ranges; in the example, which contains four source ranges, it displays *Item1, Item2, Item3,* and *Item4.* Selecting *Item1* filters the pivot table to
display only data from the first source range; selecting *Item2* filters the pivot
table to display data from the second source range, and so forth.

This default filtering system does add some value to the pivot table, because you can immediately view the contents of any of the source ranges without ever leaving the pivot table. However, it's a far less powerful tool than a custom filtering system you create yourself.

Fig. 17.13

When you let Excel create the page filter for you, the filter criteria correspond to the source ranges you used to create the pivot table.

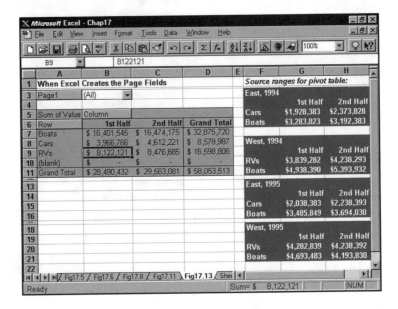

Chapter Summary

Excel contains a number of powerful consolidation tools. The most obvious is the workbook formula, which lends itself to "roll-up" summary consolidations of several identical sheets in a 3-D workbook.

Although you can also use formulas to consolidate data in sheets that aren't identical, or data that resides in different workbooks, Excel's Data, Consolidate command is usually a more appropriate tool. The Consolidate dialog box lets you point to each source range that you want to include in a consolidation, and lets you choose from a wide array of summary statistics. The Consolidate dialog box also lets you consolidate summary ranges whose columns and rows aren't in the same order, as long as the column and row headings in all the tables are identical. Finally, you can use the Consolidate dialog box to create a summary consolidation table with active links to its source ranges, although there are a few caveats involved.

Most powerful of all is the option to consolidate source ranges into a pivot table. When you create a consolidation pivot table, the PivotTable Wizard gives you the opportunity to create your own custom page filters for the table. Although this process is somewhat involved, the result is a powerful tool that can give you unexpected insights into the data contained in your source ranges.

18

Managing Different Views

It's 4:00 a.m., and you're awake and sweating. Today is the annual sales meeting, and you have to present the national sales results in front of 87 sales representatives, sales managers, and vice presidents. This time you're not going to get lost in a shuffle of overhead transparencies.

Using Excel's Group and Outline capability, you've structured a worksheet that can show or hide sales by representative, by manager, by region, and by quarter. You plan to show this worksheet on a wall projection of your computer's display. The only problem left is how to switch quickly among the different outline settings—this is not a group that waits patiently while you search for just the right combinations of detail and summary rows and columns.

If you use the View Manager, you're problem is solved. The View Manager is an Excel add-in, and not a terribly complicated one. You use it to define different ways of viewing a worksheet. You set up different views to contain different settings, such as:

- Which rows and columns are hidden, and which are displayed
- Whether a worksheet should be printed in Portrait or Landscape orientation
- Whether to show or hide row and column headings
- Whether to show or hide automatic page breaks

After you've defined one or more views, you use the View Manager to specify how the worksheet should be displayed or printed. This chapter shows you how to define your worksheet views.

Choosing Actions from the View Manager

To access the View Manager, choose View, View Manager. If you don't see the View Manager option in the View menu, you will have to install it in Excel using Tools, Add-Ins. Click the View Manager checkbox in the Add-Ins Available list box.

If you don't see the View Manager option in the Add-Ins Available checkbox, you will need to run the Setup program again, and choose to include the View Manager in the installation from your Excel disk or CD.

When you choose View, View Manager, the dialog box shown in figure 18.1 appears.

Fig. 18.1
Use the View Manager to choose a view to show or delete.

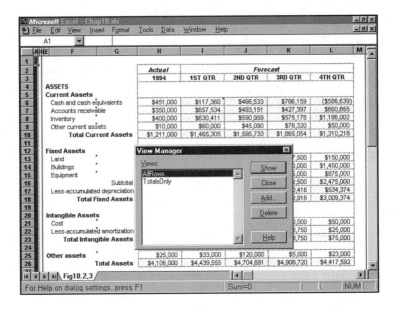

If no views are defined for the current worksheet, the Show and Delete options are not available.

Tip

A view belongs to a particular worksheet, just as does a scenario. If there are views defined for Sheet1, you do not see them in the Views box if Sheet2 is active.

Each action available from the View Manager is described below.

Showing a View

When you select a view from the Views box and choose Show, two things happen:

■ Display settings come into play, such as whether rows and columns in the active worksheet are hidden or displayed. These include many of the options you can set using Tools, Options and clicking the View tab in the Options dialog box.

■ At the time that the view was defined, certain print settings were in effect. They might well have been the default settings, or you might have specified Headers and Footers, or some other print setting. Whatever settings were selected at the time the view was defined are in effect when you show the view.

The cell formats do not change, their values are unaffected, and the displayed worksheet range remains the same (however, the cell that was active at the time the view was defined is the active cell when the view is shown).

But any rows or columns that were hidden when the view was defined are hidden when you click Show. For example, if you suppressed the display of gridlines on the worksheet when you defined the view , the gridlines vanish. And any print setting such as Print Area, Orientation (Portrait versus Landscape) or any other option that pertains to how a worksheet is printed, is activated.

This makes it very easy to switch back and forth between detail and summary views that you might have created by means of the Group and Outline item in the Data menu. If you hid any rows by means of filtered lists when you defined a view, the rows are again hidden when you show the view. You can also use the View Manager to switch between a view that displays cell formulas and one that displays cell values.

The View Manager also makes it easy to switch from print settings that are appropriate for a report—suppressed row and column headings, for example—and settings that are appropriate for development work—where you might want to show row and column headings on the printout.

Figures 18.2 and 18.3 show an example, taken from the Business Planner template. In figure 18.2, an entire screen of worksheet rows is shown.

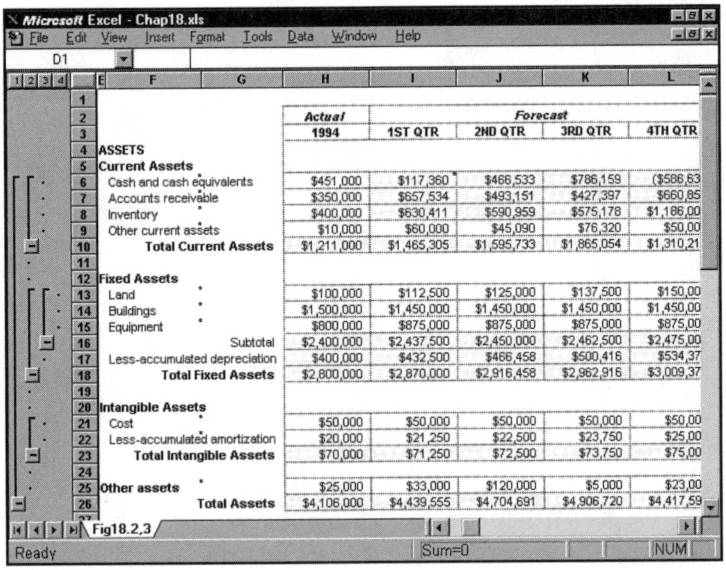

Fig. 18.2

In this view, the worksheet is outlined, but the rows are ungrouped.

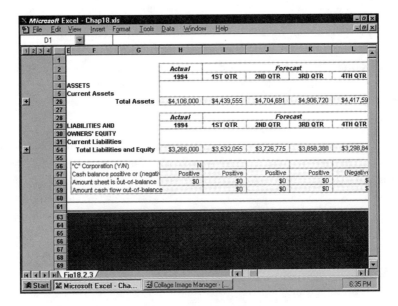

In figure 18.3, the detail rows are grouped and hidden, so only the total figures for assets and liabilities are visible.

Fig. 18.3

In this view, the detail lines are grouped.

To display these views, open the file named Chap18.xls from the companion disk, switch to the sheet named Fig18.2,3 and choose <u>V</u>iew, <u>V</u>iew Manager. The view shown in figure 18.2 is named AllRows, and that shown in figure 18.3 is named TotalsOnly.

In addition to the hidden versus displayed status of rows and columns, other display options that you can save in a view include showing or hiding:

- Automatic page breaks
- Formulas (if formulas are hidden, values are displayed, and vice versa)
- Gridlines (you can also associate particular colors with gridlines in different views)
- Row and Column headers
- Outline Symbols
- Zero Values
- Horizontal Scroll Bar
- Vertical Scroll Bar
- Sheet Tabs
- Objects (you can also choose to show an object's placeholder instead of the object itself)

To set the options listed above, choose <u>T</u>ools, <u>O</u>ptions and click the View tab. Fill or clear the appropriate checkbox for each option in the Options dialog box, and choose OK. Then, use the View Manager to define a view that keeps the settings you've just chosen, as described in the next section.

Adding and Deleting Views

Both adding and deleting views are straightforward processes. Simply set your display options as you want. Then choose <u>F</u>ile, Page Set<u>u</u>p and choose whatever printing options you want associated with a particular view. Then, follow these steps:

1. Choose <u>V</u>iew, <u>V</u>iew Manager. The View Manager dialog box appears.
2. Click <u>A</u>dd. The dialog box shown in figure 18.4 appears.
3. In the <u>N</u>ame edit box, type a descriptive name for the view.

Tip

Names such as GridsHidden or LandScape make it easier to remember which display and print settings are associated with each defined view.

4. Click either or both the Print Settings and Hidden Rows & Columns checkboxes, and choose OK.

Fig. 18.4

You can set print settings, hidden rows or columns, or both in the Add View dialog box.

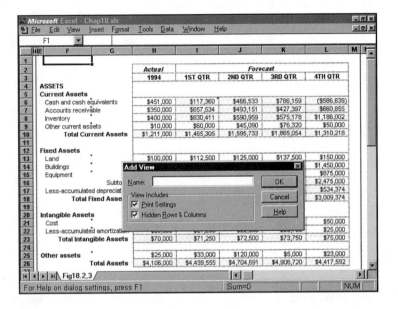

> **Note**
>
> There is no option within the View Manager to use or ignore the current display settings that are selected in the View tab of the Options dialog box or in the Page Setup dialog box. These must be set before you start the View Manager.

After you have added a view, it's a simple matter to use it: just choose View, View Manager, highlight the view you want in the Views list box, and choose Show.

To delete a view, follow the same procedure as to show a view, but choose Delete instead of Show.

Modifying a View

The Scenario Manager enables you to modify changing cells, but the View Manager doesn't offer a similar option. Instead, to modify a view, you choose the print and display settings that you want, and start the View Manager. Choose Add, and in the Name edit box retype the name of the view that you want to redefine. Choose OK, and choose OK again in response to the warning message that asks you if you want to overwrite the existing view. The old view will be changed to reflect the current settings.

Handling Special Situations: Document Protection and Page Numbering

There are two further points that you should be aware of before employing the View Manager: workbook and worksheet protection can interfere with your use of the View Manager, and a problem exists with page numbering when you print a view.

Using View Manager with Protection

When you define a view, you're setting certain options that pertain to a worksheet's display properties, possibly including whether rows and columns are hidden or displayed.

When you protect a worksheet, you might choose to protect its contents, its objects, its scenarios, or some combination of the three.

If a worksheet's contents are protected by choosing Tools, Protection, Protect Sheet, it should not be possible to hide visible rows and columns, or to display hidden rows and columns. However, this comes into conflict with the View Manager, which is capable of hiding and displaying rows and columns according to the user's choice of view.

Therefore, you can't use the View Manager to add or show a view if a worksheet's contents are protected. If you try to do so, you receive a message that you "Cannot show or define views on a protected document." In that case, if you want to use the View Manager, you will have to unprotect the sheet. You can, however, use the View Manager on a worksheet whose objects and scenarios are protected.

Similar reasoning applies to workbook protection. If you protect a workbook to prevent changes to its windows arrangement, you won't be able to use the View Manager. If you were able to do so, you could define a view with different windows display options than those in an existing view. This would conflict with the workbook's protection of its windows display, and so you are prevented from using the View Manager. To use it, you must unprotect the workbook first.

You can, however, use the View Manager in a workbook whose Structure (only) is protected. The structure of a workbook refers to adding, moving and deleting sheets. Because views belong to a particular worksheet, there is no conflict between adding or showing a view and the structure of the workbook's sheets.

View Manager and Page Numbering

When you print a worksheet that contains views by using the Report Manager (see Chapter 20), a conflict can arise. You may have several pages to print, and choose the Auto setting for First Page Number in the dialog box that appears when you choose File, Page Setup (this is the default setting).

Suppose that you also choose the Use Continuous Page Numbers option in the Add Report dialog box within the Report Manager. The conflict is that, in this case, each printed page will show 1 as its page number, instead of incrementing to 2, to 3 and so on. Here is a workaround:

1. Choose View, View Manager, and select the view that you want to print in the View Manager dialog box. Choose Show.

2. Choose File, Page Setup, and select the Page tab in the Page Setup dialog box.

3. Type the numeral **1** in the First Page Number edit box, and choose OK.

4. Choose View, View Manager and click Add in the View Manager dialog box.

5. In the Add View dialog box, reenter the name of the current view—that is, the view that was active when you modified the first page number from Auto to 1. Ensure that the Print Settings checkbox is checked, and choose OK.

6. Respond OK to the message that warns you about overwriting an existing view.

This removes the conflict between the Auto setting for the first page number and the Use Continuous Page Numbers option in the Add Report dialog box.

Chapter Summary

In this chapter, you learned about using the View Manager to switch quickly among views of a worksheet. Each view can specify a different combination of display options available from the View tab of the Options dialog box, of hidden or unhidden rows and columns, and various print options available in the Page Setup dialog box.

Worksheet and workbook protection play a part in the View Manager's availability. Under certain protection options, you are unable to add, show, or delete a view.

Views, scenarios, and the Report Manager are closely interrelated. For example, you can use the Report Manager to print views and scenarios that you have defined for a particular worksheet. These relationships are discussed in greater detail in Chapter 19.

19

Choosing Between Scenarios and Consolidations

The last several chapters have introduced two methods of managing data with Excel: scenarios and consolidations. While these two methods share some similarities, there are differences between them, and these differences tend to dictate the circumstances in which you should choose one or another. This chapter describes some of the requirements imposed and options available to help guide you in your choice of method.

Understanding the Issues

Among the issues you should consider when choosing between coalescing data with scenarios and with consolidations are:

- How you want to view the detail information
- How you want to view summary information
- The amount of data you want to make available to the active worksheet
- Maintaining links to the original sources
- The type of data you want to use

Viewing Details

Both scenarios and consolidations can take data from other worksheets or workbooks and move the data to the active worksheet. But the data are moved in different ways.

With a consolidation, all the data from the different consolidation ranges are simultaneously available on the worksheet itself. You can choose to display or hide the detail information by using the outline symbols that accompany the range of consolidated data.

With scenarios, the data in the changing cells of each scenario are not immediately visible on the active worksheet. You generally choose to change the data in the worksheet cells by selecting different scenarios with the Scenario Manager.

If it's important for you to be able to see—with as little effort as possible—the detail information that has been moved into the active worksheet, consolidate the information rather than put it into scenarios. To view all the detail information in a worksheet's scenarios—including both changing cells and result cells—it's necessary first to create either a scenario summary report or a pivot table.

However, if you want to be able to see the differential effects of source data on formulas, you should create scenarios. With one set of formulas—or even with just one formula—you can view what happens to result cells under different scenarios or combinations of scenarios. This sort of analysis is available from a consolidation, but unless the result formula happens to be one of the summary consolidation functions, you need to set up as many formulas as you have consolidation sources.

> **Tip**
>
> In a business context, it's typical to employ the Scenario Manager to create data roll-ups while a summary report is still under development. Subsequently, you might opt to use a consolidation to generate the final summary report.

Viewing Summary Functions

Of scenarios and consolidations, only consolidations make it possible to directly summarize the data *across* different sources. For example, suppose you want to examine information about product sales over a series of years. In this case, you should choose to consolidate the data sources if you want to be able to see the sum of product revenue across years. In contrast, if each scenario represents a different year, you can't view the total of product sales across all years unless you summarize the scenarios by means of a pivot table.

Consolidations also offer greater flexibility than scenarios when it comes to viewing relationships between individual values. Suppose the consolidation source for each year contains data on the number of sales representatives and total sales. By including a formula in the consolidation sources that divides total sales by total sales staff, you can consolidate the average sales revenue per sales representative.

This is more difficult to achieve by way of scenarios. Scenarios store the values of their changing cells as values, not as formulas. Although a changing cell can contain a formula when it is added to a scenario, the fact that the Scenario Manager converts the formula to a value reduces the degree of flexibility in an analysis.

Suppose that, once again, you are interested in average revenue per sales representative. Each of several worksheets contains information about sales for a given year, with a scenario that includes total revenue, number of sales representatives, and average revenue per representative. When you merge these scenarios into one worksheet, you are stuck with the original averages, even if revenue estimates change. You cannot subsequently revise the total revenue by editing the scenario and expect that the average revenue per sales representative will adjust to reflect that change.

Choosing the Amount and Type of Source Data

Consolidations enable you to bring considerably more data into a target worksheet than do scenarios. You can identify up to 255 different source ranges for one consolidation table, and the size of the combined consolidation ranges is limited only by the amount of memory installed on your computer.

Limitations on a worksheet's scenarios are different. The number of scenarios you can define is limited by available memory. But the maximum number of scenarios that can be included in a summary report is 251, and any one scenario can have no more than 32 changing cells. Clearly, you can move much more data into a consolidation range than you can into a worksheet's scenarios.

A consolidation cannot represent text data from a source range in the consolidation range; text data is represented as a blank cell in the consolidation. Scenarios, on the other hand, can deal with both text and numeric information in their changing cells.

Maintaining Links

With consolidations, you can choose to maintain links between the consolidation range and the source ranges. Therefore, if you find that you want to modify a value in a source range after creating the consolidation, you can do so, and the consolidation range will adjust accordingly.

With scenarios, there can be no link between the worksheet cell and the associated changing cell. Once the worksheet cell has been used as a scenario's changing cell, the only way to modify the changing cell's value within that scenario is to edit the changing cell itself.

A related matter is the location of the source range. You can create a consolidation from a range—and maintain links to that range—in a workbook that isn't currently open. But if you want to merge scenarios from other workbooks into an active worksheet, those workbooks must be open when you perform the merging operation.

Summarizing Scenarios and Consolidations Using Pivot Tables

You can summarize the scenarios in a worksheet by means of a pivot table, and you can use the PivotTable Wizard to summarize multiple consolidation ranges. But the *structures* of the resulting pivot tables are radically different. Suppose you have two source ranges as shown in figures 19.1 and 19.2.

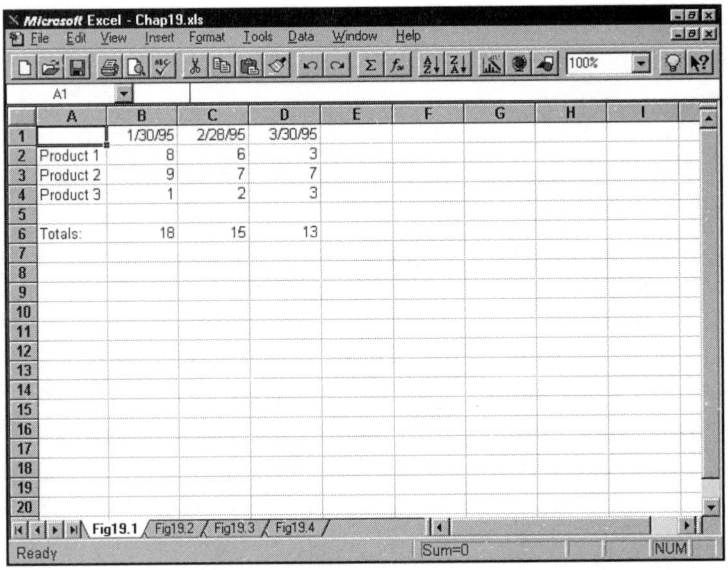

	A	B	C	D
1		1/30/95	2/28/95	3/30/95
2	Product 1	8	6	3
3	Product 2	9	7	7
4	Product 3	1	2	3
5				
6	Totals:	18	15	13

Fig. 19.1 This source range displays product sales data for the first three months of 1995.

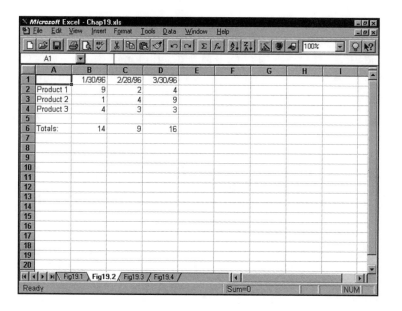

IV

Consolidations and Views

Fig. 19.2
This source range for 1996 is laid out identically to the range shown in figure 19.1.

If you create a scenario on each sheet that consists of changing cells B2:D4, you can merge them into another worksheet. On the new worksheet, you create three result cells in B6:D6, as shown in figure 19.3.

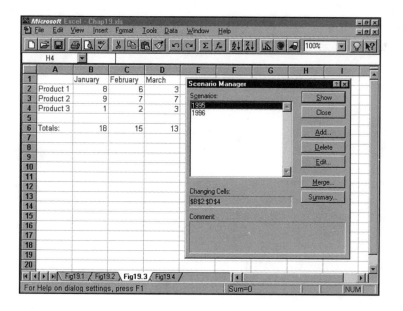

Fig. 19.3
This worksheet contains two scenarios, merged from the worksheets shown in figures 19.1 and 19.2.

Now suppose you use the PivotTable Wizard to create a pivot table, using cells A1:D4 on each of the worksheets in figures 19.1 and 19.2 as multiple consolidation ranges (see Chapter 8 for a description of this process). On the worksheet in figure 19.3, you use the Scenario Manager to create a pivot table summary of the two merged scenarios, as described in Chapter 15.

The two pivot tables—one created by the Scenario Manager, the other created by the PivotTable Wizard—are shown in figure 19.4.

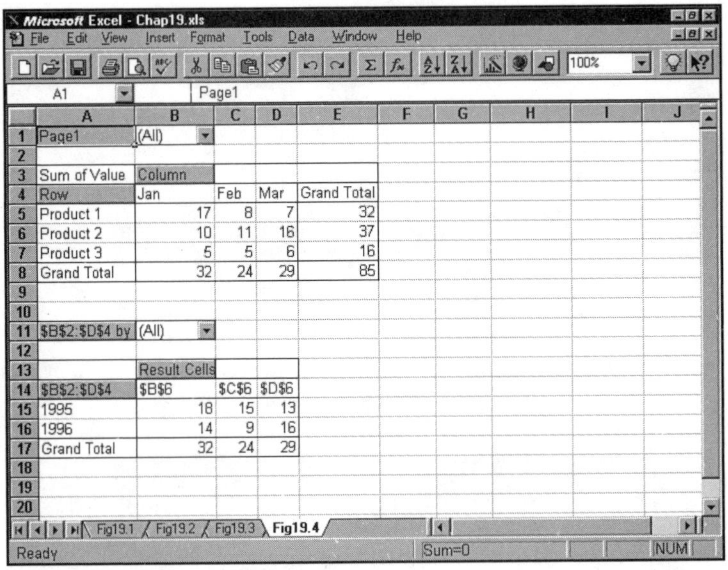

Fig. 19.4

The pivot table created by the PivotTable Wizard uses Product as the Row field; the table created by the Scenario Manager uses scenarios as the Row field.

(For clarity, the Column field of the first pivot table in figure 19.4 was grouped by month.)

Figure 19.4 shows the difference in structures of the two pivot tables. When you use the PivotTable Wizard to create a table based on multiple consolidation ranges, the resulting Row field consists of the source category labels. In contrast, the pivot table created by the Scenario Manager's Summary uses the individual scenarios as the Row field.

Tip

Especially when different scenarios are created by different contributors, the Scenario Manager's pivot table summary can be a particularly useful tool. Because each row represents a different scenario, you are in a position to check the correspondences *across* scenarios. When you are sure that contributors have provided appropriate data, you can use the PivotTable Wizard to perform the consolidation.

Therefore, if you want the Row field to represent each source range, collapsing across distinct rows in that range, use the Scenario Manager to create the pivot table. If you want the Row field to represent category labels without distinguishing between or among source ranges, use the PivotTable Wizard to summarize consolidation ranges.

Chapter Summary

This chapter discussed some of the considerations that should guide you in your choice of a method—scenarios or consolidations—to summarize information in different workbook or worksheet ranges. Among the issues to consider are how you want to view the resulting summary information, the amount of data there is to combine, whether links to the sources are desirable, and the structure of any pivot tables you use to represent the summaries.

The next chapter is the final one in this section on consolidations and views. It describes the Report Manager, a means of defining printed reports that consist of different worksheet views and scenarios.

20

Putting It Down on Paper

An important feature of any software program dedicated primarily to data management, such as Microsoft Excel or Borland dBASE for Windows, is the program's built-in report writer. The report writer arranges the records in a table (or list) into a grouping scheme that you specify; calculates statistics, such as subtotals or averages, for the groups; and then prints the full report in a neatly formatted series of pages. In many business contexts, this format for data reporting is the standard by which your reports will be measured.

You can achieve the same result in Excel, but it takes a bit more effort. Excel offers a built-in Report Manager, but it doesn't really address this need. The Report Manager is a specialized tool that allows you to organize views and scenarios into sections of a larger printed report. Instead, you combine several other Excel features in a series of steps that produce the printed output your audience expects.

If you have Access 95 on your system, there's an alternative—the Access report designer. Like the Access form designer described in Chapter 3, "Representing Business Forms on the Worksheet," the Access report designer is available through Excel's Data menu. But there's an important difference: unlike the Access form designer, which can lead the unsuspecting Excel user into a thicket of thorny technical issues, the Access report designer is a powerful tool that's simple to understand and straightforward to use.

This chapter discusses the many ways to put your data on paper, including an all-Excel solution and the speedier Access alternative. The chapter also covers a few highlights of the Page Setup dialog box, which gives you more control over the appearance of ad-hoc print jobs that you create from a list, and closes with the special reporting tasks simplified by the Excel Report Manager.

Creating a Database-Style Report from a List

When you need to create a printed report of the data in your Excel list, simply printing the list rarely is sufficient. To create a report that approximates the level of detail you find in most database programs—and displays your data in a common business format that others find easy to interpret—you use Excel's sorting and subtotaling tools. You then format the report and print it.

Figure 20.1 shows the sample sales list used to illustrate the reporting process. This section describes the steps you use within Excel to turn this list into a presentable report.

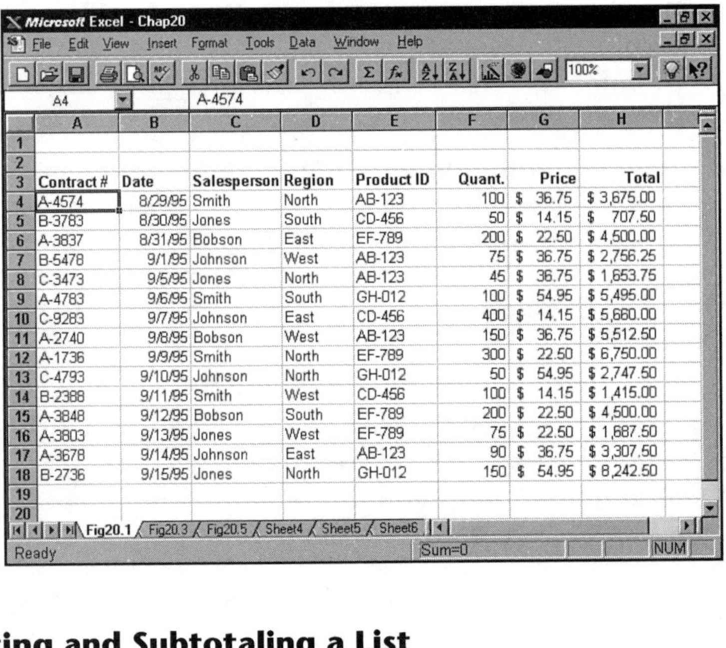

Fig. 20.1

You can use Excel's Sort and Subtotal commands to display this list in a format that approximates a database printout.

Contract #	Date	Salesperson	Region	Product ID	Quant.	Price	Total
A-4574	8/29/95	Smith	North	AB-123	100	$ 36.75	$ 3,675.00
B-3783	8/30/95	Jones	South	CD-456	50	$ 14.15	$ 707.50
A-3837	8/31/95	Bobson	East	EF-789	200	$ 22.50	$ 4,500.00
B-5478	9/1/95	Johnson	West	AB-123	75	$ 36.75	$ 2,756.25
C-3473	9/5/95	Jones	North	AB-123	45	$ 36.75	$ 1,653.75
A-4783	9/6/95	Smith	South	GH-012	100	$ 54.95	$ 5,495.00
C-9283	9/7/95	Johnson	East	CD-456	400	$ 14.15	$ 5,660.00
A-2740	9/8/95	Bobson	West	AB-123	150	$ 36.75	$ 5,512.50
A-1736	9/9/95	Smith	North	EF-789	300	$ 22.50	$ 6,750.00
C-4793	9/10/95	Johnson	North	GH-012	50	$ 54.95	$ 2,747.50
B-2388	9/11/95	Smith	West	CD-456	100	$ 14.15	$ 1,415.00
A-3848	9/12/95	Bobson	South	EF-789	200	$ 22.50	$ 4,500.00
A-3803	9/13/95	Jones	West	EF-789	75	$ 22.50	$ 1,687.50
A-3678	9/14/95	Johnson	East	AB-123	90	$ 36.75	$ 3,307.50
B-2736	9/15/95	Jones	North	GH-012	150	$ 54.95	$ 8,242.50

Sorting and Subtotaling a List

The first step in organizing an Excel list into report format is to sort it. Chapter 1, "Managing Business Data with Lists," provides a detailed explanation of the process of sorting a list within Excel, so this section focuses on the specifics of the Sort dialog box as it relates to the list in figure 20.1.

In the Sort dialog box, you make the most important choices about how your report is organized. Do you want the sections of the report to be grouped by salesperson and then by product ID? Or is it more important to group regions at the top level and then display subgroupings for salespeople?

As figure 20.2 shows, the example in this chapter uses the latter option. The list will be sorted first by region, so the major grouping of records in the report will be by region. The list will then be sorted by salesperson so that subgroups of salespeople will be in each region. The third sort field is the date. This example won't create any date groupings; instead, date is chosen as the third sort field so that within each subgroup of salespeople, the records will be sorted by date.

Fig. 20.2
The Sort dialog box is the first stop in creating a comprehensible printed report.

> **Note**
>
> The Sort dialog box contains room for only three fields, but you can sort on as many fields as your list contains. To do this, sort the list by the three least important fields, then the next three, and so on. The final sort should be on the three most important fields. For example, to sort a list on five fields, first sort on the two least important fields; then sort on the three most important fields.

As this discussion indicates, the possibilities for organizing a report are limited only by the number of fields in the list. You can choose any method of grouping and any number of subgroups simply by performing the appropriate sorting procedure on the list.

Once the data is properly sorted, it's time for the second, more subtle part of the process. Excel's Data, Subtotal command places subtotals within a sorted list for any group or subgroup within the list. The general concept is simple:

■ Create subtotals for the top-level grouping in the list.

■ Create subtotals for the highest subgroup without removing any of the existing subtotals. Repeat this step until you have created subtotals for all the subgroups in the list.

Figure 20.3 shows how the list looks after the first step is implemented; the list shows the subtotals for the top-level grouping. To get this far, you simply select a cell in the sorted list, choose Data, Subtotals, and implement the subtotal settings shown in figure 20.4.

Fig. 20.3

The sorted list with subtotals for regions, the top-level group.

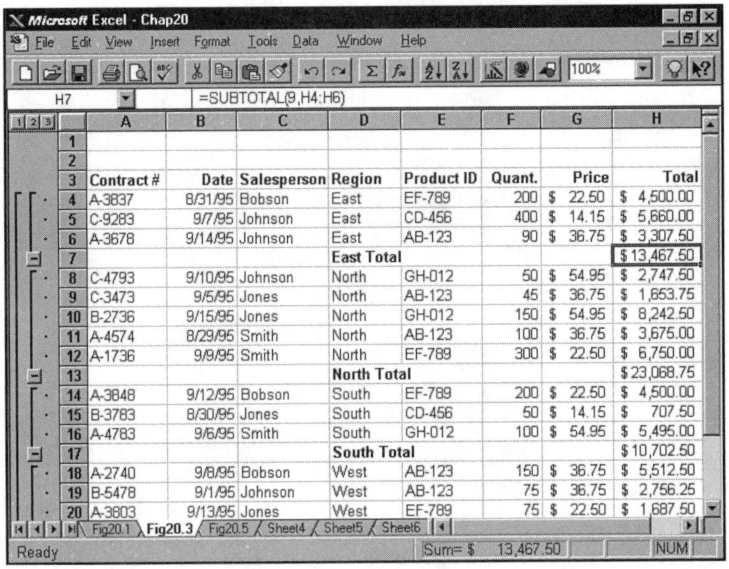

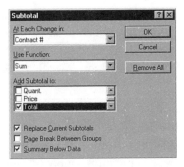

Fig. 20.4

These subtotal settings created the top-level groupings and subtotals shown in figure 20.3.

The settings shown in the Subtotal dialog box create a new subtotal in the list each time the value of the Region field changes. This is why it's important for the list to be sorted correctly. All the East records must be grouped together so that there will be only one East subtotal; all the North records must be sorted correctly so that there's only one North subtotal, and so forth. (Recall that this was the top-level, or most important, field in the sort order specified in figure 20.2.)

The Use Function drop-down list in the Subtotal dialog box lets you select from a number of subtotal statistics, including averages, counts, products, standard deviations, and more. The default choice, Sum, is by far the most commonly used in business reporting. This is the setting used to create the subtotals in figure 20.3.

Finally, there's the question of which fields to create subtotals for. You can create subtotals for as many fields as you like (although it usually doesn't make sense to create them for fields that contain text). However, adding subtotals to too many fields can clutter a report and reduce its impact. Figure 20.4 shows that this example creates a subtotal only for the crucial Total field, which shows the total amount of each sale.

The three checkboxes at the bottom of the Subtotal dialog box each play an important part in creating a report as well:

- The Replace Current Subtotals checkbox, which is selected by default, tells Excel to remove any existing subtotals before creating the new subtotals specified by the settings in the dialog box. This is convenient if you're only creating subtotals for a top-level group within a list and want to toggle between different subtotals. However, when creating subtotals for one or more subgroups, such as the Salesperson subgroup within the Region group, it's crucial to turn off this checkbox so that one set of subtotals doesn't overwrite the others.

- The Page Break Between Groups checkbox, which is deselected by default, allows you to specify that each group should fall on a different page of the printout. In the sample list shown in figure 20.3, you could specify that each region's records print on a separate page by turning on this setting. If you're creating subtotals for a list with several levels of subgroups, it usually makes sense to select this setting only for the top-level grouping, if at all.

- The Summary Below Data checkbox, which is selected, tells where to put the subtotals for each group. If you turn off this setting, Excel inserts the subtotals at the top of each group, rather than at the bottom. For most business reporting, you'll want to keep this setting selected to ensure that the subtotals appear at the bottom of the groups.

With this information in mind, there are only a few short steps to transform the list shown in figure 20.3, with its top-level grouping, to the final report shown in figure 20.5. First, another subtotal was added to the list, for the Salesperson field; the Replace Current Subtotals checkbox was deselected first so that the existing subtotals for regions are not overwritten.

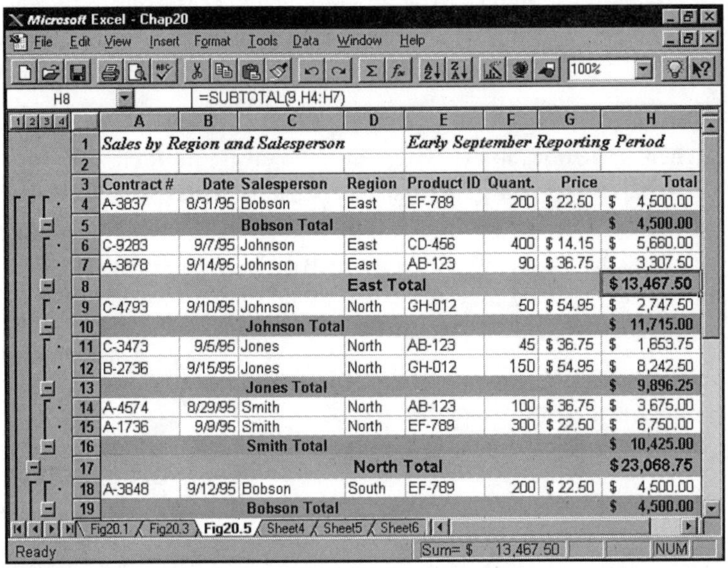

Fig. 20.5
The completed report, with an additional level of grouping, a first-page heading, and additional formatting.

Some formatting changes also make the report easier to read. For example, the subtotals created by Data, Subtotal all use the same font as the data in the original list, with a boldface attribute. Because this list contains a hierarchy of groupings, with regions at the top level and salespersons as a subgroup, the formatting was adjusted to account for this. Regional subtotals appear in a larger font to indicate that they comprise one or more subgroups.

In addition, the subtotal rows were shaded—with different shading for the top-level groups and subgroups—to make the subtotals stand out. Finally, the boldface was extended to include both the subtotal text and the subtotal value in each subtotal row.

This formatting is fairly typical of what you'll find in many business reports, but it can take time, especially for large lists with many groups and sub-groups. Excel's Format, AutoFormat command offers two settings that auto-matically take account of subtotals within a list: List 2 and List 3. To apply one of these autoformats, use these steps:

1. Select any cell in the list.
2. Choose Format, AutoFormat.
3. In the Table Format scroll list, select List 2 or List 3.
4. Choose OK.

Because the process of creating a standard business report described in the preceding pages is somewhat lengthy and involved, the following list summarizes the steps involved:

1. Choose Data, Sort to sort the list, so that the top-level groupings are the most important sort field; the first subgroup is the second most important sort field; and so on. (See Chapter 1 for a more thorough explanation of the Data, Sort command.)

2. Choose Data, Subtotals to create subtotals for the top-level group. You can create subtotals for one or more fields.

3. Choose Data, Subtotals to create subtotals for the first subgroup, taking care not to replace the existing subtotals.

4. Repeat step 3 for each subgroup that requires subtotals.

5. Format the list, possibly by choosing Format, AutoFormat and selecting the List 2 or List 3 settings in the AutoFormat dialog box.

Creating the Printout

Typically, a business report includes a formatted page-one header, such as the text in row 1 of figure 20.5, plus headers and footers on each page of the report. (Some reports omit the separate page-one header. In the example, this could be done either by deleting rows 1 and 2 of the worksheet or omitting them from the print range.) Creating the page-one header is an obvious task; you just enter the information into the appropriate cells and apply whatever formatting you want.

Entering header and footer information that appears on all pages of the printout is accomplished through the Page Setup dialog box, shown in figure 20.6. The dialog box's Header/Footer tab allows you to select from a number of predefined headers and footers in the Header and Footer drop-down lists.

To create custom headers and footers, you choose the Custom Header or Custom Footer command button in the Page Setup dialog box. Excel displays a dialog box such as the one shown in figure 20.7. The three sections of this dialog box allow you to enter text for the left, center, and right sections of the header or footer. You can then format the text in any of the sections by selecting the text, then clicking the Font button (the one with the letter A) to produce the Font dialog box.

Fig. 20.6

The Page Setup
dialog box
contains settings
for the printed
pages of your
report.

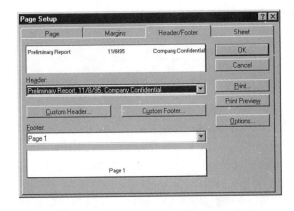

Fig. 20.7

The custom
headers and
footers you create
appear on each
page of a report.

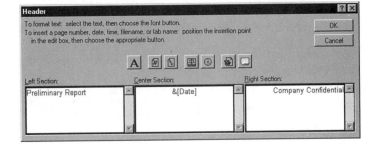

You can also use the remaining six buttons in the Header or Footer dialog
box to insert variables into the custom header or footer. The variable appears
in whichever of the three sections currently contains the insertion point. The
following list explains the meaning of each of the six buttons, moving from
left to right:

- *Pound sign.* Inserts the page number.
- *Double plus sign.* Inserts the total number of pages in the printout.
- *Calendar.* Inserts the date the report was printed.
- *Clock.* Inserts the time the report was printed.
- *Excel icon.* Inserts the file name.
- *Sheet tab icon.* Inserts the name on the tab of the sheet that contains the
  list to be printed.

With headers and footers in place, all that remains is the print command itself. When you choose File, Print, the Print dialog box shown in figure 20.8
appears.

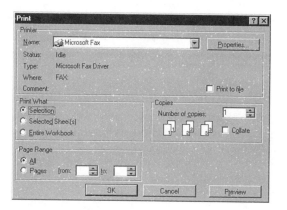

Fig. 20.8
Use the Print
dialog box to
specify what to
print and how
many copies.

By default, the Selected Sheet(s) option button is selected in the Print dialog box. If the current worksheet contains only the report you want to print, this setting is sufficient. However, if the sheet contains other entries, they too will print. To prevent this, select the cells containing the report before you choose File, Print, then use the Selection setting in the Print dialog box.

Tip

The easy way to select all cells in a report is to select one cell in the report and then press Ctrl+Shift+8. This trick works for any list, regardless of whether it contains subtotals.

Tip

You can specify that Excel print only a certain range of pages in a multipage report by using the From and To settings at the bottom of the Print dialog box.

When you have selected the print settings you want, you can choose OK to commence printing. However, in most cases it's safest to first choose the Preview button to make sure that the headers, footers, and print range you specified will produce the printout you want, with all the columns in the report safely within the page margins. You can then print the report directly from preview mode by choosing the Print button at the top of the preview screen.

Other Ways to Print Data
The brief introduction to the Page Setup dialog box in the preceding section gives you an excellent head start on nearly any custom print job you may

want to generate. The dialog box's Page, Margins, Header/Footer, and Sheet tabs contain all the settings you need to customize a print job to meet nearly any specification.

Creating ad hoc printouts of workbook data, though mundane, is an essential part of data presentation from within Excel. Pivot tables, which comprise a large portion of Excel data-management tasks, provide a prime example. There's no special command for printing pivot tables; you simply select the range containing the pivot table and then use the File, Print command.

In addition to the header/footer settings discussed earlier, some settings you're likely to use often include the following:

- *Fit to (Page tab)*. This setting compresses the font size in the printout so that the printout fits on the number of pages you specify. This setting is especially useful for smaller printouts—for example, a printout that barely spills over onto a third page can be shrunk to fit on two pages.

- *Print Area (Sheet tab)*. This setting allows you to "hard-code" a print range for the current sheet of the workbook. For example, if you know that the report you want to print always resides in range A3:H100, you can enter this as the Print Area setting for that sheet, saving yourself the trouble of specifying the range each time you use the Print dialog box, as described in the preceding section.

- *Gridlines (Sheet tab)*. This checkbox allows you to toggle off the printing of gridlines. In most business reports, it's essential to omit the gridlines.

Creating Reports from Subsets of Data

In addition to creating reports from all the records in a list, as described in the preceding sections, you can create a report from subsets of records that meet specific criteria. There are two ways to generate such subsets:

- Use the AutoFilter to filter the list in place, as described in Chapter 1.

- Use the Advanced Filter dialog box to extract copies of records that meet your criteria to a different location in the sheet, as described in Chapter 3.

Obviously, the first alternative is quicker. In addition, you don't have to turn off the AutoFilter when you print the report—even though the AutoFilter drop-down arrows display on the screen, they won't show up in the printout.

However, there are also advantages to extracting the data. For starters, you can format it however you like without changing the formatting in the original list. In addition, you can change the order of the fields in the extracted list without changing them in the original list, a technique that's described in Chapter 4, "Using Excel Databases To Organize Business Information."

Whichever method you use, printing only a subset of records can be an essential way to focus a report if the original list on which you're reporting contains more than a few hundred records.

Using the Access Report Designer

The Access report designer performs all the features described in the preceding section, and more, in a fraction of the time. As described in the introduction to this chapter, this feature performs the mundane tasks of report management—and the not so mundane tasks of implementing eye-catching, yet businesslike, formatting and styling. A further advantage is that all this takes place without requiring you to make any changes to the original list in Excel. If you have Access 95 on your system, you would be well advised to take advantage of the Access report designer whenever possible.

Note

To use the Access Report Designer, you must have Access 95 installed on your system. The AccessLinks add-in must also be activated or the Access Report command will not be available in the Data menu. To activate the AccessLinks add-in, use these steps:

1. Choose Tools, Add-Ins.

2. In the Add-Ins Available scroll list, select the AccessLinks Add-In checkbox.

3. Choose OK.

If the AccessLinks Add-In does not appear in the Add-Ins Available scroll list, follow these steps:

1. Choose the Browse command button in the Add-Ins dialog box.

2. Navigate to the Library folder of the Excel folder (which in turn is usually contained in the MSOffice folder).

3. Select the file ACCLINK.XLA.

4. Choose OK.

5. Follow steps 2 and 3 in the first set of numbered steps in this Note.

After you choose the Access Report command from Excel's Data menu, the Access Report Wizard leads you through a series of dialog boxes that are quite

easy to understand, especially if you've followed the discussion of data grouping in the earlier sections of this chapter. This section briefly describes each
step of the process.

1. Place the cell pointer in the list from which you want to create the
   report. (This example creates a report for the sample list shown in
   figure 20.1.)

2. Choose <u>D</u>ata, A<u>c</u>cess Report.

3. In the first dialog box of the Access Report Wizard, choose the fields
   that will appear on the form, as shown in figure 20.9. (It may take a few
   moments for this dialog box to appear, while Access loads.) To move
   fields from one scroll list to the other, highlight the field names in the
   <u>A</u>vailable Fields or <u>S</u>elected Fields scroll lists, then click the single-arrow
   command buttons. To move all the fields at once, click one of the
   double-arrow buttons. Choose <u>N</u>ext when you have selected the fields
   you want to appear on the report.

Fig. 20.9

The first step of
the Access Report
Wizard is to
specify which
fields you want to
use in the report.

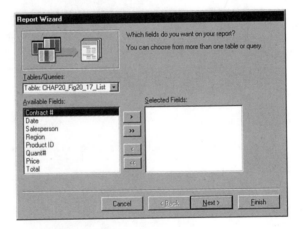

4. In the next dialog box of the Report Wizard, add grouping levels. To
   create a group, select the field on which you want to group records in
   the left scroll list, then click the right-facing single arrow. To create
   additional subgroups, repeat the process. To change the hierarchy of
   the groups, use the up- and down-facing Priority arrows in the dialog
   box. Choose <u>N</u>ext when you have specified the grouping levels you
   desire.

   (The concept of groups and subgroups was discussed in detail in the
   first section of this chapter, in which records in the sample list were

grouped by region, and then a subgroup for salespeople was created within each region. As figure 20.10 shows, the same grouping scheme is chosen in the Access Report Wizard.)

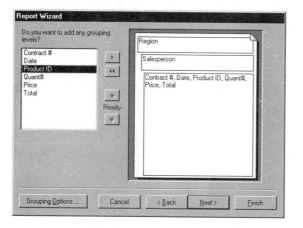

Fig. 20.10
Use this dialog box to specify how you want to group the records in a report.

5. In the next dialog box of the Report Wizard, determine how the records will be ordered within the groups (or subgroups) that you created. Figure 20.11, for example, specifies that the records are to be arranged first by date (in ascending order) and then by contract number (in ascending order). Two additional sort keys could be identified, but in a list of this size, where subgroups contain only a few records, sorting on two fields is more than sufficient.

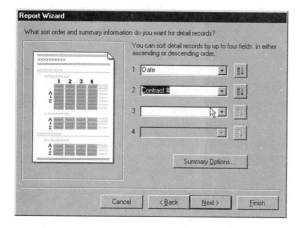

Fig. 20.11
You can specify up to four sort fields for the detail records in each group (or subgroup) of the report.

6. Determine what (if any) summary statistics you want to include for your groups and subgroups. Figure 20.12 indicates that we want to display the sum of the Total field for each group and subgroup. You access this Summary Options dialog box by clicking the Summary Options command button in the dialog box shown in figure 20.11. Choose OK to return to the third dialog box of the Report Wizard; then choose Next.

Fig. 20.12

The Summary Options dialog box lets you create statistics on any numeric field for groups and subgroups.

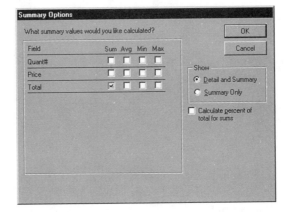

7. In the next dialog box of the Report Wizard, select the layout and page orientation for the report. The default selections shown in figure 20.13 are optimal for most business reports. You can also choose to adjust field widths so that all fields fit on a single page. This is usually optimal, but in a report with many fields, it may cause some fields to become so narrow that you can't read the data. In this case, consider a landscape orientation or eliminate some fields from the report, as described later.

Fig. 20.13

Layout and page orientation are controlled by this dialog box.

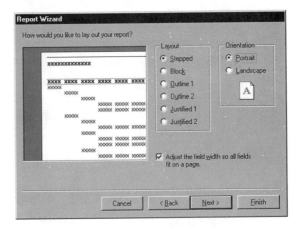

8. Select a report style in the next dialog box of the Report Wizard. All the
styles available in the dialog box are acceptable for business use. To be
conservative, the Corporate style is chosen in figure 20.14.

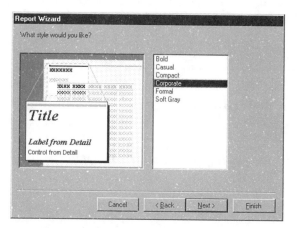

Fig. 20.14
This dialog box
determines the
style and format-
ting for the report.
All these styles are
acceptable for
business reporting.

9. In the final dialog box of the Report Wizard, specify a title for the first
page of the report, as shown in figure 20.15. From here, you can choose
to preview the report (a prelude to printing) or modify the report's
design. Choose Finish to complete the Report Wizard.

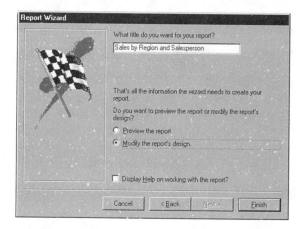

Fig. 20.15
The report name
you specify in this
dialog box appears
on the first page of
the report.

If you choose to preview the report, you see not only the structure of the report you have created, but also how the data actually appears in the report
when you print it. You can move between pages in the preview by clicking
the page-scrolling arrows in the bottom-left corner of the report window. To
print the report, simply click the Printer tool on the left end of the toolbar
above the report.

> **Note**
>
> To see more of a report preview, maximize the Microsoft Access program window and the window that contains the report. Then choose a smaller zoom factor from the Zoom drop-down list. The Fit setting displays an entire page of the report, but makes the data too small to read. The 75% setting displays about half a page, and the data is usually legible.

Modifying a Report's Design

If the report preview described in the previous section doesn't show you what you want to see, you can modify the report's design. To do so, choose View, Report Design. Access displays the report in design mode, as shown in figure 20.16.

Fig. 20.16

It's a simple matter to make small modifications in the Access report designer.

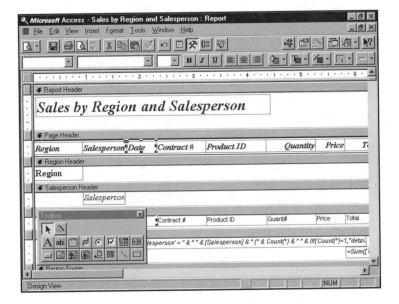

In the example in this chapter, we wanted to change the field heading "Quant." in the report (a heading taken from the original list in Excel) to the more descriptive "Quantity." To do this, the Contract # field heading was narrowed; the Product ID field heading was moved to the left; and the Quant. field heading was widened. We then double-clicked the Quant. field heading and edited the label to read "Quantity." The change will be apparent the next time we preview or print the report.

Using the report designer in this way is a simple matter, even if you've never used a database product before. It's easy to widen, narrow, move, and rearrange fields so that the report appears the way you want it to. However, the Access report designer can quickly become quite complicated, so it's usually best to stick to the basics.

Saving and Reusing a Report

When you are finished previewing, modifying, and printing a report you have created with the Access report designer, choose File, Exit. Access displays a dialog box asking if you want to save the report design you have created.

If you want to be able to use the report again, choose Yes. Access saves the report design and displays a graphical button in your workbook next to the list from which the report was created, as shown in figure 20.17. To display the report again, simply click this button.

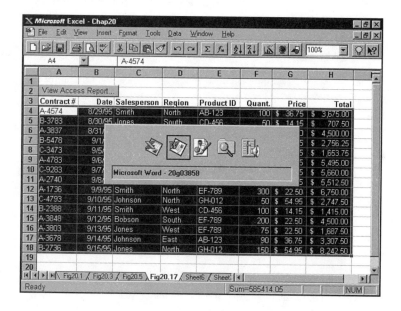

Fig. 20.17
When you save a report created in the Access report designer, a graphical button in the workbook lets you retrieve it.

You can move the View Access Report button or change the text that appears on it. To move the button, right-click it and choose Cut from the pop-up menu. Then select the new location for the button and choose Edit, Paste from the normal Excel menu.

To change the text on the View Access Report button, right-click the button, drag the mouse across the default text to select it, and type the new text.

Using the Report Manager

Excel's built-in Report Manager doesn't create output typical of business data reporting. As indicated earlier, you must use different techniques, such as Excel's sorting and subtotaling features or the Access report designer, to create such reports.

> **Tip**
>
> In Excel 95, the Report Manager command resides under the View menu. In Excel 5, the command was named Print Report and was found in the File menu.

The advantage of Excel's Report Manager is that you can use it to print out several different versions of the same workbook, which are called *sections* in Report Manager parlance. As shown in figure 20.18, each section can comprise both a scenario and a view.

> **Note**
>
> Both the View Manager and the Report Manager are Excel add-ins that must be installed on your system and activated. Otherwise, the View Manager and Report Manager commands are available on the View menu. To activate the View Manager and Report Manager add-ins, use these steps:
>
> 1. Choose Tools, Add-Ins.
> 2. In the Add-Ins Available scroll list, select the Report Manager checkbox and the View Manager checkbox.
> 3. Choose OK.
>
> If these checkboxes do not appear in the Add-Ins Available scroll list, follow these steps:
>
> 1. Choose the Browse button in the Add-Ins dialog box.
> 2. Navigate to the Library folder of the Excel folder (which in turn is usually contained in the MSOffice folder).
> 3. Select the file REPORTS.XLA.
> 4. Choose OK.
> 5. Repeat steps 2 through 4, but this time specify file VIEWS.XLA instead of file REPORTS.XLA.
> 6. Follow steps 2 and 3 in the first set of numbered steps in this Note.
>
> If the files REPORTS.XLA or VIEWS.XLA do not appear in the Library folder, chances are they were not installed on your system. Use the Excel setup program to install the necessary add-in files.

The advantages of Excel's Scenario Manager are explained in detail in Chapters 12 through 15. Views in Excel are typically used to display different levels of outlining. For example, suppose that you were using the list shown in figure 20.1. You could use the following steps to create a view named Original List:

1. Choose View, View Manager.

2. Choose the Add command button in the View Manager dialog box.

3. Enter the view name, **Original List**. Make sure that the Hidden Rows and Columns checkbox is selected.

4. Choose OK.

You could add one level of subtotals, so that grouping appears only for regions, as shown in figure 20.3. You would name this view Top-Level Subtotals. Finally, you could add another level of subtotals, creating a report with top-level groups for regions and subgroups for salespeople, as shown in figure 20.5. You would name this view All Subtotals.

You could then create a report with three sections, as shown in figure 20.18. The first section would display only the top-level subtotals; the second would display all subtotals; and the third would display the raw data from the list. A reader could then turn to the section of the printed report that contained the level of detail in which he or she was interested.

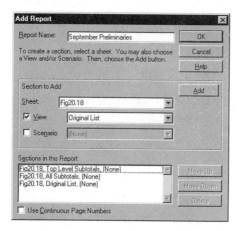

Fig. 20.18
Excel's Report Manager allows you to print different versions of the same workbook, called sections, in a single printout. The notation *(None)* at the end of each section indicates that no view was specified for any of the sections.

Whether a report's sections contain only different views or both different scenarios and different views, the steps you use to create the report are basically the same:

1. Choose View, Report Manager.

2. Choose the Add command button.

3. Type a name for the report. The report settings are saved with the workbook, allowing you to refer to this name when you want to print the report in later work sessions.

4. Use the Sheet drop-down list to specify the sheet that contains the view and/or scenario that you want to include in the report.

5. Select the named view and/or scenario that you want to include in the report.

6. Choose Add.

7. Repeat steps 4 through 6 for each section you want to include in the report.

8. Choose OK to close the Add Report dialog box.

When you close the Add Report dialog box, you return to the Report Manager dialog box. At this point, you can select a report in the Reports scroll list and choose from several options:

- To print the report immediately, choose the Print command button.

- To edit the report, such as changing the contents or the order of the sections, choose the Edit command button.

- To delete the report, choose the Delete command button.

- To add another report, choose the Add command button.

If you don't want to perform any of these tasks, choose Close to close the Report Manager dialog box. You can return to the dialog box at any time by choosing View, Report Manager from the Excel menu.

The final thing to note about the Excel Report Manager is the Use Continuous Page Numbers checkbox in the Add Report dialog box. If this checkbox is not selected (the default), each new section of the report has its own set of page numbers, beginning with page 1. If you select this checkbox, the sections are numbered continuously. For example, if the first section is ten pages long, the first page of the second section is numbered 11, and so on.

Chapter Summary

By using Excel's sorting, subtotaling, and formatting features, you can create business reports from the data in your lists that are similar to those created by database programs. You can group the data in the list in as many ways as you like; the number of subgroups you create is limited only by the number of fields in the list. You can also create reports from subsets of the records in a list by AutoFiltering or extracting records from the list and printing the results.

If you have Microsoft Access on your system, you can save time (and keep the data in your list in its original order) by using the Access report designer. Unlike the Access form designer (which is described in Chapter 3), the Access report designer is simple to use, even for someone with no previous database experience.

Excel's native Report Manager creates a more specialized report. In this kind of report, you can create several sections, each of which specifies a particular view and/or scenario that you have already created in the workbook. This is helpful if some members of an audience need to see all the data in a list, while others need to see only top-level detail. When you print the report, each of the sections is printed in sequence. You can specify whether the sections should be numbered continuously or independently.

Part V

Managing External Data Sources and Destinations

CHAPTER

21

Importing Data from External Sources

These days it's very common to find yourself receiving and analyzing data from a wide variety of sources. To make this task more challenging, management often expects this analysis to be completed instantly, or more likely, by yesterday. If you're lucky, the data your coworkers supply will be stored as Excel files, but unfortunately there are no guarantees. So the question becomes, what are the best ways to deal with non-Excel file formats? First, realize that although importing data from one application into another may seem difficult, it can usually be done. Not only can you bring data into Excel, you can usually automate much of the process. You may even be able to automate the analysis process.

What makes importing data so difficult is the multitude of data sources. Each of the source applications can export data in only a few data types, of which Excel may not be one. Happily, you'll find Excel prepared for the most difficult situations with a wide variety of techniques to access this external data, regardless of where it comes from. Despite Excel's power, it's not always possible to bring data directly from another program. In these situations it may be necessary to find a workaround, such as storing data in an intermediate file format.

In this chapter, you learn to

- Import data into Excel from many sources
- Manage the data import process
- Bring in data from ASCII files and database programs

Although importing data from one application is often a challenge, it's only the first step towards the analysis of the data. After the data has been imported into Excel, you may need to clean it up, and integrate it with the existing data. To some extent, this chapter also examines these aspects of the data transfer process. Keep in mind what you have learned about data management in the other chapters of this book.

Data Transfer Considerations

In general, you can choose from the following five basic approaches to getting data from one program to another:

- You can copy and paste information between the two programs. To do this, you can employ a number of different copy and paste commands including ones that paste graphics and/or links.

- You may be able to export the file from the source program in the file format of the target program. In this case, that means exporting or saving the source data as an Excel file.

- You may import the source file in its native format directly into the target program. Here that means opening the source data in one of the file formats that Excel can read.

- You can save the source file in an intermediate file format, one which Excel can open.

- You can query the external file from inside Excel using the MS Query add-in.

Importing Excel Data into Other Excel Spreadsheets

To better understand some of the techniques for importing data into Excel it's easiest to look at the process strictly within Excel. That is, first examine the data transfer from one Excel spreadsheet to another. Some methods for transferring data create links, and so you should also examine the options for managing those links.

A common source of data for an Excel spreadsheet is another Excel spreadsheet. To bring data into one spreadsheet from another, the first method that comes to mind is using the Copy and Paste commands. The following sections look at some alternative methods of bringing data from one spreadsheet to another. Each method has advantages and disadvantages that will dictate your choice. If you thoroughly understand all the possible methods, you can choose the one that best meets your needs in any given situation.

Using Copy and Paste

Excel is equipped with a number of copy and paste commands. Everyone is comfortable with the standard Edit, Copy and Edit, Paste commands. For example, you can do a straight copy and paste, or you can paste a picture, a linked picture, or a linked array. To appreciate the subtle differences between the various methods, an illustration is helpful. Suppose that you have the data shown in figure 21.1 in one spreadsheet, and you want to copy it to a second spreadsheet.

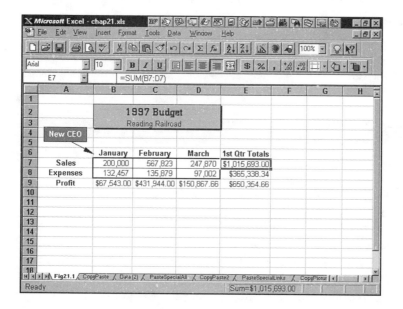

Fig. 21.1

Some budget data that you want to copy.

Notice that this spreadsheet contains cell formatting, various column widths, and graphical objects. When you use the standard Edit, Copy and Edit, Paste commands to copy this data to a new sheet or workbook, your results may not meet all of your expectations.

The main problem with this simple copy and paste technique is that the column widths are not copied during the command, and the graphic text box is resized inappropriately. Otherwise, the data is copied intact. One other important limitation with this technique is that the copied data is not linked to the source data. To solve the format related problems, you can copy the entire sheet.

There are at least three ways to copy an entire sheet:

- Select the entire sheet and choose Edit, Copy and Edit, Paste to paste to a blank sheet.
- Hold down the Ctrl key and drag and drop the sheet tab.
- Use the sheet tab shortcut menu.

You can copy more than one sheet at a time. To select adjacent sheets, click the first sheet tab and then hold down the Shift key and click the last sheet tab. All sheets between the first and last selected tabs are selected. To select nonadjacent sheets, click the first sheet tab; then while holding down the Ctrl key, click any additional sheet tabs.

Tip

To quickly copy a sheet, hold down the Ctrl key while dragging and dropping the sheet tab. To move a sheet, drag and drop the sheet tab without holding down Ctrl.

Tip

You can copy or move sheets between books by displaying both books on-screen and then using the drag and drop approach just suggested.

If you only want a picture of the data you are importing, something that looks exactly like the original but whose data can not be modified, Excel provides the Edit, Copy Picture command. You can execute this command in a number of ways, all of which produce similar results. After choosing Edit, Copy, hold down Shift and choose Edit, Paste Picture. The result is a non-dynamic graphical picture of your data.

In each copy command discussed so far, if you change the source data, the copied data does not update. If you want the copied data to reflect the most current situation, the copied data must be linked to the source data.

Retaining Links to Source Data

You can create links to your source data using a number of variations of the copy command as well as by entering formulas that reference the source data. In this section, you will look at four of these techniques: formulas, pasted links, linked pictures, and the results of using the camera tool.

You can bring your data from one spreadsheet to another sheet or workbook using formulas of the following syntax

```
=Data!B7
```

or

```
='[Excel Data.xls]Data'!$B$7
```

or

```
='D:\Spreadsheet\Data\[Excel Data.xls]Data'!$B$7
```

> **Note**
>
> By removing the absolute notation, you can copy the formula over a range of cells. By doing this, you quickly bring in large amounts of dynamically linked data. Once in, you can use all the Data commands, such as Sort, Filter, Subtotal, and Pivot Table with your data.

Another option is to use arrays to link the data. An array formula, like a regular formula, is a dynamic link to your data source, and like a regular formula it does not capture graphical objects or formats, just the raw data. However, from the standpoint of memory usage, an array is more efficient than regular formulas. One limitation of using arrays is that you cannot manipulate the individual elements of the array. To create an array formula choose Edit, Paste Special, and then click the Paste Link button.

Analyzing Data as It Is Imported

You don't need to copy all your data from one spreadsheet to another to analyze it. For example, suppose you have a large personnel database in Excel and you want to bring just the data for people in the Admin Department into another spreadsheet. You might choose any of the following commands to accomplish this task: Data, Pivot Table; Data, Advanced Filter; Data, Get External Data; or Tools, Data Analysis. On the other hand, if you want to get the data from many different spreadsheets or workbooks and create a summary area in a new spreadsheet, you should consider using the Data, Consolidate command.

Importing Data Using Pivot Tables

Pivot tables are tools that enable you to cut your data every which way, as you have seen in a number of earlier chapters. Pivot tables are used to perform advanced crosstab analysis. For more information on Pivot Tables see Chapter 7, "Understanding Pivot Tables."

Suppose you want to enable multiple users to analyze data from a single file, a pivot table might meet your needs. Pivot tables don't need to be in the file where the raw data is located. This means that the data can be maintained by one user while numerous other users analyze the data from their own pivot tables. Follow these steps to create a pivot table in a separate file from the data source:

1. Open the data source workbook and the workbook in which you want to create the pivot table.

2. Place your cursor in the data you want to analyze or highlight all of it.

3. Choose Data, PivotTable and step through the Wizard to Step 4.

4. Choose Window and then pick the file you want the pivot table to be put in from the list at the bottom of this menu.

5. Click the cell in the second workbook where you want the pivot table located. The PivotTable Wizard looks like figure 21.2.

Fig. 21.2
The PivotTable Wizard with an external reference in the PivotTable Starting Cell, in preparation for creating the external table.

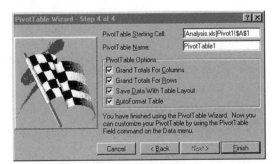

6. Click Finish.

Caution

Save all your work before attempting the preceding procedure. Creating an external pivot table may crash your system.

You will find a pivot table file on the companion disk entitled Analysis.xls, which gets its data from the Fig21.2 sheet of the Chap21.xls file, which is also on the disk. Test the flexibility by changing figures in the source file; then switch to the pivot table and choose Data, Refresh Data to see the table update.

Consolidating Data

Sometimes, instead of cutting your data into smaller pieces for analysis, you want to bring it all together to create a consolidated summary. Excel's powerful data consolidate feature enables you to bring data from many files (or sheets) into one file, possibly to create a grand total. You should refer to Chapter 17, "Consolidating Business Information," earlier in this book.

Suppose you manage four regional sales managers for a large wholesaling company. These managers are each in charge of sales in a particular region of the United States. Each quarter they submit a spreadsheet showing sales by month by product. You want to consolidate their figures into a grand total of sales by month by product. Figures 21.3 and 21.4 show two of the four spreadsheets.

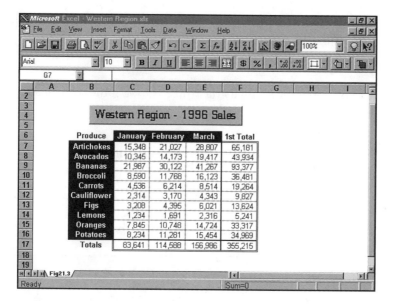

Fig. 21.3
Sales figures from the Western Region. These figures will be consolidated with three other regions to produce company wide sales figures.

Only two of the files are shown, but four are used in this example. Perform the following steps to consolidate the data from a number of workbooks or spreadsheets:

Tip

To make the process of consolidation easier, open all the source files and the summary file first.

Fig. 21.4
Quarterly sales figures from the Southern Region. Note that the Southern Region has a product list somewhat different from the Western Region.

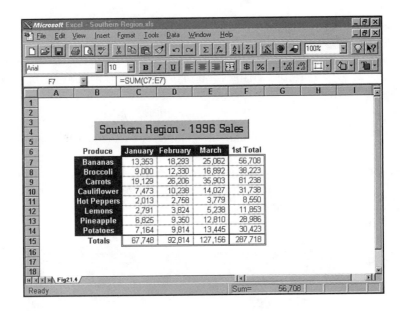

1. Select a cell in the summary file where you want the consolidated data to start.

2. Choose <u>D</u>ata, Co<u>n</u>solidate.

3. Select a type of consolidation from the <u>F</u>unction list.

4. Click in the <u>R</u>eference box.

5. Choose <u>W</u>indow and pick the first file you want to consolidate from the list of open files.

6. Select the range you want to consolidate including titles, and click <u>A</u>dd.

Note

You can control which columns and rows are consolidated by manually entering the titles in the consolidation spreadsheet prior to consolidation. When you do this, you should select consolidation ranges in the source files that do not include the titles. For example, you could have chosen to consolidate only the data for Bananas and Cauliflower for the months of January and March. To do that, you would enter those titles on the consolidation page, and then highlight the titles and the range to be filled before beginning the consolidation process.

7. Repeat steps 4 to 6 adding as many ranges as you want to consolidate.

8. If you have included the titles in the selected ranges, check the Use Labels In <u>T</u>op Row and/or <u>L</u>eft Column boxes as appropriate.

9. If you want the data to be linked to the source files, click the Create Links to <u>S</u>ource Data checkbox. Then click OK.

> **Note**
>
> To save time during the consolidation, name the data ranges in each of the source sheets before you begin. And for the best effect, use the same name in each sheet. When you're ready to select references in the Consolidate dialog box (as described earlier in step 6), click any cell in the source spreadsheet, then replace the cell address with the range name. Now, after you click the <u>A</u>dd button once, you can edit the <u>R</u>eference line to change the file name and then click <u>A</u>dd again for each of the other source files.

The end result, after adding formatting, is shown in figure 21.5. Formatting is not consolidated. Outline symbols are displayed to the left because I chose to link the data. In figure 21.5, I have hidden column C because it holds outline related information not needed for the current discussion. If you want the totals rows and/or columns to be consolidated, include them in the source range; if not, you can add totals afterwards.

The companion disk contains four files entitled Northern, Southern, Eastern, and Western Region.xls. The consolidated results are on the Fig21.5 sheet of the Chap21.xls file. The results of not linking the data can be found on the sheet Unlinked in the Chap21.xls file.

On the Disk

Data Consolidation is a powerful method of bringing in and combining data from many spreadsheets or files. Two of the strongest points of this command are its capability to consolidate source files that are not laid out identically and the capability to link to those source files. In the previous example we employed both of these features by creating links to source files that contained product lists that varied from region to region.

Fig. 21.5

The consolidation, from four files, has created an outline because we chose to create links to the source data.

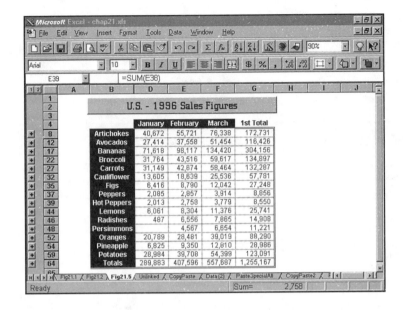

Extracting Remote Data

It's often useful to copy specific information from one file to another rather than copying an entire data range and then pulling out the portion you want. For example, suppose that you maintain a large personnel file in Excel and you want to create a file of employees who will have their ten-year anniversary in the month of January and who work in the headquarters building (which means they are in Departments 1, 4, 11, or 19). Excel's Data, Filter, Advanced Filter command can easily handle the task.

Chapter 4, "Using Excel Databases to Organize Business Information," examines the data extraction process in detail. This section looks at how to send the extracted data directly to a separate file.

Figure 21.6 shows part of a sample database. The data range including titles has been named DATA.

Figure 21.7 shows the criteria range, which has been named Crit. You can place the criteria area in either the source or target files.

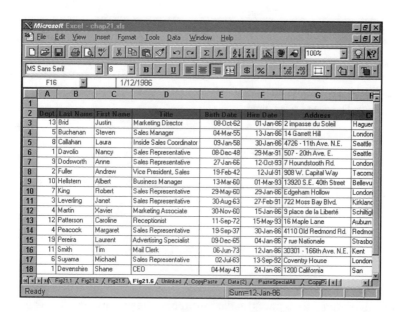

Fig. 21.6
A small portion of a spreadsheet database from which you want to extract specific records to a new file.

V

Managing External Data

Tip

Because titles in the criteria and extract ranges must be identical to those in the database, copy them, or better yet, use formula references.

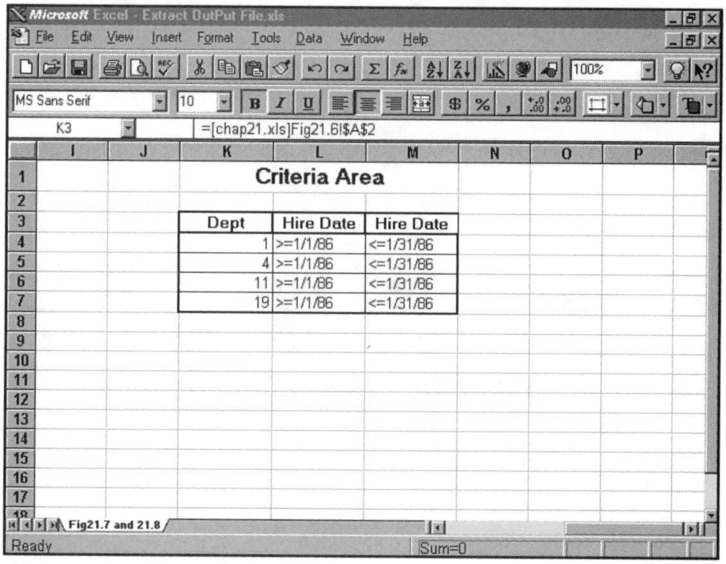

Fig. 21.7
The criteria area for the extract. Notice the formula on the edit bar. Using a formula ensures that the titles are exact matches to those in the database. Also notice the duplicate use of the Hire Date title in the criteria area to extract a range of dates.

> **Note**
>
> If you intend to repeat the extraction process many times, it is faster if you create a name in the target file that references the source file's database. Note the Refers To line of the Define Name dialog box in figure 21.8. Also, keeping the criteria area in the target file may save you time.

Fig. 21.8

The Define Name dialog box displaying a name that uses an external reference.

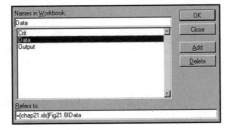

Follow these steps to extract the data from one file and insert it into another:

1. Open both the source and target files.

2. Put your cursor in an area of the target file containing at least two rows of information.

3. Choose Data, Filter, Advanced Filter.

4. In the Advanced Filter dialog box, click the Action Copy to Another Location.

5. Click in the List Range box; then Choose Window and select the source's file name from the bottom of the menu.

6. Select the database range.

   or

   If you created a name with the external reference, type the name into the List Range box.

> **Tip**
>
> You can also press F3 while on the List Range line and pick the database name from the Paste Name dialog box.

7. Click the Criteria Range box and then select the criteria range.

8. Click the Copy To box and then select the output range.

9. Choose OK. All data meeting the criteria appears in the output area, with formatting, as shown in figure 21.9.

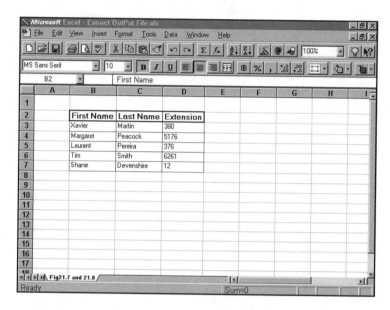

Fig. 21.9
The output area after the extract. This range is in a different file from the source data. You might find it useful to name the titles for the output range "Output."

Two files, Extract OutPut File.xls and the Fig21.6 sheet of Chap21.xls, illustrating remote extraction, can be found on the companion disk.

On the Disk

Creating an External Linked Summary Area

Up to now, this chapter has demonstrated the techniques that you might employ in a particular situation. The following example shows how you can apply a number of these techniques to develop a solution to a real-world problem. Suppose that you want to create an Excel file that summarizes data from another Excel file. Specifically, suppose that you have data laid out as shown in figure 21.10. The data area is a list of the expenses of many projects broken down by year and by department. For each project (one row of data), the expenses have been broken out into various categories such as material Cost, Fabrication, Plumbing, and Power. A specific department may be involved in many projects in a given year or none at all.

V

Managing External Data

Fig. 21.10
You want to total the expenses by department by year for each of the expense categories listed on row three.

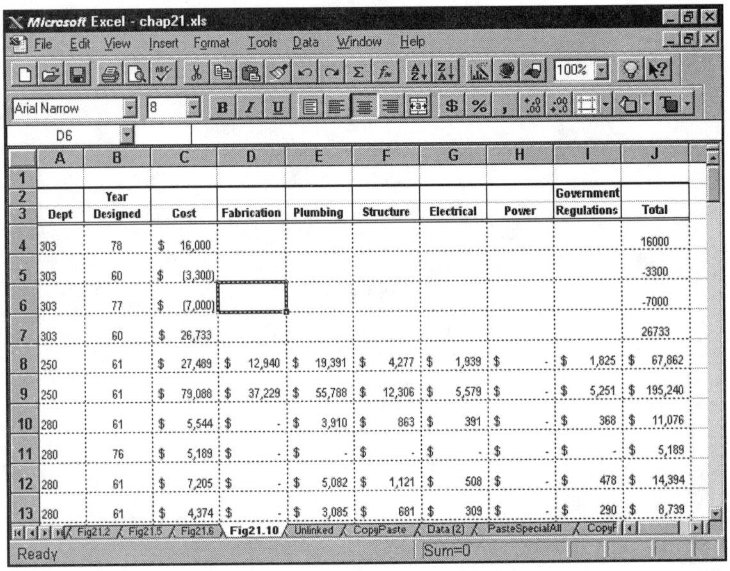

Dept	Year Designed	Cost	Fabrication	Plumbing	Structure	Electrical	Power	Government Regulations	Total
303	78	$ 16,000							16000
303	60	$ (3,300)							-3300
303	77	$ (7,000)							-7000
303	60	$ 26,733							26733
250	61	$ 27,489	$ 12,940	$ 19,391	$ 4,277	$ 1,939	$ -	$ 1,825	$ 67,862
250	61	$ 79,088	$ 37,229	$ 55,788	$ 12,306	$ 5,579	$ -	$ 5,251	$ 195,240
280	61	$ 5,544	$ -	$ 3,910	$ 863	$ 391	$ -	$ 368	$ 11,076
280	76	$ 5,189	$ -	$ -	$ -	$ -	$ -	$ -	$ 5,189
280	61	$ 7,205	$ -	$ 5,082	$ 1,121	$ 508	$ -	$ 478	$ 14,394
280	61	$ 4,374	$ -	$ 3,085	$ 681	$ 309	$ -	$ 290	$ 8,739

You want to create a summary area like that shown in figure 21.11. Your other requirements are that the summary area must be in a separate Excel workbook that is linked to the source file.

Fig. 21.11
A dynamic summary area in an external Excel file. Note the array formula on the edit line.

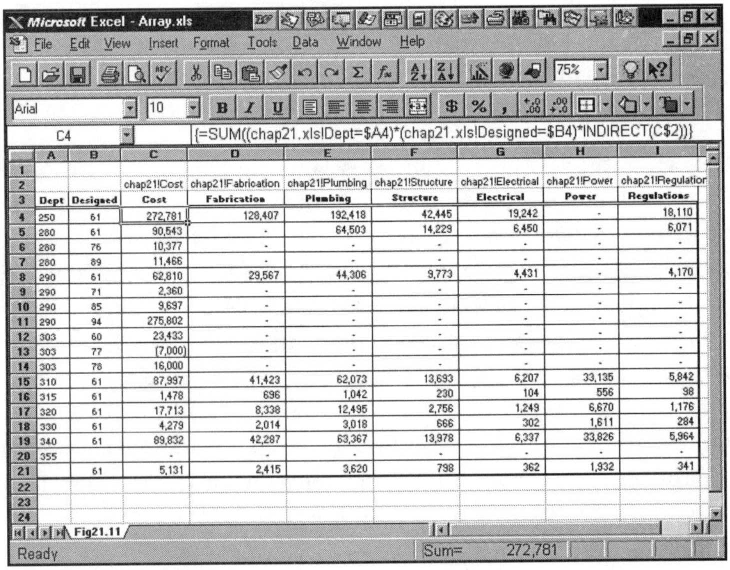

		chap21!Cost	chap21!Fabrication	chap21!Plumbing	chap21!Structure	chap21!Electrical	chap21!Power	chap21!Regulatior
Dept	Designed	Cost	Fabrication	Plumbing	Structure	Electrical	Power	Regulations
250	61	272,781	128,407	192,418	42,445	19,242	-	18,110
280	61	90,543	-	64,503	14,229	6,450	-	6,071
280	76	10,377	-	-	-	-	-	-
280	89	11,466	-	-	-	-	-	-
290	61	62,810	29,567	44,306	9,773	4,431	-	4,170
290	71	2,360	-	-	-	-	-	-
290	85	9,697	-	-	-	-	-	-
290	94	275,802	-	-	-	-	-	-
303	60	23,433	-	-	-	-	-	-
303	77	(7,000)	-	-	-	-	-	-
303	78	16,000	-	-	-	-	-	-
310	61	87,997	41,423	62,073	13,693	6,207	33,135	5,842
315	61	1,478	696	1,042	230	104	556	98
320	61	17,713	8,338	12,495	2,756	1,249	6,670	1,176
330	61	4,279	2,014	3,018	666	302	1,611	284
340	61	89,832	42,287	63,367	13,978	6,337	33,826	5,964
355		-	-	-	-	-	-	-
	61	5,131	2,415	3,620	798	362	1,932	341

Because there are many rows of data, you can start by choosing <u>D</u>ata, <u>F</u>ilter, <u>A</u>dvance Filter, which extracts the unique combination of the fields Department and Designed to the summary file.

Next, you can sort the extract list to put it in any order you need. To create the formulas that summarize the data, you could choose the DSUM function; however, in the example shown here that would require 18×7 or 126 separate criteria ranges. You might consider using a SUMIF function, but this example is too complicated for that approach. Probably the best solution for the current situation is the array formula shown on the formula bar

```
{=SUM((chap21.XLS!Dept=$A4)*(chap21.XLS!Designed=$B4)*INDIRECT(C$2))}
```

The beauty of this formula is that you only need to enter it once in cell C4 and then you can copy it to the entire summary range C4:I21. For this formula to work as written, you need to name some ranges in the source file.

The first part of the array formula (chap21.XLS!Dept=$A4) compares the value in cell A4 with each item in the range named Dept in the source file chap21.XLS. The result of this portion of the array function is a series of TRUEs and FALSEs. The next portion of this array (chap21.XLS!Designed=$B4) produces a similar array, each element of which is multiplied by its corresponding element of the first array, creating a new array of 0s and 1s. In this array, only elements that matched on both Dept and Year Designed produce 1s. Next, the INDIRECT(C$2) portion returns an array of all the values in the range of the source file named Cost. These are multiplied by either 0 or 1 depending on the results of the previous part of the formula. Finally, the resulting array is summed. Notice the use of mixed cell references in the array formula. To enter an array formula, you type the formula and hold down the Ctrl+Shift keys as you press Enter.

> ### Caution
>
> Excel's INDIRECT function requires that the source file be open for it to work. If the source file is closed and you update the links, all the formulas return #REF!. Just open the source file and everything updates correctly. If you can't have the source file open when you use the summary file, create the summary area in the source file and then reference the source file's summary area from another file using formulas of the type =Chap21.XLS!A100 or, alternatively, use the <u>E</u>dit, Paste <u>S</u>pecial, Paste <u>L</u>ink command.

Both the Chap21.XLS and the Array.xls files can be found on the companion disk.

On the Disk

Managing Excel Links

Many of the methods used in the preceding examples enable links back to the source data. This section looks at how to manage these links.

Whenever you open a file that contains links to other closed files, Excel prompts you to reestablish links. If you choose Yes, Excel reads the closed file(s) and updates the linked information. If you choose No, Excel uses the data as of the last time the links were updated.

If you want to update links to a closed file after you have opened your file, choose Edit, Links. The Links dialog box enables you to open the source files, update links, or change the source file.

> **Tip**
>
> You can quickly open linked files by selecting a linked cell and pressing Ctrl+[.

If you have used the Data, Get External Data command to bring your data into Excel, you can update the query results by placing the cursor in Microsoft Query definition range (the data brought in using Microsoft Query) and choosing Data, Refresh Data.

If you imported the data into Excel using the Data, Pivot Table command, you can refresh the pivot table by choosing Data, Refresh Data while your cursor is in the pivot table.

You can track down all the links to Excel files by using the Edit, Find command and searching for ".XLS". To save time, you can select all sheets before you use the Edit, Find command.

> **Tip**
>
> If you don't find any links using the Edit, Find command, yet the Edit, Links command shows that some exist, check the Define Name dialog box for names linked to external files.

Getting Data from Other Worksheet Applications

Excel, of course, is not the only spreadsheet program; so often you may need to import from another worksheet program such as Lotus 1-2-3 or Quattro Pro. The following sections show you how to get your data from those programs into Excel and how to deal with some of the problems that occur. Both DOS and Windows versions of these programs are examined.

Using Lotus 1-2-3 for Windows Data in Excel

There was a time, not too long ago, when virtually every PC spreadsheet user used Lotus 1-2-3, which means that there are millions of 1-2-3 spreadsheets and millions of users who want to import their 1-2-3 data into Excel. Fortunately, all versions (1 to 5) of Lotus 1-2-3 for Windows spreadsheets can be opened directly into Excel using the File, Open command. Some problems can occur with regard to graphics and macros, but because data is usually your major concern, the results are generally acceptable.

If you want to keep the 1-2-3 worksheet as an Excel file, you should save it as an Excel file using File, Save As. If you do not do this, when you save the file, it is saved as a 1-2-3 file. Anything that the 1-2-3 file contains that is added in Excel but not compatible with 1-2-3 is lost during saving.

What possible problems could you have with importing Lotus 1-2-3 files and what can you do about them? When you import a 1-2-3 spreadsheet into Excel, you receive error messages for each function that Excel can't convert. After the file is opened, Excel displays a note indicator (a red dot at the top right corner of the cell) in each cell where an error was detected. Place your mouse over the cell and the note `Formula failed to convert` appears. The value, not the formula, will be imported.

Here are some of the things you can do if Lotus 1-2-3 formulas don't translate when you open a 1-2-3 file in Excel:

- Check to see if Excel has a function that does the same thing as your 1-2-3 function.

- You can create your own formulas or functions that do the same thing as the 1-2-3 function.

- You can comment-out the formula in 1-2-3. That is, add an apostrophe in front of the formula to make it a label before importing.

- You can employ an Excel menu command to duplicate the effect of a 1-2-3 function.

- You can employ an Excel macro or Visual Basic programming (VBA) function to produce the results of a 1-2-3 function.

Let's see how some of these approaches work. Sometimes by converting a function to text before opening it in Excel, you can replace the '@ with an equal sign and have the formula work correctly. You may or may not need to change the name of the function, and if you're lucky all the arguments may work as in 1-2-3. If you need to change the function's name, consider using the Edit, Replace command if you have many copies of the function. Sometimes another option is to use an Excel format to produce the same results as a 1-2-3 function, as shown for the DATEINFO function in table 21.1. When you substitute an Excel function for a 1-2-3 function you may need to change the order of the arguments or use different arguments. Table 21.1 shows solutions for nine 1-2-3 functions that don't convert successfully.

Table 21.1   Conversion Solutions for 1-2-3 Release 5.0 for Windows File

1-2-3 5.0 for Windows @Function	Possible Excel 7.0 Solutions
@ACCRUED( )	=ACCRINT( )
@D360( )	=DAYS360( )
@DAYS360( )	Comment-out the function.
@DATEDIF(date1,date2,"format")	This function has a number of possible values for "format." Depending on the "format" you want, you can create your own formulas. For example, if format is md use the formula =DAY(date2)-DAY(date1); if it is yd use the formula =DATE(1,MONTH(date1),DAY(date1))-DATE(1,MONTH(date2),DAY(date2))
@DATEINFO(date,attribute)	This function has a number of possible "attributes." Depending on the "attribute" you may have to use a formula, a function, or simply format the cell. For example, if the attribute is 1, 2, 5, or 6, you can apply an Excel date format to the cell to accomplish the same result. Create the following custom formats DDD, DDDD, MMM, or MMMM to duplicate the above attributes.
@DB( )	Comment-out this function.
@FVAL( )	Comment-out this function and change it in Excel to the FV function.
@IPAYMT( )	=IPMT( )
@PPAYMT( )	=PPMT( )

Along with function problems with incoming 1-2-3 files, another major area of difficulty is macro conversion. Although, strictly speaking, this is not a data management issue, it is discussed briefly in the 1-2-3 for DOS section.

Getting Data from Quattro Pro for Windows

Excel does not open any Quattro Pro for Windows files (*.WB1 and *.WB2). However, there are a number of possible solutions:

- You can use Copy and Paste from Quattro Pro to Excel, or you can create a link using Excel's Edit, Paste Special, Paste Link command. If you want to create a link choose Biff3, Wk1, or Text in the As box.

- Save the Quattro Pro for Windows file as an Excel file. Quattro Pro saves your file as an Excel 3.0 file. Quattro Pro saves any formulas that it can convert to an Excel equivalent.

- Although you could save the Quattro Pro for Windows file to a DOS version of Quattro Pro that Excel can open, I strongly advise against it. Besides formula conversion problems, formatting doesn't convert well.

If you have many formulas in Quattro Pro for Windows 6.0, you may not want them converted to values when you open them in Excel. How can you save Quattro Pro for Windows 6.0's dynamic functions that don't convert into Excel equivalents? There are a number of approaches to solve this problem. Some are easy; some a little more challenging. They are similar to the options discussed for 1-2-3 for Windows.

The comment-out approach is particularly useful with Quattro Pro files because, although Excel 7.0 can't read Quattro Pro 6.0 and Quattro Pro can't save a file in Excel 7.0 format, Excel and Quattro Pro contain many of the same functions. In that case, changing the formula into text by adding an apostrophe before the @ sign can save a lot of time later. Save the file as an Excel file (3.0) and retrieve it into Excel. In Excel, replace the '@ with = and the formula will work. Because this solution is so easy, you should always try it before attempting other approaches.

Table 21.2 demonstrates a number of approaches for five Quattro Pro for Windows functions. Also, review table 21.4 on Quattro Pro 5.0 for DOS conversion solutions, later in this chapter.

Table 21.2 Conversion Solutions for Quattro Pro 6.0 for Windows Functions

Quattro Pro 6.0 for Windows @Function	Possible Excel 7.0 Solutions
@YLD2YLD(y,F1,F2,Q1,Q2)	You can create the following formula in Excel that accomplishes the same thing:=(((1+y/Q1)^F1)^(1/F2)-1)*Q2.
@YEARFRAC(date1,date2)	Comment-out the function as discussed earlier.
@MROUND(number,digits)	Comment-out the function.
@TBILLPRICE(settle, maturity,discount)	Comment-out the function.
@LINTERP(knownx's,knowny's,x)	Excel does not have a formula for calculating linear interpolations; instead you can use the following: {=IF(INDEX(knowny's,MATCH(TRUE,knowny's>=X,0)1,1)=X,INDEX(TABLE,MATCH(TRUE,knowny's>=X,0)-1,2) ,(INDEX(TABLE,MATCH(TRUE,knowny's>=X,0),2)INDEX(TABLE,MATCH(TRUE, knowny's>=X,0)-1,2))*(X INDEX(knowny's,MATCH(TRUE,knowny's>=X,0)-1,1))/(INDEX(knowny's,MATCH(TRUE,knowny's>=X,0),1)INDEX(knowny's,MATCH (TRUE, knowny's>=X,0)-1,1))+INDEX(TABLE,MATCH(TRUE,knowny's>=X,0)-1,2))}

In the Excel array formula shown in the previous table for dealing with interpolation, the knowny's and knownx's should be placed in adjacent columns—the knownx's on the left, and the entire range named TABLE.

Accessing Data in Lotus 1-2-3 for DOS

Many people still work with DOS applications or are just beginning to move to the Windows environment, so it is useful to know how to get data from those programs into Excel as well. This section examines the DOS versions of Lotus 1-2-3 and Quattro Pro.

The most practical way to get 1-2-3 releases 2.*x*, 3.*x*, and 4.*x* data into Excel is to open it in its native format. Excel translates all of 2.01's functions and most of those from other DOS versions. What it won't do is bring in all WYSIWYG colors accurately. Also, some range names that are legal in 1-2-3 are not legal in Excel. Any illegal range name will be changed; however, this could lead to serious problems in macros. Table 21.3 shows most of the functions in DOS versions of 1-2-3 that don't convert directly.

Table 21.3 Conversion Solutions for 1-2-3 for DOS Functions	
1-2-3 DOS Version @Function	**Possible Excel 7.0 Solutions**
@SOLVER	Consider using the Tools, Solver or Tools, Goal Seek commands.
@SHEETS	Use the Excel 4.0 macro function =GET.WORKBOOK or the VBA WORKBOOK(name).PROPERTY function.
@D360	=DAYS360
@DQUERY	Consider using Excel's Data, Get External Data command.

Caution

Remember that 1-2-3 macros ran with Alt + a letter. In Excel, you need to use Ctrl + the same letter. This can be a major problem because Excel's own shortcut keys use Ctrl + a letter. Only nine lowercase letters are not used by Excel. Also, keep in mind that your 1-2-3 macro shortcuts keys will override Excel's.

Managing Data from Quattro Pro for DOS

Quattro Pro for DOS version 5.0 cannot be read directly by Excel 7.0, nor can you save the Quattro Pro file as an Excel file. The best solution is the intermediate file type approach. Because this process is not what most people might expect, this section walks you through the process. Follow these steps to convert your Quattro Pro data to an intermediate file type:

1. In Quattro Pro for DOS 5.0, choose File, Save As to open the Save As dialog box.

2. Type the name of the file and include the extension of the file type you want to convert to; then press Enter. Quattro Pro automatically converts the file to the file type you specify by adding the extension.

Note

Quattro Pro 5.0 for DOS converts your file to about 30 file types including WK3 (1-2-3 3.x), WQ1 (Quattro Pro 4.0 or earlier), DBF (dBASE III, III+ and IV), DB (Paradox), and DIF (VisiCalc). Any of these types of files can be read by Excel.

V

Managing External Data

Caution

If you send your files to any file type other than a spreadsheet, none of your formulas are retained; but if data is all you want to exchange, it makes little difference which file type you choose.

You should consider all the techniques discussed in the previous sections for converting other spreadsheet functions in Excel. For example, in converting a Quattro Pro 5.0 for DOS file, table 21.4 shows some conversion solutions for functions that do not convert.

Table 21.4   Conversion Solutions for Quattro Pro 5.0 DOS Files

Quattro Pro for DOS 5.0 @Function	Possible Excel 7.0 Alternative
@MEMEMSAVAIL - this function is checking for expanded memory.	Not relevant in Windows, but may want to use =INFO("MEMAVAIL"), =INFO("TOTMEM") or =INFO("MEMUSED")@NUMTOHEX(num) =BIN2HEX(num),=DEC2HEX(num) or=OCT2HEX(num)@HEXTONUM(num) =HEX2BIN(num),=HEX2DEC(num) or=HEX2OCT(num)
@PVAL()	=PV(rate,nper,pmt,fv,type)Excel's PV function does the same job as Quattro Pro's PVAL and PV functions.
@FILEEXIST("filename")	There is no spreadsheet function to determine if a file exists; however, you can use VB DIR("path\filename") or Excel 4.0's FILES("path\filename") macro commands to determine if a file exists.

Working with Downloaded Data

More and more frequently, PC users are working with data downloaded from mainframes or other output sources that create ASCII files. There are two major categories of ASCII files that will be of interest to Excel users: *delimited* and *fixed length files*. The following two sections deal with these two file types.

Importing Delimited Files

A delimited file is one in which the data for each record is separated into fields by a delimiter such as a comma, tab, or quote. For a specific field, each record may or may not contain data of the same length; the delimiter indicates when one field ends and another begins.

One of the most common delimited files types is *comma delimited*. Follow these steps to import comma delimited files:

1. Choose File, Open or choose the Open toolbar button.

2. Select All Files (*.*) or Text Files (*.PRN; *.TXT; *.CSV) from the Files of Type drop-down list.

3. From the Look In drop-down list, select the folder where your files are located.

4. Pick the file you want to open; then choose Open.

5. If Excel needs more information, the Text Import Wizard opens, as shown in figure 21.12.

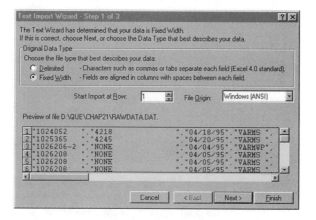

Fig. 21.12
Step 1 of the Text Import Wizard shows you what your file looks like to Excel.

6. Click Delimited to select the Original Data Type.

7. Choose Start Import at Row and enter the first row you want imported. Choose this if your file has unwanted header rows at the top of the data.

8. Select the File Origin.

9. Choose Next to move to the second step of the Wizard, as shown in figure 21.13.

Fig. 21.13

This is Step 2 of the Text Import Wizard for delimited files.

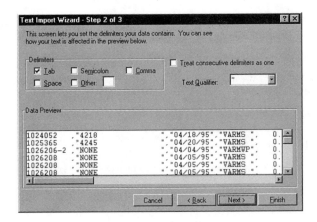

10. Click the type(s) of delimiters your file contains. You can indicate more than one type.

11. Select the type of text qualifier from the Text Qualifier drop-down list.

12. Check the Treat Consecutive Delimiters as One box if appropriate. Choose Next to reach the third step of the Wizard (not shown here).

13. Click the top of any column that you want to specify an import format for or that you want to exclude from the imported data; then choose Finish.

> **Note**
>
> If you are importing numbers or dates that you want as text, you can select a Column Data Format of Text. Also, Excel enables you to indicate the order of your date fields by selecting from the Date drop-down list. Using these options in the Wizard reduces your time needed to clean up the file later.

Once you have imported your delimited file, you probably need to clean it up and massage it before you can work with it. We'll cover this in "Preparing Data for Analysis," later in this chapter.

Fixed Length Files

Fixed length ASCII files are the second type of downloaded file of interest to you. In a fixed length file, each field is the same length for each record. That means, for example, that the first name field might be 20 characters and the last name field might be 15 characters; but those fields would be that length for all records, regardless of how long a given first or last name is.

Importing files with fixed length fields is very much like importing delimited files, in that Excel displays the Import Text Wizard and asks you to provide some information.

Follow these steps to import a file of fixed length fields:

1. Choose File, Open or choose the Open toolbar button.

2. Select All Files (*.*) or Text Files (*.PRN; *.TXT; *.CSV) from the Files of Type drop-down list.

3. From the Look In drop-down list, select the folder where your files are located.

4. Pick the file you want to open; then choose Open.

5. If Excel can't open the file directly, the Text Import Wizard opens, as shown earlier in figure 21.12.

6. Click Fixed Width to select the Original Data Type.

7. Choose Start Import at Row and enter the first row you want imported. Choose this if your file has unwanted header rows at the top of the data.

8. Select the File Origin.

9. Choose Next to move to the second step of the Wizard.

10. Show Excel where fields begin and end by adding, moving, or deleting line breaks. After this point, your screen might look like figure 21.14. Then choose Next.

> **Tip**
>
> The Data Preview window can be scrolled to show you all the columns and rows of your data. You can delete unwanted data at Step 3 if you separate useful and non-useful data with line breaks.

Fig. 21.14
Here the line breaks have been added separating useful data and setting useless data apart.

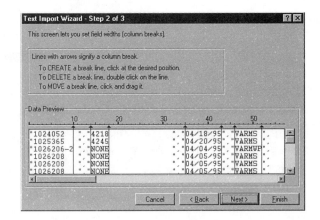

11. Click the top of any column that you want to specify an import format for or exclude from the import; then choose Finish.

If Excel can determine what your file should look like, it may bypass the Wizard.

Importing Data from Database Applications

Database programs are another common source of data for Excel users. This section explores how to get data from common PC database programs into Excel. Specifically, this sections looks at importing data from Microsoft Access, Paradox for DOS and Windows, and Lotus Approach.

Getting Access Data into Excel

Because the analytical and charting tools available in Excel far exceed those available in Access, it is often necessary to import your data from Access into Excel. You can't open an Access database directly into Excel; however, you can send the data, export it, copy and paste it, or query it from within Excel. The following sections explore some of these options.

You can send a copy of data from Access tables, queries, forms, or reports directly to Excel. Of these choices, you are most likely to send data from tables or queries; but you should try out all for types of data because you may find that you can glean something useful even from forms and reports. Follow these steps to send table data from Access to Excel:

1. Open Access and then Open an Access Database.

2. In the Database window, choose the Tables tab.

3. Select the table you want to send to Excel.

4. Choose Tools, OfficeLinks, Analyze It with MS Excel or use the OfficeLinks toolbar button, as shown in figure 21.15.

Fig. 21.15
The Access
OfficeLinks toolbar
button showing
the Analyze It with
MS Excel choice
selected.

Access creates an Excel file from the selected table's data, saves it to disk, opens Excel if it's not already open, and imports the file into Excel.

As an experiment, you should try sending a report to Excel. You may be pleasantly surprised by the results of this process. For example, figure 21.16 shows the Excel file created from an Access report. Because the Access report was grouped, the Excel file is displayed automatically as an outline.

With the preceding technique, as with copy and paste and exporting, you need to have a copy of Access to work with. If all you have is an Access database file, you are still able to bring the data into Excel by using the Get External Data command, which is discussed in the section entitled "Filtering Incoming Data" later in this chapter.

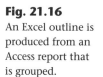

Fig. 21.16
An Excel outline is
produced from an
Access report that
is grouped.

Using Paradox for Windows Data

Like Access, Paradox is a database program from which you may want to import data. Unlike Access, Paradox files can't be opened directly into Excel. You have at least three alternatives:

■ You can use Copy and Paste from Paradox for Windows to Excel, or you can create a link using Excel's Edit, Paste Special, Paste Link command. If you want a link, choose Text in the As box. Remember that pasting a link creates an array function in Excel.

■ Paradox for Windows enables you to export to Excel. In Paradox, you choose File, Utility, Export to reach the Table Export dialog box.

> **Tip**
>
> Run a query first if you want to limit the data you are exporting to Excel; then export the Answer table or the renamed Answer table.

■ Use Excel's Data, Get External Data command.

Moving Paradox for DOS Data into Excel

As with Paradox for Windows, Excel can't read Paradox for DOS files directly. But unlike Paradox for Windows, Paradox for DOS cannot save tables as Excel files. So the best option this leaves is to use the Data, Get External Data command or use an intermediate file type for the data transfer. This section explores the intermediate file type approach.

Paradox for DOS 4.5 can export files in a number of formats including various versions of the following: Quattro, 1-2-3, dBASE, VisiCalc, and ASCII fixed and delimited. Excel can open all of these file types.

Follow these steps to export a Paradox for DOS file to an intermediate file type for Excel to read:

1. In Paradox for DOS, choose Tools, ExportImport, Export.

2. Choose the file type you want from the list.

3. Name the file and then click OK.

Using Approach Data in Excel

Approach is Lotus' database program. Excel cannot open Approach files directly, so you should consider saving your Approach data files as Excel files or use Edit, Copy and Edit, Paste. Microsoft does not provide import drivers for Approach files with MS Query in the Standard edition of Office 95, so you cannot use the Data, Get External Data command with Approach.

Using Data from Other Microsoft Programs

On some occasions it is useful to move data from other Microsoft applications into Excel. This section looks at two of those sources—Microsoft Project and Microsoft Word.

Moving Microsoft Project Data to Excel

If you use Microsoft Project, you may need to move the data into Excel to use its strong analytical and charting tools. Excel can't import Microsoft Project files directly; however, you can still move data between the two programs using any one of the following approaches:

- You can use Copy and Paste from Microsoft Project to Excel, or you can create a link using Excel's Edit, Paste Special, Paste Link command. If you want a link choose Biff4, Biff3, Biff, or Text in the As box.

> **Note**
>
> Microsoft Project determines what data gets copied to Excel by the table you are in and the rows you select. Because of this, you should design a custom table with all the fields you want to bring into Excel and then copy that table.

- You can save a Microsoft Project file as an Excel file. To do this, choose File, Save As; change the file type to Excel Workbook; and choose OK to display the Export dialog box.

Using Word Data in Excel

It is quite common to want to transfer Excel data to Word, but occasions for the reverse are rare. If you are going to copy data from Word to Excel it is most often in the form of a Word table. Two ways you can copy information between a Word table and Excel spreadsheet are as follows:

■ You can use Copy and Paste from Microsoft Word to Excel, or you can create a link using Excel's Edit, Paste Special, Paste Link command. If you want a link, choose Text in the As box.

> **Note**
>
> When you use the Edit, Paste Special, Paste Link command, Excel creates an array.

■ An alternative to choosing the Edit, Copy and Edit, Paste commands is to use drag and drop between Word and Excel. The section titled "Linking and Embedding Data in Microsoft Word" in Chapter 22 explains procedures for linking and embedding Word and Excel data.

Filtering Incoming Data

This section shows you how to use Excel's Data, Get External Data command. With this command, you can access data from a number of sources even if you can't open the source file in Excel. This command links to the MS Query add-in, so most of what you do in this section really involves Microsoft Query.

Microsoft Office Standard edition comes with drivers for querying Access, dBASE, FoxPro, Paradox, SQL server, Text files, and even Excel itself.

> **Tip**
>
> You can query Access 4.0 and 7.0 using the Access driver.
>
> The Paradox driver that comes with Microsoft Office 95 can be used to access both Paradox 4.5 DOS or Windows files.

Microsoft Query and the drivers mentioned previously are not installed automatically; you must specify that you want these features added during a Custom installation.

Assuming that you have installed all the appropriate drivers but don't find the <u>D</u>ata, Get E<u>x</u>ternal Data command available, you need to turn on the add-in or show Excel where it is. Follow these steps to add MS Query to Excel:

1. Choose <u>T</u>ools, <u>A</u>dd-Ins, Check MS Query Add-In; then check OK.

or

2. If MS Query Add-In is not on the <u>A</u>dd-Ins Available list, choose <u>B</u>rowse to locate XLQUERY.XLA. Most likely this file was installed in the MSOffice\Excel\Library\MSQuery\ folder.

Once you have installed the add-in, you can query closed external database files.

> **Caution**
>
> A number of actions in Microsoft Query may cause it to crash and even lock up your system. Always save your data before choosing the <u>D</u>ata, Get E<u>x</u>ternal Data command. Also, as soon as you return data to Excel from MS Query save your Excel file.

Follow these steps to query an external database from inside Excel:

1. Choose <u>D</u>ata, Get E<u>x</u>ternal Data to activate Microsoft Query, as shown in figure 21.17.

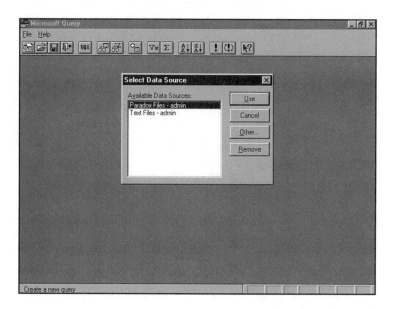

Fig. 21.17
The Microsoft Query opening screen requests you to tell it where you are going to get your data from.

V

Managing External Data

2. In the Select Data Source dialog box, choose <u>O</u>ther to display the ODBC Data Source dialog box, shown in figure 21.18.

Fig. 21.18
The ODBC Data Source dialog box allows you to see the types of drivers you have installed and enables you to pick the file type you want to use.

3. If the ODBC driver you want is not displayed in the ODBC Data Source dialog box, choose <u>N</u>ew to display the Add Data Source dialog box (see fig. 21.19). Select the driver you want from the Installed ODBC <u>D</u>rivers list; then choose OK twice.

Fig. 21.19
In the Add Data Source dialog box, you can choose from the installed drivers to add the one you want.

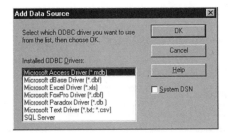

4. Select the Data Source you intend to use and click <u>U</u>se to display the Add Tables dialog box, shown in figure 21.20.

Fig. 21.20
From the Add Tables dialog box, you choose the database(s) or table(s) you want to query. In this figure, we are picking a Paradox for Windows 4.5 database.

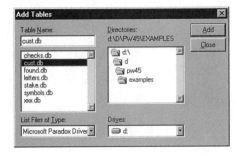

5. In the Add Tables dialog box, locate the file or table you want to query. Select the table from the Table Name list and choose Add. If you want to add additional tables to perform a relational query, select each table and choose Add. When you have added all the tables, choose Close. The Query1 form displays within Microsoft Query.

6. Add the fields you want returned by the query by double-clicking the field names in the field list.

7. Choose View, Criteria to show the query by example (QBE) grid. On the QBE grid you set the conditions that control which records (rows) of the table you see.

8. Add the field(s) you want to set criteria for to the QBE grid by dragging the field names from the field list to the Criteria Field row of the QBE grid.

9. Add criteria to the Value row of the QBE grid. Then choose Records, Query Now. The query and its result are shown in figure 21.21.

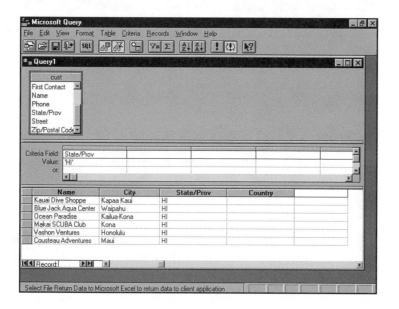

Fig. 21.21

The result of query that displays four fields from the Paradox cust database where the State/Prov field contains HI.

V

Managing External Data

10. Choose File, Return Data to Microsoft Excel to hide Microsoft Query and return to Excel displaying the Get External Data dialog box shown in figure 21.22.

Fig. 21.22

In the Get External Data dialog box, you can choose a number of options and indicate where in your spreadsheet you want the data placed.

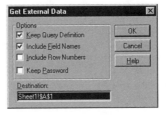

11. Choose the option you want in the Get External Data dialog box and enter the cell address for the top-left corner of the incoming data in Destination box; then click OK.

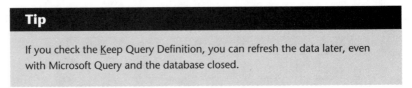

Tip

If you check the Keep Query Definition, you can refresh the data later, even with Microsoft Query and the database closed.

12. To refresh the query results in Excel, choose Data, Refresh Data.

Preparing Data for Analysis

Although you may find it relatively easy to import data files from other sources, the data is often not in an acceptable format to work with. For example, if you import TXT files from a mainframe computer, the files may need a lot of work before you can use them in Excel.

This section discusses some of the problems you may encounter and offers possible solutions. Suppose that you have just imported the fixed width file. It may not be immediately apparent what cleanup is necessary.

Some of the common problems with imported data include: an end of file character in the last active cell; many fields may be packed with trailing blanks; all numeric fields may contain an unnecessary 0 if there is no data available; and fields that appear empty often contain invisible spaces.

To remove the unwanted spaces, you can construct a formula. Note, that if you attempt to employ Excel's <u>E</u>dit, R<u>e</u>place command to clear up cells that may contain blanks, you also replace single blanks within text. For example, if one column of your data contains a mix of text and packed blanks, use of the Replace command to replace the packed blanks also turns text such as John Smith into JohnSmith. The following formula cleans up your data without this problem

```
=IF(LEN(A1)>0,TRIM(A1)&"xxx","xxx")
```

This formula uses the powerful TRIM function to remove any leading, trailing, or repeat internal spaces. Note that if TRIM finds a single internal space it does nothing to it. The trimmed result is concatenated with a random set of characters that would not be found in any of the data. If you do not concatenate the result with some text, then when you convert the formulas to values in a later step, Excel keeps numbers as left-aligned text, which is ignored in many mathematical calculations such as SUM.

The next step of the cleanup process is to convert all these formulas to values using the <u>E</u>dit, Paste <u>S</u>pecial, <u>V</u>alues command. Then you can use <u>E</u>dit, R<u>e</u>place to replace *xxx* with nothing. After this, replace any cells that contain only 0s with blanks. Replacing zeros with blanks saves memory, especially with large files. When you do this, make sure that the Find Entire Cell <u>O</u>nly option is checked. Then move the formula area over and replace all the imported data with the results of the cleanup formulas. It may also be necessary to format your data to show dates in an appropriate date format.

Automating Data Download and Cleanup

Download routines are generally repeated on a daily, weekly, or monthly basis, which strongly suggests that the entire process should be automated. Because many people still use the old 4.0 Macro language, it is included here for completeness. To open and clean up a text file with the kind of problems described in the previous section, a program similar to the one that follows could be used. Listing 21.1 shows the Excel 4.0 macro code to accomplish the entire process including download and cleanup. After the 4.0 code, the equivalent VBA code is shown. Manual recalculation cannot be on when these macros are running.

V

Managing External Data

Listing 21.1 Excel 4.0 Code for Import and Cleanup of a Mainframe Download File

```
OpenCleanDownLoadTxt
    =OPEN.TEXT("DownLoad.txt",2,1,1,1,FALSE,FALSE,
    FALSE,TRUE,FALSE,FALSE,"""",{1,1;2,1;3,3;4,1;5,1;6,1;7,
    ➥1;8,1;9,1;10,1;11,1;12,1;13,1})
    =SELECT.END(4)
    =SELECT("RC:RC13")
    =CLEAR(3)
    =SELECT("R1C14")
    =FORMULA("=IF(LEN(RC[-13])>0,
    TRIM(RC[-13])&""xxx"","""xxx"")")
    =COPY()
    =SELECT("R1C1")
    =SELECT.END(4)
    =SELECT("RC14:R1C26")
    =ERROR(0)
    =PASTE()
    =COPY()
    =PASTE.SPECIAL(3,1,FALSE,FALSE)
    =FORMULA.REPLACE("xxx","",2,1,FALSE,FALSE)
    =FORMULA.REPLACE("0","",1,1,FALSE,FALSE)
    =ERROR(1)
    =CUT()
    =SELECT("R1C1")
    =ERROR(0)
    =PASTE()
    =ERROR(1)
    =SELECT.END(4)
    =SELECT("R1C3:RC3")
    =FORMAT.NUMBER("m/d/yy")
    =RETURN()
Sub OpenCleanDownLoadTxt()

    Workbooks.OpenText Filename:="D:\que\chap21\DOWNLOAD.TXT",
    ➥Origin _
```

```
:=xlWindows, StartRow:=1, DataType:=xlFixedWidth, OtherChar _
:="""", FieldInfo:=Array(Array(0, 1), Array(11, 9), Array(14, 1), _
Array(32, 9), Array(35, 1), Array(43, 9), Array(46, 1), Array(52, 9),
Array( _54, 1), Array(61, 9), Array(62, 1), Array(69, 9), Array(70, 1),
➡Array(77, 9), _
Array(79, 1), Array(97, 9), Array(100, 1), Array(130, 9), Array(132, 1),_
Array(142, 9), Array(143, 1), Array(162, 9), Array(165, 1), Array
➡(195, 9), _
Array(198, 1), Array(218, 9))
```

This step opens the text file using the Text Wizard

```
Selection.End(xlDown).Select
Selection.EntireRow.Select
Selection.ClearContents
```

These steps clear the last line of the imported data, for example if it contained an end of file character

```
Range("N1").Select
ActiveCell.FormulaR1C1 = _
    "=IF(LEN(RC[-13])>0,TRIM(RC[-13])&""xxx"",""xxx"")"
Selection.Copy
Range("A1").Select
Selection.End(xlDown).Select
ActiveCell.Offset(0, 13).Range("A1").Select
Range(ActiveCell, "Z1").Select
On Error Resume Next
Application.DisplayAlerts = False
ActiveSheet.Paste
```

These lines enter the clean up formula in an empty column to the right of the imported data. Then the formula is copied to a range equal to the range of imported data but to the right of it

```
Selection.Copy
    Selection.PasteSpecial Paste:=xlValues,
    ➡Operation:=xlNone, _
    SkipBlanks:=False, Transpose:=False
Application.CutCopyMode = False
```

Then the formulas are converted to values, and next the xxx's and the 0's are replaced with blanks

```
Selection.Replace What:="xxx", Replacement:="",
➡LookAt:=xlPart, _
    SearchOrder:=xlByRows, MatchCase:=False
Selection.Replace What:="0", Replacement:="", LookAt:=xlWhole, _
    SearchOrder:=xlByRows, MatchCase:=False
On Error GoTo 0
Application.DisplayAlerts = True
```

V

Managing External Data

The next set of lines copy the cleaned up data on top of the original data range

```
Selection.Cut
Range("A1").Select
On Error Resume Next
Application.DisplayAlerts = False
ActiveSheet.Paste
On Error GoTo 0
Application.DisplayAlerts = True
```

Finally, one column of data is reformatted

```
Selection.End(xlDown).Select
ActiveCell.Offset(0, 2).Range("A1").Select
Range(ActiveCell, "C1").Select
Selection.NumberFormat = "m/d/yy"
End Sub
```

The error suppression code is added for two possible situations. If the paste selection is too large for undo to remain in effect, you get a prompt asking whether to continue. You may want to suppress this prompt. Second, if the Replace commands don't find items to replace, you get a message that you don't need in this situation: Cannot find matching data to replace.

Looking Up Data in Multiple Files

Often downloaded information comes from multiple files. The data in these files may need to be combined to be useful. For example, suppose that you have downloaded a file that contains a list of serial numbers of machines serviced this month. Two other downloaded files contain between them lists of model numbers corresponding to all machines ever serviced, along with other unnecessary data. You want to pull the model numbers for each of the machines serviced. If the model number is not in the first model number file, it will be in the second one. Because there are a large number of items, you want to design a way to check the first file and bring in the model number if it is there; otherwise, you want to check the second file for the model number, and if it is not in either file you want to leave the entry blank.

One solution to this problem is a single formula that looks up the desired information and returns it to the file containing the serial numbers. You may not need to look up values in two external files, however. If you can understand the solution presented here, you will be ready for any problem.

Suppose that the two external files are entitled Model1 and Model2. Each of these files has been set up so that the first column contains serial numbers, and the second column contains the model number. To make matters simple, both data ranges in the model files are named Table. Assume that, in the file with the serial numbers, the serial numbers are located in column A. The formula to accomplish this rather challenging double external lookup is as follows

```
=IF(ISERROR(VLOOKUP(A1,Model1.XLS!Table,2,0)),
➥IF(ISERROR(VLOOKUP(A1,Model2.XLS!Table,2,0)),"",
➥VLOOKUP(A1,Model2.XLS!Table,2,0)),
➥VLOOKUP(A1,Model1.XLS!Table,2,0))
```

This formula assumes that all three files are open; if either Model file is closed, the formula would include the entire path to the closed file. Note that starting with Excel version 5, the VLOOKUP function includes a fourth argument that allows you to specify that the lookup should return only exact matches, which is the case here. Once this formula is entered in a cell, such as B1, you can copy it down as far as your serial numbers extend. In situations where the preceding type of formula is employed, it is often unnecessary to retain the formulas after the data has been retrieved, in that case, you should convert the formulas to values using the Edit, Paste Special, Values command.

Chapter Summary

This chapter showed you how to import data into Excel from a wide variety of sources using a range of Excel tools. After bringing your data into Excel, you will want to analyze it. At that point you may want to read or reread many of the chapters in this book to consider how best to manipulate and analyze the imported data.

V

Managing External Data

22

Sending Data to External Sources

Although Excel gives you broad scope to manage and analyze data, you occasionally will need to export Excel data to another format, or to link an Excel workbook to another application. For example, you might have an application such as an investment portfolio manager, that doesn't recognize the XLS file format—so it can't open an Excel workbook directly. Or, you might want to take advantage of another application's word processing or graphics capabilities to display your Excel data to best advantage.

In cases like these, you save your Excel workbook in a different file format, such as ASCII text or a database format, that another application can recognize and open. You might also want to link or embed portions of an Excel workbook into another application. Then, using Excel, you can change the information in the linked document.

This chapter describes how to accomplish these tasks. It focuses on exporting data to Microsoft Access (a database management application), to ASCII files, and on linking or embedding Excel objects in other applications.

Using the Template Wizard

The Template Wizard is an add-in included in Excel 7. You use the Template Wizard to create templates for new workbooks. What's new and different about that? For years, you created templates for new workbooks and saved them in your Templates folder.

What's new is that these templates enable you to store information in external databases such as Access, dBASE, and Paradox. Alternatively, you can choose to store the information in an Excel worksheet as a list; in this way, you can enter information in one structure that's convenient for data entry, and have it stored in a list structure that's set up for retrieval or filtering.

The general flow of the process is as follows:

1. Create or open a worksheet that's formatted as you want new sheets to appear.
2. Use the Template Wizard to create a template based on your worksheet layout. Using the Wizard you can also specify such information as the type of database you want to create.
3. Open a new workbook based on your new template, and enter information in it.
4. Close or save the new workbook. The data you entered is automatically stored in the database you specified with the Template Wizard.

The usefulness of this capability lies in the fact that database management systems and Excel have different strengths. Excel is quite strong for numeric analysis tasks, offers intuitive means of data entry, and displays data attractively. Compared to database management systems, it is relatively weak for retrieving data based on criteria—and especially at maintaining links between records in different lists. Database management systems offer a few rudimentary numeric analysis capabilities; they shine when it comes to retrieving, filtering, and linking tables of data.

The Template Wizard helps you take advantage of the strengths of both applications. You can, for example, create a template that provides an analysis of the data that is entered into a worksheet. You open a new workbook based on that template and enter new data in it. When you're finished, the data is automatically swept into an external database for later retrieval, or for linkage to other data sets.

Tip

This kind of template saves your business time and grief. Users wind up entering data once only, rather than once for Excel and once for a database. You can't eliminate keystroke errors this way, but you can minimize them.

Creating a New Template

To use the Template Wizard, first install it as an add-in. If Template Wizard does not appear in the Data menu, you need to run Add/Remove Software in the Windows 95 Control Panel. During the Setup routine, modify your selection for add-in components and specify that Setup is to install the Template Wizard with Data Tracking.

When the Wizard is installed in your Excel folder, you also need to install it in Excel itself. Choose Tools, Add-Ins, and select the Template Wizard with Data Tracking checkbox in the Add-Ins Available list box. After you choose OK, Excel installs the add-in and makes it available on the Data menu.

Suppose you want to create a template to support the entry of information about payments your customers make for goods or services they purchase from you. You will eventually use this information to update your Accounts Receivable journal. Open a new workbook and design the very simple format shown in figure 22.1.

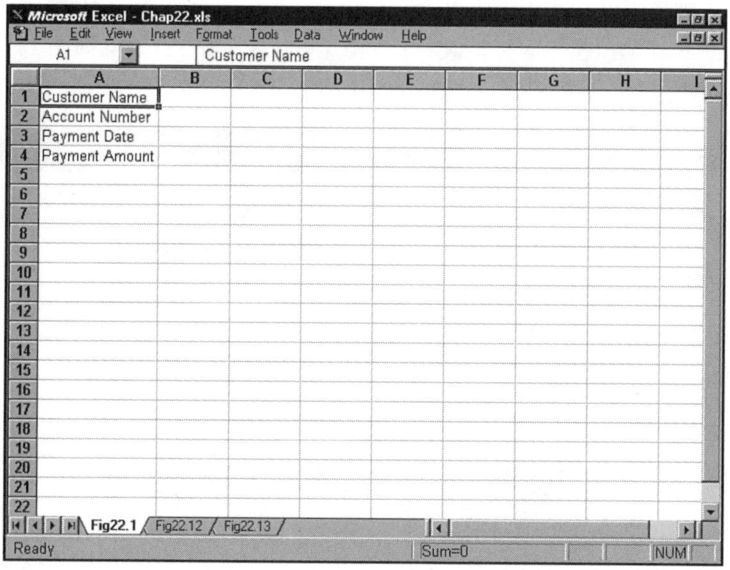

Fig. 22.1
Entries in the workbook that are the basis for a template appear in all workbooks created with that template.

After making these entries, which are no more than labels for the payment information, choose Data, Template Wizard. The first of five steps in the Template Wizard appears, as shown in figure 22.2.

Fig. 22.2
Name the workbook that's the basis for the template, and name and locate the template itself.

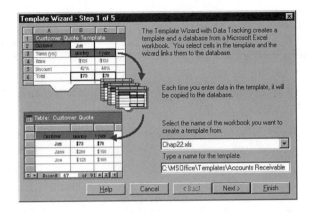

You can choose any workbook that's open as the basis for the template. Click the down arrow of the Select the Name of the Workbook You Want to Create a Template From list box to display all open workbooks. Usually, you want to base the template on the active workbook.

You can use the text edit box to define a name for the template and to redefine the path where you will store the template. If you're connected to a network, this path might be to a shared template folder.

> **Tip**
>
> Using the Windows Explorer, you can create a subfolder in your principal Templates folder. When you put an Excel template in the subfolder, its name appears as a separate tab in the File New dialog box.

After specifying the workbook, and defining the name and path to the new template, click Next. Step 2 of the Template Wizard appears (see fig. 22.3).

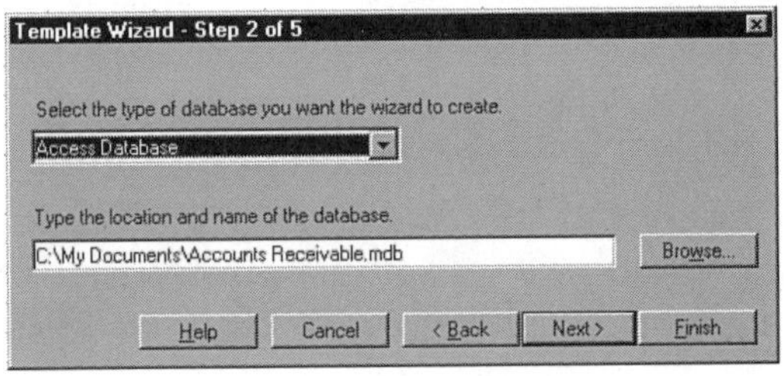

Fig. 22.3
Identify the type of database that will store information entered in a workbook that's based on the new template.

When you click the arrow by the drop-down, it displays the types of any database converters that you have installed using Setup. Use this drop-down to choose the type of database that will store the data that you enter in a workbook based on the new template.

You can also use Step 2 to define the name and path to the database that will store the data.

Note

A database like the one you're creating in this section can have only one table. You can use a database with multiple tables if it was created with its own application. (A multi-table database might have one table that contains information on customers, such as name and address, and another table that contains information on customers' payments. A unique ID that identifies a specific customer would link the two tables.)

If you want to use a database created with its application, instead of one created by the Template Wizard, click the Browse button in Step 2 to navigate to it.

After you specify the database type and define its name and path, click Next to proceed to Step 3, which is shown in figure 22.4.

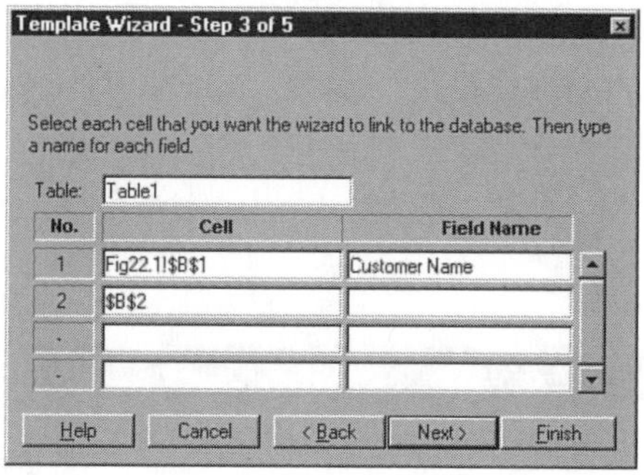

Fig. 22.4
Specify the worksheet cells that will be copied to particular database fields.

Step 3 represents the meat of the template definition process. It may look like a simple step, but there are many choices involved.

- *Sheet or Table.* If you specified that an Excel workbook will store the data, Step 3 displays the word Sheet to the left of the first text edit box. The default name in the text box is Table1. If you specified that another database file (such as Access or Paradox) will store the data, Step 3 displays the word Table to the left of the text box (as shown in figure

22.4). Again, the default name for the Table is `Table1`. In either case, you can edit the Sheet or Table name as long as the name you choose conforms to the application's rules for naming fields.

However, if you already created a database that will capture the data and specified it in Step 2, the text box becomes a drop-down, as shown in figure 22.5. This drop-down lists any tables located in that database. Use the drop-down to select from the database tables available to you.

Fig. 22.5

If the target database already exists, Step 3 of the Template Wizard displays its available tables.

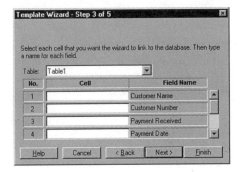

- *Cell.* Regardless of whether you specified an Excel workbook, a new external database or an existing external database to capture the data, use the column of cell boxes in Step 3 to indicate which cell in the template corresponds to which field in the database. Begin by clicking in the first cell box in Step 3, and then click in a worksheet cell to specify it. In figure 22.5, for example, you would first click the Wizard's first cell box and then click in worksheet cell B1. This indicates that a value entered in worksheet cell B1 is to be stored in Field 1 of the database.

Tip

If you want to type a cell address in a cell box rather than clicking in a cell with your mouse, make sure you enter the address as an absolute reference ($R1$C1) rather than a relative reference (R1C1).

Field Name. If the target database already exists, the names of its fields are already in the Field Name column of Step 3 of the Template Wizard (refer to fig. 22.5).

However, if the target database or workbook does not already exist, the Field Name column is blank (refer to fig. 22.4). After you enter a cell address in the

Cell column, click in the Field Name column. If, as in figure 22.4, there is a label either immediately above or immediately to the left of the chosen worksheet cell, Excel places that label in the Field Name box. You can revise that name if you want.

> **Note**
>
> Suppose the workbook that's active when you're creating the template contains actual data in the cells that will become database fields. If so, the template will contain that data. You usually don't want this—the template should usually have only the *labels* that identify the data cells, and the data cells themselves should be empty. Therefore, clear the data cells before you start the Template Wizard.

Notice the scroll bar immediately to the right of the Field Name column in Step 3. Although the dialog box displays only four fields at a time, you can specify as many fields as your application allows in a table. Use the scroll bar to move up and down through the fields you defined.

When you finish defining the relationship between the worksheet cells and the database fields, click Next to proceed to Step 4 (see fig. 22.6).

Fig. 22.6
In Step 4 of the Template Wizard you can include any additional existing workbooks in the database.

You might already have some workbooks that contain data you want to include in the database. In Step 4, you can indicate whether such workbooks exist. If they don't, select the No, Skip It button and click Next.

> **Note**
>
> The data in the workbook that's active when you start the Template Wizard does *not* automatically become part of the new database. If you use an existing workbook as the basis for the template, and if you want its data to enter the new database, make sure you have saved it so that you can select it in Step 4 of the Template Wizard.

If you do have such workbooks, select the Yes, Include button and click Next. When you do so, another dialog box (also named Step 4) appears, as shown in figure 22.7.

Fig. 22.7
Use the second instance of Step 4 to identify workbooks you want to include in the database.

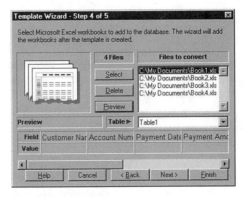

Click Select to open a dialog box similar to the File Open dialog box. Use this dialog box to navigate to locations on your disk where the workbooks that you want to include are found. When you arrive at a location, highlight the name of the workbook you want and click the Open button. The file name appears in the Files to Convert list.

When you have at least one file in the Files to Convert list box, you can click the Preview button to display its contents in the Preview area.

Remember that any additional workbooks whose data you want to move to the database must be laid out in the same fashion as is the workbook that you used in Step 3 of the Template Wizard. This is because the Wizard moves the data in, for example, cell C3 of all included workbooks into the same database field. Therefore, if C3 in Book1 contains the customer's name and C3 in Book2 contains the customer's payment amount, the database will have at least one incorrect entry in one of its fields.

The Preview area of Step 4 enables you to prevent this. When you click Preview, Excel peeks into the workbook and displays the values it contains in the cells you established in Step 3 of the Template Wizard. If everything looks correct—if the value found in the workbook corresponds to its associated field in the Preview area—you can keep the workbook available in the Files to Convert list. But if the data would be stored incorrectly in the database, you can click Delete to remove it from the list.

> **Note**
>
> The layout requirement for additional workbooks extends to additional sheets. For example, suppose you specified that cell C3 in Sheet2 of your primary workbook is to be moved to Field 2 of the database. In that case, any additional workbook must not only have a second sheet, but the second sheet must also be named Sheet2.

If, in Step 2, you identified an existing database as the target location for the data, it's possible that it contains more than one table. If so, you can use the Table drop-down list in Step 4 to select different database tables. Then use the Preview area to determine whether the layout of the currently selected workbook corresponds to the fields in each database table.

Any table might have more fields than can be simultaneously displayed in the Preview area. If all fields are not visible, the scroll box in the scroll bar flashes, which means there are more fields to view. Use the scroll bar to view additional fields.

When you finish identifying workbooks to add to the database in Step 4, click Next to proceed to Step 5 (see fig. 22.8).

Fig. 22.8
This step summarizes the information that you specified in Steps 1 through 4.

If, in the future, you want other users to receive a copy of the record added to the database, you can arrange that by clicking the Add Routing Slip button. When you do this, you can specify the addresses of the other users to notify. As Step 5 emphasizes, however, this does not occur when the Template Wizard's Step 5 completes, but later, as you add new records to the database.

> **Tip**
>
> For the Add Routing Slip option to function properly, your e-mail application must be compatible with Microsoft Exchange. If you have not installed Exchange, the Add Routing Slip button is disabled.

This section has presented a considerable amount of information, and some of it might seem confusing. Using the Template Wizard involves an active workbook, a new template, either a new or an existing database, and (possibly) existing workbooks that would contribute data to the new database. All these possibilities mean that the process can seem extremely complex the first time through.

The next section steps you through the creation of a database to give you an opportunity to practice the previous steps, examine their results, and resolve any topics you might have found confusing.

Case Study: Customer Tracking

Your company sells and services telecommunications equipment. Your Marketing department has recently acquired the Access database management system. At present, it maintains information on customers in separate Excel workbooks, one for each customer. The first sheet in each workbook contains basic customer information, and additional sheets contain information about the different products and services that the customer has purchased.

Because the product and service information is obtained from your Sales department in Excel format, Marketing wants to continue to use Excel to maintain information about specific sales. However, Marketing also intends to use Access to store, maintain, and retrieve basic customer information to target different marketing programs at particular subsets of the installed base.

The task, then, is to create a database that stores the basic customer information, and to arrange for new customers to be automatically entered in that database each time a new customer workbook is created.

Each of the workbooks that will be used to populate the new Access database is structured identically, as shown in figure 22.9.

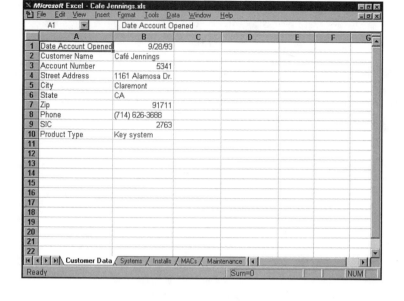

Fig. 22.9
Each row of data in the Customer worksheet will become a field in the Access database.

You choose the Cafe Jennings workbook in figure 22.9 at random from the customer workbooks that Marketing maintains and follow these steps:

1. Clear the data in cells B1:B10. You do not want this information to appear in the new template. You only want the labels in cells A1:A10 to appear.

2. Choose Data, Template Wizard. The Step 1 dialog box appears.

   Cafe Jennings.xls, the name of the active workbook, is the default workbook name in the drop-down box in Step 1. Because all customer workbooks' structure and layout are identical, you can use the default workbook as the basis for the template, so you accept the default.

3. You decide to name the template as Customers.xlt, and to store the template in the folder at the end of the path C:\MSOffice\Templates. In Step 1's edit box, enter: **C:\MSOffice\Templates\Customers.xlt**.

4. Click Next. The Step 2 dialog box appears.

5. You want to create an Access database, so select that item from the drop-down in Step 2.

6. You decide to store the database in the Access sub-folder within the MSOffice folder. In the text edit box in Step 2, enter: **C:\MSOffice\Access**.

7. Click Next. The Step 3 dialog box appears.

8. Click in the Cell box for field No. 1, and then click in cell B1 of the Customer Data worksheet in the file named Cafe Jennings.xls.

9. Click in the Field Name box for field No. 1. Excel automatically enters the name Date Account Opened as the default field name, which you accept.

10. Repeat steps 8 and 9, above, for fields No. 2 through 10. When you finish entering the information for the tenth field, the dialog box appears as shown in figure 22.10.

Fig. 22.10
Because a cell address can belong to any sheet in the base workbook, the Template Wizard qualifies the cell address with its sheet name in the Cell box.

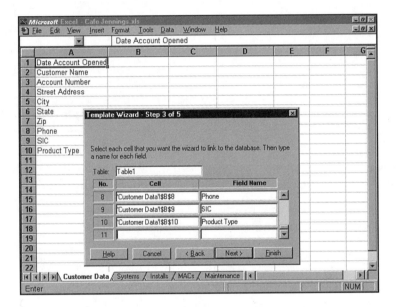

11. Click Next. The Step 4 dialog box appears. Here you can include other workbooks in the database when it is first created. You decide to include the other customer workbooks that Marketing has provided, so you select Yes.

12. Click Next. The second instance of the Step 4 dialog box appears. Click Select.

13. The Select Files to Convert dialog box appears. Navigate to where you stored the files for Chapter 22 from the companion disk, and select Both Cafe Jennings.xls And Outdoor Sports.xls. Choose Open.

14. The previous Step 4 dialog box returns and now contains Outdoor Sports.xls in the Files to Convert list box. Highlight that entry and choose Preview. The customer data for Outdoor Sports, Inc., appears in the Preview area (see fig. 22.11). Use the horizontal scroll bar to confirm that the data are in the correct locations.

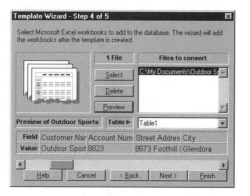

Fig. 22.11
Not all cell values
align well with the
field boxes in Step
4 of the Template
Wizard.

> **Tip**
>
> The individual field boxes in the Preview area are sometimes not large enough
> to display the full value from the associated worksheet cell. Make allowance for
> this when you visually confirm their values.

15. Click Next. The Step 5 dialog box appears, summarizing information
about the name and location of the template and database files. Click
Finish.

Now that you have created the database, you can use Microsoft Query or
open the database with the Access application to check the contents of the
file.

Saving Data in Other Formats

Excel provides several options for saving workbooks or worksheets in other
formats. You can access these options by choosing File, Save As and clicking
the Save as Type drop-down list. Some of the formats available are directly
compatible with other spreadsheet and database applications such as 1-2-3,
Quattro/Pro, and dBASE; others are different types of ASCII formats.

If you choose to save a workbook in 1-2-3 format, you can save the entire Excel workbook as 1-2-3 version 3 or 4. (Version 3 saves the worksheets and
charts only.) In all other cases, only the active Excel sheet is saved. To save
the entire Excel workbook, you need to activate each sheet in turn, choose
File, Save As, and save the active sheet in the chosen format.

There is a special step to take before attempting to save a worksheet in dBASE
format. Prior to saving the worksheet, choose all columns that contain data

(put your mouse pointer over the leftmost column's header, hold down the mouse button, and drag right to the final used column). Then choose Format, Column, AutoFit Selection. If the contents of a cell are not fully visible because the column is not wide enough, any contents you can't see are not saved to the dBASE file. When you AutoFit columns, their width is adjusted to fully display the longest value in the column.

Several ASCII text file formats are available that structure the text file in different ways. These formats are particularly useful when you want to move data from Excel to a DOS application (one that runs in the DOS environment but not in Windows) or an application such as Quicken or CapTool that does not directly recognize the Excel file format.

Suppose the active worksheet appears as shown in figure 22.12.

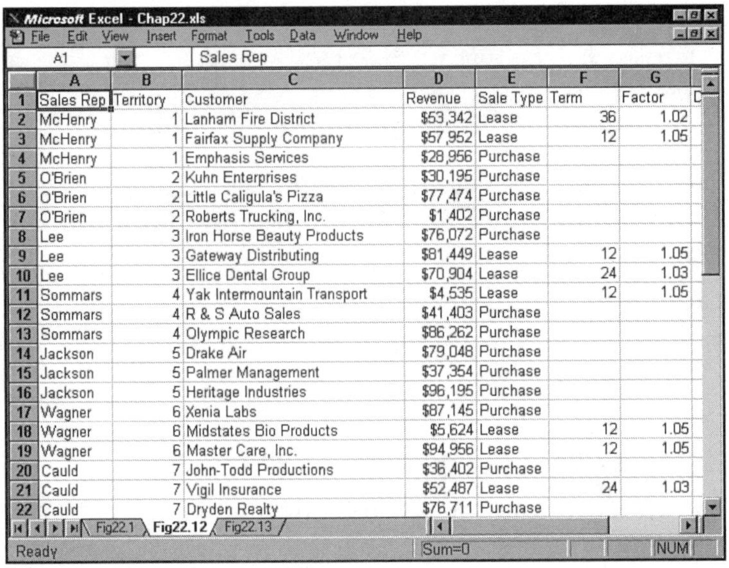

Fig. 22.12
This worksheet appears differently when saved as an ASCII file, depending on the text type that you choose.

	A	B	C	D	E	F	G
1	Sales Rep	Territory	Customer	Revenue	Sale Type	Term	Factor
2	McHenry	1	Lanham Fire District	$53,342	Lease	36	1.02
3	McHenry	1	Fairfax Supply Company	$57,952	Lease	12	1.05
4	McHenry	1	Emphasis Services	$28,956	Purchase		
5	O'Brien	2	Kuhn Enterprises	$30,195	Purchase		
6	O'Brien	2	Little Caligula's Pizza	$77,474	Purchase		
7	O'Brien	2	Roberts Trucking, Inc.	$1,402	Purchase		
8	Lee	3	Iron Horse Beauty Products	$76,072	Purchase		
9	Lee	3	Gateway Distributing	$81,449	Lease	12	1.05
10	Lee	3	Ellice Dental Group	$70,904	Lease	24	1.03
11	Sommars	4	Yak Intermountain Transport	$4,535	Lease	12	1.05
12	Sommars	4	R & S Auto Sales	$41,403	Purchase		
13	Sommars	4	Olympic Research	$86,262	Purchase		
14	Jackson	5	Drake Air	$79,048	Purchase		
15	Jackson	5	Palmer Management	$37,354	Purchase		
16	Jackson	5	Heritage Industries	$96,195	Purchase		
17	Wagner	6	Xenia Labs	$87,145	Purchase		
18	Wagner	6	Midstates Bio Products	$5,624	Lease	12	1.05
19	Wagner	6	Master Care, Inc.	$94,956	Lease	12	1.05
20	Cauld	7	John-Todd Productions	$36,402	Purchase		
21	Cauld	7	Vigil Insurance	$52,487	Lease	24	1.03
22	Cauld	7	Dryden Realty	$76,711	Purchase		

- If you choose Formatted Text (Space delimited) (*.prn), the text file separates the worksheet's columns with spaces. The number of spaces between values depends on the width of the column when you save the worksheet, and the length of the value in a given column.

- If you choose Text (Tab delimited) (*.txt), the ASCII file separates the worksheet's columns with tabs.

- If you choose CSV (Comma delimited) (*.csv), the ASCII file separates the worksheet's columns with commas.

- If you choose DIF (Data Interchange Format) (*.dif), the ASCII file saves the contents of each cell on a different line, interleaved with information about whether the cell contains text or a numeric value.

- If you choose SYLK (Symbolic Link) (*.slk), the ASCII file saves the contents of each cell on a different line, along with formatting information about the cell.

In each case, if you save a worksheet as text, the ASCII file contains values in place of any formulas and functions contained in the Excel worksheet.

If you subsequently open an ASCII file with the .prn or .txt extension from within Excel, the Text Wizard appears and guides you through options such as how to format columns. If you open an ASCII file with the .csv, .dif, or .slk extension, Excel bypasses the Text Wizard.

If you use VBA, you can exert more control over the format of an ASCII file to which you want to output Excel data. The formats provided in the File, Save As dialog box are rigid, and at times you might want a slightly, or even dramatically, different ASCII representation. Further, VBA enables you to output data from different worksheets into one ASCII file.

Suppose you have a workbook that contains a customer's account number in cell A1 of Sheet1, and the customer's outstanding account balance in cell A1 of Sheet2. Here is an example of how you could use VBA to output the account number and account balance to an ASCII file named CUSTOMERS.TXT

```
Option Explicit
Sub WriteTextToDisk()
Dim FileNumber As Integer
Dim OutputData As String
Dim InputData As String
```

The first few statements of this VBA subroutine require that all variables be declared explicitly, declare the subroutine, and declare three necessary variables. The next statement

```
FileNumber = FreeFile()
```

assigns to the integer variable `FileNumber` the next available number for an external file. This is a useful safeguard should you have more than one such file open simultaneously. Several file-handling commands, such as `Write` and `Input`, require that you refer to a file by its number. By obtaining the next available file number, you can ensure that you're dealing with the correct file.

Next, you open the file for some operation such as input or output. This statement

```
Open "CUSTOMERS.TXT" For Append As #FileNumber
```

opens a file named CUSTOMERS.TXT in the current folder for output from Excel. The file name could also include a path specification, such as "C:\MyDocuments\CUSTOMERS.TXT."

Specifying Append in the statement means that if the file already exists, new data that is written to it will start at the current end-of-file. If the file does not exist before the Open statement is executed, CUSTOMERS.TXT is opened as a new file.

Then, the VBA variable OutputData is set equal to the value in cell A1 of the active workbook's worksheet named Sheet1, and that value is written to the output file CUSTOMERS.TXT, represented by the variable FileNumber

```
OutputData = ActiveWorkbook.Sheets("Sheet1").Cells(1, 1)
Write #FileNumber, OutputData
```

The output operation is repeated for the value in cell A1 of the active workbook's worksheet named Sheet2

```
OutputData = ThisWorkbook.Sheets("Sheet2").Cells(1, 1)
Write #FileNumber, OutputData
```

Remember, if you want to save this file using the File, Save As dialog box, you can't save the data from Sheet1 and from Sheet2 in the same ASCII file. Using this method allows you to do so.

Then, you close the output file for the output operations

```
Close #FileNumber
```

You can view the contents of what you wrote to CUSTOMERS.TXT using the remaining code

```
FileNumber = FreeFile()
Open "CUSTOMERS.TXT" For Input As #FileNumber
```

The Open statement makes the file accessible for input to Excel by use of the keyword Input, as distinct from the earlier Open statement which used the keyword Append. Then, the code loops through each line in the text file, displaying each line's contents in a message box

```
Do Until EOF(FileNumber)
    Input #FileNumber, InputData
    MsgBox InputData
Loop
```

```
Close #FileNumber

End Sub
```

and after the loop terminates, it closes the file and ends the subroutine.

Linking and Embedding Data in Microsoft Word

It frequently happens that you have an Excel worksheet that you want to represent, in whole or in part, in a Word document. An example that's frequently cited is a Word document being prepared as a report. You use Word to create the report's text and you use Excel to provide the charts, figures, or tables in the text. There are several ways to do this; the method you choose should be guided in part by what you want to happen *after* you move the worksheet information to the Word document.

> **Note**
>
> This process is termed Object Linking and Embedding, or OLE (pronounced "olay"). You can use it with any application that supports OLE. Because both Word and Excel are included in the Microsoft Office suite, this section describes OLE as you would use it with those applications. The basic approaches and procedures are, however, the same regardless of the target OLE application.

There are also choices based on where you start the process: in Excel or in Word. This section also describes your options when you might select a particular option.

Differentiating Between Embedded and Linked Objects

An *object* is something you put into an Excel worksheet, a Word document, or any other file. In the Excel context, examples of objects are pictures you draw on the worksheet using the Drawing toolbar, charts you place in the worksheet, list boxes created on the worksheet, and so on.

More broadly, an object can be the Excel worksheet itself, a collection of cells from a worksheet, or anything you place on a worksheet.

When you *embed* an object such as Excel worksheet into a Word document, you can see the object in the document just as it appears in Excel. You can manipulate it; you can change a cell's format, edit its value, modify formulas, and so on.

When you *link* an object, you can do all the things you can with an embedded object. The difference is that an active link is maintained between the object as it's represented in Word and the object as it exists in Excel. So, if the object's characteristics (a cell value, for example) change in Excel (the source application), its characteristics are automatically updated in its Word representation (see fig. 22.13).

Fig. 22.13
Cell A1 in the Excel worksheet is linked to the Word document. When the value of cell A1 changes in Excel, its value automatically changes in Word.

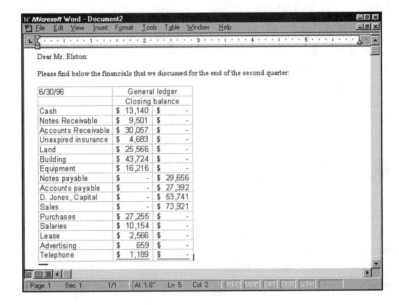

With Excel active, if you change the value of cell A1, the linked object in the Word document reflects the change. This is not true of an embedded object.

There are tradeoffs involved in the choice between linking and embedding—both come with a cost.

- If the object is a very large one, consider linking it. When you embed an object, you actually create a copy of the object in the target application, one that is saved with the target file. Unless you subsequently discard the object's source (for example, by deleting a workbook), you save two copies of the object—perhaps unnecessarily.

- Is the object incomplete? For example, if the object is an Excel worksheet, is all the necessary data current? If not, consider linking it. During the time the data in Excel is being completed, maintaining a link means that the object's representation in Word will be as current as possible.

> **Tip**
>
> Many business processes require constant updating. Suppose you're tracking annual sales results. During the year, you could link a Word document that describes current standings to an Excel workbook that contains the actual dollar results. In this way, the Word document is constantly updated as new data enters the Excel workbook.

- If the source file could become unavailable, consider embedding the object. Suppose you want to include an Excel worksheet that is someone else's responsibility—perhaps someone on your LAN—in a Word file. If you use linking, and that someone suddenly decides to delete the file, then there's nothing to link to. But if you embed the object, you create a copy of it that stays with the Word document. And you can always modify or maintain an embedded Excel object yourself by means of Excel.

- Are you on a *really* tight schedule? If so, consider embedding the object. When you open a Word document that contains links, you usually want the links to be updated. If there are many links to many different Excel workbooks, the update can take some time. You can opt to update the links manually rather than automatically—this saves a little time—but if you do so it's easy to forget to update the links.

As noted at the beginning of this section, you can start either the linking or embedding process in either Excel or Word. The next four sections describe the possible combinations of events: establishing a link from Excel into Word, linking from Word to Excel, and embedding from either application.

Using Excel to Link to Word

If you are linking an Excel object to Word, it's best to start with Excel if the object is something other than a complete worksheet or workbook. If you start with Excel, you can select the object, such as a range of cells, that you want to link. If you start with Word, you must select a complete file; you can subsequently limit the scope of the linked object, but it's easier to do so at the outset.

Figure 22.14 shows an Excel worksheet and a Word document, with worksheet cells A1:C20 linked to the Word document.

Fig. 22.14
To link a subset of a workbook into Word, it's easiest to start the process from Excel.

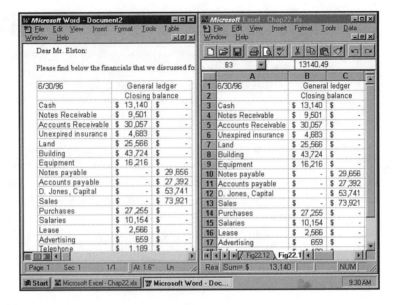

To create this link, follow these steps:

1. With both Word and Excel open, activate Excel and select the source workbook.

2. Highlight cells A1:C20, and choose <u>E</u>dit, <u>C</u>opy.

3. Switch to Word, select the point in the document where you want to insert cells A1:C20, and choose <u>E</u>dit, Paste <u>S</u>pecial. The Paste Special dialog box appears (see fig. 22.15).

4. In the <u>A</u>s list box, choose Microsoft Excel Worksheet Object.

5. Select the Paste <u>L</u>ink checkbox, and choose OK.

The cells are now pasted into the Word document, and the link is established. If you worked your way through this example, you will find that you can now activate Excel, change a value in the range A1:C20, and see it immediately change in the Word document.

Suppose you now close the Word document and save the changes. Switch to Excel, and change some value in A1:C20. Now, switch back to Word and open the Word document. You can see the change reflected in the linked object.

And suppose you now switch back to Excel and choose <u>F</u>ile, E<u>x</u>it (saving changes to the Excel workbook if necessary). Then, with Word active, double-click the linked object to select and open it for editing. Excel starts again and opens the source workbook. You can now make changes to the source range that are immediately reflected in Word's linked object.

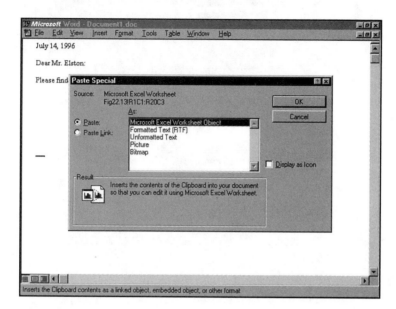

Fig. 22.15
Define the nature of the object—linked or embedded—in the Paste Special dialog box.

Note

In all cases—linking, embedding, starting from Excel, starting from Word—you can choose to display the object as the Excel icon instead of as the object itself. In the Paste Special dialog box, check the Display as Icon checkbox.

Displaying the object as an icon is a good way to save screen space. It's also a useful technique when the Excel object acts as a box in a flowchart—you can hide the specifics within the icon, and display them by double-clicking the icon when you are ready to view them.

Using Word to Link to Excel

The previous section advised you to begin with Excel to create a link to Word. On occasion, though, you might find it expedient to begin from Word. Suppose your computer is memory-sparse or you have as many applications open as you can handle, and Excel is not presently running. In that event, you can insert an existing Excel worksheet from its location on your disk into a Word document. To do so, follow these steps:

1. With the Word document active, choose Insert, Object. The Object dialog box appears. Click the Create from File tab (see fig. 22.16).

Fig. 22.16
Here you can
insert an object
that already exists
on your disk.

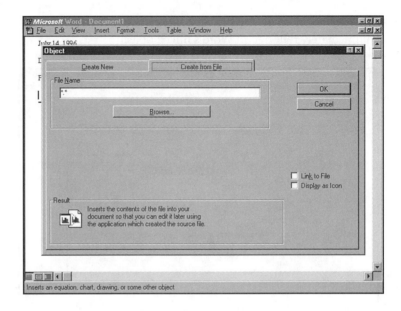

2. Unless you want to type the entire path and file name in the File Name text box, click the Browse button.

3. Navigate to the location of the workbook you want to insert, and choose OK. The Object dialog box reappears.

4. To create a link to the file, select the Link to File checkbox. Click OK.

If your computer doesn't have enough memory, you will notice your disk working as Word accesses the workbook you identified in step 3. Eventually, the contents of the first sheet in the workbook will appear. If you watch the Windows 95 taskbar during this process, you will see that Excel itself does not open during the insertion process.

There are two special characteristics you should be aware of if you initiate the process from Word instead of from Excel:

■ The worksheet is inserted starting at the first used cell and ending at the last used cell—or, if an object such as a chart exists in the worksheet, it is inserted so the object can be displayed. If there is more in the worksheet than can successfully be displayed, Word displays only as much as it physically can in its window.

■ The sheet that is displayed from the chosen workbook is the active sheet. That is, if the workbook has more than one sheet, the one that is displayed is the one you would see if you opened the workbook using Excel. This sheet, of course, need not be the first sheet in the workbook.

Suppose you inserted an Excel worksheet object, whether by starting the process in Word or in Excel. You have chosen to link the object to the Excel workbook, and in the Word document you see cells A1:C20. Subsequently, you want to change the display to B3:C20. To do so, follow these steps:

1. Select the linked object in the Word document.

2. Choose Edit, Links. The Links dialog box appears (see fig. 22.17).

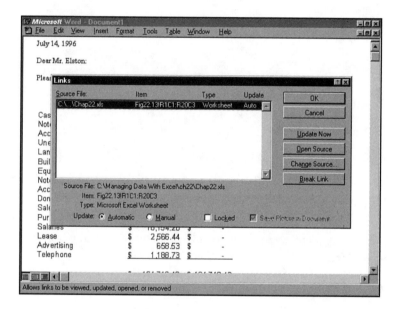

Fig. 22.17
Use the Links dialog box to change how the links update, as well as to change or break existing links.

3. In the Source File list box, select the file whose link you want to modify.

4. Click the Change Source button. The Change Source dialog box appears (see fig 22.18).

5. In the Item text box, type **Sheet1!R3C1:R20C3** (you can also use A1 notation: Sheet1!A3:C20).

6. Choose Open. The Links dialog box returns. Choose OK.

The object displays again according to the change you made in the Item text box.

Tip

You can also use this method to change which workbook, or worksheet in the workbook, Excel displays. For example, in the Item text box, you could change Sheet1!A1:C20 to Sheet2!A1:C20.

Fig. 22.18

The Open button does not fully open the selected file—it simply dismisses the dialog box after you modify some aspect of the link, such as the item to display.

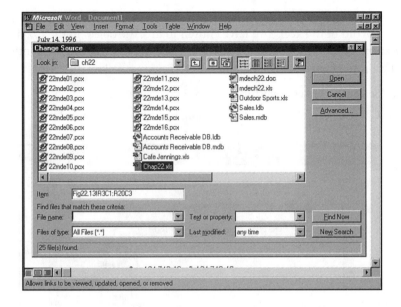

Embedding from Excel or from Word

The procedures you use to embed, rather than link, an object into Word from Excel are nearly identical to those used to link objects. Starting from Excel, you select the object you want to embed, choose Edit, Copy, switch to Word, and choose Edit, Paste Special. The only procedural difference is that you do not select the Paste Link checkbox.

Or, if you prefer to start from Word, choose Insert, Object. Click the Create from File tab, navigate to the location of the file that you want to embed, choose the file, choose OK in the Browse dialog box, and choose OK in the Object dialog box. The only difference is that you do not select the Link to File checkbox.

The real differences are in what happens after the Excel object is embedded in the Word document:

- If you make a change to the Excel source object, the change is *not* reflected in the object as it's represented in the Word document. Similarly, if you make a change to the embedded object, the change is not reflected in the source.

- If you double-click a linked object, Excel opens if it is not already running. This is because you are working with a link to the Excel source. But if you double-click an embedded object, Excel does not open, although you can edit the embedded object. You can change cell values, insert new formulas—virtually anything you could do in an Excel cell, because you have access to Excel menu commands.

Figure 22.19 shows what happens when you double-click an Excel object that's embedded in a Word document.

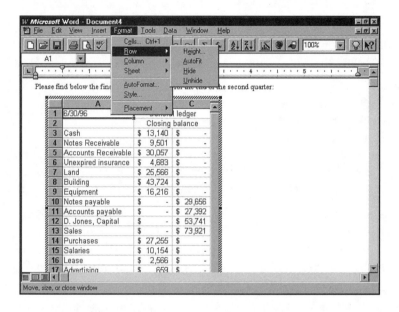

Fig. 22.19
Word's usual menus are replaced by Excel menus when you edit an Excel object embedded in a Word document.

If the Excel object in figure 22.19 were *linked* to the source, double-clicking it would activate Excel. But because the object is *embedded*, the menus display Excel menu items, even though you can still see Word in the title bar. (The File and Window menus retain the appearance and functions that are normal for Word.) You also have access to Excel's toolbars, scroll bars, and sheet tabs.

Working with Microsoft Access

Excel 7 provides an add-in named AccessLinks you can use for these purposes:

- Create an Access form to enter data
- Use a form created in Access to enter data
- Create a report form, using the Access Report Wizard
- Modify an Access report
- Convert an Excel list or database to an Access database file

To use any of these capabilities, you must have Microsoft Access installed on your computer, and you must have the AccessLinks add-in installed in Excel.

If you have Access installed, but you do not see Access Form, Access Report, and Convert to Access in the Excel Data menu, you need to install the AccessLinks add-in. Use the same steps described at the start of this chapter for installing the Template Wizard, both as to running Setup and as to installing the add-in with Tools, Add-Ins.

Keep in mind that if you do not have Microsoft Access installed on your computer, you can still save data from an Excel workbook to an Access database by using the Template Wizard.

This section focuses on converting an Excel list to an Access database.

Converting a List

The Convert to Access option on the Data menu is mildly misleading. When you choose that option, the Link Spreadsheet Wizard starts. It doesn't convert Excel data into a standalone Access database, but creates a new Access database that is *linked* to the data in the Excel worksheet.

Linked Access databases don't offer all the flexibility offered by stand-alone databases. You can't, for example, modify the field length or data type of a linked field in Access. And you can't create links between Access database tables when you begin from Excel and choose Convert to Access.

Nevertheless, this is a convenient method to create an Access database from your Excel workbook. With a linked database, you can modify the data in Excel cells either from Excel, with the linked workbook open, or from Access, with the linked database open.

To create a linked Access database from a worksheet list, follow these steps:

1. Save the workbook.

> **Note**
>
> You can't use AccessLinks to convert a list in an unsaved workbook to an Access database, because AccessLinks actually creates *links* between the workbook and the resulting Access database. The workbook must be saved for AccessLinks to establish the linkages.

2. Select a cell in the list. AccessLinks begins by identifying the range occupied by the list, and it cannot identify the range if the active cell is outside the range.

3. Select Data, Convert to Access. The Convert to Microsoft Access dialog box appears (see fig. 22.20).

Fig. 22.20
You can choose to create a new Access database or to add to an existing database.

4. Choose between creating a new database and adding to an existing database. To continue with this example, choose the Ne̲w Database button and choose OK.

5. The Access window appears. At this point, wait for the Link Spreadsheet Wizard to start.

6. The first step of the Link Spreadsheet Wizard appears (see fig. 22.21).

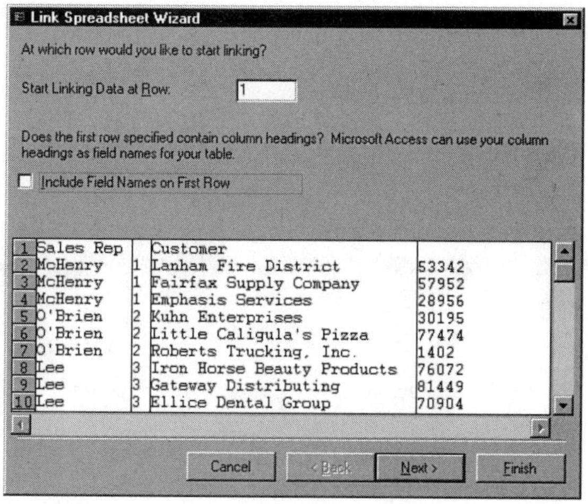

Fig. 22.21
Excel list headers can become field names in the Access database.

7. If the data range that was chosen in step 2 contains a header row, select the I̲nclude Field Names on First Row checkbox. Access treats the values in the first row as field names. Click Ne̲xt.

8. The second step of the Link Spreadsheet Wizard appears. Name the table and click Fi̲nish.

The conversion process has a few results beyond simply creating a new database:

■ A text box is placed in your Excel worksheet that tells you the name and location of the new Access database.

■ The Link Spreadsheet Wizard creates a *linked* Access database. Conceptually, this is similar to the links discussed in the previous section between Excel and Word. The Access database contains links to the worksheet cells, rather than the actual data values.

■ Access defines the database fields according to the type of data you have in each column of the original Excel list; this restricts the nature of the information that Access can display. For example, suppose worksheet column A contains a header in row 1 and numbers only in rows 2 through 20. If you now change the value in cell A2 to a text value, Access can't display the text value because it defined the field as numeric.

■ Because the files are linked, you can't use Access to change fundamental properties of the database table's fields.

■ If, at the end of the conversion process, you close the source workbook, Excel can't open the workbook again until you close the linked Access database.

After you finish creating the new database, you can view it by clicking the file's Maximize button in the Access window. If necessary, choose View, Datasheet in Access. Figure 22.22 shows the data sheet.

Fig. 22.22
You can change the values in a linked database from Access as long as you enter the same kind of data that's already in the field.

Sales Rep	Territory	Customer	Revenue
McHenry	1	Lanham Fire District	$53,342.00
McHenry	1	Fairfax Supply Company	$57,952.00
McHenry	1	Emphasis Services	$28,956.00
O'Brien	2	Kuhn Enterprises	$30,195.00
O'Brien	2	Little Caligula's Pizza	$77,474.00
O'Brien	2	Roberts Trucking, Inc.	$1,402.00
Lee	3	Iron Horse Beauty Products	$76,072.00
Lee	3	Gateway Distributing	$81,449.00
Lee	3	Ellice Dental Group	$70,904.00
Sommars	4	Yak Intermountain Transport	$4,535.00
Sommars	4	R & S Auto Sales	$41,403.00
Sommars	4	Olympic Research	$86,262.00
Jackson	5	Drake Air	$79,048.00
Jackson	5	Palmer Management	$37,354.00
Jackson	5	Heritage Industries	$96,195.00
Wagner	6	Xenia Labs	$87,145.00
Wagner	6	Midstates Bio Products	$5,624.00
Wagner	6	Master Care, Inc.	$94,956.00

Sheet1 : Table — Record: 1 of 23

You can also view the table layout by choosing View, Table Design. This view, shown in figure 22.23, shows that you can't change all the properties of a linked table.

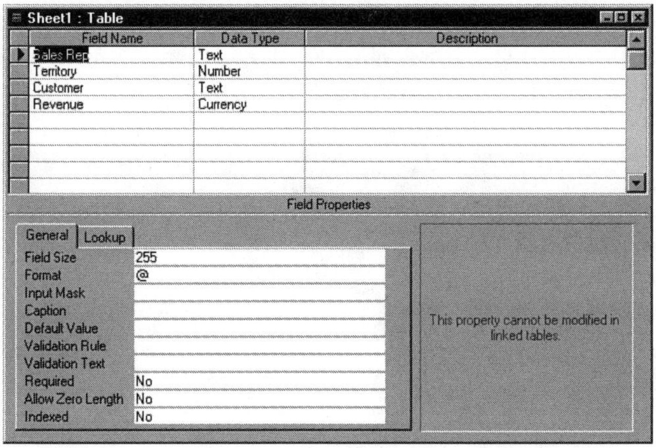

Fig. 22.23
If you need to
modify table
properties, it's best
to create a
standalone Access
database.

If you want to perform actions such as linking two tables in an Access database with a common field, or changing the field size of a table's field, you must start from Access—not from Excel—and create a database that stands alone—not one that is linked to an Excel source. This process is described in the following section.

Importing an Excel Worksheet into Access

To exert greater control over the structure of an Access database based on an Excel workbook, start with Access instead of Excel. Doing this means you can directly control table properties and the nature of the relationships among the database tables.

The data shown in figure 22.24 can be stored more efficiently in an Access database than in an Excel workbook because each record describes a sales opportunity, and there are three sales opportunities for each sales representative.

Because the sales representative's name and territory are redundant information, they can be stored by Access in a table that's separate from the sales information. Then, if the two tables are linked by a single common field, the values in that field are the only ones that need to be repeated. The lengthy sales representative information need not be repeated in the table that contains the sales information, and that results in more efficient data storage.

Another reason for storing the sales representative data in a separate table is to maintain its integrity. Especially when lengthy information is keyed repeatedly, it's typical for typing errors to occur. By keeping information about the sales representatives in a separate table, all that's needed to link data about a particular sale to data about the sales representative is a unique key— the common field mentioned previously.

Fig. 22.24

You can save space by storing the representatives' names and territories once only.

	A	B	C	D	E	F	G	D
1	Sales Rep	Territory	Customer	Revenue	Sale Type	Term	Factor	
2	McHenry	1	Lanham Fire District	$53,342	Lease	36	1.02	
3	McHenry	1	Fairfax Supply Company	$57,952	Lease	12	1.05	
4	McHenry	1	Emphasis Services	$28,956	Purchase			
5	O'Brien	2	Kuhn Enterprises	$30,195	Purchase			
6	O'Brien	2	Little Caligula's Pizza	$77,474	Purchase			
7	O'Brien	2	Roberts Trucking, Inc.	$1,402	Purchase			
8	Lee	3	Iron Horse Beauty Products	$76,072	Purchase			
9	Lee	3	Gateway Distributing	$81,449	Lease	12	1.05	
10	Lee	3	Ellice Dental Group	$70,904	Lease	24	1.03	
11	Sommars	4	Yak Intermountain Transport	$4,535	Lease	12	1.05	
12	Sommars	4	R & S Auto Sales	$41,403	Purchase			
13	Sommars	4	Olympic Research	$86,262	Purchase			
14	Jackson	5	Drake Air	$79,048	Purchase			
15	Jackson	5	Palmer Management	$37,354	Purchase			
16	Jackson	5	Heritage Industries	$96,195	Purchase			
17	Wagner	6	Xenia Labs	$87,145	Purchase			
18	Wagner	6	Midstates Bio Products	$5,624	Lease	12	1.05	
19	Wagner	6	Master Care, Inc.	$94,956	Lease	12	1.05	
20	Cauld	7	John-Todd Productions	$36,402	Purchase			
21	Cauld	7	Vigil Insurance	$52,487	Lease	24	1.03	
22	Cauld	7	Dryden Realty	$76,711	Purchase			

To create an Access database from the workbook shown in figure 22.24, follow these steps:

1. Close Excel if you want. It isn't necessary to have Excel running when you create the Access database.
2. Start Access. The Microsoft Access dialog box appears (see fig. 22.25).
3. Select the Blank Database button and choose OK.

Fig. 22.25

Choose Blank Database to initiate a new file.

4. The File New Database dialog box appears. Enter a name for the data-base in the File <u>n</u>ame edit box, or accept the default name. Navigate to a new location if you want and choose Create.

5. The Database window appears. Choose <u>N</u>ew. The New Table dialog box appears (see fig. 22.26).

6. Select Import Table Wizard and choose OK.

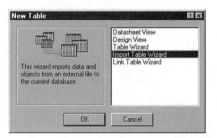

Fig. 22.26
Various wizards are available when you choose <u>N</u>ew in the Database window.

7. The Import dialog box appears. Use it to navigate to the folder where you stored the workbook Chap22.xls, from this book's companion disk. Select Microsoft Excel (*.xls) from the Files of <u>t</u>ype drop-down. Select Chap22.xls, and choose Import.

8. The Import Spreadsheet Wizard starts. Select the Show Named <u>R</u>anges button and choose SalesData (see fig 22.27). This is a named range in the Chap22.xls, consisting of the data in B1:I49 of the sheet named Fig22.12, and containing all the sales data with the exception of the names of the sales representatives. Click <u>N</u>ext.

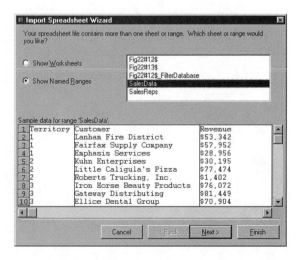

Fig. 22.27
You can choose an existing named range in an Excel workbook as the data to import into the Access database.

V

Managing External Data

9. In the Wizard's next step, select the Include Field Names on First Row checkbox, and click Next.

10. The next step in the Wizard lets you change field names, indicate whether to index a field, or skip a field (see fig. 22.28). In this example, you don't need to change or modify any of these choices. Click Next.

Fig. 22.28
Name, index, or skip fields with this step in the Import Table Wizard.

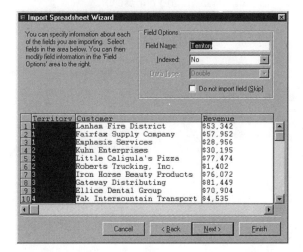

11. The Wizard's next step lets you determine a primary key for the table (see fig. 22.29). A primary key has a variety of uses, but one is to uniquely identify each record in the table. Select the Let Access Add Primary Key button. Doing this causes Access to add an ID field. Click Next.

Fig. 22.29
Even if you won't use a table's primary key to join to another table, you should usually create one anyway so that you can uniquely identify particular records.

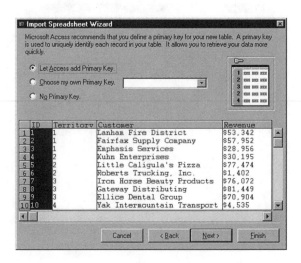

12. In the Wizard's final step, name the table SalesData and click Finish.

You have now created a table named SalesData in the Access database, whose records were imported from an Excel worksheet. The table has a primary key, and it omits the name of the sales representative.

You should now repeat steps 5 through 12 to create another table in the database. Two steps should be done differently, though. In step 8, choose SalesReps as the named range instead of SalesData. The SalesReps name refers to the range K1:L17 in the sheet named Fig22.12 and contains only unique sales representative names and territories (there is exactly one sales representative for each territory). And, in step 12, name the table SalesReps before choosing Finish. When you finish, name the database Sales.

The end result is an Access database named Sales with two tables, SalesData and SalesReps. Each table has a field named Territory. You can use this field to join the two tables. To see the effect of doing so from within Excel, exit Access and start Excel. Then, follow these steps:

1. Choose Data, Get External Data. If you don't see the Get External Data option, you have to install the Microsoft Query add-in as described in Chapter 8.

2. The Select Data Source dialog box appears. Choose MS Access 7.0 Database from the Available Data Sources list box, and then choose Use.

3. The Select Database dialog box appears. Navigate to the location where you stored Sales.mdb. Select it and choose OK.

4. The Add Tables dialog box appears. Select SalesData from the Table list box and click Add. Then select SalesReps and click Add. When you see that both tables appear in the Query window, choose Close.

5. Choose Table, Joins. The Joins dialog box appears. See figure 22.30.

> **Note**
>
> The options in the Join Includes area of the Joins dialog box define how to handle situations where not all records in one table can be matched to all records in another table. In the present example, the choice makes no difference because each record in each table has a matching Territory value in the other table.

Fig. 22.30

Use the Joins dialog box to define how to relate two different tables to one another.

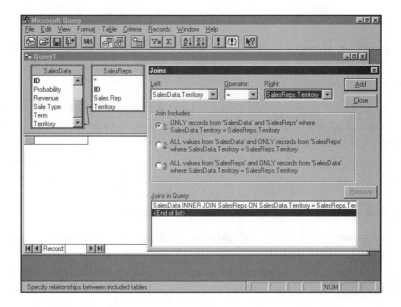

6. In the Joins in Query list, select the line that reads `SalesReps INNER JOIN SalesData ON SalesReps.ID = SalesDataID`. Click Remove. This breaks the join between the two tables on their primary keys: you don't want to join them on this basis because the primary keys do not join the tables on the basis of equality of the Territory field.

7. In the Left drop-down list, choose SalesData.Territory. In the Right drop-down list, choose SalesReps.Territory. This creates a join between the two tables, associating a record in SalesData with a record in SalesReps when the two records have the same value for Territory. Click Add, then choose Close.

8. In the SalesData table, double-click Customer, and then double-click Revenue. In the SalesReps table, double-click SalesRep. The result you see in the data pane of the Query window is shown in figure 22.31.

9. If you now want to return the data to the Excel worksheet, choose File, Return Data to Microsoft Excel. The Get External Data dialog box appears, giving you the chance to keep the query definition, to include field names in the worksheet, to include row numbers, and to keep any password associated with the database. You can also specify the worksheet destination for the data. After you have selected any of these options, choose OK.

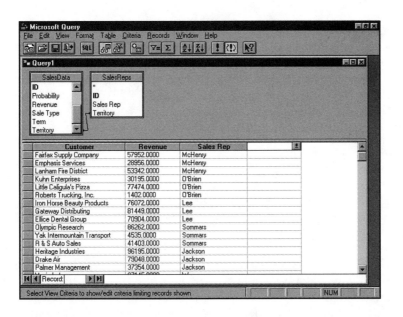

Query returns from the database any fields that you chose in step 8, and all records identified by the query.

> **Tip**
>
> There are many kinds of information that can be stored more efficiently in a database management system than they can in an Excel workbook. Examples include inventory (join product counts to product descriptions by means of a product code), major projects (join information about subsidiary processes to the overall project), and assets (join information about specific equipment to classes subject to identical depreciation regulations).

This section described how to create and populate an Access database from an Excel workbook and how to immediately to return its data to another Excel workbook. It would be unusual for you to do so in reality. The three main points of this section were:

- To illustrate both processes.
- To verify that the data you import into an external database is returned to Excel properly by using Query.
- To demonstrate how you can use tables and table joins to avoid storing the same information repeatedly.

Chapter Summary

It's appropriate that this final chapter of *Managing Data with Excel* focuses on managing data outside of the Excel context. The preceding chapters discussed how to manage data using Excel's worksheet functions, menu commands, and VBA code. But there are many data management processes that Excel is not designed to accomplish—at least, not in the most straightforward way possible.

However, you can still use Excel to collect and analyze data, and subsequently export the data in another format for further management and analysis. This chapter described how to move Excel data into Microsoft Access databases and how to save Excel data in the most widely accepted format: ASCII files.

You have also seen how to link and embed Excel files into Word documents. The procedures described apply, with only slight differences, to any application that supports OLE. The chapter also described how to link an Excel worksheet to an Access database. Remember that you can create or add to an Access database (and other database management applications) without actually having the application installed on your computer or network by using the Template Wizard. However, to link an Excel workbook to an Access database, you must have Access installed.

We hope that you find this book of use as you continue to manage your business's data and that your revenues and profits continue to grow.

What's on the Disk

The disk included with this book contains all the worksheets that are depicted in the book's figures. This makes it easy for you to practice the data management examples described in the text. The disk also contains files in various other formats—such as Access, ASCII text and Paradox—for you to use if you want to practice moving data in and out of Excel, and to and from other applications.

There are also several VBA routines that have already been coded for you. These VBA routines are discussed, line by line, in the associated chapters of the book. They are described briefly in this appendix.

The disk is organized with a folder for each chapter. Each folder contains many workbooks that the chapter uses. These workbooks usually contain worksheets that are named for the chapter and figure that displays their contents. For example, Chapter 22 has, among others, a figure 22.13. You can find the worksheet for that figure in the workbook named *Chap22.xls*, and the name of the worksheet itself is *Fig22.13*.

A few chapters refer to workbooks that are not depicted in the book's figures. You will also find those workbooks in the disk's folder for the associated chapter.

Moving Files to Your Hard Disk

Follow these steps to install the files from the *Managing Data with Excel* companion disk:

1. Put the companion disk into your floppy drive. (We are assuming your floppy drive is drive A. If not, use the correct drive letter in step 3.)

2. Choose Start and then Run.

3. In the Open text box, type **a:\install** and click OK.

4. Optional: Specify an alternate drive and folder for the program to install the files to.

5. Click Unzip.

6. After the files are unzipped, click OK and then click Close. The Companion disk files are now on your hard drive in the directory MDEXCEL (or in a directory you've specified).

VBA Modules and Subroutines

As mentioned earlier, the disk contains several VBA subroutines you can use to speed up the execution of different data management tasks. These subroutines are provided in editable format—that is, they were not converted to add-ins—so you can modify them to suit your particular data management requirements.

You'll find line-by-line discussions of the modules in their associated chapters. Brief overviews are provided here.

VBA and Pivot Tables

The workbook named Chap10.xls contains three VBA modules. The first shows you how to create a pivot table from worksheet data. The second shows you how to create a pivot table that's based on external data: specifically, an Access database. And the third places list boxes on a worksheet so a user can structure a pivot table, display it, and clear it without resorting to the PivotTable Wizard.

VBA and the Scenario Manager

The workbook named OAR.xls (short for *Opportunity Analysis Report*) in Chapter 16's folder contains a VBA module named Top3Accounts. It shows you how to use VBA to create scenarios on different worksheets, merge them into one worksheet, create a summary pivot table from the scenarios, and then extract information you can use in decision-making from the pivot table summary.

Index

embedding with
AccessLinks add-in,
447-457
external database query,
413-417
extracting from text file
for pivot table,
184-185
filtering from database
applications (Get Data
command),
412-417
grouping/ungrouping in
pivot table control
fields, 157-160
importing
delimited files,
404-406
fixed length files,
407-408
from other database
applications,
408-411
from other worksheet
applications,
398-399
using pivot table,
387-388
importing to other Excel
spreadsheets, 384-385
analyzing data while
importing, 387-397
creating external
linked summary
area, 395-397
extracting remote
data, 392-395
link management,
398-399
retaining links to
source data,
386-387
using copy and paste,
385-386
linking and embedding
in Microsoft
Word, 439

linking Microsoft Word
to Excel, (special
worksheet
characteristics),
443-444
linking to Microsoft
Word from Excel,
441-443
locating in multiple
downloaded files,
420-421
managing data from
Quattro Pro for DOS,
conversion solutions
for version 5.0,
403-404
OutputData variable,
438
refreshing in pivot
tables, 163-166,
180-181
storing in external
databases (Template
Wizard), 423-424
storing in other formats,
435-439
working with
downloaded data for
worksheets, 404
worksheet
consolidation, 321-322
**data cache
(introduction), 177**
data cells
altering with formulas
in worksheets, 273-274
display options (pivot
tables), 139-141
introduction, 133
maximum number in
pivot tables, 139
renaming after
altering, 278
data fields
customizing, 153-157
pivot tables, 210-204

data forms, 49-56
calculated fields, 52-53
closing, 50
creating, 51-53
Access Form
Designer, 56-57
Access FormWizard,
57-60
design, 60-63
filtering lists, 54-56
list headings, 52
maximum number of
fields (columns), 51
navigating lists, 53-54
opening, 50
properties, 60-61
**data management
(Scenario Manager
tool), 249**
Data menu commands
Access Form, 58
Consolidate, 326-333
Filter, 20
Form, 50
Group and Outline, 33
Sort, 12
Subtotal, 361
Table, 35, 38, 40
**data sheets (creating
Scenario Summary), 301**
**data source (specifying
for PivotTable Wizard),
142-143**
data tables
arrays (recalculating
data tables), 43-44
AutoFilter control,
45-46
case study, 41-42
deleting, 44-45
editing, 44-45
one-variable compared
to two-variable, 36-39
static copies, 45
two-variable, 38-42

O

objects
advantages/
disadvantages of
linking and
embedding, 440
differentiating between
linked and embedded,
439-441
introduction, 439
**ODBC Data Source dialog
box, 414**
OFFSET function, 91-96
on-sheet controls
creating, 85-88
lists
management, 88-89
retrieving data, 84-89
running macros, 88-89
selecting, 86
one-variable data tables
AutoFilter control,
45-46
compared to two-
variable, 39
creating, 36-38
**Option Base 1 statement
(VBA), 223**
**Option Explicit
statement (VBA), 214**
**Options command (Tools
menu), 31**
Options dialog box, 31
**organizing (Sort dialog
box), 361**
**Outline capabilities
(managing different
views), 343-350**
outlines, 32-33
creating, 33
displaying details, 33
hiding details, 33
OutputData variable, 438
overwriting data, 70

P

**Page Break Between
Groups checkbox
(Subtotal dialog
box), 363**
page fields
creating multiple fields
in pivot tables,
204-207
customizing in pivot
tables (PivotTable
Wizard), 204-207
**page fields (pivot tables),
introduction, 134-135**
**page filters, creating with
step 2b (PivotTable
Wizard), 334**
**Page Setup dialog
box, 365**
Custom Header/Footer
command, 365
customizing printed
data, 367-368
Fit to option, 368
Gridlines option, 368
Print Area option, 368
Paradox format, 459
passwords
breakers, 108
protecting files, write
reservation password,
108-110
paste command
Edit Menu, 45, 63
importing data into
Excel spreadsheets,
385
analyzing data while
importing, 387-397
retaining links to
source data,
386-387
**Paste Special command
(Edit menu), 91-92, 97**

**Paste Special dialog box,
99-100**
**Paste Special menu
commands**
Add, 100
Skip Blanks, 100
Transpose, 97
Values, 101
pivot tables
analyzing in terms of
revenue, 231-232
applying custom sort
orders, 167-168
as a data source,
advantages, 177
building with VBA,
213-217
bypassing query during
construction, 218-222
cell display options,
139-141
column fields, 130-132
consolidating, step 2b
(PivotTable Wizard),
334-340
contingency analysis,
232-238
control fields,
customizing, 151
creating
from external source,
181-189
from list, 170
multiple page fields,
204-207
with VBA
(Opportunity case
study), 305-318
creating/modifying with
VBA, 210-213
customizing
control field
subtotals, 149-151
data fields, 153-157,
201-204
formats, 146-148

Complete and Return this Card
for a *FREE* Computer Book Catalog

Thank you for purchasing this book! You have purchased a superior computer book written expressly for your needs. To continue to provide the kind of up-to-date, pertinent coverage you've come to expect from us, we need to hear from you. Please take a minute to complete and return this self-addressed, postage-paid form. In return, we'll send you a free catalog of all our computer books on topics ranging from word processing to programming and the internet.

Mr. ☐   Mrs. ☐   Ms. ☐   Dr. ☐

Name (first) ☐☐☐☐☐☐☐☐☐☐☐☐   (M.I.) ☐   (last) ☐☐☐☐☐☐☐☐☐☐☐☐☐☐☐☐☐☐☐☐

Address ☐☐☐☐☐☐☐☐☐☐☐☐☐☐☐☐☐☐☐☐☐☐☐☐☐☐☐☐☐☐☐☐☐☐☐☐☐☐☐

City ☐☐☐☐☐☐☐☐☐☐☐☐☐☐☐☐☐☐   State ☐☐   Zip ☐☐☐☐☐ ☐☐☐☐

Phone ☐☐☐ ☐☐☐ ☐☐☐☐   Fax ☐☐☐ ☐☐☐ ☐☐☐☐

Company Name ☐☐☐☐☐☐☐☐☐☐☐☐☐☐☐☐☐☐☐☐☐☐☐☐☐☐☐☐☐☐☐☐☐☐☐

E-mail address ☐☐☐☐☐☐☐☐☐☐☐☐☐☐☐☐☐☐☐☐☐☐☐☐☐☐☐☐☐☐☐☐☐☐☐

1. Please check at least (3) influencing factors for purchasing this book.

Front or back cover information on book .... ☐
Special approach to the content .... ☐
Completeness of content .... ☐
Author's reputation .... ☐
Publisher's reputation .... ☐
Book cover design or layout .... ☐
Index or table of contents of book .... ☐
Price of book .... ☐
Special effects, graphics, illustrations .... ☐
Other (Please specify): _____ ☐

2. How did you first learn about this book?

Saw in Macmillan Computer Publishing catalog .... ☐
Recommended by store personnel .... ☐
Saw the book on bookshelf at store .... ☐
Recommended by a friend .... ☐
Received advertisement in the mail .... ☐
Saw an advertisement in: _____ ☐
Read book review in: _____ ☐
Other (Please specify): _____ ☐

3. How many computer books have you purchased in the last six months?

This book only .... ☐   3 to 5 books .... ☐
2 books .... ☐   More than 5 .... ☐

4. Where did you purchase this book?

Bookstore .... ☐
Computer Store .... ☐
Consumer Electronics Store .... ☐
Department Store .... ☐
Office Club .... ☐
Warehouse Club .... ☐
Mail Order .... ☐
Direct from Publisher .... ☐
Internet site .... ☐
Other (Please specify): _____ ☐

5. How long have you been using a computer?

☐ Less than 6 months   ☐ 6 months to a year
☐ 1 to 3 years   ☐ More than 3 years

6. What is your level of experience with personal computers and with the subject of this book?

	With PCs	With subject of book
New	☐	☐
Casual	☐	☐
Accomplished	☐	☐
Expert	☐	☐

Source Code ISBN: 0-7897-0385-8

7. Which of the following best describes your job title?

Administrative Assistant .... ☐
Coordinator .... ☐
Manager/Supervisor .... ☐
Director .... ☐
Vice President .... ☐
President/CEO/COO .... ☐
Lawyer/Doctor/Medical Professional .... ☐
Teacher/Educator/Trainer .... ☐
Engineer/Technician .... ☐
Consultant .... ☐
Not employed/Student/Retired .... ☐
Other (Please specify): _____ ☐

8. Which of the following best describes the area of the company your job title falls under?

Accounting .... ☐
Engineering .... ☐
Manufacturing .... ☐
Operations .... ☐
Marketing .... ☐
Sales .... ☐
Other (Please specify): _____ ☐

9. What is your age?

Under 20 .... ☐
21-29 .... ☐
30-39 .... ☐
40-49 .... ☐
50-59 .... ☐
60-over .... ☐

10. Are you:

Male .... ☐
Female .... ☐

11. Which computer publications do you read regularly? (Please list)

_____
_____
_____
_____
_____
_____
_____
_____
_____
_____

Comments: _____
_____
_____

Fold here and scotch-tape to mail.

About the Companion Disk

The companion disk includes:

Tools for automating database management tasks with VBA code

Fully developed Excel workbooks that you can incorporate into your own data management challenges

Every chapter has a corresponding Excel workbook on the companion disk. All case studies and figures that employ worksheet data are replicated in these workbooks. We recommend that you install these files on your computer when you begin the book, to make it easier for you to follow along with instruction sets and to understand the case studies more fully.

Licensing Agreement

By opening this package, you are agreeing to be bound by the following:

This software is copyrighted and all rights are reserved by the publisher and its licensers. You are licensed to use this software on a single computer. You may copy the software for backup or archival purposes only. Making copies of the software for any other purpose is a violation of United States copyright laws. This software is sold as is, without warranty of any kind, either expressed or implied, including but not limited to the implied warranties of merchantability and fitness for a particular purpose. Neither the publisher nor its dealers and distributors nor its licensers assume any liability for any alleged or actual damages arising from the use of this software. (Some states do not allow exclusion of implied warranties, so the exclusion may not apply to you.)